MELANCHOLY DUTY

ARCHIVES INTERNATIONALES D'HISTOIRE DES IDÉES

INTERNATIONAL ARCHIVES OF THE HISTORY OF IDEAS

154

MELANCHOLY DUTY
The Hume-Gibbon Attack on Christianity

by
STEPHEN PAUL FOSTER

MELANCHOLY DUTY

The Hume-Gibbon Attack on Christianity

by

STEPHEN PAUL FOSTER

Central Michigan University,
Mount Pleasant, U.S.A.

KLUWER ACADEMIC PUBLISHERS
DORDRECHT / BOSTON / LONDON

A C.I.P. Catalogue record for this book is available from the Library of Congress

B
1499
.R45
F67
1997

ISBN 0-7923-4785-4

Published by Kluwer Academic Publishers,
P.O. Box 17, 3300 AA Dordrecht, The Netherlands.

Sold and distributed in the U.S.A. and Canada
by Kluwer Academic Publishers,
101 Philip Drive, Norwell, MA 02061, U.S.A.

In all other countries, sold and distributed
by Kluwer Academic Publishers,
P.O. Box 322, 3300 AH Dordrecht, The Netherlands.

Printed on acid-free paper

Printed in the Netherlands

To my Father—Howard Foster

TABLE OF CONTENTS

PREFACE AND ACKNOWLEDGMENTS

This book is a study of the work of two formidable critics of Christianity—the Scottish infidel, David Hume, and the author of the magisterial *Decline and Fall of the Roman Empire*, Edward Gibbon. Their work in many important respects represents the culmination of philosophic history, a monumental eighteenth-century achievement of thought which conjoined empirical philosophy, methodological naturalism, and critical historiography. Christianity, both as a social-political institution and a historical and moral interpretation of the world, was the central object of their trenchant and often hostile criticism. Their writings form, if you will, a complementary critique of Christianity. Philosophic history was in part a profound reaction against the intellectual and moral domination of the church, and Hume and Gibbon have emerged as the most gifted and insightful of that elite community of Enlightenment thinkers in Great Britain that pushed historical inquiry into confrontation with eighteenth-century Christianity. Gibbon deeply admired Hume—twenty-six years his elder—and sought to emulate him. The skeptical Hume crafted his philosophical attacks upon centerpiece Christian notions such as miracles and immortality of the soul. His philosophical productions, moreover, were accompanied by the *History of England*, a massive work of cultural history which also dealt heavily with the politics of Christianity. Gibbon, though, set his own course and became *the* historian of the Roman empire. He amassed an unparalleled stock of historical erudition and, with the skill of the consummate ironist, cast the central elements of Hume's philosophical criticism into an iconoclastic, skeptical history of Christianity itself, a version that was unhappy reading for faithful believers.

No other full length work that I am aware of deals with the complementary features of the work of Hume and Gibbon in the complete range of its confrontation with Christianity. Christianity is a historical religion, and Hume and Gibbon made history itself a problem for the defenders of the Faith. This book explores in depth the efforts of Hume and Gibbon—self-consciously refining and employing the canons of philosophic history—to confront Christianity both epistemologically and morally, and attempts to show just how deeply both of these thinkers were preoccupied with the social and political dimensions of their own religion, that is, the religion that defined and dominated European culture. Epistemologically, *Christian history* came under their attack. The Divine plan of redemption for man, including Christ's entry into human history, was cast into doubt, an effect of Hume's "Of Miracles" and Gibbon's "infamous" chapter fifteen of the *Decline and Fall*. Morally, the *history of Christianity* became the history of fanaticism and superstition. The conduct of Christians—in extreme—was a huge object of interest for Hume and Gibbon: their history of Christianity focused on the perversity of its practitioners.

In chapter fifteen of the *Decline and Fall* Gibbon speaks of the "melancholy duty" of the historian whose task it is to describe religion as it is discovered among "a weak and degenerate race of beings." Evidence of Gibbon's melancholia is found throughout the *Decline and Fall,* and it is most bitter and eloquent in its explorations of Christianity's shortcomings. Likewise, the steady rhythms of Hume's normally calm and detached prose are usually broken only when he confronts the fanaticism of sectaries or the superstition of monks. The melancholy duty of which Gibbon speaks carries with it an aspect of inevitable disillusionment, the result of the historian's discovery and articulation of the profound disparity between human aspiration and achievement. In their confrontation with Christianity disillusionment was the central legacy.

The scholarship on Hume and Gibbon is, of course, voluminous and far ranging. I am particulary in dept to the work of Donald Livingston. His *Hume's Philosophy of Common Life* in my view is a profound and masterful interpretation of Hume's philosophy, one of the few general treatments of him that completely integrates his historical with his philosophical work. For the work of Duncan Forbes, J. Pocock and Ernest Gellner I am also appreciative. Gibbon remains a perennial subject of interest for historians, literary theorists and other scholars. In recent years David Jordan and David Womersley have made major contributions to understanding the formation of Gibbon's thoughts. Womersley has recently edited a fine and long overdue critical edition of the *Decline and Fall of the Roman Empire.* Unfortunately, it appeared too late for use in this book.

A shorter version of chapter three of this book was previously published as "Edward Gibbon and the Anti-Miracle Man: Hume's 'Of Miracles' at Work in The *Decline and Fall of the Roman Empire,"* *The Modern Schoolman* 71, no. 3 (March 1994), and other small portions of the work were earlier published as "Different Religions and the Difference They Make: Hume on the Political Effects of Religious Ideology," *The Modern Schoolman* 66, no. 4 (May 1989). I gratefully acknowledge the permission of the editor of *The Modern Schoolman* to use that material.

I wish to offer my thanks and appreciations to those individuals who helped me in many ways, both directly and indirectly, with the writing of this book. To William C. Charron I owe a special debt. As a teacher he was enthusiastic, rigorous, and demanding. In the high standards he set for himself he was exemplary. As a mentor he was kind and encouraging. He also made helpful comments and suggestions on the manuscript. Thanks to Tom Moore for his generous assistance in this project. Also a special thanks to Jane Tilmann, who provided me with tireless assistance and evinced unwavering cheerfulness through many drafts of the manuscript. Finally, it is with great affection that I acknowledge the contributions of my wife Barbara and my daughters Alyson and Rebecca. Without their steady support, enthusiasm, and good humor throughout my labors, I could not have completed this work.

ABBREVIATIONS
(See Bibliography for full references)

The Works of Edward Gibbon

EE   *The English Essays of Edward Gibbon*, edited by Patricia Craddock.

DF   *The History of the Decline and Fall of the Roman Empire*, in seven volumes edited by J. B. Bury.*

Letters-G   *The Letters of Edward Gibbon*, in three volumes, edited by J. E. Norton.**

Memoirs   *Memoirs of My Life*, edited with and Introduction by Betty Radice.

MW   *The Miscellaneous Works of Edward Gibbon*, in five volumes, with occasional notes and narrative by John, Lord Sheffield.**

The Works of David Hume

Dialogues   *The Dialogues Concerning Natural Religion*, edited by John Valdimir Price.

EHU   *Enquiry Concerning Human Understanding*, edited by L. A. Selby-Bigge, 3rd edition.

EPM   *Enquiry Concerning the Principles of Morals,* edited by L. A. Selby-Bigge, 3rd edition.

Essays   *Essays Moral, Political and Literary*, edited by Eugene F. Miller.

HE   *The History of England From the Invasion of Julius Caesar to the Revolution in 1688*, in six volumes.**

HGB   *The History of Great Britain: The Reigns of James I and Charles I*, edited by Duncan Forbes.

Letters-H   *The Letters of David*, in two volumes, edited by J. Y. T. Greig.**

NHR   *The Natural History of Religion*, edited by Wayne Colver.

Treatise   *A Treatise of Human Nature*, edited by L. A. Selby-Bigge, 2nd edition.

*   All citations to the *Decline and Fall* will include, in order: chapter number, volume number to the Bury edition, and page number. Thus, e.g., (DF-5, I, 118.) I have included chapter numbers for those readers using a different edition of the *Decline and Fall.*

** Volume numbers will be designated by Roman numerals.

CHAPTER ONE

INTRODUCTION:
HUME, GIBBON, AND THE ATTACK ON CHRISTIANITY

I. Hume, Gibbon, and Christianity

[L]et us confirm [Gibbon] in his own opinion of his book by showing, in the first place, that it has one quality of permanence—it still excites abuse.

Virginia Woolf

Nineteen ninety four marked the two hundredth anniversary of Edward Gibbon's death. When he expired at the age of fifty-six Gibbon had already enshrined his literary immortality in the three thousand pages of the *Decline and Fall of the Roman Empire*, the Enlightenment's most celebrated and "notorious" work of history. Gibbon's often harsh treatment of the conduct of the early Christians, his skepticism of miracles, and his hostility toward institutional Christianity caused the notoriety and marked him as an enemy of the Christian religion. Since the publication of volume one in 1776, the *Decline and Fall* has remained continuously in print.[1] Two hundred years after its completion in 1788 this work still entices the interpreters and exegetes who grapple with its deliberately elusive style and supremely artful modes of insinuation.[2]

Reading the *Decline and Fall* near the end of the ferociously ideological twentieth century brings an additional appreciation for its author's independence of thought and gifted eloquence. Gibbon remains the consummate anti-ideologue; humorous, fair-minded, individualistic in character, and audaciously ironic. It is

---

[1] A three volume Modern Library series of the *Decline and Fall* is still in print as is an Everyman's Library series. Also, a critical, three volume edition of the *Decline and Fall*, edited by David Womersley was published in 1994 by Allen Lane, Penguin Press. This edition appeared too late for use in this work. All reference to the *Decline and Fall* in this work are to the Bury edition.

[2] See Patricia Craddock, *Edward Gibbon: A Reference Guide* (Boston: G. K. Hall, 1987). This guide contains approximately 2,000 annotated citations of works (books, articles, reviews) on Gibbon published between 1761 and 1985. Craddock has also published a two volume biography of Gibbon: *Young Edward Gibbon: Gentleman of Letters* (Baltimore: The Johns Hopkins University Press, 1982); and *Edward Gibbon: Luminous Historian, 1772-1794* (Baltimore: The Johns Hopkins University Press, 1989). There are a number of major works on Gibbon published in the last forty years, the most notable in my view being: Harold Bond, *The Literary Art of Edward Gibbon* (Oxford: Clarendon Press, 1960); David Jordan, *Gibbon and his Roman Empire* (Urbana, IL: University of Illinois Press, 1971); and David Womersley, *The Transformation of the Decline and Fall of the Roman Empire* (Cambridge: Cambridge University Press, 1988).

tempting, as a quick aside, to compare Gibbon's eighteenth-century narrative to one of the epic histories of the twentieth century, Leon Trotsky's *History of the Russian Revolution*. In remarkable contrast to Gibbon's work, which conveys an acute appreciation of human fallibility (including his own) and a deliberate ambiguity and openness to interpretation, Trotsky's immense and entertaining history impresses the reader nevertheless with its arrogance, conviction of omniscience, and doctrinal rigidity.[3]

Gibbon's work still exudes controversy. Both what he wrote about Christianity and the manner in which he wrote it were probably more controversial than anything else he ever did. The *Decline and Fall* orchestrates a persistent criticism of Christianity around the theme of human fallibility. Gibbon's Christianity is often a tale of perversity chronicling the deeds of a contemptible variety of poseurs, opportunists, hypocrites, and fanatics. Readers of the *Decline and Fall* were confronted with Gibbon's thesis that Christianity abetted the socially disintegrating forces at work on the Roman empire, a major cause of the initial outraged provoked by the book.[4] The *Decline and Fall*, however, endures as an arresting metaphor for the conflict of good and evil, a metaphor cast in baleful, cataclysmic, world-historical terms. Rome, the cradle of the rule of law, the repository of civilized values, tragically crumbles under the sustained assaults of the barbarians on its borders, the gradual corruption of its political institutions, and the subversive effects of Christianity.[5] Near the end of his long historical journey Gibbon lugubriously summarizes in just nine words his immense project: "I have described the triumph of barbarism and religion." (*DF-71*, VII, 321)

Much has been written about Gibbon's rough handling of historical Christianity and his often cynical, contentious representation of the workings of institutional religion. This book, however, contemplates his presentation of the history of Christianity in the *Decline and Fall* in light of the philosophy of David Hume, particularly Hume's naturalistic interpretation of religion's effects on

---

[3]Consider the unintended irony of Trotsky's harangue against the Mensheviks and Social Revolutionaries during the Bolshevik consolidation of power in 1917. "You are pitiful isolated individuals; you are bankrupts; your role is played out. Go where you belong from now on—into the *dustbin of history*." Leon Trotsky, *The History of the Russian Revolution*, trans. Max Eastman (New York: Monad, 1932), 3: 311, italics added.

[4]See Shelby T. McCloy, *Gibbon's Antagonism to Christianity* (Chapel Hill, NC: University of North Carolina Press, 1933). McCloy covers numerous critics of Gibbon including attacks by Gibbon's contemporaries as well as latter detractors.

[5]See Michael Grant, *The Fall of the Roman Empire* (New York: Macmillan, 1990) for a short, highly readable analysis of the causes of the fall of the Roman Empire. Of Gibbon's analysis Grant writes (xi): "[h]undreds of reasons have been suggested for the collapse of the Roman West. Some indication of their variety can be obtained from reading Edward Gibbon's superb and never truly superseded *History of the Decline and Fall of the Roman Empire (1776-88)*."

society and politics. Gibbon, as we shall see, was inspired by Hume's work and saw him as a model of the "philosophic historian."[6] Hume and Gibbon were indeed fierce critics of Christianity. Hume's critique of it stems from an epistemological perspective that redefines norms of rationality as they apply to theological argumentation and religious belief. A Christian believer, Hume concludes at the end of his "Of Miracles," "subverts all the principles of his understanding." (*EHU*, 131) The Christian faith and human reason, Hume argues, are incompatible. Behind Gibbon's criticism of Christianity is a naturalistic interpretation of the historical events of Christianity's rise out of pagan Rome's decline. Gibbon shared Hume's skepticism of miracles and like Hume rejected the rationality of theology. Gibbon, as we shall also see, used the history of Islam to criticize Christianity. Gibbon wrote what turned out to be a historical critique of Christianity with all the philosophical implications of a naturalistic outlook. Hume's writings brought to bear a philosophical critique of Christianity that relied on a richly historical view of religion. Hume wrote history as well as philosophy, and his *History of England* is not only a political history of England but an ecclesiastical history and a history of enthusiasm and superstition as well. Hume and Gibbon in their writings thus subjected the full range of human motivations and interests to naturalistic assumptions and unceremoniously withdrew religion's long and jealously guarded exemption from scrutiny as a cultural manifestation of wholly human aspirations and designs. Characteristic of both Hume and Gibbon was a consciously employed philosophical skepticism used to deflate claims for religious truth and certainty, especially the truths of Christianity. The writings of Hume and Gibbon could not but be interpreted by the bulk of their contemporaries, and many who succeeded them, as an attack on the Faith.

Their critique of historical Christianity make Hume and Gibbon major contributors to the secularizing of the modern world. They regarded themselves and each other as "philosophic historians"—as members, if you will, of an intellectually and morally elite society that advanced the freedom of thinking and resisted ecclesiastical authority. Their contributions, moreover, were complementary. Hume was foremost a philosopher, in fact the greatest of the eighteenth-century English-speaking philosophers. Gibbon was primarily a historian who had imbibed the philosophical outlook of the Scottish Enlightenment

---

[6]See Geoffrey Keynes, *The Library of Edward Gibbon: A Catalogue*, 2nd ed., (n.p.: St. Paul's Bibliographies, 1980), 156, for a list of Hume's works actually owned by Gibbon. Cited are two editions of *The History of England*, a copy of the *Dialogues Concerning Natural Religion*, and three editions of *Essays and Treatises on Several Subjects* which contain the *Natural History of Religion* and the two *Enquiries*. Gibbon cites all of these works in the *Decline and Fall*. I am inclined to doubt that Gibbon read the *Treatise*. It is not shown to be in his library, and I find no citations to it in his writings.

as exemplified by Hume.[7] His creative mind was concentrated on his historical enterprises: indeed, Gibbon viewed himself as *the* historian of the Roman empire.[8] He read and digested vast amounts and amassed an encyclopedic knowledge of geography, numismatics, theology, and church and military history. In the *Decline and Fall* there are approximately 8,000 footnotes, 3,000 of them citing to secondary sources. As one recent biographer has observed: "[i]t would be possible to compile a comprehensive and entertaining critical bibliography of European historical writing from the second century A.D. to the eighteenth century from Gibbon's notes alone."[9]

As well, Gibbon possessed an extraordinary capacity for absorbing and creatively synthesizing the intellectual labor of many kinds of thinkers and writers—historians, antiquarians, theologians, and philosophers—a talent that was instrumental in the production of his vast edifice of historical literature and learning.[10] Gibbon's fine editor, J. B. Bury, writes that Gibbon's work is "marked

---

[7]A comment should be made on the stylistic differences between Hume and Gibbon. Duncan Forbes contrasts, somewhat misleadingly in my view, the smooth style of Hume's narrative that "moves fast on welded rails," to that of Gibbon, who, as Virginia Woolf (quoted by Forbes) says, leaves the reader "for hours on end mounted on a celestial rocking-horse which, as it gently sways up and down, remains rooted to a single spot." Duncan Forbes, introduction to *The History of Great Britain: The Reigns of James I and Charles I*, by David Hume (Middlesex, England: Penguin, 1970), 10. The difference in style is not, I believe, so much the speed of movement. Both cover vast historical distances quickly and with economy. Gibbon's manner is more elegant, studied, and artfully ironic and subtle, whereas Hume is less ironic, more direct and prosaic.

[8]See "Gibbon Becomes 'The Historian of the Roman Empire,'" in 'Chapter One' of Jordan's, *Gibbon and His Roman Empire*. Jordan describes how Gibbon retrospectively interpreted his life as *the* historian of the Roman empire. And, Martine Watson Brownley, "Gibbon's Memoirs: The Legacy of the Historian," *Studies on Voltaire and the Eighteenth Century* 201 (1982):210. "Gibbon's challenge was to establish the proper relationship in his narrative between his career as a historian and his life as a private man. He did not intend to remove personal concerns completely from the *Memoirs*; he simply wanted to focus only on those aspects of his private life which illuminated the emerging historian." Also, see Catherine N. Parke, "Edward Gibbon by Edward Gibbon," *Modern Language Quarterly* 50, no. 1 (March 1989): 23-37.

[9]J. W. Burrow, *Gibbon* (New York: Oxford University Press, 1985), 100. In contrast to Gibbon, Hume's *History of England* is perfunctorily documented. See A. W. Ward and A. R. Walling, eds., *Cambridge History of English Literature* (New York: G. P. Putnam's Sons, 1913), 10: 321-22. "[I]t cannot be contended that he [i.e., Hume] took full advantage of such authorities as were then accessible: he seems to have been content with those under his hands in the Advocates Library; he was not critical as to their comparative value; and he was careless in his use of them."

[10]Gavin DeBeer, *Gibbon and His World* (London: Thames and Hudson, 1968), 72, summarized Gibbon's synthesizing capacities most aptly. "Far from conforming to the facile view which would make Gibbon a disciple of French eighteenth-century rationalism, he picked his way independently, as Giuseppe Giarrizzo has recently shown, learning method and technique from Bayle, gathering material from Tillemont, taking a select little from Montequieu, opposed to Voltaire, Rousseau and the *Encylopedistes*, judiciously influenced by Hume and Robertson, and supplied by his inexhaustible fount of knowledge, tempered by an artistry and expression all his own."

by ecumenical grasp, extraordinary accuracy, and striking acuteness in judgment."[11] J. M. Robertson admiringly observes that Gibbon almost completely escaped self-contradiction, rarely forgetting what he had written. "In all his History I recall only one repetition."[12] Gibbon was single-mindedly and wholeheartedly devoted to being the historian of the Roman empire. It took him a lifetime to write the *Decline and Fall*—lavishing on it the attention of his researches. James Cotter Morison, one of Gibbon's early twentieth-century biographers, eloquently summarizes how appropriate Gibbon's personality, character, and experience were for the massive intellectual project he undertook. "[T]he place was open for a writer who should unite all the broad spirit of a comprehensive survey, with the thorough and minute patience of a Benedictine; whose subject, mellowed by long brooding, should have sought him rather than he it; whose whole previous course of study had been an unconscious preparation for one great effort which was to fill his life."[13]

Philosophic history was an eighteenth-century synthesis of empirical philosophy and critical historiography that, not surprisingly, took a severely critical view of Christianity's role in the development of Western civilization: Hume is the culmination of the *philosophic* side of it; Gibbon the *historic*. The comparisons to be drawn of Hume's critical philosophical genius with Gibbon's iconoclastic historical assault on institutional Christianity in the *Decline and Fall* make the consideration of them together intriguing, controversial, and essential.[14]

Philosophic history, dutifully practiced with a professed disinterested, self-critical determination to understand the past, represented for Hume and Gibbon the triumph of the philosophical quest. Properly studied, history could yield truth, truth with a morally instructive value. But truth is elusive and, what Hume calls "just" philosophy (philosophy not corrupted by "enthusiasm", i.e., religious emotion), is difficult to practice because, in part, of the perennial corruptibility of human nature. Religion plays a huge role in this corruptibility because of its capacity to arouse intense passion and the propensity of passion to move those under its influence toward the rationalization of power and the subversion of norms of self-restraint. And so the interplay of philosophic history and religion remains an important, perhaps the most important consideration in understanding what Hume and Gibbon were all about as philosophic historians. Gibbon's narrative in

---

[11]*Encyclopedia Britannica*, 11th ed., s.v. "Gibbon."

[12]J. M. Robertson, *Gibbon* (London: Watts and Co., 1925), 85.

[13]James Cotter Morison, *Gibbon*, (London, Macmillan, 1904), 102-3.

[14]Jordan, *Gibbon and His Roman Empire*, and, Womersley, *The Transformation*, are recent major works dealing with the influences on Gibbon's work, and both scrutinize the Hume-Gibbon connection. Also, a doctoral dissertation from Germany has been recently published on Hume and Gibbon. M. Andreas Weber, *David Hume und Edward Gibbon: Religionssoziologie in der Aufklarung* (Frankfurt am Main: Hain, 1990).

the *Decline and Fall* builds up to a confrontation with the apologists of early Christianity over the question of the church's miraculous origins as he echoes the skepticism registered by Hume's "Of Miracles."

The intellectual relationship of Gibbon and Hume[15] bears significantly upon an overlooked but consequential aspect of Hume's own extraordinary career—his special role as a philosophical mentor. Hume took a keen, personal interest in the scholarly development and progress of his friends and was a powerful influence on them.[16] Adam Smith and Edward Gibbon are two of the more luminous beneficiaries of his tutelage. At the age of eighteen Smith wrote to his friend William Cullen: "I should prefer David Hume to any man for a colleague; but I am afraid the public would not be of my opinion."[17] At this young age Smith could comprehend Hume's genius but was intimidated by public disapprobation of Hume's reputation for irreligion. Smith though became and remained a close and life-long friend of Hume and eulogized him as "approaching as nearly to the idea of a perfectly wise and virtuous man, as perhaps the nature of human frailty will admit." (*Letters*-H, II, 452)

Hume was Gibbon's senior by twenty-six years and advised the bi-lingual Gibbon to write his history in English rather than French (*Letters*-H, II, 170-171).[18]

---

[15]A number of major works on Gibbon attempt not only to show the historiographical and philosophical connections of Gibbon to Hume, but attempt an interpretation of Hume against which Gibbon can be measured. This is the case with Jordan, *Gibbon and His Roman Empire*, and Womersley, *The Transformation*.

[16]Gladys Bryson, *Man and Society: The Scottish Inquiry of the Eighteenth Century* (1945; reprint, New York: Augustus M. Kelley, 1968), 2. In Hume's Scottish circle was "a group of scholars working at the same set of problems over the period of a century. Standing head and shoulders above them all was David Hume, pivot and provocation to the group."

[17]Adam Smith, *The Correspondence of Adam Smith*, ed. Ernest Campbell Mossner and Ian Simpson Ross (Oxford: Clarendon Press, 1987), 5.

[18]"Why," Hume gently scolds in a letter to Gibbon commenting on a manuscript on the history of the Swiss revolution he had written in French, "do you compose in French, and carry faggots into the wood, as Horace says with regard to the Romans who wrote in Greek?" Hume then states two reasons why he thinks Gibbon should write in English. The first is practical, and it shows that Hume was quite prescient with regard to the future of the English language. "Our solid and increasing establishments in America, where we need less dread the inundation of Barbarians, promise a superior stability and duration to the English language." The second reason is a methodological, and in my view, a more interesting one. Hume is worried that Gibbon's more figurative and poetic French may compromise his efforts. "Your use of the French tongue has also led you into a style more poetical and figurative, and more highly coloured, than our language seems to admit of in historical productions: for such is the practice of French writers, particularly the more recent ones, who illuminate their pictures more than custom will permit us." (*Letters-H*, II, 170-71) The "highly coloured" language might lend some inappropriate emotive nuance or convey an ambiguity that could impair his history. See also J. E. Norton, *A Bibliography of the Works of Edward Gibbon* (London: Oxford University Press, 1940), 42, where Norton notes that Hume advised Gibbon's publisher, Strahan, on improvements for the *Decline and Fall*.

It was Hume's congratulatory letter on the publication of volume one of the *Decline and Fall* that Gibbon proudly proclaimed, "overpaid the labour of ten years." (*Memoirs*, 160)   Hume's professed ruling passion was by his own confession "the pursuit of philosophy and general learning."   This intellectual passion had profound social manifestations in the life-long philosophical friendships and acquaintances Hume happily maintained.   His warm and lively correspondence reveals many aspects of his leadership in an influential philosophical community.[19]   Around Hume were gathered a circle of friends and acquaintances who with him launched the Scottish Enlightenment.[20]   The "infidel" Hume also consorted with Scottish clergy such as Hugh Blair and Alexander Carlyle who helped shield him from the wrath of their less tolerant colleagues.[21]   Hume's philosophical community helped provide Gibbon with inspiration, encouragement and, most importantly, a philosophical model which shaped his historical thinking.[22]

Hume's mentorship is thus highly suggestive in this regard.   Hume, a towering philosopher and a superb historian, was *the* ideal philosophic historian for Gibbon to emulate.[23]   His *History of England* was popular and excited both praise and denunciation all over Europe, particularly in France.[24]   Hume was also read in

---

[19]Hume's influence was not limited only to Britain and to France, where his history and essays were enormously popular. His ideas were also influential in the development of American political thinking. See Gary Wills, *Explaining America: The Federalist* (New York: Penguin, 1981), a detailed study of the impact of Hume's essays on Madison and Hamilton and the *Federalist Papers*, and also by Gary Wills, *Inventing America: Jefferson's Declaration of Independence* (New York: Vintage Books, 1978).

[20]It should be noted that the Scottish Enlightenment was not a feature of all of Scotland. See Anand C. Chitnis, *The Scottish Enlightenment: A Social History* (London: Croom Helm, 1976), 4-5. "Despite the ascription 'Scottish', the Enlightenment was not apparent all over Scotland; nor did it flower with equal vigour in those parts of the country where it appeared. Its location was essentially that limited geographical area of the central, lowland belt bounded by Glasgow in the west and Edinburgh in the east but also taking in the cities and universities of Aberdeen. It was an urban movement and its intimacy was prompted, and its progress facilitated, by the forms of social and intellectual expression that towns and urban living encouraged."

[21]Ernest Campbell Mossner, *The Life of David Hume*, 2nd ed. (Oxford: Clarendon Press, 1980), 363, 579-80.

[22]In the *Decline and Fall* we find citations, accompanied with high praise, to the work of Hume, Smith, and Robertson.

[23]Donald Livingston, *Hume's Philosophy of Common Life* (Chicago: University of Chicago Press, 1984), 210, writes: "[n]o philosopher of Hume's stature has made a contribution to history equal to that of his monumental *History of England*." Many aspects of Hume's philosophy and history are debatable. This assessment is not.

[24]For a study of the influence of Hume's *History of England* on political thought in France, see Laurence Bongie, *David Hume: Prophet of the Counter-Revolution* (Oxford: Clarendon Press, 1965).

America.[25] Thomas Jefferson studied Hume and was initially taken with him ("Several of Hume's Political essays are good," he wrote to Thomas Randolph in 1790). Yet, twenty years later in a letter to Colonel William Duane, Jefferson (enamored with the French Revolution and put off by Hume's lament for Charles I and his excoriation of the Puritan radicals) reviled Hume's *History of England.* Hume "still continues to be put into the hands of all our young people, and to infect them with the poison of his own principles of government."[26] Gibbon, though, deeply admired Hume, cited him authoritatively in his work and, as J. G. A. Pocock points out, paid Hume the ultimate compliment by referring to him as the "Scottish Tacitus."[27] Hume's *Essays,* both *Enquiries, The Natural History of Religion,* and *The History of England* are all cited by Gibbon in the *Decline and Fall.*

The critical way in which Gibbon deals with Christianity in the *Decline and Fall* takes on a greater level of philosophical and historical comprehensibility when placed against the backdrop of Hume's philosophy and the Scottish Enlightenment.[28] Hugh Trevor-Roper writes that Gibbon "intellectually was not an Englishman."[29] Gibbon's short stay at Oxford was the least intellectually stimulating, most slothful period of his life. By his own contemptuously tinged recollection, the fourteen months with the "monks at Magdalen" were "the most idle and unprofitable of my whole life." (*Memoirs,* 76) At the age of forty-six Gibbon left England where he never felt completely at home and took up quarters in Lausanne (where he had been exiled by his father as a young man) to finish his history.

It was the philosophically precocious Scots with whom Gibbon identified and whose ideas on religion and society he put to historical use. (Hume, Robertson, and Gibbon have come to be known as the triumvirate of philosophic historians) In his

---

[25]Bryson, *Man and Society,* 3. In America "Hume, as accepted text was anathema, but as a target he was everywhere used."

[26]*The Life and Selected Writings of Thomas Jefferson,* ed. Adrienne Koch and William Peden (New York: Random House, 1944), 497, 606.

[27]J. G. A. Pocock, "Gibbon's *Decline and Fall* and the World View of the Late Enlightenment," in *Virtue, Commerce, and History: Essays on Political Thoughts and History, Chiefly in the Eighteenth Century* (Cambridge: Cambridge University Press, 1985), 147.

[28]See David Allan, *Virtue, Learning and the Scottish Enlightenment: Ideas of Scholarship in Early Modern History* (Edinburgh: Edinburgh University Press, 1993), 9-10. "It would certainly be no departure from the orthodoxy to suggest that the historical writings associated with the Enlightenment provide the central testament of the eighteenth-century Scottish achievement. On this much at least all current historians could probably agree. In their historical works the great literati gathered the evidence and deduced the explanatory schemes upon which their definitive pronouncements on political economy and social development would ultimately rest."

[29]Hugh Trevor-Roper, "Gibbon and the Publication of the *Decline and Fall of the Roman Empire,* 1776-1976," *The Journal of Law and Economics* 19, no. 3 (Oct. 1976): 492.

discussion of the Crusades in the *Decline and Fall* Gibbon credits the Scots with a great philosophical contribution in the understanding of the development of European civilization in the late middle ages. "On this interesting subject, the progress of society in Europe, a strong ray of philosophic light has broke from Scotland in our own times; and it is with private as well as public regard that I repeat the names of Hume, Robertson, and Adam Smith." (*DF-61*, VI, 465, n.89) Gibbon also pays high compliments to the Scottish Enlightenment historians by comparing them favorably to the Italians. "Fra Paolo and Davila, were justly esteemed the first historians of modern languages, till, in the present age, Scotland arose to dispute the prize with Italy herself." (*DF-70*, VII, 308, n.101) In 1777, a year after publication of volume one of the *Decline and Fall* and a year after the death of Hume, Gibbon wrote to William Robertson, "When I ventured to assume the character of historian, the first the most natural, but at the same time the most ambitious wish which I entertained was to deserve the approbation of Dr Robertson and Mr Hume, two names which friendship united and which posterity will never separate." (*Letters*-G, II, 152) Gibbon describes the unforgettable impression that the histories of Hume and Robertson left upon him. "The old reproach, that no British altars had been raised to the Muse of history, was recently disproved by the first performances of Robertson and Hume, the histories of Scotland and of the Stuarts. I will assume the presumption to say that I was not unworthy to read them: nor will I disguise my different feelings in the repeated perusals. The perfect composition, the nervous language, the well turned periods of Dr. Robertson inflamed me to the ambitious hope, that I might one day tread in his footsteps: the calm philosophy, the careless inimitable beauties of his friend and rival [David Hume] often forced me to close the volume, with a mixed sensation of delight and despair." (*Memoirs*, 114) Here by self-declaration are Gibbon's modern day models.

Gibbon was bewitched by Hume and his "calm philosophy." Hume's writings embodied ideals Gibbon strove to emulate—detachment and moderation, quintessential marks of philosophic history. Hume looked to history as a mine for philosophical truth, and he was one of the first historians who viewed it in a completely secular perspective. It was a perspective in striking conflict with a widely held Christian providential historical outlook.[30] His contemporaries Benjamin Stillingfleet, David Hartley, and even William Robertson himself, construed the history of the human race as consistent with the biblical account of man's descent from Adam and Eve. Even the weight of Newton was behind the

---

[30]Richard Popkin, "Hume: Philosophical Versus Prophetic Historian," in *David Hume: Man-sided Genius*, ed. Kenneth R. Merrill and Robert W. Shahan (Norman, OK: University of Oklahoma Press, 1976), 83.

biblical view of history. (Ibid., 83) Yet Hume rejected the biblical outlook with its miracles and prophecies and set the stage for the nineteenth-century approach to the Bible as a historical document subject to the canons of literary and historical criticism.[31]

Hume's work thus was to have profound philosophical and historical implications for thinking about religion, particularly Christianity as a great historical religion. Leslie Stephen in *The History of English Thought in the Eighteenth Century* notes that the publication of Hume's work marks one of the major turning points in the history of thought.[32] Stephen also comments that Hume's theory of morality strikes down attempts to deduce theology as a regulative principle of conduct.[33] Gibbon followed in this vein and wrote against Christian theology by ridiculing it, by making its history a record of fanaticism and folly. His ridicule was both artful and hurtful and was read as an attack on the traditional Christian beliefs deeply held by his fellow countrymen. England at the time of the publication of the *Decline and Fall* was a profoundly Christian society. "The salient fact for the social historian of eighteenth-century England is that Christian belief is initially almost universal, a belief calling attention to the history of a chosen nation conceived as a family or group of families, with a Holy Family as its culmination; a faith whose established Church taught obedience, humility and reverence to superiors with unanimity and consistency down the decades."[34] However, the underpinning of the Christian outlook was under heavy, critical scrutiny by major philosophers such as Hume. Immortality of the soul, the foundations of the Christian religion in the miraculous, and the reality of a good, omniscient creator were central features of the Christian outlook and were the targets, for one, of Hume's criticism. Preceded by the English deists who attacked

---

[31]Peter Addinall, *Philosophy and Biblical Interpretation: A Study in Nineteenth-Century Conflict* (Cambridge: Cambridge University Press, 1991), devotes an entire chapter (Chapter 2, "David Hume") to Hume's religious naturalism and the impact of it on biblical interpretation in the nineteenth century.

[32]Leslie Stephen, *History of English Thought in the Eighteenth Century* (London: Smith, Edder and Co., 1902), 1: 311. Stephen says that: "Hume's reasonings [on theological issues] were, until very recent times, the single example in our literature of a passionless and searching examination of the great problem." See Ernest Gellner, *Plough, Sword and Book: The Structure of Human History* (Chicago: University of Chicago Press, 1988), 113-44 for a discussion of the major impact of Hume's insights on religion and society. Also see George E. Davie, *The Scottish Enlightenment and Other Essays* (Edinburgh: Polygon, 1991), 68, for an assessment of Hume's impact on the history of thought. "The radicals' criticism of Hume's philosophy as too pusillanimous to rise to the bright vision of the material utopia is thus offset by this alternative assessment of him as being, in the weighty words of Adam Smith 'by far the most illustrious philosopher and historian of the present age' . . . ."

[33]Stephen, *History of English Thought*, 1: 314

[34]J. C. D. Clark, *English Society 1688-1832: Ideology, Social Structure and Political Practice During the Ancien Regime* (Cambridge: Cambridge University Press, 1985), 87.

the notion of revealed religion, Hume was busy developing what turned out to be a secularist perspective with its rejection of the literal truth of the Bible and its doubts about the rationality of theology.[35] Hume formulated his critical, skeptical philosophy prior to writing his *History of England*. The *Treatise* and *Enquiry Concerning Human Understanding* were written between 1736 and 1751. The first *Enquiry* contained "Of Miracles" the themes of which are echoed by Gibbon in chapter fifteen of the *Decline and Fall* and bear upon his interpretation of the history of Christianity.

James Cotter Morison attributes Gibbon's loss of orthodoxy to the influence of Hume and Pierre Bayle, the seventeenth-century French skeptic.[36] Gibbon's "irreligion" was also blamed on his contact with Hume and Voltaire.[37] The *Decline and Fall*, however, possesses a distinctive philosophical orientation historically linked to Hume and deals with Christianity in a naturalistic fashion that parallels Hume's. Frank Manuel, writing of Hume's influence on Gibbon's thinking, is absolutely emphatic: "[i]n my judgment, it was Hume's influence that was more pervasive in the formation of the philosophical historian . . . . Gibbon treasured praise from the dying Hume above all other appreciations, and he kept quoting the words of approval to all his correspondents . . . . But it was no single work of Hume that dominated Gibbon: it was the man and his writing in their totality that were congenial to him and set Hume above all the contemporary writers."[38]

As a philosophic historian, one of Gibbon's major challenges was to deal "philosophically" with Christianity. Christianity had a key role in the decline and fall of the Roman empire: Gibbon sought to explain that role and, understandably, was reluctant to accept the interpretations of the early Christian apologists. The impartial distance for which Gibbon strived came at the cost of a confrontation with apologetic-Christianity. Apologetics meant partiality—the apologist remains suspect because of interested motives, and hence must always be unphilosophical in Gibbon's estimation. Gibbon therefore was relentlessly skeptical in looking at the claims of the early Christian apologist: such skepticism attempted to achieve a detached and rigorous philosophical perspective. Moreover, this skepticism was

---

[35]Stephen, *History of English Thought*, 1:309-10.

[36]Morison, *Gibbon*, 68.

[37]McCloy, *Gibbon's Antagonism to Christianity*, 162, 198. Also see Edgar Wind, *Hume and the Heroic Portrait: Studies in Eighteenth-Century Imagery*, ed. Jaynie Anderson (Oxford: Clarendon Press, 1986), 29-30, for an account of the eminent Josuah Reynolds' portrait of James Beattie, *Essay on Truth*, painted to celebrate Beatties' victory over Hume's skepticism with his work, *Essay on Truth*. In the portrait is a "winged Genius" casting Hume, Voltaire, and, some allege, Gibbon into the abyss.

[38]Frank E. Manuel, "Edward Gibbon: Historien-Philosophe", in *Edward Gibbon and Decline and Fall of the Roman Empire*, ed. G. W. Bowersock, John Clive, and Stephen R. Graubard (Cambridge, MA: Harvard University Press, 1977), 173.

used to exorcize the transcendental causality in history that was a foundational element of the Christian view and to inaugurate a naturalistic interpretation of the past.

James Noxon has noted that in Hume's writings more of his pages deal in some way with religion than any other topic.[39] The justification of religious belief was not the exclusive concern of Hume. He also dwelt upon the stamp that religious belief imprints on the human personality and character and upon religion's effects on social and political institutions.[40] In short, Hume's interest in religion extended to its widest ranging impact on human culture. The centrality of religion is an equally salient feature of Gibbon's history. Pocock observes that: the "*Decline and Fall*, from beginning to end . . . is profoundly concerned with the capacity of religion in its various forms to stabilize, to destroy, and to reconstitute the fabric of civilized society; so that history is largely determined by religion, and religion—while reduced from the sacred to the secular dimension—is one of the greatest phenomena of history."[41] Hume viewed religion as a derivative rather than a primary or basic aspect of human nature. In the *Natural History* he wrote that: "[t]he first religious principles must be secondary; such as may easily be perverted by various accidents and causes, and whose operation too, in some cases, may, by an extraordinary concurrence of circumstances, be altogether prevented." (*NHR*, 25) This has extremely important implications for a historian of civilization such as Gibbon. Because religion takes on unique and varied configurations, ("easily perverted by various accidents and causes"), it is important for the historian to uncover those historical contingencies that shape a particular religion. Religion in Hume's approach was something the philosophical historian should consider in its contingent forms, a phenomenon to be reviewed entirely as a manifestation of human nature, empirically understood. Moreover, such empiricism entailed a rejection of rationalized foundations of religious belief insofar as the objects of religious belief, i.e., supernatural objects, were beyond the reach of direct sense experience.[42]

Within the panoramic, thousand-year course of late classical and medieval history provided by the *Decline and Fall* are the momentous aspects of religion's

---

[39]Noxon, "Hume's Concerns with Religion," in *David Hume: Many-Sided Genius*, 59.

[40]Duncan Forbes, *Hume's Philosophical Politics* (Cambridge: Cambridge University Press, 1975), 61, n.1 says: "[n]o one, at any rate, can deny his [i.e., Hume's] life long concern with every aspect of it [i.e., religion]: philosophical, ethical, psychological, sociological and historical."

[41]J. G. A. Pocock, "Superstition and Enthusiasm in Gibbon's History of Religion," *Eighteenth-Century Life*, n.s. 8, no. 1 (October 1982): 83.

[42]Hume's philosophy, interestingly enough, appealed to nineteenth Century German fideists. See Isaiah Berlin, "Hume and the Sources of German Anti-Rationalism," in *Against the Current: Essays in the History of Ideas*, ed. Henry Hardy (New York: Penguin, 1980), 162-87.

impact on morals and politics. History, as the philosophic historian envisions it, provides an instructive and entertaining spectacle which dramatizes the human dimensions of morality and religion. Religious beliefs and practices are major objects of interest because they are so instrumental in the developing character of social and political institutions.[43]   Indeed, Gibbon viewed religion largely in political and social terms. In one of his summational, self-evaluative pauses in the *Decline and Fall*, Gibbon says: "I have reviewed, with diligence and pleasure, the objects of ecclesiastical history, by which the decline and fall of the Roman empire were materially affected . . . ." (*DF-49*, V, 261)   The diligence is apparent in Gibbon's somewhat reluctantly drawn, less than wholesome picture of Rome's early Christians. Hume's own *History of England*, while a constitutional history, can also be read as an elaborate treatise on the relation of politics and religion.[44]

Religion though in its private, more individualistic aspects seemed to escape Hume and Gibbon. J. B. Black properly, perhaps, disparaged both Hume and Gibbon for their supposed incapacity to comprehend and appreciate the inner-spiritual qualities of Christianity.[45]   As both Hume's critics and defenders acknowledge, he was hostile to Christianity, particularly the Calvinist variant of his own country, a consequence in part of his own direct experience.   Hume's biographer, Ernest Mossner, notes that the "rigorous 'Scottish Sabbath' of the dawning eighteenth century . . . with its early morning family prayers, its two long services and sermons at the Kirk, and its severe restrictions upon personal freedom, must occasionally have struck even the most godly as depressing and gloomy."[46] The Scotland of Hume's birth was a religiously rigid and often gloomy scene, and it was ruled by an ecclesiastical tyranny that dominated every facet of national life.[47]   Hume's own boyhood parish, Chirnside, though located in the relatively

---

[43]Mary Fearnley-Sander, "Philosophical History and the Scottish Reformation: William Robertson and the Knoxian Tradition," *The Historical Journal* 33, no. 2 (1990): 323-38, argues that the philosophical history of Scottish Enlightenment, for all its modernity, stands in a relationship of continuity to the Knoxian Reformation tradition of historical writing, a relationship based on an assumption of the primacy of religion in its shaping of Scottish culture.

[44]See Stephen Paul Foster, "Different Religions and the Difference They Make: Hume on the Political Effects of Religious Ideology," *The Modern Schoolman* 46, no. 4 (May 1989): 253-74.

[45]J. B. Black, *The Art of History* (New York: F. S. Crofts and Co., 1926), 104-5, 169-73.

[46]Mossner, *Life of David Hume*, 33.

[47]Henry Grey Graham, *The Social Life of Scotland in the Eighteenth Century* (1901; reprint, New York: Benjamin Blom, Inc., 1971). See Chapters: "Religious and Ecclesiastical Life, Parts I & II" and "Theological Opinions and Teaching," for extensive detail on the religious background and climate of Hume's Scotland. Also, see Henry Buckle, *On Scotland and the Scotch Intellect*, ed. H. J. Hanham (Chicago: University of Chicago Press, 1970), 241. "In no other Protestant country, have they [the clergy] exercised such control over the universities; not only the doctrines taught, but also the mode of teaching them, being, in Scotland, placed under the supervision of the Church . . . . Over grammar-schools, the clergy possessed an authority fully equal to that which they had in the universities. They also appointed

tolerant Merse, was reputed to be a bastion of fanaticism.[48] John Knox during his Geneva exile had, as Hume notes, "imbibed from Calvin a fanaticism which augmented his native ferocity," and it was a cold fanaticism which took deep roots in the Scottish character. Calvin's doctrine of total depravity was a national preoccupation, and its observable effects on the Scots were manifest, as Henry Grey Graham notes, in their "melancholy despair" and "reckless vice."[49] While the religious moderates in the Scotland of Hume's youth were gaining authority in the Kirk, the Covenanter spirit was the prevailing one.[50] The religious climate in which Hume found himself, with its pervasive Calvinistic rigor and angst, was focused on the afterlife and on the prospect of eternal torment as the consequence of not being saved.[51] Such a profound effect by religious ideas on the lives of his own people could not have failed to arouse the criticism of a thinker like Hume. Given the pervasiveness of religion in everyday life and Hume's interests and inclinations, he seemed destined to confront and confound the eighteenth-century Christian view of human nature.[52]

Though not as hostile to Christianity as Hume, Gibbon was, apparently, largely devoid of religious feeling and highly suspicious of religious emotion. Gibbon, says Walter Bagehot, "objected to Christianity because it was the intensest of religions."[53] J. B. Bury, writes that, "so far as every sort of religious yearning or aspiration was concerned, his poverty was almost unique."[54] This is probably so. Both Hume and Gibbon disliked and distrusted the emotional side of religion. But they were hardly unique among eighteenth-century thinkers in this regard. Locke, as one scholar has noted, had bequeathed to eighteenth-century philosophers and theologians an almost pathological aversion to religious emotion.[55] Even the most

---

and removed, at their own pleasure, teachers of every grade, from village schoolmasters to tutors in private families."

[48]Shirley Robin Letwin. *The Pursuit of Certainty: David Hume, Jeremy Bentham, John Stuart Mill, Beatrice Webb* (Cambridge: Cambridge University Press, 1965), 22.

[49]Graham, *Social Life of Scotland*, 399. "That such a creed should be taught in all its nakedness could not fail to have disastrous effects on the morals which the preachers condemned—leading some to melancholy despair, others to reckless vice, and in the 'elect' to indifference as to conduct and duty."

[50]Letwin, *The Pursuit of Certainty*, 19.

[51]Graham, *Social Life of Scotland*, 404-13. The uncertainty of salvation, Graham suggests, was the cause of lifelong apprehension and a whole dismal train of terror-induced mental pathologies.

[52]Letwin, *The Pursuit of Certainty*, 27. "Having discovered the pretensions of the Kirk, and of religious enthusiasts in general, Hume bound himself to undermine them."

[53]*Collected Works of Walter Bagehot*, 8 vols., ed. Norman St. John-Stevas (Cambridge, MA: Harvard University Press, 1965), 1:385.

[54]*Encyclopedia Britannica*, 11th ed, s.v. "Gibbon."

[55]Gerald R. Cragg, *Reason and Authority in the Eighteenth Century* (Cambridge: Cambridge

conventional theologians stressed the rationality of God and eschewed "enthusiasm." The stodgy, orthodox enemy of Hume, William Warburton, Bishop of Glouchester, condemned the popular evangelist John Wesley as a "dangerous enthusiast." (Ibid., 156.)

The enduring controversy surrounding the thought of Hume and Gibbon is due, more than for any other single reason, to the implications of that thought for Christianity. Their books were viewed with resentment and vexation by the orthodox.[56] On March 18, 1776 Hume wrote from his deathbed to Gibbon in order to congratulate him on his recently published first volume of the *Decline and Fall*. Embedded in the amity of congratulations, however, was a warning: "I own I was a little curious to see how you would extricate yourself from the Subject of your two last Chapters [fifteen and sixteen]. I think you have observ'd a very prudent Temperament; but it was impossible to treat the Subject so as not to give Grounds of Suspicion against you, and you may expect that a Clamour will arise." (*Letters*-H, II, 310) Hume's curiosity was not idle, and his prediction was on the mark. The "Subject" to which Hume refers is Christianity. In spite of the "prudent temperament" (quite obviously for Hume a very important consideration in writing about religion), a "clamour" did indeed arise! Gibbon had brought a storm of religious controversy down upon himself.

Hume was regarded by many of his fellow Scots as a writer of abominable books that disparaged Christianity. (*Essays*, xxxvii) He expressed doubt about miracles, questioned Christianity's cherished centerpiece doctrine of immortality, and ridiculed Scotland's own Protestant hero, John Knox, as a rustic, stone-hearted bigot. The account of Knox's conduct in the *History of England* made Hume extremely unpopular. "[A]ll the godly in Scotland abuse me," Hume casually remarked to Adam Smith, "for my account of John Knox and the Reformation." (*Letters*-H, I, 306) Hume's letters to his close friends are full of deprecatory remarks about orthodox Christianity, particularly with reference to the clergy. To Gilbert Elliot he wrote: "[b]ut the Priests are so jealous, that they cannot bear to be touched on that Head [as objects of humor]; and for a plain Reason: Because they are conscious they are really ridiculous." (*Letters*-H, I, 153) The popular eighteenth-century evangelist and founder of Methodism, John Wesley referred to Hume as "the most insolent despiser of truth and virtue that ever appeared in the

---

University Press, 1964), 10.

[56]"Right from the beginning, Gibbon's sneering and cynical interpretation of the triumph of Christianity drew fire from ecclesiastical critics; most of these, however—Prebendary Travis, Davis, Apthorp, Dr Randolph and 'poor Chelsum'—were nonentities who merely let off blanks. But weightier figures were also to register their disapproval. Coleridge dismissed Gibbon's prose style as meretricious . . . ." Roy Porter, *Edward Gibbon: Making History* (London: Weidenfeld and Nicolson, 1988), 3.

world."[57] Hume's irreligion cost him teaching chairs at Edinburgh and Glasgow universities.[58] There was also a movement to excommunicate him from the national church. It was unsuccessful mainly because of the efforts of his liberal clergy friends to protect him. (*Letters*-H, I, 224)[59] Hume was dismayed to learn that the revered Frances Hutcheson had opposed his appointment to the Chair of Moral Philosophy at Edinburgh University referring to him as "a very unfit Person for such an Office." (*Letters*-H, I, 58) Hume's writings were scandalous and viewed as pernicious corrosives on the moral cement of eighteenth-century society.

Gibbon, like Hume, was loathed by the orthodox. He had blamed the otherworldly preoccupations of Christianity for the decline of the Roman empire, heaped scorn and abuse on the church, and sneered at the entirety of monasticism as a dreary, superstition-ridden enterprise.[60] The *Decline and Fall* compares Christianity invidiously with both the pagan religions of Rome and the religion of Islam. Edinburgh University's Dr. Thomas Bowdler suitably edited the *Decline and Fall* in order to make it safe for the young. He purged "all passages of an irreligious or immoral tendency."[61] Bowdler's editorial services were highly valued as Britain at this time was gripped by the fear of irreligion.[62] As early as 1783, even before its completion, the *Decline and Fall* was placed on the Catholic Church's *Index librorum prohibitorum*. Pope Benedict XV retained it there as late as 1917.

The hostility with which the writings of Hume and Gibbon were greeted bears heavily upon the critical interpretation of their works. In the introduction to a major work on the philosophy of Hume, Donald Livingston writes that Hume is unique among modern philosophers in that his work tends to provoke "antimonic"

---

[57]Quoted from Hugh Trevor-Roper, "The Historical Philosophy of the Enlightenment," in *Studies on Voltaire and the Eighteenth-Century* 27, 1669.

[58]Mossner, *Life of David Hume*, 153-62, 246-49.

[59]For an account of the attempt by members of the Scottish national church to excommunicate Hume and Lord Kames, see Mossner, *Life of David Hume*, 336-55.

[60]Jordan, *Gibbon and His Roman Empire*, 120, says, Gibbon "began with the assumption that barbarism and Christianity destroyed the Roman empire. This thesis loses its importance in the later volumes, and with his increasing sophistication about historical causation, Gibbon also abandons his deliberate hostility to Christianity." I don't believe that Jordan is right here in his claim that Gibbon abandoned his hostility toward Christianity in the later volumes. Gibbon's hostility toward Christianity was qualified from the beginning. It is the fanaticism and then the institutional corruption of Christianity that draws his criticism throughout the *Decline and Fall*. In the later volumes we find Gibbon at his most scathing in his narrative dealing with Christianity, particularly in treatment of the Crusades. See for example, the *Decline and Fall*, chapter 58.

[61]Quoted from McCloy, *Gibbon's Antagonism to Christianity*, 304.

[62]Womersley, *The Transformation*, 107, 109. Also see, John Redwood, *Reason, Ridicule and Religion: The Age of Enlightenment in England, 1660-1750* (London: Thames and Hudson, 1976). Much of this work treats the great fear of anti-religion in England.

interpretations. "More than any other modern philosopher," writes Livingston, "Hume has appeared as the construct of the conceptual frameworks that interpreters have imposed upon him."[63] He cites as examples Capaldi's ranking of the *Treatise* with Kant's *Critique of Pure Reason* in marked contrast with H. A. Pritchard who dismissed it as a clever, perverse work. Worth adding is that Bertrand Russell viewed Hume's philosophy as a sort of mopping up operation in the wake of Locke and Berkeley ("He represents in a certain sense, a dead end"), and he completely denigrated Hume's *History of England* as the spiteful work of a Tory bigot.[64] It is also important to emphasize that Hume's historical work has been as widely praised and roundly condemned as his philosophical work.

One of the reasons that Livingston gives for this remarkable tradition of exegesis with what he calls the "out of focus picture of Hume's achievement" is the unevenness with which Hume's philosophical and historical works have been studied. Contrary to a wide and longstanding view of Hume's philosophy, Livingston argues that his historical and philosophical works must be read as an integral whole in order to understand him properly.[65] While I believe that Livingston is correct in his assessment, there is an additional important reason that accounts for this great diversity of value attached to Hume's writings. It is the same reason that Gibbon's work, even to this day, has been greeted by the exegetes in an antimonic vein. Like Hume, Gibbon tends to appear as "the construct of the conceptual frameworks that interpreters have imposed upon him." Gibbon "still excites abuse," as Virginia Woolf says. Gibbon's work was widely excoriated, and his person was the object of ridicule and calumny. Joseph Ward Swain, one of Gibbon's biographers, writes that during his lifetime Gibbon "was the victim of an exceptional amount of malicious gossip and slander . . . . He also had the misfortune to fall into disfavour with some the ablest retailers of gossip in his day. Dr. Johnson disliked him, Boswell loathed him, Horace Walpole held him up to ridicule, and countless lesser wits followed in the train of these masters."[66] "Gibbon," jeered Richard Porson, one his early critics, "was never failing in natural

---

[63]Livingston, *Hume's Philosophy of Common Life*, 1.

[64]Bertrand Russell, *A History of Western Philosophy: And It's Connection with Political and Social Circumstances from the Earliest Times to the Present Day* (New York: Simon Schuster, 1945), 660. Of Hume's *History of England*, Russell casually writes: "Hume's *History of England* . . . devoted itself to proving the superiority of Tories to Whigs and of Scotchmen to Englishmen: he did not consider history worthy of philosophic attachment." Such a remark makes it difficult to believe that Russell ever read the work, nor does it seem likely that he was familiar with Hume's essays.

[65]Livingston, *Hume's Philosophy of Common Life*, 1-3. This is also the view of John Danford, *David Hume and the Problem of Reason: Recovering the Human Sciences* (New Haven, CT: Yale University Press, 1990), who argues a similar position.

[66]Joseph Ward Swain, *Edward Gibbon the Historian* (New York: St. Martins Press, 1966), 8.

feeling except when women were to be ravished and Christians to be martyred."[67]
Woolf herself was one of the abusers. She found the *Decline and Fall* cliched,
dull, predictable. Gibbon's fame, she grumbled, came from journalists who liked
to imitate him.[68] Christopher Dawson, while more appreciative, regarded Gibbon's
history as somewhat superficial and lacking in an understanding of the nature of
the fundamental changes that had brought down the Roman empire.[69] Arnold
Toynbee faults Gibbon for his inability to discern in the history of Rome larger
historical patterns. This inability, he argues, vitiates the attempt of the *Decline and
Fall* to create a perspective of decline and disintegration. "Gibbon," Toynbee
writes, "fails to recognize the two historical truths that the *Pax Augusta* was a
disintegrating Hellenic Society's tardy response to the challenge of a four-hundred-
years-long Time of Troubles, and that the weak points, as well as the strong points,
of the Roman Empire only become intelligible when they are viewed against this
historical background . . . ."[70]

Yet the fulsome praise and admiration for Gibbon's work were and are no less
in force. Both Hume and William Robertson greatly admired the style and learning
of the *Decline and Fall*. Robertson "tested" a portion of Gibbon's 8,362 references
and relinquished to Gibbon his self-proclaimed title of most industrious historian.
"Before you [Gibbon] began your historic career, I used to pride myself in being
at least the most industrious historian of the age; but now, alas! I can pretend no
longer even to that praise."[71] Hume himself lauded Gibbon. In his letter of
congratulations, written in the last months of his life, he wrote: "[w]hether I
consider the Dignity of your Style, the Depth of your Matter, or the Extensiveness
of your Learning, I must regard the Work as equally the Object of Esteem; and I
own, that if I had not previously had the happiness of your personal Acquaintance,
such Performance, from an Englishman in our Age, would have given me some
Surprize." (*Letters*-H, II, 309)

Hume's remarks are remarkably wide-sweeping in their expression of
approval. The style, the content, and Gibbon's erudition are all elements that
deeply impressed the dying Hume. Hugh Trevor-Roper writes that the nineteenth-
century historian, Thomas Carlyle "hated Gibbon for having shattered the
comfortable, unquestioned philosophy in which he had been brought up."[72] Some,

---

[67]Quoted from Bagehot, *Collected Works*, 1: 386.

[68]Virginia Woolf, *"The Historian and 'The Gibbon'* in *Collected Essays"* (New York:
Harcourt Brace and World, 1967), 1: 115.

[69]Christopher Dawson, "Edward Gibbon: Annual Lecture on a Master Mind, Henriette Hertz
Turst," *Proceedings of the British Academy*, (1934), 176.

[70]Arnold Toynbee, *A Study of History* (London: Oxford University Press, 1954), 9: 746.

[71]Quoted from Porter, *Edward Gibbon: Making History*, 73.

[72]Trevor-Roper, "Gibbon and the Publication of the *Decline and Fall of the Roman Empire*,

like Carlyle, found Gibbon's treatment of Christianity offensive and mean spirited. Yet, who could doubt his unsurpassed erudition or his indefatigable application? Cardinal Newman, whom Lytton Strachey notes in his *Eminent Victorians*, "feasted on the worldly pages of Gibbon,"[73] came to lament that "the chief, perhaps the only English writer who has any claim to be considered an ecclesiastical historian, is the unbeliever Gibbon."[74]   Trevor-Roper, it should be noted, viewed Gibbon's achievement as a singular event in the intellectual history of the West. "Gibbon is a man whom one never forgets . . . the perusal of his work forms an epoch in the history of one's mind."[75] The ancient historian Arnaldo Momigliano says that "we owe it to Gibbon that the problem of the relations between Christianity and the political and social developments of Europe has come to stay in European historiography."[76] Gibbon's penetration into the history of Christianity was sufficiently profound to alter, as Momigliano notes, its very historiography.

I believe the reason the works of both Hume and Gibbon have provoked such dichotomies of interpretive and evaluative response is that they cast upon Christianity a pervasive shroud of doubt which touches upon all of its significant features, the epistemological (the knowledge of religious truth), the moral (the practice of religious truth), and the historical (the origins of religious faith). Neither of the two in comparison to some of their French philosophe counterparts directly or dogmatically attacked Christianity.   Hume and Gibbon slyly built "escape hatches" into their critiques of Christianity. Hume's epistemology didn't rule out miracles, just a rational justification for their belief. Gibbon's five secondary causes, which explained Christianity's success in naturalistic terms, were nevertheless pronounced by him to be secondary causes. That Gibbon was harshly critical of Christianity is undeniable; that he had no use for it is certainly not the case.[77] Though derided by some of his critics as a heathen protégé of Voltaire,

---

1776-1976," 504.

[73]Lytton Strachey, *Eminent Victorians* (New York: G. P. Putnam's Sons, 1918), 37.

[74]Quoted from Porter, *Edward Gibbon: Making History*, 134.

[75]Trevor-Roper, "Gibbon and the Publication of the *Decline and Fall of the Roman Empire*, 1776-1976," 505.

[76]Arnaldo Momigliano, *Studies in Historiography* (London: Weidenfeld and Nicolson, 1966), 52.

[77]Paul Turnbull, "The 'Supposed Infidelity' of Edward Gibbon," *The Historical Journal* 5, no. 1 (March 1982): 23-41. Gibbon's ambivalence toward Christianity has been commented on by various interpreters. Turnbull, however, advances an extreme "revisionist" thesis arguing that Gibbon was actually a Christian. The argument, completely unconvincing in my view, relies on some strained interpretations of a couple of letters and deathbed conversion reports, and overlooks the bulk of his writings about Christianity. Turnbull's article, however, is a good example of the dichotomous modality of interpretation surrounding Gibbon, particulary in the context of Christianity. Was Gibbon an infidel or a Christian?

Gibbon chastises the French deist for his sloppy historical writing and his anti-Christian partiality. "In his own way, Voltaire was a bigot, an intolerant bigot." (*DF-67*, VII, 146, n.15)[78] Gibbon, in fact, eschewed the atheism of his French contemporaries as dogmatic and motivated by arrogance. "Yet I was often disgusted with the capricious tyranny of Madame Geoffrin, nor could I approve the intolerant zeal of the philosophers and Encyclopedistes, the friends of d'Olbach and Helvetius: they laughed at the scepticism of Hume, preached the tenets of atheism with the bigotry of dogmatists, and damned all believers with ridicule and contempt." (*Memoirs*, 136) Thus, Gibbon sympathetically linked himself to the skeptical Hume. But the skepticism, particularly with regard to religion, was serious, not flippant. Gibbon regarded the scoffing of the likes of Voltaire and Helvetius as demeaning to the subject and intentions of the philosophic historian.[79]

The Hume-Gibbon attack on Christianity provoked doubt, doubt at least that Christianity could be articulated and defended by means of human rationality and that its history demonstrated its truth. They did not offer an alternative secularized faith to the one they were criticizing, unlike the Jacobin attackers of Christianity in France with their religion of humanity, or later the Bolsheviks in Russia with their vision of the socialist workers' paradise. They did not provide doctrinal alternatives to Christianity, merely doubt about Christianity's own. Thus it is the sheer doubt, the agnostic outcome of their work that in part creates the space for the extensive range of interpretative response. The doubts they raised about Christianity rebounded upon them. Their motives, their characters, the dangerous consequences of their ideas all became rich areas for speculation and extrapolation. The significance for Christianity of the moral and epistemological questions that Hume had raised was immediately apparent. He was, like Gibbon, savaged by a number of his prominent contemporaries including Samuel Johnson, James Boswell, and James Beattie for imputed motives of vanity and arrogance in his skeptical undermining of Christian-based morality. "Johnson's standard line about Hume and infidels in general was that they were motivated by vanity, which

---

[78]R. R. Palmer, *Catholics and Unbelievers In Eighteenth-Century France* (Princeton, NJ: Princeton University Press, 1939), 7, also comments on Voltaire's bigotry and intolerance. "Fréron, a conservative and Catholic journalist, was called by Voltaire, in a single work, a scribbler, scoundrel, toad lizard, snake, spider, viper's tongue, crooked mind, heart of filth, doer of evil, rascal, impudent person, cowardly knave, spy, and hound. He found his journal gagged, his income halved and his career ruined by the concerted attacks of the philosophers."

[79]J. G. A. Pocock, "Gibbon and the Idol Fo: Chinese and Christian History in the enlightenment," in *Sceptics, Millenarians and Jews*, ed. David S. Katz and Jonathon I. Israel (Leiden: E. J. Brill, 1990), 19. "In his remarks about Bayle, and even more about Voltaire, it is a constant that mere scepticism is unscholarly because flippant, and flippant because unscholarly; and behind all his jokes and innuendoes about theologians lies an unalterable determination that this critical investigation of theology must be maintained and not given up."

prevented them from seeing the truth. Hume, he told Boswell, was a 'man who has so much conceit as to tell all mankind that they have been bubbled [i.e., deceived] for ages, and he is the wise man who sees better than they.'"[80] Hume, it seems, had ignobly kicked out the religious props of moral life and left nothing but a smug, self-centered skepticism that would be of little use to anyone but a philosopher. "Hume and other infidels," said Boswell, "destroyed our principles and put nothing firm in their place." (Ibid., 36) Boswell, incidentally, made a similar complaint about Gibbon's dissimulated attack on Christianity, referring in his *Life of Johnson* to the *Decline and Fall* as a work "which, under the pretext of another subject, contained much artful infidelity."[81]

Hume late in his life expressed bitterness with the abuse he believed himself to have endured from the "bigoted" English literati. In a letter to his friend and publisher William Strahan he writes: "[c]onsidering the Treatment I have met with, it would have been very silly for me at my Years to continue writing any more; and still more blameable to warp my Principles and Sentiments in conformity to the Prejudices of a stupid, factious Nation, with whom I am heartily disgusted . . . . For as to any Englishman, that Nation is so sunk in Stupidity and Barbarism and Faction that you may as well think of Lapland for an Author." (*Letters*-H, II, 269) Hume had identified himself morally with the pagan skeptics, rejected the religion of his countrymen, and spent his life writing philosophical and historical works that were critical of it. He understandably was an object of abuse for his efforts and, again, was understandably resentful. "Thus, Hume was an angry man in the mid-1770s—angry, above all, with English 'zealots' such as Johnson and other members of the London literary-intellectual world. The celebration of Beattie and the attacks on his own work were proof to Hume that religion was not only false but harmful; it ruined one's mind because it soured the 'natural' affections and inflamed the passions."[82] Hume was hostile to and uncomprehending of the transcendental and otherworldly orientation of Christianity.

Gibbon's own writing about Christianity is so oblique, so marked by ironic implication, that attempts to characterize his critique of Christianity in any simple, obvious way do him an injustice. A modern critic writes that: "Gibbon's attack on Christianity was more offensive in manner than incisive in content. There was little sustained argument but much innuendo."[83] Such a judgment can hardly stand after carefully considering Gibbon's treatment of miracles in the *Decline and Fall* and

---

[80]Stephen Miller, "The Death of Hume," *Wilson Quarterly* 30 (summer 1995): 35-36.

[81]Quoted from Thomas Jemielity, "Gibbon Among the Aeolists: Islamic Credulity and Pagan Fanaticism in *The Decline and Fall*," *Studies in Eighteenth-Century Culture* 19 (1989): 165.

[82]S. Miller, "Death of Hume," 36-37.

[83]Cragg, *Reason and Authority*, 152.

its historiographical implications for Christianity.   Gibbon had added historiographical doubts to the moral and epistemological ones. Certainly Gibbon is a master of innuendo, but his narrative is crafted to present the evidence for his interpretation of events in a manner that confronts the received outlook in a persistently disturbing and unsettling manner. The strong reaction that Gibbon provoked with his critical handling of "The Progress of Christianity" in chapter fifteen attests to the disturbing quality of his critical perspective and gives credence to the claim of another critic that he had, in effect, put Christianity in a new, uncomfortable, and defensive position by forcing Christian apologists to deal on his terms, to consider the doubts he raised about the origins of this historical religion.[84]

Of Gibbon, Bury writes that upon returning from his Lausanne exile, he "easily settled into a sober, discreet, calculating Epicurean philosopher, who sought the *summum bonum* of man in a temperate, regulated, and elevated pleasure."[85] Bury's Gibbon is similar to Hume in his moral identification with the skeptical pagan philosophers. Gibbon, however, in my view, was less antagonistic toward Christianity generally than Hume and had more appreciation for its contributions.[86] For one thing, Gibbon came to rely heavily upon and appreciate the labors of annalists and historians like the Catholic Le Nain de Tillemont and the Protestant Johannes Mosheim. "[T]he historian Mosheim is full, rational, correct, and moderate." (*DF-47*, V, 104 n.1) High praise for the usually critical Gibbon. For another, Gibbon was willing to credit Christianity in some instances with advancing civilization.[87]   While chapter thirty-seven of the *Decline and Fall* opens with a scathing critique of the monks in the East, later in the chapter Gibbon celebrates the conversion of the Goths to Christianity. "The progress of Christianity has been marked by two glorious and decisive victories: over the learned and luxurious citizens of the Roman empire; and over the warlike Barbarians of Scythia and

---

[84]Thomas W. Africa, "Gibbon and the Golden Age," *The Centennial Review* 3, no. 3 (summer 1963): 280-81.

[85]*Encyclopedia Britannica*, 11th ed., s.v. "Gibbon."

[86]See David Dillon Smith, "Gibbon in Church," *Journal of Ecclesiastical History* 35, no. 3 (July 1984): 452-63, for an account of Gibbon's church attendance and some of his general views on Christianity. "[W]e know that [Gibbon] dutifully sat in the family pew at Buriton, occasionally attended services elsewhere and was indeed something of a connoisseur of sermons." (452)

[87]Also, Letwin, *The Pursuit of Certainty*, 18, observes that: "[t]he Reformation [in Scotland] had not, as in England, reduced religion to a political and individual concern. Instead it replaced Catholicism with another complete interpretation of all the facts of existence." This would suggest that Hume was less open to appreciating Christianity's value and was reacting against a much more pervasive and powerful ecclesiastical system of authority than existed in Gibbon's England and Switzerland. "There was nothing anywhere to brighten the atmosphere of gloom and hopelessness in which the grimmest sort of religion flourished." (19)

Germany, who subverted the empire and embraced the religion of the Romans."
(*DF-37*, IV, 81) Christianity wrought a civilizing effect upon the barbarous Goths.
"The Goths were the foremost of these savage proselytes; and the nation was
indebted for its conversion to a countryman, or, at least to a subject, worthy to be
ranked among the inventors of useful arts, who have deserved the remembrance
and gratitude of posterity." (*DF-37*, IV, 81-82)[88] Gibbon did see great social value
in Christianity, however, with regard to its truth, he remains agnostic.[89] Here
Gibbon's philosophic skepticism prevails. Religion at its best for Gibbon elevates
human sociability by creating the images, ceremonies, and myths that help give
expression to spiritual aspirations and by refining those strong passions that
manifest the potential to heighten enmity and conflict.[90] Proper religion strengthens
social traditions by giving them the vestments of respect.

In what sense, if any, can we say that Hume and Gibbon were personally
"religious"? Both, I believe, had completely rejected Christianity which they saw
as a long historical vacillation between fanaticism and superstition. They doubted
away, as we shall see, Christianity's miracles and were generally skeptical about the
claims of revealed religions. Hume's religious views have been described,
somewhat misleadingly in my view by Livingston, as a "philosophical theism."
(Ibid., 332) Any theism attributed to Hume should be rigorously qualified so as to
account for what is essentially an agnosticism with regard to any possible
knowledge of God. (*Treatise*, 633, n.1) Gaskin's characterization of Hume as an
attenuated deist--an atheist from the Christian perspective--is probably more
accurate or descriptively appropriate than Livingston's.[91] If Hume could in any way

---

[88]W. H. C. Frend, "Edward Gibbon (1737-1794) and Early Christianity," *Journal of
Ecclesiastical History* 45, no. 4 (October 1994): 670, points out Gibbon's praise for the Christian
conversion of the Goths.

[89]Pocock, "Gibbon and the Idol Fo," 18. "Although it is pretty clear that at some point Gibbon
ceased to be what is meant by a believer, it has to be constantly born in mind that he was a child of the
Protestant, not the Voltarian Enlightenment, and that the two are very different in both origin and spirit."
Pocock adds that Gibbon's "Protestant" orientation helps innoculate him against the "extremes of popery,
predestination and puritan fanaticism or 'enthusiasm.'"

[90]D. Smith, "Gibbon in Church," 460. "Nevertheless public worship seemed to Gibbon
essential in maintaining 'the religious sentiments of a people,' even if such elevated minds as those of the
poet or the philosopher might be able to sustain their devotion merely by private 'prayer, meditation and
study.' And the interruption of the practice of public worship, he said, 'may consummate in the period
of a few years, the important work of a national revolution.' The church was indeed one of the props of
Gibbon's society to which it should lend both stability and moral support. It was in this respect that the
pulpit had an important role to play." Also, see Livingston, Hume's *Philosophy of Common Life*, 329-
334, for a discussion on "True Religion," for Hume. Much of Livingston's discussion could be applied
to Gibbon as well.

[91]J. C. A. Gaskin, *Hume's Philosophy of Religion*, 2nd ed. (Highlands, NJ: Humanities Press
International, 1985), 222.

be characterized as religious it would be in the sense that he would lend support to and show respect for forms of religious expression that help sustain the traditional moral order. Custom plays a large role in Hume's moral philosophy and religious custom can and often does have value for him. Hume was not like some of his French contemporaries, militantly atheistic and categorically hostile to all religion. He was sympathetic to the dignified religious bearing of Charles I. The effect of Hume's philosophical theism, says Livingston, "is to endorse a deeply traditionalistic and conservative view of social and political order."[92] This is essentially correct, I believe, and it applies to Gibbon as well. Whatever religious feeling they might have had was expressed as public morality and manifested in a veneration for the ancient and traditional rituals that gave cohesion and order to moral and social affairs. Both Hume and Gibbon approbated the classical moralists like Epicurus who, though skeptical participated in the rituals of their countrymen out of respect.

II. Christianity and the "Conservatism" of Hume and Gibbon

Virtue without terror is powerless.

---

[92]Livingston, Hume's Philosophy of Common Life, 332.

II. Christianity and the "Conservatism" of Hume and Gibbon

Virtue without terror is powerless.

M. Robespierre

The Hume-Gibbon attack on Christianity was a feat of a philosophically refined, self-critical moralism. It was self-critical in the sense that these philosophic historians were employing their insight and erudition to attack the religious foundations of their own culture. Certainly Hume and Gibbon viewed themselves as moralists, and their critique of Christianity possesses a moral perspective and a style characteristic of iconoclastic writers. However, in attempting to grasp and characterize that perspective one is led inevitably to that tendentious generality known as the "Enlightenment"—the very term itself a masterpiece of historico-moral imagery—and a consideration of the array of associated aspirations and ideals its admirers celebrate or illusions and malignancies its detractors castigate. The Hume-Gibbon critique of Christianity was of course a conspicuous piece of Enlightenment iconoclasm that brought criticism to bear on all aspects of contemporary culture. Art, commerce, education, politics, etc., were seen by Enlightenment thinkers to be hampered and oppressed by the long-established, jealously regarded authority of the church.[93] The church was the enemy. (Ibid., xviii)[94] However, because the Enlightenment as a historical, moral, and philosophical abstraction lends itself to sweeping characterizations with tendentious ideological implications, it is important to qualify the "Enlightenment thinking" of Hume and Gibbon, particularly as it relates to their criticism of Christianity.[95]

---

[93] See Paul Hazard, *European Thought in the Eighteenth Century: From Montesquieu to Lessing*, trans. J. Lewis May (New Haven, CT: Yale University Press, 1954), particularly Chapter one, "The Ubiquitous Critic." "In London, a very learned man, John Arbuthnot by name, gathered some of the leading intellectuals of the day about him, and together they founded one of the queerest sodalities every heard of. They called it the Scriblerus Club, and its object was to throw ridicule on every kind of literary ineptitude and incompetence. It seemed to give notice to the Europe of 1713 that the spirit of criticism was abroad in the world." (3)

[94] Hazard writes: "[i]t was more than a reformation that the eighteenth century demanded, it was the total overthrow of the Cross, the utter repudiation of the belief that man had ever received direct communication from God; of the belief, in other words, in Revelation. What the critics were determined to destroy, was the religious interpretation of life."

[95] Consider Peter Gay's own self-admitted tendentiousness. "[T]he amiable caricature drawn by liberal and radical admirers of the Enlightenment has been innocuous: the naïveté of the Left has been far outweighed by the malice of the Right. Still, like the conservative view, the liberal view of the Enlightenment remains unsatisfactory and calls for revision. And so scholars have turned to polemics. I have had my share in these polemics, especially against the Right, and I must confess that I have enjoyed them. But the time is ready and the demand urgent to move from polemics to synthesis." Peter Gay, *The*

One helpful suggestion for making such a qualification comes from Ernest Gellner who contrasts the "British style of Enlightenment" with the "French or Romance style."[96] Gellner articulates the difference between the two, respectively, in terms of ratifying and analyzing important social and political changes that *had* occurred, the "Enlightenment of the reformed," as against angry protestations that changes be made, i.e., the "Enlightenment of the unreformed." (Ibid., 115) The bifurcation thus expressed is richly suggestive: the French philosophes with their hatred for *l'Ancien Régime* stand in contrast to the self-congratulatory British, proud of their own political heritage. While gradualist social and political reform followed in the wake of Britain's Enlightenment—no civil wars, no revolutions, expanded enfranchisement—from France's ensued a revolution, regicide, a reign of terror, and Napoleon. The astute early twentieth-century sociologist Elie Halévy observes that the deposition of James II forced moderation and toleration upon the British religious establishment, and thus the government did not face a ferocious anti-clerical intelligentsia intent on imposing its own secular but rigorous ideology. "[T]he ministers of the Nonconformists sects, which had come into being at the time of the civil and religious wars and had until then been centers of Illuminism, seemed to relax their Calvinist intransigence. Content at having contributed to the overthrow of the catholicizing Stuart dynasty and having secured legal toleration for the practice of their faith, they turned their backs on fanaticism and became, in matters of doctrine, open-minded and rationalist."[97]

Gellner's British-French Enlightenment-contrast is useful in arguing for a "conservative" character for the British Enlightenment of which Hume and Gibbon were dominant figures.[98] The characterization of Hume and Gibbon as conservatives raises a number of issues. "Conservative" can be used to characterize a person's political and social thought, attitude, and conduct.[99] Thus

---

Enlightenment: An Interpretation. Vol. 1, *The Rise of Modern Paganism* (New York: W. W. Norton, 1966), ix.

[96]Gellner, *Plough, Sword and Book*, 115-16.

[97]Elie Halévy, *The Birth of Methodism in England*, trans. and ed. Bernard Semmel (Chicago: University of Chicago Press, 1971), 34-35.

[98]The argument for Hume as a political conservative has been made by a number of his twentieth-century interpreters. Livingston, *Hume's Philosophy of Common Life*; David Miller, *Philosophy and Ideology in Hume's Political Thought* (Oxford: Clarendon Press, 1981); Frederick G. Whelan, *Order and Artifice in Hume's Political Philosophy* (Princeton, NJ: Princeton University Press, 1985); and Sheldon S. Wolin, "Hume and Conservatism," in *Hume: A Re-evaluation*, ed. Donald W. Livingston and James T. King (New York: Fordham University Press, 1976), 239-56, all affirm for Hume's conservatism. John B. Stewart, *Opinion and Reform in Hume's Political Philosophy* (Princeton, NJ: Princeton University Press, 1992), argues against all of these writers.

[99]All of my discussion on conservatism in Hume and Gibbon acknowledges Livingston's cautionary remarks about the difficulty involved in using terms like "liberal" and "conservative." See

it is important to be precise and accurate about what features of their thought, attitudes, and modes of conduct would make it reasonable to characterize Hume and Gibbon as conservatives. They unquestionably were both enthusiastic supporters and admirers of the British Constitution. Hume had incurred the wrath of Whig historians who resented him, the historian of England, "who had presumed to shed a generous tear for the fate of Charles I and the Earl of Strafford." Gibbon reviled the French Revolution and concurred with Burke's denunciation of the French radicals who toppled *l'Ancien Régime.* Yet, as philosophic historians, Hume and Gibbon were both highly critical of Christianity and thus they were, in contrast to many religious conservatives like Burke, philosophically radical.[100] "The fascination of Hume's political thought," says David Miller, "lies in seeing how a revolutionary philosophy is combined with an establishment ideology to yield what is probably the best example we have of a secular and sceptical conservative political theory."[101] Three separate but related issues emerge to form a case for the consideration of Hume and Gibbon as *conservative* critics of Christianity: Hume's support of the British constitution and his rejection of the radical Whig's right to revolution; the political theorizing of Hume and Gibbon within the context of the French Revolution; and the anti-Christian feature of the thought of Hume and Gibbon and its implication for conservative political thinking.

Donald W. Livingston, "On Hume's Conservatism," *Hume Studies* 21, no. 2 (November 1995), 152. "[T]hese terms ["liberal" and "conservative"] have not only changed their meaning over time, they are highly contested terms, being in their very nature partisan expressions the expectations of which cannot entirely escape a political commitment."

[100]See Anthony Quinton, *The Politics of Imperfection: The Religious and Secular Traditions of Conservative Thought From Hooker to Oakshott* (London: Faber and Faber, 1978). Quinton distinguishes secular from religious conservatism in British political thought: Hume and Gibbon would be examples of the former, Burke the latter. Quinton argues (13-14) that religious conservatives tend to stress the *moral* imperfection of human beings while the secular conservatives stress the *intellectual* limitations. This is an extremely important distinction and one often overlooked in the argumentation over Hume's conservatism. Stewart, *Opinion and Reform,* argues—contra Livingston, Miller, and Wolin—against a conservative interpretation of Hume by making Burke the paradigm of conservative thinkers and then showing—what no one will dispute—that Hume differs in fundamental ways from Burke. "Never does Hume renounce reflection; never does he, with Burke, recommend a policy of simply following inherited tradition, a policy that is 'the happy effect of following nature, which is wisdom without reflection, and above it.'" (219) This is certainly the case. However, Hume's conservatism, following Quinton's distinction, is rooted in his view of the limits of rationality. Burke's defense of the status quo was largely on religious grounds—Burke's "wisdom" is that of revealed Christianity. Hume did not, as Stewart rightly asserts, embrace uncritically *any* long established status quo. Hume's conservatism is, as will be argued below, best understood in the historical context of the French Revolution, and it is quite plausible to suggest that Hume would have, like Gibbon, been highly critical of the destruction of *l'Ancien Régime.*

[101]D. Miller, *Philosophy and Ideology in Hume's Political Thought,* 2.

The British Constitution and the Right to Revolution

Hume was an admirer and defender of the British Constitution. He viewed it as a long term, largely successful experiment in balancing both of the primary, but antithetical ingredients necessary for an enduring, stable, political order—authority and freedom. Hume warmly approbated the British Constitution in his writings. "The plan of *liberty* is settled; its *happy effects* are proved by experience; a long tract of time has given it *stability*; and whoever would attempt to overturn it, and to recall the past government or abdicated family, would, besides other more criminal imputations, be exposed, in their turn, to the reproach of faction and innovation." (*Essays*, 501, italics added) Note the boast of the "happy effects" of "liberty" and the resulting stability offered by the British Constitution. "Innovation" and similar locutions are almost always terms of disapprobation for Hume when he discusses politics. "Let us cherish and improve our ancient government as much as possible," he admonishes in his essay "Principles of Government," "without encouraging a passion for such dangerous novelties." (*Essays*, 36) "Novelties" refer in this context to a hypothetical proposal to shift greater power to the House of Commons in emulation of the Dutch Republic. When Hume contemplates political history, he almost always comes down on the side of tradition and established governments. Here are observations he makes in the *History of England* in reflecting on the role of religious dissenters during the reign of Elizabeth: "[i]n the particular exertions of power, the question ought never to be forgotten, *What is best*? But in the general distribution of power among the several members of a constitution there can seldom be admitted any other question than, *What is established*? . . . . If any other rule than established practice be followed, factions and dissensions must multiply without end: and though many constitutions, and none more than the British, have been improved even by violent innovations, the praise bestowed on those patriots to whom the nation has been indebted for its privileges ought to be given with some reserve, and surely without the least rancour against those who adhered to the ancient constitution." (*HE*, IV, 184-85, original italics) Note again Hume's aversion and disdain for innovations in politics, much of which lie in his overall pessimism and a concern for the vulnerability of institutions which depend upon the shifting passions of human nature.[102]

Consider also Hume's comment on the destruction wrought by the "innovative" Puritans during the English civil war: "[a]uthority, as well as liberty,

---

[102]See J. G. A. Pocock, *The Machiavellian Moment: Florentine Political Thought and the Atlantic Republican Tradition* (Princeton, NJ: Princeton University Press, 1975), 494. "It should be stressed . . . that Hume continued to regard the British constitution as a compromise between absolute monarchy and popular republic, and rated high the chances that it would gravitate toward one extreme or the other in the end."

is requisite to government; and is even requisite to the support of liberty itself, by maintaining the laws, which can alone regulate and protect it. What madness, while everything is so happily settled under ancient forms and institutions, now more exactly poised and adjusted, to try the hazardous experiment of a new constitution, and renounce the wisdom of our ancestors for the crude whimsies of turbulent innovators!" (*HE*, V, 77) Here is the great emphasis on authority, an element, Hume argues, that is necessary for a stable government and ultimately liberty itself. Experimentation of the kind Hume speaks of here constitutes a repudiation of ancestral wisdom. Authority is eroded by the turbulence of religious enthusiasts who jettison the tested, the known, and the established for the airy aspirations of reckless innovators.

In his "Of the Original Contract" Hume took aim at the radical Whig case for a right to revolution on the basis of an original contract broken by a usurpating sovereign. "Let not the establishment at the *Revolution* deceive us, or make us so much in love with a philosophical origin to government, as to imagine all others monstrous and irregular." (*Essays*, 472) Hume is apprehensive about the intrusion into politics by philosophy, i.e., he is wary of "philosophical" theories which make exclusive normative claims about what constitutes legitimate government. The "original contract," upon which government was supposed to be founded, was a central piece of Whig political philosophy. "They [the original contract theorists] affirm, that all men are still born equal, and owe allegiance to no prince or government, unless bound by the obligation and sanction of a *promise*." (*Essays*, 469) Hume was intent on discrediting Whig ideology because he believed it to be pernicious. "In reality, there is not a more terrible event, than a total dissolution of government, which gives liberty to the multitude, and makes the determination or choice of a new establishment depend upon a number, which nearly approaches to that of the body of people." (*Essays*, 472)

The radical Whig original contract theorizing from Hume's perspective was defective both theoretically and practically. Theoretically, the original contract rested on what Hume pejoratively referred to as a "metaphysical" doctrine, i.e., a construct of philosophizing without experience. The original contract doctrine, as Hume points out in "Of the Original Contract," has little do with political history or political experience. "But would these reasoners look abroad into the world, they would meet with nothing that, in the least, corresponds to their ideas, or can warrant so refined and philosophical a system." (*Essays*, 469-70) Almost everywhere in the world one looks, princes and governors lay claim to obedience, and subjects comply with no thought or recognition of a contract or compact that binds the prince and gives the right of revolution in its abeyance. Such philosophizing produces paradoxes or conundrums that violate common sense and common practice. "And nothing is a clearer proof, that a theory of this kind is erroneous, than to find, that it leads to paradoxes, repugnant to the common sentiments of mankind, and to the practice and opinion of all nations and all ages." (*Essays*, 486) What follows from the perspective of the "common sentiments of mankind" in the wake of the original contract theory is a glaring inconsistency between the way many or most governments are founded and operate and the way they are supposed to be constituted and supposed to operate. The theoretical norm, in effect, is removed from or untouched by practical reality. The original contract theorist affirms "*that absolute monarchy is inconsistent with civil society, and so can be no form of civil government at all; and that the supreme power in a state cannot take from any man, by taxes and impositions, any part of his property, without his own consent or that of his representatives.*" (*Essays*, 486-87, original italics) Such theorizing in Hume's view is vitiated by its incapacity to account for so much of the political experience that is reflected in actual practice. "What authority any moral reasoning can have, which leads into opinions so wide of the general practice of mankind, in every place but this single kingdom, it is easy to determine." (*Essays*, 487)

The second defect of original contract theorizing is practical. A theory that affirms and supports a right to revolution is in Hume's view dangerous and reckless. In order for governments to exist and provide whatever benefits they can for their subjects they need authority more than anything else. Without that authority, without the opinion on the part of the governed that the government possesses some legitimate claim to their allegiance, power is simply up for grabs, a process which is often sanguinary and destructive. In "Of the Coalition of Parties" Hume writes: "[b]ut the people must not pretend, because they can, by their consent, lay the foundations of government, that therefore they are to be permitted, at their pleasure, to overthrow and subvert them." (*Essays*, 499) A right to revolution is, as noted above, dangerous, and it is unnecessary. It is dangerous in Hume's view because it gives encouragement to political innovators, chronic discontents, and opportunists, and it is unnecessary because if a prince or governor is sufficiently egregious—offering no protection or benefit to his subjects—he will be overthrown. "Nor is any one, when he reads of the insurrections against Nero or Philip the Second, so infatuated with party-systems, as not to wish success to the enterprize, and praise the undertakers." (*Essays*, 490) No one, Hume might argue, really *needs* a right to revolution.

In his "Origin of Government" Hume points out that all governments represent a dynamic balance in some fashion or other of liberty and authority. "[L]iberty," Hume says, is the "perfection of civil society," but authority, in a sense, is more basic and primary in that it is the necessary condition for the existence of civil society, i.e., a society that operates under some set of political rules. (*Essays*, 41) "[B]ut still authority must be acknowledged essential to its [civil society's] very existence: and in those contests, which so often take place between the one and the other, the latter may, on that account, challenge the preference." (*Essays*, 41) Authority is the foundation of the political order and Hume, as we can see, attaches great importance to it. Herein lies one important element of Hume's conservatism.

Hume's disdain for radical Whig revolutionary ideology and rhetoric and his proclivity for established authority raise the issues of his own support for the Protestant Settlement of 1689 and the consistency of his conservative affirmation for established authority. In his "Of the Protestant Succession" Hume concedes that the displacement of the Stuarts by the Hanoverians set a dangerous precedent in its rejection of the established family. "Would not every popular leader put in his claim at every vacancy, or even without any vacancy; and the kingdom become the theatre of perpetual wars and convulsions?" (*Essays*, 503-04) The Hanoverian succession did what every departure from precedent and established norm does, namely, significantly raise the risk of bringing on a sanguinary and protracted power struggle. Yet, Hume rejects the Jacobite claims for the Stuarts and Whiggishly affirms the Hanoverian succession. In a letter to Henry Home, Hume mentions his essay and its Whig proclivities. "The conclusion [of "Of the Protestant Succession"] shows me a Whig, but a very sceptical one." (*Letters*-H, I, 111)

The *kind* of Whig that Hume is, though, is a conservative, establishment, mid-eighteenth-century Whig, a skeptical one, as he notes, who rejects the Jacobite arguments for the return of the Stuarts. Hume, in effect, takes up an establishment line and argues for the Protestant Settlement. The Settlement has been vindicated by its success. "[T]he whole force of our constitution has always fallen to one side, and an uninterrupted harmony has been preserved between our princes and our parliaments. Public liberty, with internal peace and order, has flourished almost without interruption: Trade and manufactures, and agriculture, have encreased: The arts, and sciences, and philosophy, have been cultivated. Even religious parties have been necessitated to lay aside their mutual rancour." (*Essays*, 508) The pivotal issue in Hume's analysis is the religious question. Religion had been the main source of political contention throughout the seventeenth century: Hume had written about this with considerable passion. It was the main cause of the civil war and the fall of Charles I, and it was the principle reason for James II's abdication of the throne and exile. Why not, given their long-reaching claims to the throne, bring the Stuarts back? "The disadvantages of recalling the abdicated family consist chiefly in their *religion*, which is more prejudicial to society than that established amongst us, is contrary to it, and affords no toleration, or peace, or security to any other communion." (*Essays*, 506, italics added) Religion was indeed the biggest problem with the Stuarts.   Roman Catholicism had been defeated by Cromwell and his Puritans. A Roman Catholic prince in England, whether in 1689 or 1745, would have been a prince of a minority religion and a widely hated one at that. This, as Hume argues in the *History of England*, was simply a recipe for tyranny or civil war. "[H]e [i.e., James II] persisted in asserting, that he never meant to subvert the laws, or procure more than a toleration and an equality of privileges to his Catholic subjects. . . . And such was his zeal for proselytism, that, whatever he might at first have intended, he plainly stopped not at toleration and equality; he confined all power, encouragement, and favour, to the Catholics. Converts from interest would soon have multiplied upon him . . . . And, on the whole, allowing this king to have possessed good qualities and good intentions, his conduct serves only, on that very account, as a stronger proof, how dangerous it is to allow any prince infected with the Catholic superstition to wear the crown of these kingdoms." (*HE*, VI, 305-06) Hume is quite clear and unequivocal here: Roman Catholic princes, no matter how well intentioned, would not be able to rule effectively over Great Britain.

Hume's objection to the Catholicism of the Stuart's had nothing to do with the its theological or doctrinal features: it was purely political. A zealot prince of a minority religion would destabilize the civil order. Hume had in fact greatly sympathized with the earlier Stuarts (James I and Charles I) whom he saw to be victims of Puritan religious fanaticism. Indeed, it was Hume's sympathy for the Charles I that earned him his reputation as a Tory historian.[103] Hume, however, strived valiantly not to be a "party historian," Tory or Whig. Rather as Mossner says: "the practical lessons of history that he [Hume] teaches are colored by a cautionary skepticism concerning the likelihood of continuous human progress that belongs to what may with equal justice be called the large, non-party, Conservative tradition." (Ibid., 235) This characterization of Hume's political, "practical lessons" is consistent with Hume's claim to be a "very sceptical" Whig. Thus, Hume's sympathy for the early Stuarts and castigation of the fanatical Puritanism that routed Charles I, and his support for the removal of James II and the installation of William and Mary are all of a consistent, conservative piece. The enemy for Hume was radical, philosophical religion.

Hume, Gibbon and the French Revolution

Hume's attachment to the British Constitution—with its balance of liberty and authority—set him in contrast to the French philosophes and the absolutist

---

[103]See, Ernest Campbell Mossner, "Was Hume a Tory Historian? Facts and Reconsiderations," *Journal of the History of Ideas* 2 (1941): 225-36.

tendencies of their philosophical theorizing that inspired a loathing for *l'Ancien Régime* and the radical attack on it. The philosophes' cure for the disease of the old order—at its center an "unreformed," absolutist, truth-monopolizing church—was its own secularized version of ideological absolutism.[104] "[T]he 'French' or Romance style, whether in the form of the doctrine of the Encyclopaedist, in Comtian positivism, or in its prolonged later addiction to Marxism, is drawn precisely to some such counter-doctrine and counter-church. It is drawn to systems built of mundane, naturalistic or historicist elements, but one, in its general architecture and spirit, mirroring all too faithfully that which it would repudiate and replace."[105]

Thus, the characterization of Hume (and Gibbon, as we will see) as conservative is perhaps best argued and appropriately understood in the context of the ideological climate of the French Revolution and its historical aftermath.[106] Conservatism, as Livingston argues, "is not a timeless disposition to defend the status quo but a historically limited movement that appears on the scene only to defend a certain sort of value and to combat a certain sort of enemy. Although differing widely on many things, conservatives have agreed about the enemy: the violent intrusion of rationalistic metaphysics into politics." (Ibid., 308) Livingston defines conservatism as a "doctrine of limits, in particular a doctrine of the limits beyond which philosophical criticism of social and political order cannot go." (Ibid.) Although he died thirteen years before the onset of the French Revolution, Hume, Livingston argues, had worked out the criticism of what he saw as the violation of politics by philosophy; the French Revolution being an egregious example of such a violation (what Livingston calls a "metaphysical rebellion"). Edmund Burke, of course, went on to articulate a critique of the French

---

[104]Note the remarks of Robert Darnton, "In Search of the Enlightenment: Recent Attempts to Create a Social History of Ideas," *Journal of Modern History* 33, no. 1 (March 1971): 116, who contrasts French anticlericalism with the lack of it in Protestant countries like England. "How incompatible were Christianity and the Enlightenment, in any case? They were enemies in France, but there philosophy fed on persecution and a tradition of anticlericalism absent in Protestant countries."

[105]Gellner, *Plough, Sword and Book*, 116. Also see Raymond Aron, *The Opium of the Intellectuals,* translated by Terence Kilmartin (New York: Doubleday, 1957), 215. "Thanks to the double success of the Reformation and Revolution, in the sixteenth and seventeenth centuries, the British Intellegensia never found itself in conflict with the Church and the ruling class."

[106]Livingston, *Hume's Philosophy of Common Life*, 307. "To understand the conservative mind and Hume's relation to it, we should begin with what self-professed conservatives have said about their position. Erik von Kuehnelt-Leddihn, a contemporary Austrian conservative, views his own thinking as a criticism of various forms of what J. L. Talmon has called 'totalitarian democracy,' a way of thinking that Kuehnelt-Leddihn traces to the French Revolution: 'the roots of the evil are historically-genetically the same all over the Western World. The fatal year is 1789, and the symbol of iniquity is the Jacobin Cap.'"

Revolution[107] and its "metaphysical rebellion," but Hume, claims Livingston, "should be thought of as the first conservative philosopher."[108] Hume's *History of England* and his political essays were taken up by French conservatives after the Revolution as powerful documentation to support the Counter-Revolution.[109]

What does it mean though in the context of Hume's philosophic history to speak of limitations to philosophical criticism of the social and political order? What, in effect, is metaphysical rebellion, and what is wrong with it? Metaphysical rebellion is the penetration of politics by "metaphysics," by a system of ideas resistant to reformation or reshaping by experience. Those engaged in metaphysical rebellion attempt to impose their philosophical theories into moral practice in the absence or defiance of the constraints of experience, experience conformed by common opinion. "All the philosophy," says Hume, ". . . [t]herefore, in the world, and all the religion, which is nothing but a species of philosophy, will never be able to carry us beyond the usual course of experience, or give us the measures of conduct and behaviour different from those which are furnished by reflections on common life." (*EHU*, 146) Note that for Hume philosophy and religion are all of a piece. Philosophy, like religion, goes bad when it sets itself against or remains indifferent to experience. Superstition and enthusiasm are what Hume calls "corruptions of true religion." (*Essays*, 73) The corruption Hume speaks of is a corruption of politics by metaphysics. Superstition—in its quest to perpetuate by coercion its metaphysical system—sets up priest-ridden, despotic political orders where inquisitions are carried out, where freedom is suppressed. Enthusiasts, energized by their metaphysical utopian visions, overturn established political orders and impose their own equally oppressive dictatorships. Hume's favorite example of this is Cromwell's New Model army driven by the fanatical hatred of Romanism. In both cases we have a metaphysical rebellion, i.e., a penetration of politics by "metaphysics," by a system of ideas resistant to reformation or reshaping by experience. Philosophy emulates corrupted religion when its practices come to resemble those of corrupted religions,

---

[107]Livingston, "On Hume's Conservatism," 154. "Burke argued that the revolution in France should not be viewed as a legitimate demand for reform but as the self-serving work of a corrupt philosophical consciousness whose world inversions had flattened out the landscape of inherited cultures and customs making the very notion of reform unintelligible."

[108]Livingston, *Hume's Philosophy of Common Life*, 310. "In Hume's philosophy, however, we find a conceptual structure designed to rebut revolutionary thought and capable of explaining in broad outline the conservative view of legitimate social and political order." Also, on the relationship of Hume's conservatism to Burke's, see Wolin, "Hume and Conservatism," 252-53. "Hume's analytical conservatism prepared the way for Burke in many respects. Although the latter possessed a conviction and passion which Hume lacked, many of the same materials had been worked over in Hume's writings."

[109]Bongie, *David Hume, Prophet of the Counter-Revolution*. This is pointed out by Livingston, *Hume's Philosophy of Common Life*, 310.

when philosophy becomes "sectarian," i.e., resistant to modification or correction from experience.[110] Corrupted modern philosophy takes its form in utopianism. One can reasonably argue, I believe, that Hume would have viewed the Jacobins in much the same way as he did the seventeenth-century Puritans who toppled Charles I—as fanatical, impassioned theorizers who, on the basis of an untested system of belief, would sweep away an established order.

Hume makes a crucial distinction between the kind of technical or scientific knowledge in which the opinion and knowledge of experts should prevail over what he calls "general opinion," and the moral knowledge in which the opposite is the case. "[T]hough an appeal to general opinion may justly, in the speculative sciences of metaphysics, natural philosophy, or astronomy, be deemed unfair and inconclusive, yet in all questions with regard to morals, as well as criticism, there is really no other standard, by which any controversy can ever be decided." (*Essays*, 486) Moral standards (as well as aesthetic ones) are derived from, established by, and confirmed by the broad experience of many people; not by select coteries of professional thinkers. Moral wisdom develops slowly from the refinement of historical experience. Philosophy or abstract theorizing about virtue and goodness have little direct efficacy in producing virtuous people. "[G]eneral virtue and good morals in a state, which are so requisite to happiness, can never arise from the most refined precepts of philosophy, or even the severest injunctions of religion; but must proceed entirely from the virtuous education of youth, the effect of wise laws and institutions." (*Essays*, 55) Wise laws and institutions come into place across generations and have an almost slow experimental character.

The context of the French Enlightenment and the ideological climate of 1789 have a particular significance when Hume is placed in opposition to J. J. Rousseau. With some risk of oversimplification, Hume and Rousseau can be construed as Enlightenment antipodes. Rousseau's *Contrat Social* provided the philosophical and ideological ammunition for the conduct of the Revolution, and his enigmatic character and career personify the metaphysical rebellion to which Hume was so resistant.[111] Hume and Rousseau were almost exact contemporaries. Rousseau was born a year after Hume and survived him by two, and though like Hume, he died over a decade prior to the onset of the Revolution, Rousseau is

---

[110]Livingston, *Hume's Philosophy of Common Life*, 311-13.

[111]See Gordon H. McNeil, "The Cult of Rousseau and the French Revolution," *Journal of the History of Ideas* 6, no. 2 (1945): 197-212. McNeil writes (206) that the "*Contrat social* itself was published thirteen times between 1792 and 1795, and one edition was appropriately issued in pocket Bible size for the use of the soldiers defending *la patrie*. Collections of extracts were equally popular, the editor of one of them expressing the hope that the *Contrat social* rather than the sword would overthrow the thrones of Europe."

closely associated—ideologically—with it.[112] Virtually every aspect of a Hume-Rousseau comparison is emblematic of conflicting or contrary values, from their characters and personalities to their philosophical views on the foundations of society and morality. Hume, warm, sociable, and affable, a man who was nurtured by deep and life-long friendships, stands in stark comparison to the sentimental but unstable Rousseau, who seemed to be incapable of forming normal attachments to others. Hume's life stands out in its propriety, continuity, stability, and sociability; while Rousseau's is the embodiment of alienated genius, characterized by insecurity, rootlessness, and narcissism. Even their memoirs provide a remarkable contrast suggesting how their characters and personalities point in two profoundly different moral directions. Hume's "My Own Life," succinct and artfully understated, is intended to speak to his life's work and passion (his writings) and his reputation, as these two things are integrally connected. It is his final, summative pronouncement on his career as a moral philosopher. It concludes: "though most men anywise eminent, have found reason to complain of calumny, I never was touched, or even attacked by her baleful tooth: and though I wantonly exposed myself to the rage of both civil and religious factions, they seemed to be disarmed in my behalf of their wonted fury." (*Essays*, xli) Not exactly true, but this is consistent with Hume's character and demeanor. Stoical and detached, Hume made every attempt, even at the end, to set himself apart personally from religious passion and political controversy. Hume sought to be both honorable and conventionally respectable. "My friends never had occasion to vindicate any one circumstance of my character and conduct . . . ." (*Essays*, xli) Rousseau's prolix *Confessions* is a masterpiece of romantic self-presentation. His act of confession was itself revolutionary in its depths of frankness, an attempt to set himself in opposition to norms of an artificial society he despised.

When the two philosophers encountered each other they managed to initiate a ridiculous and infamous quarrel that turned into a *cause célèbre*. The quarrel itself was a remarkable phenomenon of philosophical polarity in which many major Enlightenment figures in both France and England came to choose sides in what was simultaneously an amusing and serious affair.[113] Hume initially befriended the

---

[112]See Gordon H. McNeil, "The Anti-Revolutionary Rousseau," *American Historical Review* 58, no. 4 (July 1953): 808-823, and Aram Vartarian, "The French Enlightenment and Its Nineteenth-Century Critics," *Studies in Burke and His Time* 18, no. 1 (winter 1977): 3-26.

[113]Dena Goodman, "The Hume-Rousseau Affair: From Private *Querelle* to Public *Procès*," *Eighteenth-Century Studies* 25, no. 2 (winter 1991-92): 171-201. Also Mossner, *Life of David Hume*, devotes a chapter, "Jean-Jacques Rousseau," to the quarrel. F. L. Lucas, *The Art of Living: Four Eighteenth-Century Minds* (New York: Macmillan Co., 1960), 20, writes of the quarrel: "[h]ere one may symbolically see the sanity of the Enlightenment attacked, bewildered, and baffled by that romantic, neurotic, fanatic frenzy which was to erupt in French Revolution and Romantic revival; to be checked awhile by the material solidity of the nineteenth century; and to devastate with yet wilder irrationalism the

hapless, bohemian Rousseau, arranged to bring him and his dog, Sultan, to England, and even secured for him a pension from George III. Hume, however, unwittingly managed to get mixed up in a practical joke played on Rousseau by Horace Walpole. Rousseau blamed Hume and in addition accused him of malice and treachery—figments of his paranoid imagination. Hume, initially incredulous, took exception and the quarrel ensued.[114] D'Holbach had forewarned Hume about Rousseau: "*Je vous le dis franchement, vous allez rechauffer un serpent dans votre sein.*"[115]

The theory of the social contract, however, is the pivotal philosophical point of this emblematic comparison of Hume with Rousseau. The comparison turns on the extent to which the social and political views of each of these two are conditioned and shaped by historical thinking. How one views history in large part determines the value one attaches to the *conservation* or *repudiation* of existing institutions. Hume's "Of the Original Contract" provides an initial point of contrast. "Did one generation of men go off the stage at once, and another succeed, as is the case with silk-worms and butterflies, the new race, if they had sense enough to choose their government, which surely is never the case with men, might voluntarily, and by general consent, establish their own form of civil polity, without any regard to the laws or precedents, which prevailed among their ancestors. But as human society is in perpetual flux, one man every hour going out of the world, another coming into it, it is necessary, in order to preserve stability in government, that the new brood should conform themselves to the established constitution, and nearly follow the path which their fathers, treading in the footsteps of theirs, had marked out to them." (*Essays*, 476-77) Hume, arguing against the contractarian view of political legitimacy, attempts to show that such a view implies the necessity for a continuous re-invention of those "laws and precedents" that significantly regulate social conduct. Hume makes the historical point that institutions possess an enduring character beyond that of any particular person or generation, and that the historical shape of an institution—its production over time of legal, social, and moral constraints—indeed is the profound advantage it offers. What is not explicit here, but what Hume stresses elsewhere throughout his writings and particularly in his history, is that without the various conventions of social restraint life is

---

first half of the twentieth."

[114]The quarrel became a public debate with, as noted, philosophers taking up sides. See Daniel Gordon, *Citizens Without Sovereignty: Equality and Sociability in French Thought, 1670-1789* (Princeton, NJ: Princeton University Press, 1994), 163. "It is not difficult to establish why people like Suard, d'Alembert, and Lespinasse favored Hume over Rousseau. Apart from the fact that Rousseau's accusations were a fraud, Hume was more appealing because he was a recognized defender of politeness and civilization, whereas Rousseau their greatest critic."

[115]Quoted from Lucas, *The Art of Living*, 21.

brutish. The rules of restraint do not come easily to human beings who are by nature egoistical and practically short-sighted. Hume would be completely resistant to any notion of a noble savage and is philosophically and anthropologically distant from Rousseau's view of human beings whose essential goodness is corrupted by social institutions. *"L'homme est né libre, et partout il est dans les fers,"* Hume would have found to be perversely paradoxical.[116] Hume's confidence in the humanizing value of the artifices of civilization, such as rules of property, stands in diametrical opposition to Rousseau's suspicion of them and ambivalence toward them. Sheldon Wolin notes that for Hume: "[h]istorical time imparted to social arrangements a qualitative element. Time implied experience, and experience in turn provided the motive for gradual adjustment. Conversely, the greatest calamity was violent change, which worked to snap the close union which history had fashioned between an institution, its utility, and its duration. In contradicting the nature of time and experience, sweeping change could not adapt institutions according to utility; for utility, in political matters, was inseparable from time and experience."[117]

Rousseau in contrast with Hume argues that every generation must give its consent in order for a government to be legitimate. *"Il faudrait donc, pour qu'un gouvernement arbitraire fût légitime, qu'à chaque génération le peuple fût le maître de l'admettre ou de le rejeter: mais alors ce gouvernement ne serait plus arbitraire."*[118] This, of course, is precisely what Hume rejects. Rousseau's argument for the social contract fails to appreciate that history—embodying, as it does, time and experience—creates legitimacy, gradually and incrementally. "When a new government is established, by whatever means, the people are commonly dissatisfied with it, and pay obedience more from fear and necessity, than from any idea of allegiance or of moral obligation. The prince is watchful and jealous, and must carefully guard against every beginning or appearance of insurrection. Time by degrees removes all these difficulties and accustoms the nation to regard, as their lawful or native princes, that family which at first, they considered as usurpers or foreign conquerors." (*Essays*, 474-75) The key element

---

[116]Rousseau had told Hume that he regarded *Du Contrat Social* as his best work. Hume quite disagreed. "I think this work [*La Nouvelle Héloïse*] his [i.e., Rousseau's] masterpiece; tho' he himself told me, that he valu'd most his *Contrat Sociale*; which is as preposterous a Judgement as that of Milton, who preferd the Paradise regaind to all his other Performances." (*Letters-H*, II, 28) In a letter to Turgot Hume spoke of Rousseau's writings as essentially full of sophistry. "I always esteemed his Writings for the Eloquence alone and . . . looked on them, at the bottom, as full Extravagance and of Sophystry. I found many good Judges in France and all in England, of a like Opinion." (*Letters-H*, II, 91)

[117]Wolin, "Hume and Conservatism," 247.

[118]Jean-Jacques Rousseau, *Du Contrat Social*, ed. Ronald Grimsley (Oxford: Clarendon Press, 1972), 109.

here is the passage of time and the accretion of history: time insidiously transforms both perceptions and behavior on the part of the prince and the people.[119] "The original establishment was formed by violence, and submitted to from necessity. The subsequent administration is also supported by power, and acquiesced in by the people, not as a matter of choice, but of obligation. They imagine not, that their consent gives their prince a title: But they willingly consent, because they think, that, from long possession, he has acquired a title, independent of their choice or inclination." (*Essays*, 475) Hume thus describes political legitimacy as a nuanced outgrowth of an historical process in contrast to Rousseau who views it categorically and abstractly.[120] *"Puisque aucun homme n'a une autorité naturelle sur son semblable, et puisque la force ne produit aucun droit, resent donc les conventions pour base de toute autorité légitime parmi les hommes."*[121] Rousseau seems to emerge in contra-distinction to Hume as a profoundly anti-historical thinker, and it is easy to understand why critics of the French Revolution seized upon his work as embodying an anti-historical destructive rationale for the wholesale repudiation of the *l'Ancien Régime*.[122] "As Taine was to remark, echoing Burke, the new state was to be a state of men without history. In this specific sense, he was right. History was to be given a fresh start, as Barère proclaimed to the National Assembly."[123] Indeed, Rousseau's thinking is traditionally associated with the

---

[119]Robert Nisbet, *Conservatism: Dream and Reality* (Minneapolis, MN: University of Minnesota Press, 1986), 23. "Basic to conservative politics is its view of the role of history. 'History' reduced to its essentials is no more than experience, and it is from conservative trust in experience over abstract, and deductive thought in matters of human relationships that its trust in history is founded."

[120]See Michael Oakeshott, *Rationalism in Politics and Other Essays* (Indianapolis, IN: Liberty Press, 1991), 84, for observations on Rousseau's efforts to achieve a political theory devoid of contingency. "The problem of how to achieve infallibly correct political decisions, how to make infallibly just laws, how to be ruled by a mistake-proof will, devoid of contingency, is one to which Rousseau continually returns." Rousseau's problem, as Oakeshott notes, is that the absence of any contingencies, historical or otherwise, prevents the theory from going in any possible normative or explanatory direction. "But the nemesis which overtook Plato, overtook Rousseau also. A mistake-proof *volonté général* is substituted for deliberative discourse (which must always be liable to error), but it is found to have no instructions whatever for interpreting any actual political situation or about the response to be made to it." Oakeshott's reasoning here is similar to Hume's in his rejection of the original contract as a normative theory of political obligation.

[121]Rousseau, *Du Contrat Social*, 108.

[122]McNeil, "The Cult of Rousseau," writes (205-6) that the "Jacobins are usually considered followers of Rousseau, and there is some justification for this. His admirers were to be found in all parts of the party. There was the radical Marat, who was said to have been one of the few to know and appreciate the *Contrat social* before the Revolution. Of the Dantonist moderates, Hérault de Séchelles and Camille Desmoulins were disciples. But Maximilien Robespierre was both the most famous Jacobin and the most famous disciple of them all. His religion of the Supreme Being may very well have been derived, at least in part, from Rousseau . . . ."

[123]J. S. McClelland, "Introduction" to *The French Right From De Maistre to Maurras*, ed.

radical elements of the French Revolution such as Marat and is often excoriated by conservative critics of the Revolution. "We are not the converts of Rousseau," exclaims Burke.[124]

Gibbon, unlike Hume, did not write essays or treatises on political and social philosophy. He did, like Hume, affirm the British Constitution: "Britain perhaps is the only powerful and wealthy state which has ever possessed the inestimable secret of uniting the benefits of *order* with the blessings of *freedom*." (*MW*, III, 560.) Gibbon notes the accomplishment of the British government's balance of those same antithetical values that Hume stresses; order or authority against freedom or liberty. Gibbon echoes Hume's esteem for the British political traditions: "I acknowledge with pleasure and pride the good sense of the English nation, who seem truly conscious of the blessings which they enjoy; and I am happy to find that the most respectable part of opposition has cordially joyned in the support of 'things as they are'." (*Letters*-G, III, 265) Gibbon, as we shall see, was horrified by the French Revolution.

Gibbon's political views must be extrapolated from his history and his correspondence. Hume, as noted above, was long dead by 1789, but Gibbon then was living in Lausanne and, observing the Revolution from nearby, concurred with Burke's diagnosis of the "French disease." In a 1791 letter to Lord Sheffield, he wrote that "Burke's book [*Reflections on the Revolution in France*] is a most admirable medicine against the *French disease*, which has made too much progress even in this happy country. I admire his eloquence, I approve his politics, I adore his chivalry, and I can even forgive his superstition." (*Letters*-G, III, 216, italics added)[125] Burke was tainted a bit, it seems, by a certain affinity for superstition, but not nearly enough to overcome Gibbon's admiration for his conservative political principles. Gibbon shared Burke's disdain for the revolutionaries and their doctrine of equality, and his contempt for the unfolding "metaphysical rebellion." Writing to Lord Sheffield in December of 1789, he descants upon the progress of the revolution. "Their King brought a captive to Paris after his palace had been stained with the blood of his guards: the Nobles in exile, the Clergy plundered in a Way which strikes at the root of all property, the capital an independent Republic, the union of the provinces dissolved, the flames of discord kindled by the worst of men (In that light I consider Mirabeau), and the honestest of the Assembly, a set

---

J. S. McClelland (New York: Harper and Row, 1970), 19.

[124]Edmund Burke, *Reflections on the Revolution in France* (Indianapolis, IN: Bobbs-Merrill, 1955), 97.

[125]Nearly twenty years earlier Gibbon supported a petition in the House of Commons that relieved clergymen, lawyers, and physicians from the obligation to subscribe to the Church of England's Thirty-Nine Articles. Burke opposed this petition, a fact mentioned by Gibbon in one of his letters. (*Letters*-G, I, 305)

of *wild Visionaries* (like our Dr. Price) who gravely debate and dream about the establishment of a pure and perfect democracy of five and twenty millions, the virtues of the golden age and the primitive rights and equality of mankind which would lead in fair reasoning to an equal partition of lands and money." (*Letters*-G, III, 184, italics added) Gibbon's reproachful observation is full of pathos and conveys a pervasive sense of violation and destruction. The institutions of the ancient kingdom lie in ruins; the political order is shattered; the conflict has promoted the dregs and unleashed the worst human elements. This bitter, impassioned denunciation of the French eleuthromaniacs ("wild Visionaries") captures the essence of Gibbon's conservative outlook and its distrust of theorists such as the non-conformist minister Richard Price, whom he sees as a corrupted, sectarian philosopher, unconstrained by historical experience. Gibbon clearly was disgusted by radicals such as Mirabeau who presided over the dismantlement of institutions, which, though flawed, were nevertheless worthy of preservation and reform. "The French nation had a glorious opportunity, but they have abused and may lose their advantages. If they had been content with a liberal translation of our system, if they had respected the prerogatives, of the crown and the privileges of the Nobles, they might have raised a solid fabric on the only true foundation, the natural Aristocracy of a great Country." (*Letters*-G, III, 184)

Gibbon also rejected the perfectionism reflected in the thinking of radicals such as Price and was quick to ridicule his egalitarianism. "My own contempt for the wild & mischievous system of Democracy will not suffer me to believe without positive proof that it can be adopted by any man of a sound understanding and historical experience." (*Letters*-G, III, 337) History, Gibbon opines, argues in condemnation of democracy. As noted above, Gibbon was very much an admirer and supporter of the British Constitution, and he had served in Parliament as a sound establishment Whig.[126] The French, he complained in a letter to Lord Sheffield in 1791, "spread so many lyes about the sentiments of the English nation, that I wish the most considerable men of all parties and descriptions would join in some public act declaring themselves satisfied with, and resolved to support, our present constitution." (*Letters*-G, III, 216) Gibbon despised the levelling ideology and feared what the spread of French equality would mean for his own status. "Most of the crimes," he writes, "which disturb the internal peace of society are produced by the restraints which the necessary, but unequal laws of property have

---

[126]For an extensive discussion of Gibbon's political views and orientation, see, H. T. Dickinson, "The Politics of Edward Gibbon," *Literature and History* 8, no. 4 (1978): 175-96. Dickinson writes (179), that: "[t]hey [the establishment Whigs] appreciated the benefits of limited government and they were ready to protect every subject's rights under the rule of law, but they were implacably opposed to any attempt to democratize the constitution. As a staunch defender of the existing constitution and prevailing political order, Gibbon was a conservative or establishment Whig."

imposed on the appetites of mankind, by confining to a few the possessions of those objects that are coveted by many." (*DF-4*, I, 93) In comparison with most others Gibbon's station in life was enviable, and he knew it. (Ibid.)[127] "When I contemplate the common lot of mortality, I must acknowledge that I have drawn a high prize in the lottery of life." (*Memoirs*, 173) The Revolution, Gibbon feared, would engulf Europe and eventually ruin the happy life he had built in Lausanne. "I begin to fear that Satan will drive me out of the possession of Paradise . . . . Where indeed will this tremendous inundation, this conspiracy of numbers against rank and property, be finally stopped? Europe seems to be universally tainted, and wherever the French can light a match, they may blow up a mine." (*Letters*-G, III, 287-88) Like Hume's, Gibbon's conservatism has significance within the historical context of the French Revolution. His affinity with Burke and his revulsion for British sympathizers like Price and French democrats like Mirabeau arise out of a social and political perspective that embraces hereditary monarchy and an aristocracy of privilege, and links political rights to the possession of property.[128] The French could have emulated the British and built a constitutional monarchy upon a solid natural aristocracy of privilege.

In the *Decline and Fall* Gibbon offers a defense of hereditary monarchy which employs a mode of reasoning resonate with Hume's. How, Gibbon proposes, should the succession of authority work in a state? This is obviously an extremely important question in a work that features the chaos coming out of the crumbling political institutions of Imperial Rome. "In the cool shade of retirement, we may easily devise imaginary forms of government, in which the sceptre shall be constantly bestowed on the most worthy by the free and incorrupt suffrage of the whole community. Experience overturns these airy fabrics, and teaches us that in a large society the election of a monarch can never devolve to the wisest or to the most numerous part of the people." (*DF-7*, I, 181)

Thus deployed is a Hume-like characterization of the work of philosophy as "the reflections of common life, methodized and corrected." The "cool shade of retirement" is an otherworldly image for philosophy unconstrained by experience, by history. Common life experience counteracts the illusions of such an idealized view of political succession. A hereditary monarchical form of government,

---

[127]Dickinson, writes of Gibbon's view of his lot: "Gibbon was fully conscious of his good fortune in being born a member of the propertied élite and he feared all schemes which might rob him of these advantages."

[128]See David Womersley, "Gibbon's Unfinished History: The French Revolution and English Political Vocabularies," *The Historical Journal* 35, no. 1 (1992): 63-89. Womersley cites (73) three main features of Gibbon's political convictions: an hereditary monarch is superior to an elected one because it avoids faction and tumult; a natural aristocracy of a country is its true foundation; and political rights appropriately and happily coincide with the possession of property.

though, as Gibbon notes, is a fair target for abuse and ridicule, is actually the best. Why? It is unlikely that in a large society the selection or election of "the most worthy" will be the actual outcome decided by what Gibbon calls the "multitude" who are subject to the vicissitudes of passion. It is not simply that Gibbon lacks confidence in the common people which, as an eighteenth-century aristocrat, he did. Worthiness, or what might be termed moral merit, is inherently contentious and, with such an enviable prize at stake, the process of determining "the most worthy" would stimulate passionate and dangerous contention. "[O]ur more serious thoughts will respect a useful prejudice, that establishes a rule of succession, independent of the passions of mankind; and we shall cheerfully acquiesce in any expedient which deprives the multitude of the dangerous, and indeed the ideal, power of giving themselves a master." (*DF-7*, I, 181) Gibbon's problem with "the most worthy" principle of succession is that it neither defines nor outlines any actual predictable *process* of selection: it leads away rather than toward agreement and in so doing ultimately makes force decisive. "The army is the only order men sufficiently united to concur in the same sentiments, and powerful enough to impose them on the rest of their fellow-citizens; but the temper of soldiers, habituated at once to violence and to slavery, renders them very unfit guardians of a legal or even a civil constitution." (*DF-7*, I, 181-82)

The major advantage of an hereditary monarchy is, simply put, that it is an obvious solution to the problem of succession. It provides a means for the convergence of agreement—on who should rule—and thus reduces the danger or need for resorting to conflict or force. "The superior prerogative of birth, when it has obtained the sanction of time and popular opinion, is the plainest and least invidious of all distinctions among mankind. The acknowledged right extinguishes the hope of faction, and the conscious security disarms the cruelty of the monarch." (*DF-7*, I, 182) For Hume, the *opinion* of legitimacy is what is crucial in creating the conditions of political legitimacy. "It is . . . on opinion only that government is founded; and this maxim extends to the most despotic and most military governments, as well as to the most free and most popular." (*Essays*, 32) Like Hume, Gibbon recognizes that the *opinion* of legitimacy remains the critical element in the stability of government. Gibbon commends heredity as a principle for the recognition of authority and of the transfer of power, not for any intrinsic reasons and not because he believed that it would necessarily guarantee that the best would rule, but merely because of its convenience as a salient point for agreement. What is critical is not so much who is the object of agreement to possess power but that there is a commodious way for essentially egoistic individuals to agree at all. Agreement is hugely important: making agreement easy to achieve is equally so. Gibbon's argument for hereditary monarchy is congruent with Hume's disquisition on the Protestant succession.

Religious and Secular Conservatism

Though we have set the conservatism of Hume and Gibbon in the context of a British, as distinct from a more radical French Enlightenment ideology, it is also important to refine the conservatism of Hume and Gibbon insofar as it has a direct bearing on their attack on Christianity. Conservative politics, particularly the conservative reaction to the French Revolution, is typically closely linked to a profoundly religious outlook. The French Catholic right ferociously attacked everything associated with the anti-Christian tendencies of the philosophes, particularly, as noted above, Rousseau.[129] Burke's conservatism was likewise religious as well as political. The French Revolution for him was not merely an attack on a social-political order; it was an assault on Christianity and the moral order it upheld. Moreover, in his *Reflections on the Revolution in France,* Burke had argued that religion is the foundation of the moral and political order. "We know, and it is our pride to know, that man is by his constitution a religious animal; that atheism is against, not only our reason, but our instincts; and that it cannot prevail long."[130]

The conservatism of Hume and Gibbon is, however, distinctively secular in its philosophical basis in contrast with conservatives, like Burke, who argue that the authority for the moral norms and sanctions of a society or community must come from an affirmation of eternal religious truths. Hume's critique of the original contract theory helps provide a key to understanding how this secular philosophy and establishment ideology combine. Duncan Forbes has observed that Hume's utilitarian justification for government along with his repudiation of the original contract theory is part and parcel of his rejection of the "religious hypothesis." Hume's critique of the original contract was another piece of his attack on Christianity. "The contract theory which Hume attacked rested on some supernatural sanction; for the contractarians, the promise, unlike government, was not just one more invention in the interests of society, that is, human society in the 'lower' or 'narrower' sense, which for Hume is its only meaning. The obligation to keep faith, according to the 'fashionable system', would hold even if there were no such thing as society in Hume's sense at all."[131]

---

[129]For a representation of attacks on the French Revolution from the French Right, ranging from the eighteenth century through the twentieth, see McClelland, ed. *The French Right.*

[130]Burke, *Reflections on the Revolution in France,* 103.

[131]Forbes, *Hume's Philosophical Politics,* 67.

Forbes' observation is most important, particularly since it stresses the impact of Hume's ideas about religion on the formulation of his theory of political obligation and bears out as well the consistent and pervasive secularizing tendency of his thinking.   Hume's critique of the original contract theory, Forbes acknowledges, is well known. Less obvious has been how heavily that critique rests on a rejection of the "religious hypothesis." "[W]ithout his critique of the religious hypothesis he has only scotched the snake, not killed it." (Ibid., 66) Hume's criticism of the original contract does not simply reflect a different conception of human political behavior or a variant concept of political obligation: it moves profoundly against a larger, theologically grounded view of the world.

Hume's explanation of how governments actually come into being and how they are maintained takes theology out of politics in a manner analogous to his wholesale rejection of rationalism in religion. Human beings, Hume observes, are flawed by a kind of practical myopia: they tend to prefer short-term satisfaction over long-term gains.[132] "[F]ew are successful in the pursuit [of happiness]. One considerable cause is the want of strength of mind, which might enable them to resist the temptation of present ease or pleasure, and carry them forward in search of more distant profit and enjoyment." (*EPM*, 239) The climb from barbarism to civilization is in part a practical education in how to contend with this perennial human weakness. Even though individuals may understand the long-term value of curbing their natural avarice and the importance of correcting a built-in partiality, human inclination with all its practical short-sightedness works against such restraint. Hume puts it this way. "All men are sensible of the necessity of justice to maintain peace and order; and all men are sensible of the necessity of peace and order for the maintenance of society. Yet, notwithstanding this strong and obvious necessity, such is the frailty or perverseness of our nature! it is impossible to keep men, faithfully and unerringly, in the paths of justice . . . . This great weakness is incurable in human nature." (*Essays*, 38)

While this great weakness is incurable, however, it can, to use Hume's term, be "palliated." This palliation involves the creation of general rules of conduct. Hume here speaks of the "necessity of justice," i.e., of the need for there to be general rules which apply to everyone and which support the social order. Having rules and someone whose generally acknowledged job it is to enforce them provides a degree of security and predictability of conduct. Trust and cooperation emerge. A system of rules, once in place and enforced with some relative consistency, is to a degree sufficient to obviate the practical short-sightedness which characterizes the human condition and which is attended with so many

---

[132]For an extensive analysis of this kind of practical myopia recognized by Hume, see John G. Cross, *Social Traps* (Ann Arbor, MI: University of Michigan Press, 1980).

practical disadvantages. Without rules and some assurance of consistent enforcement this necessity does not obtain and there is no security for life and property. Government in its most elemental and primal form imposes order by punishing or threatening to punish rule breakers. Thus government in Hume's view comes to be approbated through its capacity to enforce rules and encourage behavior that is limited through norms of self-restraint. Without self-restraining norms little can be achieved beyond the most rudimentary forms of existence. The Hobbesian "war of all against all" characterizes human interaction in the absence of self-restraint and rule-conformity: life is "nasty, brutish, and short." Human beings are eminently social, the most social perhaps of all creatures, and all their possibilities for happiness and greatness lie in inventing and practicing the arts of cooperative endeavor and discovering the vast utility of mutual assistance and trust.

Political institutions, Hume argues, imperfect as they are, create the minimal foundations for rule-conformity with respect to security of person and property and thus provide the necessary stability and security for civilization to emerge and endure. Civilization, Duncan Forbes says, is for Hume mainly a political or legal concept. Civilized people are the inventors of institutions that give rise to law and liberty.[133] "Of all men that distinguish themselves by memorable achievements," Hume says, "the first place of honour seems due to Legislators and founders of states, who transmit a system of laws and institutions to secure the peace, happiness, and liberty of future generations." (*Essays*, 54) Hume's enthusiasm for the state is not as an end in itself but as a means—involving primarily the encouragement to rule-conformity—to secure peace and create the conditions for people to enjoy liberty. Politics is the arena where human beings make their great social achievements as active participants in the process of rule creation. Living by rules is what enables people to curb their more violent passions and escape their destructive consequences. Hume, in speaking of the means of attaining happiness in one of his essays, says that: "[w]hen . . . we have fixed all the rules of conduct, we are *philosophers*: When we have reduced these rules to practice, we are *sages*." (*Essays*, 149, original italics) Governments provide for the enforcement of certain kinds of rules[134] which make human behavior regular and predictable. That in turn

---

[133]Forbes, *Hume's Philosophical Politics*, 296.

[134]Hume's rules are "rules of justice" which refer to norms that define mainly the economic and material conditions of society; norms that give rise to promise-keeping which make contractual relations possible and ultimately provide for commerce and exchange, and norms that establish the security of property. A society in which promises are broken with impunity and in which property has little security quite obviously can generate little of economic value, and ultimately little of cultural, civilized worth. Hume actually formulates three rules of justice: "the stability of possession, of its transference by consent, and of the performance of promises." On the "strict observance of those three laws," Hume says, "the peace and security of human society entirely depend." (*Treatise*, 526)

provides a basis for human reciprocity, reliability, trust, and cooperation. Thus, it is in the limitations of human nature that we find the originative forces for the invention of government, an agency whose fundamental role is that of a rule enforcer. "It is evident," says Hume, "that, if government were totally useless, it never could have place, and that the sole foundation of the duty of allegiance is the *advantage*, which it procures to society by preserving peace and order among mankind." (*EPM*, 205, original italics) The assertion is explicit. The entire basis ("the sole foundation") for political allegiance is utility ("the advantage, which it procures to society"). Hume casts off the original contract theory of political obligation because the notion of an original contract presupposes a pre-existing social order which has created contract-obeying sanctions. "We are bound to obey our sovereign, it is said; because we have given a tacit promise to that purpose. But why are we bound to observe our promise?" (*Essays*, 481) The original contract theory of obligation puts the cart before the horse, so to speak: a legal-political order with all its attendant norms must exist in order for the notion of a contract to have any meaning.

Gibbon, as a skeptical philosophic historian, likewise views government, its origins and operations, without benefit of the religious hypothesis. His observations and musings about the decline of the Roman state advance no notion of a theological sanction for governmental authority.[135] Like Hume, Gibbon holds to a utilitarian principle for the foundation of government. Magistracy, he says, draws credit upon itself entirely insofar as it enforces laws curbing the egoistic, unrestrained, and immoderate tendencies of individuals, tendencies which destroy security and undermine mutual cooperation. "To maintain the harmony of authority and obedience, to chastise the proud, to protect the weak, to reward the deserving, to banish vice and idleness from his dominions, to secure the traveler and merchant, to restrain the depredations of the soldier, to cherish the labours of the husbandman, to encourage industry and learning, and, by an equal and modern assessment, to increase the revenue without increasing the taxes, are indeed the duties of a prince." (*DF-65*, VII, 73)

The "duties of the prince," the application of government authority, in effect, is to oppose the egoistic, self-preferring tendencies of human nature. The emphasis of Gibbon's remarks here is on security, especially the security of property. However, more generally, there remains an underlying focus on the human proclivity for continuous overreaching in nearly every aspect of life. Restraints, it

---

[135]Dickinson, "The Politics of Edward Gibbon," 181. "[Gibbon] was convinced that civil government was an artificial construct made by man and was not a divinely-ordained institution imposed upon man by God . . . . Gibbon believed that there was no evidence to show that civil governments were ever created by original contracts and no proof that even Britain could trace her constitution to an ancient and immemorial past."

appears, need to be built in at almost every level of social existence, from chastising the proud and arrogant to limiting government expenditure which creates the need to increase taxes. Government's primary value is to contain corruption. In describing the barbaric state of early Germany, Gibbon says that: "[c]ivil governments, in their first institutions, are voluntary associations for mutual defence. To obtain the desired end it is absolutely necessary that each individual should conceive himself obliged to submit his private opinion and actions to the judgment of the greater number of his associates." (*DF-9*, I, 242) Espoused here is an evolutionary view of government with self-defense through collective action as the originative self-interested motive. The obligation referred to is simply a reference to the dictates of prudence. In speaking of the Trajan and the Antonines Gibbon alludes to abuses of power but in no way calls into question their authority. "The obedient provinces of Trajan and the Antonines were united by laws and adorned by arts. They might occasionally suffer from the partial abuse of delegated authority; but the general principle of government was *wise*, *simple*, and *beneficent*." (*DF-2*, I, 31, italics added) Gibbon's assessment does not in any way consider the situation in contractual terms, but rather on the overall benefit conferred by the administration of Trajan and the Antonines. The wisdom, simplicity, and beneficence that Gibbon attributes to the principle of government would apply primarily to the administration of the laws. The "wisdom" of the government, Gibbon would seem to suggest, means that the laws could be justified from their usefulness and appropriateness. The "simple" quality of the general principle of government suggests that it was easy to perceive this usefulness, and the "beneficent" quality also implies that this principle was predominately good and decent. Government, clearly for Hume and Gibbon, has its foundation in utility, and the normative political philosophy of both thinkers is decidedly secularist in its foundation and orientation. This secularism sets them apart from religious conservatives like Burke, and thus the conservatism attributed to them is one, as Miller notes, that combines a revolutionary philosophy (revolutionary in the sense of being at odds with, in this case, the predominate Christian world view) with an establishment ideology, i.e., an ideology that defends property and monarchy, and supports a constitution that embodies social hierarchy and opposes democracy. However, because this revolutionary philosophy is skeptical of the establishment religion it thus poses a threat to the establishment. And therefore the philosophic skepticism can rightly be accused of eroding important social norms and undermining the social order—just what a conservative would strive to avoid. (Recall above the bitter accusations of Johnson on the effects of Hume's infidelity.) "[I]n morals and politics," warns Miller, "scepticism may have a disturbing effect by undermining convictions that are necessary to the maintenance of normal social and political life."[136] Some of these convictions may indeed be expressed in the form of religious beliefs.

Much of what we make of this issue turns, once again, on the theme of the corruption of religion (by superstition and enthusiasm) and philosophy (by sectarianism and utopianism) and the effects of those corrupted enterprises on politics. The harmful impact of corrupted religion and philosophy on society is greatly a matter of the intractability of metaphysical and theological claims to define reality in some ultimate and authoritative sense combined with the volatility of the kind of emotion that accompanies deep religious or philosophical insights. Assertions of theological or metaphysical truth (about the Gods and what they approbate), Hume and Gibbon would argue, cannot be demonstrated, and hence any apparatus (theological or metaphysical) beneath the religious belief remains forever contentious: controversy of this nature is unresolvable and inherently so. Religious beliefs cannot be defended as knowledge claims. "But to all Appearance the Sentiment of Stockholm, Geneva, Rome ancient and modern, Athens, & Memphis, have the same Characters. And no thinking man can implicitly assent to any of them; but from the general Principle, that as the Truth in these Subjects is beyond human Capacity." (*Letters*-H, I, 151) The multiplicity of religions with their conflicting assertions attests to the difficulty of establishing a theological system that can withstand controversy. Yet, the passionate intensity with which people cling to religious belief is a near universal phenomenon. Indeed, this fervid certitude about the status of the "invisible world" accounts for some of the most extremes in human conduct.

Religion also has a history—demonstrated widely in the history of Christianity—of emotive volatility which in conjunction with the attendant theoretical contentiousness arouses profound antagonisms and brings on doctrinal or sectarian conflict. Believers claim to possess certain knowledge that is, ultimately, uncertain, and then seek to make that knowledge the indisputable cornerstone of social and political conduct. Religions which are new or relatively late on the scene may be especially menacing because of the overweening confidence engendered by the religious emotion. Supremely confident, highly enthused religious believers are great threats to established societies: Hume's seventeenth-century Puritans and Gibbon's early Christians and Muslims are major historical examples of the danger that zealots of parvenu religions can pose to society. Eighteenth-century Anglicanism was more to Hume's and Gibbon's liking because, generally speaking, the attachment to it was less emotional and its observances staid and conventional.

---

[136]D. Miller, *Philosophy and Ideology in Hume's Political Thought*, 36.

In regard to the danger that philosophic skepticism can pose to society, it is important to stress the fact that the skepticism of Hume and Gibbon is *speculative* not *practical*.[137] At the metaphysical and epistemological level Hume and Gibbon are relentless in applying their skeptical arguments. This is a counter to the arrogance of reason. However, in practical (moral and political) matters, Hume argues that the skepticism which repudiates the value of established traditions, including established religions, is pernicious because those traditions represent arbitrary but agreed-upon means for achieving social goals and expressing social aspirations: skepticism applied to these simply undermines practical, established methods of cooperation.[138] Tradition, custom, and the institutions that are in place by sheer virtue of their persistence and endurance and usefulness vindicate themselves. Imperfect though they are, they provide consensus and guidelines for action. Hume and Gibbon anathematize the rejection of tradition on the basis of speculation that is impervious to common life experience. What we see then in the thought of Hume and Gibbon is their iconoclastic skepticism relating to individual knowledge claims and distrust of metaphysics and their conservative confidence in, and endorsement of, established custom. Hume's naturalistic epistemology argues for the primacy of custom as the determinant of belief and as the guidepost for practical living. "Custom then is the great guide of human life. It is that principle alone which renders our experience useful to us, and makes us expect, for the future, a similar train of events with those which have appeared in the past." (*EHU*, 44) Hume and Gibbon indeed preferred the pagan religions based solidly on custom, myth, and tradition over the philosophical religions (monotheistic in character) like Christianity that, as we will see in later chapters, developed a systematic, logical, and ultimately an exclusive claim to be believed. It was the philosophical religions with their insistence on conformity of belief that disturbed society. Gibbon in fact ridicules the theological controversies that unfold with the

---

[137]Stewart, *Opinion and Reform*, 203. "The view, now in vogue, that Hume was a conservative in his moral and political philosophy results from the opinion, inculcated by generations of professors, that Hume's chief concern was to dethrone reason; that opinion, however, ignores the purpose for which he advocated the experimental method. Moreover, it cannot be pleaded that he was either reticent or obscure about his reformist intentions." I would agree completely that Hume never dissimulated his interest in social reform. However, whatever is to made of Hume's so-called aspiration to "dethrone reason" is, it seems to me, beside the point, with respect to the issue of Hume's conservatism. Hume conservatism, in my view, lies in his critique of the intrusion of metaphysics or theology into politics. Stewart argues as if conservatives must be opposed to critical reform of social institutions, with a complete embrace of custom or tradition. This is not the case: even Burke supported the American colonists in their revolution against the Crown.

[138]David Fate Norton, *David Hume: Common-Sense Moralist, Sceptical Metaphysician* (Princeton, NJ: Princeton University Press, 1982), 53, says: "Hume maintains a common-sense morals, but at the same time he outlines and supports a sceptical metaphysics."

development of Christianity throughout the *Decline and Fall*. They are almost always accompanied by civil strife and contention. Yet he writes with a great respect for the pagan skeptical philosophers who dissimulated their attachment to the ancient religions, and coins a metaphor, "the philosophic smile," that captures the benign and respectful dissimulation in demeanor and attitude of the philosopher who contemplates the customary rituals of his countrymen. The smile is knowing and benevolent and is an element of the philosopher's respect for the venerable traditions. Religion's usefulness, i.e., its capacity for stabilizing institutions and supporting norms of self-restraint is what commends it to Gibbon.[139] Gibbon strives mightily in the second chapter of the *Decline and Fall* to impress on the reader how much the pagan religions of Rome contributed to its political and social stability. His effort in this regard deliberately sets up a counterpoint to his later account of Christianity's damage to the Roman institutions and mores and its destruction of classical pagan virtue.

The rule of law and respect for traditions, including the traditional religions, had a powerful conserving, regulative value and were what helped to make Rome into a great civilization. The parvenu Christians with their after-life preoccupations were driven by zeal and fanaticism and a contempt for tradition and ancient belief. This zeal marks the recrudescence of barbarism. He speaks of the Christians in the late fourth century: "[b]ut, in almost every province of the Roman world, an army of fanatics, without authority and without discipline, invaded the peaceful inhabitants; and the ruin of the fairest structures of antiquity still displays the ravages of *those* Barbarians, who alone had time and inclination to execute such laborious destruction." (*DF-28*, III, 209, original italics) With the italicized "those," Gibbon makes his point that the early Christians were indeed barbarians. Against the majesty of Roman civilization are launched the new destroyers and ravagers, incognizant, as barbarians always are, of the value and beauty in the structures they dismantle forever. These new Christian barbarians lack what all barbarians, with their immoderation and unrestraint, lack, "authority" and "discipline." Cooperation, security, and progress emerge from an awe of established authority expressed in the respectful adherence to norms of self-restraint. Human beings as moved primarily by passion are constrained from their tendency for overreaching by the habits of rule conformity, not by reason.[140] Without the authority to establish these habits and the discipline to maintain them,

---

[139]Charles Norris Cochrane, *Christianity and Classical Culture: A Study of Thought and Action from Augustus to Augustine* (London: Oxford University Press, 1944), 101, notes that with the Romans, the "spirit of official religion was utterly pragmatic. Accordingly it becomes purely irrelevant to inquire into its substantial truth or falsehood." Gibbon's own spirit is classical in this regard.

[140]Forbes, *Hume's Philosophical Politics*, 24-26.

the security and trust needed to develop and nurture civilized institutions are unrealizable. Thus, Hume and Gibbon were not hostile to religion as such, but to philosophical religions that elevated the importance of doctrine or ideology over custom and tradition.

Hume's *History of England* and Gibbon's *Decline and Fall* are histories of civilization, and they embody the conservative temperament and outlook of their authors in their attempts to show how fragile and vulnerable are the conventions that support continuity and stability in social institutions. They do so, however, in somewhat different ways. Hume traces the emergence of a free people out of the early historical mist of barbarism. It is the story of the evolution of norms of self-restraint and the emergence of the rule of law and constitutionality. The *History of England*, which begins with the "rude and turbulent" Roman Britains immersed in ignorance and superstition, culminates in the Revolution of 1688, out of which came "the best system of government, at least the most entire system of liberty that ever was known amongst mankind." (*HE*, VI, 317) Hume's account reads as a long, difficult, and ultimately successful trans-generational struggle of the British people to escape the limitations of barbarism and to establish stable traditions that guarantee political and religious authority.

Gibbon's account is tragic. His history of civilization moves in the opposite direction from Hume's, a story of the gradual enervation of a civilization, its ravagement by religious sectarians and fanatics, its descent into despotism, and its ultimate collapse. Gibbon sees the benign effects of moderation embodied in the conservative institutions and traditions of Rome where the "gentle, but powerful influence of laws and manners had gradually cemented the union of the provinces." (*DF-1*, I, 1) Yet Rome slowly crumbles as the laws and manners lose their binding, restraining force.[141]

The *Treatise* states that the "practice of the world goes further in teaching us the degrees of our duty, than the most subtile philosophy, which was ever yet invented." (*Treatise*, 569) Philosophic history is for Hume and Gibbon the fitting alternative for the corrupt "subtile philosophy" with its otherworldly possibilities. Philosophic history studies the "practices of the world" in an attempt both to understand the extent and limits of human nature and to prescribe those duties in the world. In contemplating the Hume-Gibbon critique of Christianity it becomes apparent that their resort is indeed to the "practices of the world" and the

---

[141]See Peter Brown, "Gibbon on Culture and Society," in *Edward Gibbon and 'The Decline and Fall of the Roman Empire,'* 42. Brown says that: "to be effective, in Gibbon's view, institutions and legal systems had to be firmly swaddled in an integument of prejudices and values." He adds that in the *Decline and Fall* there is a theme of "leakage of reality" which refers to the gradual, insidious creeping in of folly which gradually destroys institutions. This gives a dramatic tension to the *Decline and Fall*: institutions may teeter on the edge for generations before they are finally lost.

"reflections of common life." These are the sources of their theorizing on the impact of religion and society and the spectacular career of Christianity. The history of the Christian religion at its most desperate moments is paradigmatic of the destructiveness that ensues from a philosophical-theological perspective that repudiates the corrective possibilities offered by common life experience. "But what must a philosopher think," says Hume, "of those vain reasoners, who, instead of regarding the present scene of things as the sole object of their contemplation, so far *reverse the whole course of nature*, as to render this life merely a passage to something farther . . . ." (*EHU*, 141, italics added) This reversal of "the whole course of nature" with its concomitant devaluing of the natural order is at the bottom of Hume's and Gibbon's critique of Christianity.[142]

---

[142]Livingston, *Hume's Philosophy of Common Life*, points this out in, chapter eleven, "Politics and Providential History." Livingston writes, (300): "[b]elief in providential history is not only dangerous, it is perverse because it requires that we 'reverse the whole course of nature, as to render this life merely a passage to something farther.'"

CHAPTER TWO

PHILOSOPHIC HISTORY AND THE CRITIQUE OF ORTHODOXY

I. Philosophic History

Above all, historical composition requires the power of resisting the instinct of religious zeal, which prompts one to cry down what one finds to be false, and to embellish what one thinks to be true.

Pierre Bayle

David Hume and Edward Gibbon were self-proclaimed philosophic historians. Philosophic history challenged Christianity's authority to make the past theological, i.e., the study of God's work in human history. The gospel proclaiming Christ's participation in history as a man is indeed an affirmation of theological-historical truth. Thus, philosophic history in its confrontation with theological history was momentous in its rebellion against Christianity. "Any ecclesiastical historian who believes in Christianity is bound also to be a theologian," observed Arnaldo Momigliano.[1] Christian history was inherently theological in conception, requiring a persistent interweaving of fact with dogma and an insistence on the transcendental significance of that period of time in which Christ came and participated in human events. (Ibid., 138) Philosophic history was persistently skeptical about the transcendental causes at work in history and inevitably antagonistic toward Christian dogma.[2] Hugh Trevor-Roper writes that: "[s]ince the Renaissance, European writers had sought to discover general causes in history to replace the theological determinism of the Middle Ages, and the theologians had invariably resisted these attempts."[3]

History as an instrument of knowledge was being pushed and pulled toward explanations of reality that were fully incommensurable: history unfolded according to a spiritual causality and hence was the exclusive province of the theologian, or it was a process that operated by natural causality and thus was the occupation of the philosophic historian. The theological history that philosophic

---

[1] Arnaldo Momigliano, *The Classical Foundations of Modern Historiography* (Berkeley, CA: University of California Press, 1990), 137.

[2] Arnaldo Momigliano, "Introduction. Christianity and the Decline of the Roman Empire," in *The Conflict Between Paganism and Christianity In the Fourth Century: Essays edited by Arnaldo Momigliano,* ed. Arnaldo Momigliano (Oxford: Clarendon Press, 1963), 3. "There is an anti-Christian note in Montesquieu which becomes loud in Voltaire and loudest of all in Gibbon's *Decline and Fall.*"

[3] Hugh Trevor-Roper, [i]ntroduction to *The Decline and Fall of the Roman Empire* (New York: Alfred A. Knopf, 1993), 1:lv-lvi.

history was to challenge was long in the making, well entrenched, and brilliantly executed. As Arnaldo Momigliano points out: "[t]he spade-work in Christian chronology was done long before the fourth century. The greatest names involved in this work, Clemens Alexandrinus, Julius Africanus, and Hippolytus of Rome, belong to the second and third centuries. They created the frame for the divine administration of the world; they transformed Hellenistic chronography into a Christian science and added the lists of the bishops of the most important sees to the list of kings and magistrates of the pagan world. They presented history in such a way that the scheme of redemption was easy to perceive."[4] The challenge to the presentation of the scheme of redemption and the "theological determinism" of Christian historiography identifies the highly distinctive, empirically oriented feature of philosophic history which finds its most accomplished practitioners in Hume and Gibbon. Gibbon hailed Tacitus as the progenitor of philosophic history, "the first of historians who applied the science of philosophy to the study of facts." (*DF-9*, I, 230)[5] In Gibbon's praise is the suggestion of an opposition to a view of history as a divinely-governed unfolding of events. But Tacitus's attention to the facts, by itself, hardly distinguishes him from the Christian-apologist historians, and to suggest a simple dichotomy that pits fact-oriented anti-apologists like Gibbon against fact-indifferent Christian apologists would be seriously misleading. The apologist historian, Momigliano argues, is very much concerned with historical facts. As the apologist presents the case for the Faith he "knows that at any point he will be challenged. The questions with which he deals are controversial. And the controversy is never one of pure dogma or of pure fact—the two are interrelated."[6] The issue is not the facts as such but the Christian supernatural interpretation and presentation of them. This is what Gibbon came to dispute. It is the application of "the science of philosophy" *to* the facts that speaks for Tacitus's genius. Gibbon's appreciation for Tacitus lies in the latter's ability to recognize the depths and specialties of human deviancy and his lack of illusions about the conduct of human beings when pursing and wielding political power. These were the facts Tacitus, as a historian, was willing to address. Tacitus was a theorist of despotism, a phenomenon of obvious intense interest to Gibbon.[7] "Tacitus's real aim was to unmask the imperial rule, in so far as it was government

---

[4]Momigliano, " Pagan and Christian Historiography in the Fourth Century A.D.," *Conflict Between Paganism and Christianity*, 83-84.

[5]See Jordan, *Gibbon and His Roman Empire*, 172-83, for a discussion of Gibbon's admiration of Tacitus and the extent to which he attempted to emulate him.

[6]Momigliano, *Classical Foundations of Modern Historiography*, 137.

[7]See Roger Boesche, "The Politics of Pretence: Tacitus and the Political Theory of Despotism," *History of Political Thought* 8, no. 2 (summer 1987): 189-210, for an excellent discussion of Tacitus as a theorist of despotism.

by debasement, hypocrisy, and cruelty."[8] In Tacitus Gibbon choose a classical progenitor who was adept at recognizing the rationalization of power and the corruption of ideology. "The deeper he [Tacitus] looks, the more evident the contrast becomes between reality and appearances, between deeds and words in human behaviour." (Ibid., 118) So it is with Gibbon, who, philosophically mindful and historically alert to the flaws of human nature, attempts to sort out appearance from reality in his story of Christianity's part in the decline and fall of Rome.[9]

Philosophic history was *l'histoire raisonné* as opposed to *l'histoire simple*, which meant that it was not to be just a compilation or chronology of events but an explanation of past human action based on a theory of human nature.[10] Human nature was to be understood naturalistically, as a part of nature, displaying a regularity of operations and subject to laws that make human behavior explainable. Philosophic history was a mode of philosophic explanation. A theory of human nature as a basis of explanation for the past was in fact what made the philosophic historian philosophic. With its naturalistic methodological constraints, human nature as a construct of philosophic history would of necessity move into direct conflict with a supernaturally conditioned religious view of human nature. History became a prominent Enlightenment battle theater featuring a contest between a naturalistic-philosophic and a theological-religious perspective of human nature: human beings as purely natural creatures versus human beings as major participants in a supernatural order. R. R. Palmer points out that the increasingly empirical and rational character of eighteenth-century argumentation forced the traditional Catholic polemicists to try to meet their anti-Christian attackers with their own evidentiary methods—appealing to, and sorting out factual evidence—a game they were bound to lose. With the growing empiricism of the eighteenth century, there was a departure of apologists, Palmer argues, from a historical perspective grounded in a tradition based on a collective memory of sacred events. Historical evidence for them existed primarily to confirm that collective memory. "Despite all the writings of Augustine and Bousset, it was only in the eighteenth century that critical historical inquiry, based on evidence, became a foundation of religious

---

[8]Momigliano, *Classical Foundations of Modern Historiography*, 117.

[9]It is worth noting that the title pages of Books One and Two of Hume's *Treatise* bear an epigraph by Tacitus: *Rara temporum felicitas, ubi sentire, quae velis; & quae sentias, dicere licet.* "Seldom are men blessed with times in which they may think what they like and say what they think." Hume also, apparently, admired Tacitus and intended to do his own philosophical unmasking. Hume's use of epigrams has been analyzed by Paul Russell, "Epigram, Pantheists, and Freethought in Hume's *Treatise*: A Study in Esoteric Communication," *Journal of the History of Ideas* 54, no. 4 (October 1993): 659-73.

[10]Bongie, *David Hume: Prophet of the Counter-Revolution*, 4.

apologetics."[11] Christian history, as Palmer points out, was based on tradition, and "tradition," as he says, "is always in effect an instrument of present authority." (Ibid., 58)

The philosophic historians not only pressed for a secularized view of what had been a Christian view of the past, but they also tended to look at religious experience itself through the lens of secularism thus naturalizing or de-sacralizing the sacred. They advocated a radical reconsideration of religion—both of its claims to truth and of its value to society and its regulation of human conduct. Religious phenomena (religious belief, conduct, and institutions) were to be contemplated in a causal, naturalistic sense. The philosophic historian regarded religion as an important aspect of human culture subject to the same kind of critical scrutiny as the other manifestations of cultural life,[12] a repudiation of the medieval construction of knowledge represented in hierarchies of value.[13] The extensive critical reviewing and weighing of theological opinions and religious doctrine in the *Decline and Fall* do not represent Gibbon's quest to discover or demonstrate theological truth but instead his attempt to show the effects of theological thinking and theorizing on the history of the Roman empire and ultimately on the shape of modern Europe. History in its engagement with theology becomes a theater of irony for Gibbon. Theological ideas and religious ideals, as they make their way through history, influence conduct and shape institutions, often in ways that no one intends—hence the irony. The indifference to theological truth marks Gibbon's abandonment of a privileged interpretive standpoint of any particular religion, including Christianity.[14] Gibbon's critics—the more perceptive ones anyway—recognized that his indifference to theological truth was a major threat to Christianity.

Philosophic history thus came inevitably into confrontation with the Christian view of history as the work of divine providence. This confrontation is one of the most salient features of the Enlightenment and indicative of the profound shift in thinking that Hume and Gibbon helped to bring about. Ernst Cassirer writes that

---

[11]Palmer, *Catholics and Unbelievers In Eighteenth-Century France*, 53..

[12]Louis Kampf, "Gibbon and Hume," in *English Literature and British Philosophy: A Collection of Essays*, ed. S. P. Rosenbaum (Chicago: University of Chicago Press, 1971), 112.

[13]See Earnest Gellner, *Reason and Culture: The Historic Role of Rationality and Rationalism* (Cambridge, MA: Blackwell, 1992), 61. Gellner writes that one of the salient features of the history of modern rationality (Post-Cartesian rationality) is that *all* phenomena become subject to the regular conventions of rational inquiry. No phenomenon is permitted to claim a special status and dictate the methods of investigation into its claims.

[14]Kurt Rudolf, *Historical Fundamentals, and the Study of Religions* (New York: Macmillan, 1985), 34. Rudolf says that: "[f]or the historian of religions, there is, strictly speaking, no 'religion' at all." This seems to be the case for Gibbon. He writes about religions but entertains no religion with a privileged perspective.

the philosophy of the Enlightenment confronted history as a problem, one primarily in the "field of religious phenomena." In so doing, Enlightenment thinking "was forced to draw new conclusions and to make new demands, which in turn opened up the whole horizon of the historical world."[15] One of the casualties of the Enlightenment's confrontation with history was the certainty of religious truth. Quarrels over particular dogmas or the content of particular doctrines become less important than criticism over what constitutes the actual nature of belief.[16] Part of what Gibbon actually did as a self-proclaimed philosophic historian and a surreptitious critic of Christianity was to immerse the historical truths of Christianity in doubt and ultimately to make Christian doctrine less credible than it had previously been. The "evangelical bluestocking," Hannah More exclaimed upon Gibbon's death: "[h]ow many souls have his writings polluted! Lord preserve others from their contagion!"[17] Doubt and faith are incompatible: this is one of the reasons why the *Decline and Fall*, an instrument of doubt, was received by Christians with such hostility and why it was a major piece of the bitter eighteenth-century polemics surrounding Christianity.[18] Leslie Stephen, at the distance of nearly a century from the appearance of Gibbon's work, wrote that Gibbon struck Christianity "by far the heaviest blow which it had yet received from any single hand. What he did was to bring the genuine spirit of historical inquiry for the first time face to face with the facts."[19] Stephen's observation about Gibbon seems to echo the latter's praise for Tacitus. Chapters fifteen and sixteen of the *Decline and Fall* remain the most controversial and provocative portions of the work and for a fairly obvious reason: they represent Gibbon's critical, naturalistic attempts to grapple with Christianity's self-protective, supernatural world view.

Gibbon's history of the Roman empire appeared at a time when Christian theology still dominated the interpretation of human experience and the perspectives of history. However, Christianity was increasingly being driven on

---

[15]Ernst Cassirer, *The Philosophy of the Enlightenment*, trans. Fritz C.A. Koelln and James P. Pettegrove (Boston: Beacon Press, 1951), 196.

[16]Cassirer, *Philosophy of the Enlightenment*, 136. "The controversy from now on is no longer concerned with particular religious dogmas and their interpretation, but with the nature of religious certainty; it no longer deals with what is merely believed but with the nature, tendency, and function of belief as such."

[17]Quoted from Porter, *Edward Gibbon: Making History*, 111.

[18]Roy Porter, "Gibbon, the Secular Scholar," *History Today* 36 (September 1986): 49, writes: "Gibbon's history stepped outside this holy circle [of the Church]. His onslaught against religion didn't merely expose theological sophistries and the ambitions to plant the Cross on the Capitol. Rather, he turned traditional histories on their head, or more properly, on their feet. Human history was not a divine puppet-theatre. On the contrary, the history of religion had to be seen as an expression—indeed, an aberration—of the history of man."

[19]Stephen, *History of English Thought*, 1:449-50.

the defensive from two fronts. First, the powerful explanatory engine of modern science in the seventeenth century had greatly increased confidence in the efficacy of unaided reason and observation and helped stage the Enlightenment and set the foundations for a secular culture in which the role and importance of the transcendent would be strongly contested.[20] Second, European Christianity had to contend with the barbarism and disgrace of two centuries of Catholic-Protestant fratricide that, in addition to the physical warfare and destruction, had expended vast amounts of polemical energy on the battlefields of theology and metaphysics. The Enlightenment had spawned a young, robust, and confident naturalism that posed a serious threat to the church's long established and jealously guarded intellectual and moral authority. Eighteenth-century Christianity, with its competing sects, was still viewed harshly by historians like Hume and Gibbon as a dogmatic, apologetic endeavor. From the standpoint of the theologian engaged in theological disputation, history was not supposed to be practiced as a dispassionate pursuit because it served thoroughgoing apologetic ambitions.[21] History's purpose was to advance doctrine and vanquish disbelief, and it was valued primarily as a weapon of sectarian polemics. It is virtually impossible to overemphasize how closely the subject of religion is tied to philosophic history, a connection that has its greatest significance in the attempt of philosophic historians such as Hume and Gibbon to challenge the Christian view of history and to discredit both the method and message of Christian apologetics. In his first *Enquiry* Hume wrote: "[t]here is no method of reasoning more common, and yet none more blameable, than, in philosophical disputes, to endeavour the refutation of any hypothesis, by a pretence of its dangerous consequences to religion and morality." (*EHU*, 96) Hume is emphatic here: the philosophic reasoning of his time was dominated ("no method of reasoning" is "more common") by special pleading for religious doctrine, in spite of its apparent failure ("yet none [is] more blameable"). Gibbon too attacked the special pleading of religious apologists. "[A] great part of the errors and corruptions of the Church of Rome may fairly be ascribed to this criminal dissimulation of the ecclesiastical historians." (*EE*, 304) The "dissimulation" to which Gibbon refers is the hagiographical writings of the church historians who, Gibbon complains, happily overlooked all the shortcomings and failings of their subjects. "The success of these *didactic* histories, by

---

[20]See Charles Coulston Gillispie, "Science and the Enlightenment," in *The Edge of Objectivity: An Essay in the History of Scientific Ideas* (Princeton, NJ: Princeton University Press, 1960), 151-201.

[21]For a short but superb discussion on the background of skepticism and its impact on the study of history leading into the eighteenth century, see Richard Popkin, "Skepticism and the Study of History," in *David Hume: Philosophical Historian*, ed. David Fate Norton and Richard H. Popkin, (Indianapolis, IN: Bobbs-Merrill and Co., 1965), ix-xxxi.

concealing or palliating every circumstance of human infirmity, was one of the most efficacious means of consecrating the memory, the bones, and the writings of the saints of the prevailing party . . . ." (EE, 304, original italics) Note the two connected themes: the reality of human limitations ("infirmity") and the corrupted motivation of the "ecclesiastical historians" which make their representations of the past unreliable. Clearly, this anti-apologetic thrust was a major component of philosophic history.

Understanding the philosophic history of Hume and Gibbon as an attempt to repudiate the theological determinism of the Christian view of history and advance a naturalistic interpretation of human affairs is critical in developing a more general understanding of the significance of their attack on Christianity. This becomes evident with the exploration of three interrelated themes that dominate their works and make them highly distinctive achievements: impartiality and moralism, skepticism, and human nature and causality in historical explanation.

Impartiality and moralism in philosophic history

Hume and Gibbon were preoccupied with impartiality as the defining normative feature of their intellectual lives. In his musings in *My Own Life*, Hume, with some pride, reflects that: "I thought, I was the only Historian, that had at once neglected present power, Interest, and Authority, and the Cry of popular Prejudice." (*Essays*, xxxvii)[22] Power, interest, authority, and prejudice are powerful forces inimical to *philosophic* history, i.e., history as a philosophically guided, systematic attempt to report the truth about the human past. For the philosophic historian, impartiality was seen to be a central governing norm. Its purpose was to control the investigation and evaluation of historical events by a disciplined, self-correcting regard to power, glory, ambition, and the like. Discerning and telling the truth about the past (what the philosophic historian claimed to be about) is not an easy, unimpeded process. Impartiality requires a persistent, self-conscious review of all those typical interests and motives that might diminish the capacity for recognizing and reporting the truth.

Noted above was Gibbon's high esteem for Tacitus as the "first" philosophic historian. Tacitus opens his *Annals* with a bitter denunciation of the falsification of history of the Augustan age by the "rising tide of sycophancy" (*gliscente adulatione*). "[T]he histories of Tiberius and Caligula, of Claudius and Nero, were falsified through cowardice while they flourished, and composed, when they fell,

---

[22]See Victor G. Wexler, *David Hume and the History of England* (Philadelphia: American Philosophical Society, 1979), for an iconoclastic work that argues that Hume's claims, and those of his interpreters such as Duncan Forbes, for impartiality are exaggerated. Wexler contends that Hume's major motivation was less impartiality than his desire to discredit Whig historians.

under the influence of still rankling hatreds."[23] Tacitus, lamenting the betrayal of the truth through corrupted motives, pledges to write of the Augustan age "without anger and without partiality" (*sine ira et studio*). Gibbon made his high estimation of impartiality quite apparent in his "Vindication," written specifically to defend himself against charges that he had deliberately twisted historical facts to serve partisan purposes. "I adhered to the wise resolution of trusting myself and my writings to the candour of the public, till Mr. Davies of Oxford presumed to attack not the faith, but the good faith, of the historian." (*Memoirs*, 161) Gibbon wrote the "Vindication" with great reluctance after the publication of his first volume of the *Decline and Fall* in 1776 had created a furor. Davies had aroused Gibbon's ire not because he disputed aspects of his work (many had done that) but because he impugned his motives and his honesty (the "good faith of the historian"). "The different misrepresentations, of which he has drawn out the ignominious catalogue, would materially affect my credit as an historian, my reputation as a scholar, and even my honour and veracity as a gentleman." (*EE*, 234) In the "Vindication," Gibbon articulates the primacy that impartiality has for the philosophic historian. "If we skilfully combine the passions and prejudices, the hostile motives and intentions, of the several theologians, we may frequently extract knowledge from credulity, moderation from zeal, and *impartial truth* from the most disingenuous controversy. It is the right, it is the duty of a critical historian to collect, to weigh, to select the opinions of his predecessors; and the more diligence he has exerted in the search, the more rationally he may hope to add some improvement to the stock of knowledge, the use of which has been common to all." (*EE*, 277-78, italics added)

Thus described are the systematic, self-correcting activities that are supposed to guide and control the work of the "critical historian." Gibbon was most assiduous in this regard. "[Gibbon's] position as the impartial historian," writes commentator Harold Bond, "enables him to quote the adversaries on either side against each other and produce the exact measure of approbation he wishes."[24] The "Vindication" also credits Hume as a historian who stands above theological factionalism. "Since the origin of Theological Factions, some Historians, Ammianus Marcellinus, Fra-Paolo, Thuanus, Hume, and perhaps a few others, have deserved the singular praise of holding the balance with a steady and equal hand." (*EE*, 299)

Gibbon attempted a mediation between theological or providential history, which is dogmatic, and pyrrhonian history, which denies the possibility of objective

---

[23]Tacitus, *The Annals*, trans. John Jackson, Loeb ed., 3 Vols. (Cambridge, MA: Harvard University Press, 1931), 243-45.

[24]Bond, *Literary Art of Edward Gibbon*, 123.

historical truth. Both the providential and the pyrrhonian are motivated by party or sectarian considerations. (Ibid., 57-58)[25] Gibbon sought to apply consistent and systematic historiographical principles related to the assessment of source material and documentation and rescue history from what he saw as a doctrinal, apologetic servitude.[26] A critical, non-sectarian bent combined with the desire to create a true and impartial narration of events would, in sum, characterize for Gibbon the ideal historian.[27] In order to achieve this ideal the historian must overcome credulity, superstition, prejudice, personal inclination, party interest, all those forces potentially at work in the human personality which rival critical, disinterested, truth-seeking capacities.[28]

The philosophical historian was a "moralist." Philosophic history, Hume and Gibbon at times remind us, is supposed to "amuse" and "instruct." Both the amusement and the instruction have a moral purpose. The moral teaching of history is closely connected to the norm of impartiality. In his *Enquiry Concerning the Principles of Morals*, Hume wrote: "[t]he notion of morals implies some sentiment common to all mankind, which recommends the same object to general approbation, and makes every man, or most men, agree in the same opinion or decision concerning it." (*EPM*, 272) The moral realism is apparent. More remarkable though is the emphatic claim that makes it obvious that Hume extends this commonality of moral sentiment to judgments of history. "It also implies some sentiment, so universal and comprehensive as to extend to all mankind, and render the actions and conduct, even of the persons the most remote, an object of applause or censure, according as they agree or disagree with that rule of right which is

---

[25]Bond states that Gibbon's literary form in the *Decline and Fall* was modeled after Aristotle's rhetorical panegyric or epideictic style of address which involves praise and blame. In assigning praise and blame, impartiality is particularly important since the fair attribution of praise or blame requires a neutral, judge-like impartiality. In many respects the historian is like a judge.

[26]See, DeBeer, *Gibbon and His World*, 72-73, for a discussion of Gibbon's limitations in the critical methods of source criticism.

[27]Peter Gay, *Style in History* (New York: W. W. Norton, 1974), 31.

[28]Leo Braudy, *Narrative Form in History and Fiction* (Princeton, NJ: Princeton University Press, 1970), 13, writes that: "[a]lthough Gibbon is similar to Hume in many ways, he is a better historian because, perhaps taking his cue from Fielding, he departs from Hume's *false ideal of detachment*." (italics added) This is one of the more remarkable and, in my view, highly questionable claims of Braudy's "revisionist" interpretation of Hume and Gibbon. The claim that Hume's ideal of detachment is false reflects a rather dogmatic epistemological perspective and flies in the face of Hume's remarkable achievement of highlighting the importance of attempting to transcend party and sectarian motivation in the writing of history. Also, it is not obvious, as Braudy suggests, that Gibbon *did* depart from his frequently stated ideal of detachment or impartiality in the writing of history. In Chapter forty-seven of the *Decline and Fall*, Gibbon opens with a long footnote critically evaluating his sources for their partiality. Braudy never states just when Gibbon departs from this ideal, nor does he cite any text in Gibbon's writings where he repudiates it, explicitly or implicitly.

established." (*EPM*, 272) Hume is clear here—"all of mankind" and "even of the persons the most remote"—that the conduct of historical persons is open to and invites moral judgment.

In making moral judgments, the historian, playing the moralist role, takes up a disinterested, *impartial* perspective.[29] "He must here, therefore, depart from his private and particular situation, and must choose a point of view, common to him with others; he must move some universal principle of the human frame, and touch a string to which all mankind have an accord and symphony." (*EPM*, 272)[30] This common point of view which links together, as Hume goes on to call it, "the party of humanity," is marked by the language used. "When a man denominates another his *enemy*, his *rival*, his *antagonist*, his *adversary*, he is understood to speak the language of self-love, and to express sentiments, peculiar to himself, and arising from his particular circumstances and situation. But when he bestows on any man the epithets of *vicious*, or *odious* or *depraved*, he then speaks another language, and expresses sentiments, in which he expects all his audience are to concur with him." (*EPM*, 272, original italics)

Hume takes pains to make this distinction between "self-love" and a common, i.e., universal, "moral" perspective. But it is the linkage of *language* to this universal *moral perspective* that drives the moralism—with its entertaining, instructive intentions—in Hume's philosophic history. The difference in language, so Hume argues, is evidence of a strong basis in human nature for the existence of this common, disinterested perspective that stands out as the moral point of view. "The distinction, therefore, between these species of sentiment being so great and evident, language must soon be moulded upon it, and must invent a peculiar set of terms, in order to express those universal sentiments of censure or approbation, which arise from humanity, or from views of general usefulness and its contrary." (*EPM*, 274) Here Hume asserts a kind of human inventiveness relative to the phenomenon of morality itself that involves, in perhaps a developmental, evolving way, the formation of a language that enables human beings to transcend self-interested perspectives and express moral feelings and ideas. "Virtue and Vice become then known; morals are recognized; certain general ideas are formed of human conduct and behaviour; such measures are expected from men in such

---

[29]D. Miller, *Philosophy and Ideology in Hume's Political Thought*, 57. "Hume argues that moral judgements nevertheless have a basis in human nature, and are not merely the expression of arbitrary conventions enforced by social and political pressure."

[30]See Elizabeth S. Radcliffe, "Hume on Motivating Sentiments, the General Point of View, and the Inculcation of 'Morality,'" *Hume Studies* 20, no. 1 (April 1994): 37-58 for a discussion of two quite different interpretations of Hume's moral theory, the "sentimentalist" version and the "ideal observer" reading. The "ideal" or "impartial observer" is closer to the one suggested here, although Radcliffe does attempt a mediation of the two.

situations. This action is determined to be conformable to our abstract rule; that other, contrary. And by such universal principles are the particular sentiments of self-love frequently controlled and limited." (*EPM*, 274) Human beings, it appears, have at their disposal a moral vocabulary which can be used to articulate standards of behavior for which there is in human nature near universal approval. This moral vocabulary is what the philosophic historian must be able to use appropriately and impartially so as to make his history truly morally instructive and entertaining. "Vicious," "odious," and "depraved," the "epithets" Hume cites above as choice examples of moral language, are exactly the kinds of words one finds put to use in his history. They are words which are very efficacious in arousing strong feelings. Hume seeks in his history to arouse that universal sentiment of approbation or censure in the contemplation of the action of historical figures—a fundamental part of history's moral instruction. The historian attempts to speak with the impartial voice of humanity—divorced from sect, party, or any particular interested motive. Consider these observations of Hume on the Irish massacre of 1641 in his *History of England*. "But death was the slightest punishment inflicted by those rebels: all the tortures which wanton cruelty could devise, all the lingering pains of body, the anguish of mind, the agonies of despair, could not satiate revenge excited without injury, and cruelty derived from no cause. To enter into particulars would shock the least delicate humanity. Such enormities, though attested by undoubted evidence, appear almost incredible. *Depraved nature* even *perverted religion*, encouraged by the *utmost licence*, reach not to a pitch of ferocity; unless the pity inherent in human breasts be destroyed by that contagion of example, which transports men beyond all the usual motives of conduct and behaviour." (*HE*, V, 62, italics added)

With "depraved nature," "perverted religion," "utmost licence," Hume, the philosophic historian, is performing his role as moralist, in this instance arousing in the readers strong feelings of moral condemnation. Hume attempts to speak with a characteristically eighteenth-century propriety (not wanting to "shock" with "particulars" even "the least delicate of humanity"), but more importantly with impartially, not as a Protestant or Catholic, or with any particular sectarian or national identity, but as a member of the party of humanity condemning the cruelty and destructiveness of fanaticism and observing how much fanaticism unhinges those normal standards of human decency, i.e., "the usual motives of conduct and behaviour." The moral perspective sought by Hume, and, as we will see by Gibbon, comes from the historian's disposition, or at least the *attempt* to achieve the disposition, of impartiality. The impartial disposition—a difficult and worthy achievement—runs counter to a strong and persistent natural inclination to take the interested perspective. "It seems certain, both from reason and experience, that a rude, untaught savage regulates chiefly his love and hatred by the ideas of private utility and injury, and has but faint conceptions of a general rule or system of behaviour." (*EPM*, 274, n.1) Impartiality is a norm developed by civilized people who gradually learn how to distinguish between a perspective which is peculiar to oneself, and that in which fellow human beings will concur with her or him. "But we, accustomed to society, and to more enlarged reflections, consider . . . that, in general, human society is best supported on such maxims: and by these suppositions and views, we correct, in some measure, our ruder and narrower passions. And though much of our friendship and enmity be still regulated by private considerations of benefit and harm, we pay, at least, this homage to general rules, which we are accustomed to respect, that we commonly pervert our adversary's conduct, by imputing malice or injustice to him, in order to give vent to those passions, which arise from self-love and private interest." (*EPM*, 274-75, n.1)

The force of private interest is persistent, insidious, and relentless even in dissimulating the motives of self-interest with the *use* of disinterested moral language. Yet, as Hume notes, personal bias pays tribute to general, impartial rules by cloaking itself in the language of justice—just as the liar indirectly honors the ultimate value of truth by attempting to pass off his lie as true. Herein lies the challenge for the philosophic historian as moralist—to counter those self-delusional passions arising from "self-love" and "private interest." In the context of writing history, this means attempting to overcome sectarian or party interests because sectarian ideals, no matter how sublime, can easily be tied to motives of ambition and self-interest. The spiritual yearnings so strongly associated with religion are in a widely proclaimed, self-appointed opposition to human material aspirations. Yet institutionalized religion is often infused with motives of power and ambition, motives that dramatically conflict with the sectarian's preoccupation with the transcendent and all of its ramifications for selfless idealism and hope for redemption. This dramatic conflict in human aspiration, with its possibilities for both the comic and the tragic, is not only the major source of the entertainment offered by history, but also the focal point of moral instruction.

The sectarian or party ideologue emerges for Hume and Gibbon as the nemesis of the impartial philosophic historian. Consider again the "Vindication": "The historian must indeed be generous, who will conceal by his own disgrace, that of his country or his religion." (*EE*, 303) Gibbon's aspiration as a moralist is to transcend potentially interested perspectives such as those of party or sect and to take up what Hume calls "a point of view, common to him with others." (*EPM*, 272) The philosophic historian attempts to be an "impartial spectator," writing history that reflects moral judgements as they would be made by mankind.

Through impartiality history achieves its central purpose, instruction. Once more, the "Vindication": "[w]hatever subject he [i.e., the historian] has chosen, whatever persons he introduces, he owes to himself, to the present age, and to posterity, a just and perfect delineation of all that may be praised, of all that may excused, and of all that must be censured. If he fails in the discharge of his important office, he partially violates the sacred obligations of truth, and disappoints his readers of the instruction which they might have derived from a fair parallel of the vices and virtues of the most illustrious characters." (*EE*, 303) Here is the connection, drawn by Gibbon himself, between the historian's guiding norm of impartially in the cause of truth-seeking and the historian's role as a moralist. The violation of the norm of impartiality destroys the capacity to fulfill the morally instructive role. Gibbon was well aware of the complexities of human motivation, particularly those surrounding the religious aspects of human experience, and the *Decline and Fall* evinces Gibbon's concerted, but sometimes unsuccessful, efforts to resist the facile characterization of the motives of historical personages. The cynical attribution of certain kinds of motivation to match certain types of people is the work of party hacks and corrupted religious apologists.

Gibbon's determination to exert impartiality is acutely obvious in his observations on the life of Muhammad. The strong and easy temptation that Gibbon resists is simply to dismiss Muhammad as a fraud. "Of his last years, ambition was the ruling passion; and a politician will suspect that he secretly smiled (the victorious impostor!) at the enthusiasm of his youth and the credulity of his proselytes." (*DF-50*, V, 401). More is suggested here than might be immediately thought, and Gibbon's comment is less cynical than it initially appears. Muhammad himself, only in the reflective moments of his later years, grasps the happy coincidence of his own powerful religious passions and his willing, believing followers. The next sentence makes this clear: "[a] philosopher will observe that *their* credulity and *his* success would tend more strongly to fortify the assurance of his divine mission, that his interest and religion were inseparably connected, and that his conscience would be soothed by the persuasion that he alone was absolved by the Deity from the obligation of positive and moral laws." (*DF-50*, V, 401-402, original italics) "Their credulity" and "his success" are obviously connected. But it takes a philosopher—an impartial philosophic historian in this case—Gibbon argues, to sort out the complex workings of the elements of interest, ambition, and belief. Muhammad is *both* believer and imposture. The success of his own act, as evidenced by the growth of his followers, makes him a believer.

Christianity provides a case that parallels Muhammad and Islam. The entirety of chapter twenty of the *Decline and Fall* deals with Constantine, for obvious reasons. Constantine, more than any other single individual, represents the institutionalization of Christianity. His conduct, personality, and character form an essential piece of historical Christianity.[31] Constantine's Christianity is a complex phenomenon for the historian because his pivotal role in the church's history is so much an object of scrutiny for apologists and anti-Christian detractors and because the actual events of his conversion are so involved and drawn out. Gibbon concedes that it might be tempting, particularly for critics of the Catholic Church, to dismiss the conversion of Constantine as sheer and utter opportunism. "The protestant and philosophic readers of the present age will incline to believe that, in the account of his own conversion, Constantine attested a wilful falsehood by a solemn and deliberate perjury. They may not hesitate to pronounce that, in the choice of religion, his mind was determined only by a sense of interest; and that (according to the expression of a profane poet) he used the altars of the church as a convenient footstool to the throne of the empire." (*DF-20*, II, 324-25) In similarity to his assessment of the motives and character of Muhammad, Gibbon shows great awareness of the complexity of religious motives and passions and resists the temptation to become rigid and categorical in his interpretation. "A conclusion so harsh and so absolute is not, however, warranted by our knowledge of human nature, of Constantine, or of Christianity. In an age of religious fervour, the most artful statesmen are observed to feel some part of the enthusiasm which they inspire." (*DF-20*, II, 325) Note well that Gibbon's framework of interpretation is a theory of human nature with certain assumptions about human motivation and human action. As with Muhammad, Constantine's motivation is believed to be partly self-interest, partly sincere belief. Gibbon is simply unwilling to make important historical figures serve as ideological props for historians or apologists: he neither wants to play the part of uncritical apologist nor that of hostile, dogmatic detractor. In fact, we can see Gibbon attempting to move away from sectarian perspectives and consider the events here, the career of Constantine, in a naturalistic perspective, a way that takes into account the complexities of human nature, religious passion, and individual personalities.[32]

---

[31]David Jordan, "Gibbon's 'Age of Constantine' and the Fall of Rome," *History and Theory: Studies in the Philosophy of History* 8, no. 1 (1969): 78. "The age of Constantine was especially important for Gibbon because it marked the official establishment of Christianity in Europe, and Christianity was being hotly debated in the Enlightenment."

[32]Jordan, "Gibbon's 'Age of Constantine' and the Fall of Rome," 77-78, argues that Gibbon did not succeed in an impartial consideration of Constantine. "Gibbon's view of the age of Constantine rests ultimately on his philosophic assumptions; and his antagonism to Christianity, which is far more complex than most commentators think, is a major ingredient in this philosophy . . . . Placid indifference, the detachment Gibbon recommended to all who would call themselves philosophers, he himself lacked in all discussions of religion, let alone fanaticism and religious enthusiasm. He would have us believe that he viewed religion with philosophic indifference. But philosophic indifference could hardly generate the

Skepticism in philosophical history

The philosophic historian's quest for an impartial, disinterested, moral point of view has an affinity with another distinctive feature usually associated with philosophic history, namely skepticism.[33] Impartiality, as we have seen, involves an effort to step out of perspectives that are dominated by sectarian thinking and that are influenced by party and sectarian interests. The skepticism of the philosophic historian is a moderate, or what Hume calls a "mitigated" skepticism. "There is, indeed, a more *mitigated* scepticism or *academical philosophy*, which may be both durable and useful, and which may, in part, be the result of this Pyrrhonism, or *excessive* scepticism, when its undistinguished doubts are, in some measure, corrected by common sense and reflection." (*EHU*, 161, original italics) Pyrrhonism, or excessive skepticism, is, in Hume's view, an overreaction to credulity, a repudiation of the self-correcting possibilities of common experience. The durability Hume boasts of for his moderate skepticism lies in this underlying support of common experience: its usefulness—unlike Pyrrhonism, which is so radical in its doubts that it can have no practical significance—lies in its awareness of human corruptibility and its self-conscious opposition to the powerful tendencies of human credulity, which unopposed, resist the sometimes obtrusive endeavors of truth-seeking. "The greater part of mankind are naturally apt to be affirmative and dogmatical in their opinions; and while they see objects only on one side, and have no idea of any counterpoising argument, they throw themselves precipitately into the principles, to which they are inclined; nor have they any indulgence for those who entertain opposite sentiments." (*EHU*, 161)

The phenomenon of the formulation of belief, particularly religious belief, has some interesting features. First is the sheer dominating character of passion relative to belief.[34] Second is the natural, intense antagonism engendered by the contemplation of a belief that contradicts or opposes one's own. Not only are most people naturally "dogmatical," as Hume says, but they also possess a fierce natural resistance to altering or discarding a belief, a phenomenon manifest in the strong

---

passion that informs his treatment of Christianity and Constantine." I think that Jordan overstates Gibbon's impassioned discussion of religion. Certainly Gibbon was antagonistic to Christianity, but as Jordan himself suggests, this antagonism is complex. His harsh treatment of Constantine reflects his concern as a moralist to disapprobate the political corruption of Christianity. Other major political-Christians in the *Decline and Fall* (Athanasius, for example) fare much better.

[33]For an excellent scholarly study of the role that skepticism plays in early modern theological polemics see Richard H. Popkin, *The History of Scepticism From Erasmus to Spinoza* (Berkeley, CA: University of California Press, 1979).

[34]Addinall, *Philosophy and Biblical Interpretation*, 22, says of Hume: "[h]is aim was to show that self-conscious human reasoning does not have the significance in human thinking and experience which it is generally assumed to have, and that its contribution to knowledge is and must be more limited than has often been supposed."

resentment a believer feels in the face of disbelief. "To hesitate or balance perplexes their understanding, checks their passion, and suspends their action. They are, therefore, impatient till they escape from a state, which to them is so uneasy: and they think, that they can never remove themselves far enough from it, by the violence of their affirmations and obstinacy of their belief." (*EHU*, 161) Gibbon echoes this notion in chapter fifteen. "The decline of ancient prejudice exposed a very numerous portion of human kind to the danger of a painful and comfortless situation. A state of scepticism and suspense may amuse a few inquisitive minds." (*DF-15*, II, 59) Disbelief or uncertainty is uncomfortable, and violent affirmations serve as self-protective reactions to doubt. Skepticism acts as a corrective to this natural inclination to indulge in the "obstinacy of belief." "But could such dogmatical reasoners become sensible of the strange infirmities of human understanding, even in its most perfect state, and when most accurate and cautious in its determination; such a reflection would naturally inspire them with more modesty and reserve, and diminish their fond opinion of themselves, and their prejudice against antagonists." (*EHU*, 161) Hume urges skepticism, it seems, for three basic reasons, one of which is intellectual and two of which are moral: (1) as a counteraction to dogmatism, which, if invincible, inhibits the self-corrective possibilities in thinking and reasoning, (2) as a counterpoise to arrogance which promotes a heightened mutual viciousness in sectarian rivalry, and (3) as a means to make the thinking of antagonists less the object of visceral resentment by reducing a natural prejudice against them.

Hume directs his skepticism primarily at religious belief. Why? It is in religious matters that human reasoning often overreaches and asserts itself in its most dogmatic extremes. Religious beliefs are the work of the human imagination and are pursued without the encumbrance or limits of sense experience. "The *imagination* of man is naturally sublime, delighted with whatever is remote and extraordinary, and running, without control, into the most distant parts of space and time in order to avoid the objects, which custom has rendered too familiar to it." (*EHU*, 162, original italics) Skepticism brakes this natural overreaching tendency. It executes a philosophical purpose in countering the dogmatical approach to belief. Philosophers are supposed to be the opposites of dogmatists. "It must, however, be confessed that this species of scepticism, when more moderate, may be understood in a very reasonable sense, and is a necessary preparative to the study of philosophy, by preserving a proper impartiality in our judgements, and weaning our mind from all those prejudices, which we may have imbibed from education or rash opinion." (*EHU*, 150) Philosophic history with its skeptical orientation, opposes theological history and attacks the work of theological historians as dogmatic, sectarian, and ultimately corrupted by the self-interested passions and motives so typical of sectarians.

We see thus the close relationship between impartiality and skepticism: impartiality involves the repudiation of the sectarian perspective; the skeptic practices a tentativeness of belief thus depriving himself or herself of the absolute certainty of belief. Absolute certainty of belief is the defining, quintessential feature of the sectarian. Skepticism of the moderate kind functions as a corrective to the accumulation of prejudiced perspectives and careless reflection. Human beings in all of their imperfection, it seems, have a quite natural, inevitable tendency to gather up and entertain mistaken, faulty, and erroneous opinions. All sorts of influences may come into play: sectarian prejudices, bad education, sloppy thinking, etc.

Gibbon's *Decline and Fall* puts into full play his rendition of skeptical, anti-apologetic history.[35] Chapter fifteen opens *sotto voce*: "[a] candid but rational inquiry into the progress and establishment of Christianity may be considered as a very essential part of the history of the Roman empire." (*DF-15*, II, 1) Indeed! The skeptical and impartial orientation that Gibbon intends is already implicit in this opening sentence with the carefully muted phrase, "candid but rational inquiry." Candid turns out to be something of a euphemism: Gibbon's account of Christianity's "progress and establishment" focuses with intense skepticism on the miraculous origins of Christianity. In the next, the sixteenth chapter, Gibbon develops a skeptical attack on the martyrdom claims of the early Christians. Both the miracles of the early church (proof of its Divine origins) and the dimensions of its persecution (the evidence of Christian moral suffering) are cast into doubt: Christianity is diminished. All of this is in direct opposition to the Christian apologist-historians.[36]

But there is another important dimension to the skepticism that Gibbon practices that takes him beyond Hume. This is found in sections of the *Decline and Fall*, such as chapter forty-seven, in which Gibbon delves deeply into the doctrinal history of Christianity. Christian theology turns out to be for Gibbon, quite

---

[35] J. G. A. Pocock writes of Gibbon that: "[h]is early conversion to Catholicism and the subsequent growth of his irreligious skepticism separated Gibbon from the traditions of Anglican scholarship, which might well have claimed him otherwise; and he attached himself instead to the unfolding patterns of Enlightenment historiography, an international style in many respects, to which nevertheless the Scottish school was imparting a development both local and universal, and of great intellectual power." Pocock, "Between Machiavelli and Hume: Gibbon as Civic Humanist and Philosophical Historian," in *Edward Gibbon and the 'Decline and Fall of the Roman Empire,'* 103.

[36] Jaroslav Pelikan, *The Excellent Empire: The Fall of Rome and The Triumph of the Church* (San Francisco: Harper and Row, 1987), 39, "Gibbon was deliberately setting his work apart from the piety and orthodoxy of the apologists who had treated this subject matter before him and who, of course went on treating it in their own fashion long after him . . . ."

entertaining—at the expense of the dignity of the theologian—as well as instructive. One of the major areas of impact of the Christian religion is the invention of what Gibbon calls "theological science," a vast construction of the mind that becomes very important to the institutional development of Christianity. Christian theology is a subject that, in contrast to Hume, seems to interest Gibbon greatly. In fact, Gibbon writes the history of Christian doctrine so as to deflate it, that is to dispose the reader to contemplate the entire Christian theological edifice with amusement and skepticism. Gibbon, in effect, uses doctrinal history—immerses the reader in it in fact—in order to induce skepticism, generally, about theology. Chapter forty-seven (about seventy-five pages in the Bury edition) is an extraordinary study of Christian doctrine which ranges from the fifth through the seventeenth centuries. The opening two sentences of the chapter give a sense of how this doctrinal study is to unfold: "[a]fter the extinction of paganism, the Christians in peace and piety might have enjoyed their solitary triumph. But the principle of discord was alive in their bosom, and they were more solicitous to explore the nature, than to practice the laws, of their founder." (*DF-47*, V, 103) Here are two of the incipient themes of the chapter: that Christian ideals of "peace and piety" might have prevailed and that religious harmony was possible. But speculation—preoccupation with the inherently unresolvable details of what Gibbon calls the "invisible world"—sparks doctrinal conflagration. Hinted at is the futility of this exploration of Christ's nature. As the chapter unfolds, beginning with the "Theological History of the Doctrine of the Incarnation," the reader takes Gibbon's guided tour through a veritable maze of conflicting speculative permutations on Christ's nature. To the Ebionites he is a pure man: "[i]f they had courage to hail their king when he appeared in a plebeian garb, their grosser apprehensions were incapable of discerning their God, who had studiously disguised his celestial character under the name and person of a mortal." (*DF-47*, V, 104) To the Docetes he was a pure god: "[m]any among the Gentile proselytes refused to believe that a celestial spirit, an undivided portion of the first essence, had been personally united with a mass of impure and contaminated flesh; and, in their zeal for the divinity, they piously abjured the humanity, of Christ." (*DF-47*, V, 107) There seems to be an endless number of these unreconcilable dichotomies, and we weave through even more twists and turns. "A more substantial, though less simple, hypothesis was contrived by Cerinthus of Asia, who dared to oppose the last of the apostles. Placed on the confines of the Jewish and Gentile world, he laboured to reconcile the Gnostic with the Ebonite, by confessing in the same Messiah the supernatural union of a man and a God: and this mystic doctrine was adopted with many fanciful improvements by Carpocrates, Basilides, and Valentine, and heretics of the Egyptian school." (*DF-47*, V, 110) The incarnation doctrine wends through its historical path on a convoluted course constructed by Gibbon that highlights all the instabilities and peculiarities that permeate human nature. Its career, far-fetched and unpredictable, is as varied and colorful as humanity itself. Gibbon then describes that point in history when a doctrinal consensus is achieved: "[i]n the beginning of the fifth century, the *unity* of the *two natures* was the prevailing doctrine of the church. On all sides it was confessed that the mode of their co-existence could neither be represented by our ideas nor expressed by our language." (*DF-47*, V, 113, original italics) So, after the labyrinthine exposition, the entire business turns out to be beyond comprehension. The history of theology, Gibbon seems to want the reader to realize, is itself so infested with all the typical outgrowths of human opportunism, aggrandizement, and folly that the much-vaunted status of its ambitious truth-claims deserves to be soundly deprecated. Gibbon's elaborate doctrinal studies thus bring to fruition in a very particular and dramatic way the skeptical perspective at work. Skepticism, adroitly employed, helps to keep the philosophic historian faithful to the norm of impartiality. Also, skepticism, insofar as it deflates self-serving ideologies and ridicules ignorance, makes history entertaining and morally instructive.

Causality and human nature in philosophic history

Philosophic history was conceived by its practitioners to be a search for the causes of those events that make up the unfolding course of the human past. "But the most usual species of connection," says Hume, "among the different events which enter into any narrative composition is that of cause and effect . . . ."[37] Gibbon, in setting up his iconoclastic chapter sixteen, says: "[t]o separate (if it be possible) a few authentic, as well as interesting, facts from an undigested mass of fiction and error, and to relate, in a clear and rational manner, the *causes*, the extent, the duration, and the most important circumstances of the persecutions to which the first Christians were exposed, is the design of the present chapter." (*DF-16*, II, 77, italics added)

By "cause," as it applies to history, Hume means a certain observable regularity between human motives and human actions. "It is universally acknowledged that there is a great uniformity among the actions of men, in all nations and ages, and that human nature remains still the same, in its principles and operations. The same motives always produce the same actions: The same events follow from the same causes." (*EHU*, 83) This uniformity of motive and action is a necessary assumption, Hume argues, since without it the world of particularity

---

[37]This quote comes from the Hendel edition of Hume's first *Enquiry* (Indianapolis, IN: Bobbs-Merrill, 1955), 34, which contains a section appended to "Section III, "Of the Association of Ideas," that is not in the Selby-Bigge edition.

can never be surmounted. "But were there no uniformity in human actions, and were every experiment which we could form of this kind irregular and anomalous, it were impossible to collect any general observations concerning mankind; and no experience, however accurately digested by reflection, would ever serve to any purpose." (*EHU*, 85) Without the assumption of uniformity in human actions, history could never amount to more than rudimentary antiquarianism and offer no moral instruction. Without a theory of human nature there is no moral point of view and both Hume and Gibbon were moralists in the sense that they believed that history was to be *morally* instructive.

Philosophic history in Hume's conception thus operates with the assumption of a causal relation between motives and actions. This causal relation is seen to hold across cultures and throughout history and thus permits the historian to move from his expostulations, based on his own direct experience in analyzing and explaining human actions, to extrapolations about those of other peoples in other times.[38] This notion of a uniformity in human action, a uniformity of human nature, if you will, guides the philosophic historian in the attempt to sift out true accounts of the past. Without it there are no standards or guidelines for sorting out the tall tales (the concocted, twisted, and fabricated stories) from the true ones. "And if we would explode any forgery in history, we cannot make use of a more convincing argument, than to prove, that the actions ascribed to any person are directly contrary to the course of nature, and that no human motives, in such circumstances, could ever induce him to such a conduct." (*EHU*, 84)

Human activity and behavior, the material of history, so to speak, are sufficiently uniform to make history explainable by reference to general patterns, according to the philosophic historian. Like the physical order, human conduct is governed by general, uniform laws which make it, to a certain extent, predictable. Philosophic history thus operates with the principle of uniformitarianism, i.e., the historian assumes that human nature, at a high and abstract level of generality, is uniform, and therefore that historical events, even at vast distances of time are commensurable to some degree with the present. Also, philosophic historians, viewing human beings as natural agents in a natural order, explained human conduct as a phenomenon governed by the causality of nature. As the new, mechanistic philosophy of nature of the seventeenth century did not resort to supernatural explanation to account for the behavior of physical objects, so the philosophic historian of the eighteenth century rejected supernatural explanation. Societies, the object of historical study, are complex ordered units subject to a

---

[38]James Farr, "Hume, Hermeneutics, and History: A 'Sympathetic 'Account," *History and Theory: Studies in the Philosophy of History* 17, no. 3 (1978): 288, says that Hume gives "a psychological analysis of the causal connection and a methodological analysis of causal explanation."

variety of natural and "moral" (human/social) influences that account for their nature.[39]

The stress Hume places on the uniformity of human nature leads him to statements that are temptingly and easily fed into a highly mechanistic interpretation of his philosophy and historiography that precludes an appreciation of the important individual and cultural human differences. "Mankind are so much the same, in all times and places, that history informs us of nothing new or strange in this particular. Its chief use is only to discover the constant and universal principles of human nature, by showing men in all varieties of circumstances and situations, and furnishing us with materials from which we may form our observations and become acquainted with the regular springs of human action and behaviour." (*EHU*, 83) This notorious historiographical rumination has been quoted frequently in the long debate over how to read Hume's philosophy of history and, even more generally, what to make of Hume's Enlightenment philosophy. Interpreters such as J. B. Black have seized upon it in their arguments that Hume operated with a philosophy that precluded any genuine appreciation for historical uniqueness.[40] This mechanistic, anti-historical interpretation of Hume's thinking has a long tradition that goes back at least to R. G. Collingwood and continues through Black, Frederick Meinecke, and most recently, David Womersley.[41]

Given Gibbon's close philosophical linkages to Hume (Gibbon at the very least confessed to his aspiration to be a philosophic historian in the tradition of Hume), and his great admiration for Hume's work and the Scottish Enlightenment, his major interpreters find themselves trying to come to terms with the Hume-Gibbon relationship and what it means in assessing Gibbon's place in the ranking of Enlightenment historians. Meinecke, for example, looks at Hume and Gibbon as great but typical Enlightenment historians whose model of natural causality inhibited the development of an insightful appreciation of human diversity and individuality manifested through history.[42]

More recently, Womersley's interpretation of Gibbon as a historian is linked directly to what he sees as Hume's failed Enlightenment historiography.

---

[39]See, Trevor-Roper, "The Historical Philosophy of the Enlightenment."

[40]Black, *Art of History*, 101. Black here says that Hume works with a "false and mechanical psychology."

[41]Forbes, *Hume's Philosophical Politics*, 102, defends Hume against historicists like Black, Collingwood, and Meinecke, who charge him with a constricted, mechanized view of human nature which lacks a concrete, differentiating historical imagination, a defect also laid by some at Gibbon's door.

[42]Frederich Meinecke, *Historism: The Rise of a New Historical Outlook*, trans. J. E. Anderson (New York: Herder and Herder, 1972). See specifically, Chapter five, "Enlightenment Historiography in England."

Womersley argues that Gibbon began his labor on the *Decline and Fall* closely resembling Hume in his attempt to see the workings of history causally, as a demonstration of fixed, immutable principles of human nature.[43] However, during the twenty-year course of the work, Gibbon supposedly moved away from this Humean perspective to become increasingly fascinated with the particulars of historical experience and less concerned with human nature and causality. "The assumptions of causal investigation thus have only dwindling pertinence in the history of the later empire." (Ibid., 208) Womersley's Gibbon, then, starts out in the Humean Enlightenment camp of historiography preoccupied with an abstract, uniform view of human nature and emerges at the end of the *Decline and Fall* with a kind of *Verstehen* perspective. Gibbon, "transforms his idea of history from a tableau transparent to the penetrating vision of the philosopher to a chiaroscuro procession in which the flashes of illumination measure the profundity and magnitude of the surrounding shadows." (Ibid., 233) Gibbon, in effect, abandons the philosophic part of philosophic history, i.e., the desire to discern causal explanations in history based upon some fixed notion of human nature. Womersley's account of Gibbon charts the course of his liberation from the tyranny of Hume's philosophic history and its presumption of uniformity in human nature and preoccupation with causality. This leaves Gibbon free to explore human beings and human societies in their full variance and individuality without the arrogant presumption and myopic constraint of some eighteenth-century, European-dictated norm of a fixed human nature.[44] This interpretation of Gibbon is directly linked to Womersley's view of the limitations of Hume's historiography. Gibbon breaks the mold and achieves genuine historical insight while Hume fails. Womersley's criticism of Hume here is part of a larger critique of Enlightenment historiography of which Hume is the paradigm case. Enlightenment historiography, critics such as Womersley contend, is defective because of a overly mechanized view of human behavior which abstracts away important historical differences. Moreover, the relationship between history and a fixed view of human nature remains problematic for Hume because his assumptions pertaining to human beings—as abstract, universal generalities—are timeless, that is, *a-historical.*

---

[43]Womersley, *The Transformation*, 2-38.

[44]See David Wooton, "Narrative, Irony, and Faith in Gibbon's *Decline and Fall*," *History and Theory: Studies in the Philosophy of History*, Theme Issue No. 33, *Proof and Persuasion in History* (1994): 102. Wooton challenges Womersley's claim that Gibbon's philosophic and hence skeptical view of religion evidenced early in the *Decline and Fall* dramatically dropped away in the later books. "Womersley requires us to believe that there is more than one occasion when Gibbon described what a philosopher would think yet did not intend to identify his own views with those of the philosopher. It would be tedious to show how this involves a misreading of Gibbon, who never (I would argue) became, as Womersley seems to think, uncritical of the miraculous."

"Thus Hume's historiography," Womersley argues, "rests on a huge begging of the question. It purports to result in knowledge of human nature; yet the historian must already possess such knowledge before he can begin to examine his material."[45]

Does Hume though, really beg the question? Only if knowledge of human nature begins with and is understood as a completely abstracted, a-historical knowledge, is it problematical to say how it connects with history. But human nature in Hume's conception, as Livingston argues, must be comprehended narratively, that is, historically. One cannot philosophize about human experience without a narrative (hence historical) framework. "Timeless principles are abstractions from ideas associated narratively. But, most important, the moral world (the world of human action) is the product of ideas associated narratively, and so has, ontologically, a narrative structure. Historical understanding, then, is internal to any understanding of the existences that populate the moral world."[46] Livingston's interpretation dissolves the dichotomy of a timeless understanding versus a historical world that seems to put Hume into the question-begging dilemma posed by Womersley.[47] Hume *begins* his study already immersed in a narrative framework. He becomes a philosophical historian through a self-conscious process of correction of perspective.[48] This process is guided by the norm of impartiality, the canon for the philosophical historian. It is no accident, I believe, that some of the most prominent detractors of Hume's history argue that he took up history for extrinsic reasons (e.g., making money, achieving literary prominence) after his philosophical *Treatise*, in Hume's own words, "fell deadborn from the press."[49] Such argumentation puts a biographical and personal twist on

---

[45]Womersley, *The Transformation*, 34.

[46]Livingston, *Hume's Philosophy of Common Life*, 5.

[47]See also, Simon Evnine, "Hume, Conjectural History, and the Uniformity of Human Nature," *Journal of the History of Philosophy* 31, no. 4 (October 1993): 589-606, for a discussion of Hume's supposed anti-historical, timeless view of human nature. Evnine attempts to show that Hume's view of human nature does accommodate historical diversity and change.

[48]Womersley, *The Transformation*, 182-91, 195-96, argues that it is in the last three volumes of *Decline and Fall* that Gibbon dramatically moves away from "causal" philosophic historiography to an embrace of particularity. In contrast to Womersley who sees great development and improvement in the latter half of the *Decline and Fall*, many of Gibbon's interpreters, Bury being the most notable, have tended to view it as a much inferior production, given Gibbon's lack of knowledge of the languages of the original sources.

[49]Ernest Campbell Mossner, "Philosophy and Biography: The Case of David Hume," *Philosophical Review* 59, no. 2 (April 1950): 184-85, points to a longstanding mode of Humean exegesis that attributes his move from writing philosophy (the *Treatise* as a very young man) to history to base and vainglorious motives. "The questioning of Hume's motives, of his intellectual and moral integrity, began with some of his contemporaries in the second half of the eighteenth century." Mossner then goes on to cite several eighteenth-century critics of Hume, Warburton for example, and some nineteenth-century ones as well, including J. S. Mill and T. H. Huxley. Also, there are twentieth-century writers who impugne his

Hume's life that adds further support for a bifurcated interpretation of his philosophy and history. Even Hume's *interest* in history and his motives for writing it are supposed to be extrinsic and disjointed. (Ibid., 186-87)[50] We know now that this is not the case; Hume's interest in history is at least co-terminus with the publication of the *Treatise* when Hume was in his late twenties.[51]

Womersley does say that "the essence of Hume's views on historical narrative is that composure, and the perspective conferred by distance, yield insight."[52] This is indeed the case. The composure amounts to a mastery of emotion; distance helps achieve that. This is an essential part of that self-conscious process of correction. Livingston describes this process: "The moral philosopher, then, cannot bracket out narrative structure without bracketing out the moral world itself. He can understand the narrative world and himself only by learning to think narratively. Consequently, there must be a standard for correcting narrative judgments. This is not to say, however, that the moral philosopher must think only in a narrative way. He must still try to achieve a tenseless and universal perspective of the moral world by reference to whatever abstract principles of morals, aesthetics, religion, politics, law, and the like are defensible. But none of these abstract principles are defensible unless they are abstractions from and are applicable to some narrative order which has been already properly understood, that is, understood through narrative judgments critically determined by the standards of correct narrative thinking."[53]

Womersley's interpretation of Gibbon's supposed abandonment of philosophic history, with its assumptions of causality and a fixed human nature, fails to recognize in Gibbon's history the profound philosophical interplay, suggested here

---

motives such as Victor Wexler, cited above.

[50]Mossner cites John Herman Randall's disparagement of Hume's character. "Hume wrote for two motives: to make money, and to gain a literary reputation . . . . Philosophy was after all a rather narrow field; so he turned to history and wrote a good Tory history of the Stuarts because the Whigs were in power . . . ."

[51]See, Victor Wexler, "David Hume's Discovery of a New Scene of Historical Thought," *Eighteenth-Century Studies* 10, no. 2 (winter 1976/77): 185-86. "[Hume] maintained that it was not until his election as keeper of the Library of the Faculty of Advocates in Edinburgh in 1752, that he 'formed the plan of writing the History of England.' Yet Hume first began to think about writing history at an earlier date. Between the publication of the *Treatise* in 1739 and his election to the post at the Library, Hume wrote several essays that were actually excursions into historical writing. 'Of the Rise and Progress of the Arts and Sciences' (1742) and 'Of the Populousness of Ancient Nations' (1751), two of Hume's arguments in behalf of cosmopolitan culture and modern civilization, are based on historical observation. Even the rather shallow essay 'Of the Study of History' (1742), which he later termed 'frivolous' and deleted from all editions of his works after 1746, gives evidence that he was concerned with history as a genre."

[52]Womersley, *The Transformation*, 25.

[53]Livingston, *Hume's Philosophy of Common Life*, 251-52.

by Livingston, of the "tenseless and universal perspective" with the "narrative order." Gibbon, in practicing philosophical history, interweaves a universal and abstracted perspective of human nature with a narrative order rich in the particulars of human historical experience.

Even though, as Womersley suggests, Gibbon may have come to a manifestly greater understanding of the rich variance in historical life than Hume,[54] the *Decline and Fall* possesses an overpowering narrative unity that links it to a salient Enlightenment ideal—the value of human freedom.[55] Civilization, heralding itself as an achievement of tried and tested norms of self-restraint, emerges out of barbarism but remains a characteristically fragile achievement.[56] Though civilization accumulates beneficent wisdom and conserving habits, barbarism remains a perennially dark and lurking presence. Thus in the *Decline and Fall* we find an elaborate interplay of the antithetical forces associated with barbarism and civilization played out: freedom contests with despotism; rule of law with arbitrary will and anarchy; ignorance and superstition with art and science; prosperity, security of property and refinement of taste and manners with illiteracy, poverty, and coarseness.[57]

The *Decline and Fall* is a haunting account of the loss of freedom and the horrors of tyranny. The demise of the classical Roman civilization was, in a sense, history's greatest lesson.[58] In the very opening lines of his book Gibbon insinuates his theme of corruption. Traces of decline in the great Roman civilization are perceptible to the philosophic historian: "[i]n the second century of the Christian Æra, the empire of Rome comprehended the fairest part of the earth, and the most civilized portion of mankind. The frontiers of that extensive monarchy were guarded by ancient renown and disciplined valour. The gentle, but powerful

---

[54]Wooton, "Narrative, Irony, and Faith in Gibbon's *Decline and Fall*," 103, argues that Gibbon did have a more acute sense of historical diversity than did Hume. I believe that this is indeed the case.

[55]Gay, *The Rise of Modern Paganism*, 3, writes: "[t]he men of the Enlightenment united on a vastly ambitious program, a program of secularism, humanity, cosmopolitanism, and freedom, above, all freedom in its many forms . . . ."

[56]See Francois Furet, "Civilization and Barbarism in Gibbon's History," in *Edward Gibbon and 'The Decline and Fall of the Roman Empire*, 162. Furet says: "what fascinates Gibbon about Roman civilization is not so much that in it lay the foundations of Europe, but that it was so fragile, as fragile perhaps as Europe's civilization now was."

[57]See Craddock, *Edward Gibbon: Luminous Historian*, 19. She notes that after the first three chapters of the *Decline* the "readers have two necessary points of reference before them: the greatness achieved by absolute power and a unified world, with its vulnerability; and the greatness open to shared power and a free world, with its greater vulnerability."

[58]J. W. Burrow, *Gibbon* (New York: Oxford University Press, 1985), 38. Burrow here writes of the long moralizing tradition of Roman history.

influence of laws and manners had gradually cemented the union of the provinces. Their peaceful inhabitants enjoyed and abused the advantages of wealth and luxury. The image of a free constitution was preserved with decent reverence. The Roman senate appeared to possess the sovereign authority, and devolved on the emperors all the executive powers of government." (*DF-1*, I, 1) Into this initially bright, idyllic description of Rome's near perfect greatness creeps the insidious, melancholy imagery of decay, like a rich musical chord drifting slightly off key. At first glance all is well, but Gibbon's impeccable precision in the choice of his words and his deft balance of phrasing begins to convey in the fourth and fifth sentences a slight uneasiness centering on the hinted-at disparity between appearance and reality.[59] The institutions are not as healthy as they appear.[60] With the real power located in the emperors, despotism is already slowly closing its grip. Thus, from the very beginning, Gibbon places grey shadows of tyranny over his pages. In chapter three Gibbon presents the artful usurpation of Augustus, its destruction of the rule of law, and the transformation of Rome from a republic to a military dictatorship. "The tender respect of Augustus for a free constitution which he had destroyed can only be explained by an attentive consideration of the character of that subtle tyrant . . . . His virtues, and even his vices, were artificial; and according to the various dictates of his interest, he was at first the enemy, and at last the father, of the Roman world." (*DF-3*, I, 78) Augustus is the "enemy" of Roman freedom and the "father" of Roman despotism. Gibbon, as is fitting and appropriate for the philosophic historian, captures the essence of profound but imperceptible human and institutional transformations.

The final chapters of the *Decline and Fall* reverberate with Gibbon's melancholic reflections on the completeness of Rome's servitude—freedom lost. "In Rome the voice of freedom and discord is no longer heard; and, instead of the foaming torrent, a smooth and stagnant lake reflects the image of idleness and servitude." (*DF-70*, VII, 309) Here, near the end of Gibbon's long journey, is a deeply poignant moment. Rome's imperial greatness has vanished. In its place is the ecclesiastical tyranny of the effete late-medieval popes. Of Rome's leaders now: "[t]he successful candidate is drawn from the church, and even the convent;

---

[59]W. E. H. Lecky, "Edward Gibbon," in *Warner Library* (New York: Warner, 1917), 11: 6273, writes that: "Gibbon excels all other English historians in symmetry, proportion, perspective and arrangement . . . ." This is an excellent example of that balance and symmetry.

[60]See F. W. Walbank, *The Aweful Revolution: The Decline of the Roman Empire in the West* (Toronto: University of Toronto Press, 1969), 46-47. "Thus behind the rosy hue of Gibbon's picture of a prosperous Antonine world we are in a position to detect a least one notable weakness—the almost complete stagnation of technique." Walbank argues that Gibbon's description of the prosperity under the Antonines needs considerable qualification: there were major stagnating forces, in effect, since the time of Augustus, particularly slavery which was a major deterrent to technical innovation.

from the mode of education and life the most adverse to reason, humanity, and freedom." (*DF-70*, VII, 310) It is worth noting that Hume's ghost still haunts Gibbon late in the *Decline and Fall*. Gibbon attaches a footnote to these pages gently chiding Hume. "Mr. Hume . . . too hastily concludes that, if the civil and ecclesiastical powers be united in the same person, it is of little moment whether he be styled prince or prelate, since the temporal character will always predominate." (*DF-70*, VII, 309, n.105) Hume, it seems, underestimates the potential danger of religious tyranny. Nevertheless, Gibbon is thinking about Hume as he closes out his final lament of freedom's loss.

Thus the universal perspective of freedom comes inevitably into play as Gibbon finishes his tragedy. The theme of freedom is inextricably bound up with his narrative and provides the moral point of reference for the entire work—from beginning to end. Without some notion of a constant and universal human nature, it is difficult to understand why an ideal such as freedom could come to bear so pervasively and poignantly in Gibbon's work.[61] What point is there for the historian to celebrate the achievement of some great value or decry its loss to people who are not in some fundamental way like the historian?

---

[61] A somewhat pedestrian point that seems to belie Womersley's claim that Gibbon abandons causality is that approximately the last twenty pages of the *Decline and Fall* are given over by Gibbon to support his claim of four principal causes of the ruin of Rome. "I can discern four principal causes of the ruin of Rome, which continued to operate in a period of more than a thousand years." (*DF-71*, VII, 317) Gibbon is not only affirming causes (discovered by himself the historian) but that they are at work for an entire millennium.

II. Irony and Philosophic History

I had rather risk my fortune with such authors as Mr. Gibbon, Dr. Robertson, D. Hume, etc. than be the publisher of a hundred insipid publications.

Thomas Cadell (Hume's & Gibbon's publisher)

The relationship of philosophic history to religion is complex, and this relationship accounts in large part for the continuing fascination of Enlightenment historiography. From the pervasiveness of the religious perspective on the world in the eighteenth century, however, there came great power in the form of a religiously controlled view of the world, including the very important historical world. From one's view of the world follows life's prescriptions respecting how to interpret life's experiences, how to conduct oneself, what claims one may lay to the world's goods, etc. Much of the power and authority of eighteenth-century Christianity's derived from its jealously controlled monopoly on interpreting its own status and role. But understanding religion—understanding in the sense of a critical, dispassionate perspective on it—also meant resisting and challenging its self-interpreting control and ultimately its prescriptive authority. In order to study religion as an objective historical phenomenon, it was necessary to approach it with a critical posture that was in reality a threat to its own interpretational monopoly. How could it be otherwise? And so philosophic history developed, understandably, in the face of a deep and pervasive hostility to any effort to look skeptically or critically at Christianity. Thus, the actual writing of philosophic history was uniquely shaped by a self-consciousness of its operation in enemy territory. Philosophic history, while much impressed by and absorbed with religion, undeniably worked to undermine its authority—a rich and intriguing piece of irony.

It is in this challenge to the authority of religion, and in particular to Christianity, that irony can be understood as a key element of the major polemical, critical thrust of philosophic history. Irony echoes with many nuances in philosophic history's skepticism toward religious beliefs and fuels its moralist ambitions. Leo Strauss in his eloquent *Persecution and the Art of Writing* argues that the perennial character of philosophy is its dangerous consequences for the established social order, its threat to popularly accepted dogmas.[62] If so, then, when philosophy is put into practice it may invite a hostile response, even persecution. Strauss writes that persecution cannot prevail against public expression if one is skillful at "writing between the lines." (Ibid., 24) Gibbon was extraordinarily skillful at writing between the lines. He makes an allusion to this

---

[62]Leo Strauss, *Persecution and the Art of Writing* (Glencoe, IL: Free Press, 1952), 21.

in his "Vindication." "Writers who possess any freedom of mind, may be known from each other by the peculiar character of their style and sentiments; but the champions who are inlisted in the service of Authority, commonly wear the uniform of the Regiment." (*EE*, 286)   Note how he pits himself against those "champions" of "authority." Philosophical freedom, therefore, "freedom of mind," is marked by a distinctive style.[63]   Thus we have Gibbon himself alleging a profound connection between a writer's style and his disposition for truth telling.

Writing between the lines, perfecting an inimitable style that was distinctive in its resistence to authority, was for Hume, and even more so for Gibbon, a matter of irony. The adroit irony that is so much a part of Gibbon's highly distinctive style is a means to attack, provocatively but safely, the champions of authority and to undermine prevailing orthodoxies. "Irony," as defined by Hayden White, "is the linguistic strategy underlying and sanctioning skepticism as an explanatory tactic, satire as a mode of emplotment, and either agnosticism or cynicism as a moral posture."[64]   This definition succinctly captures the strategic use of irony in both Hume and Gibbon. Skepticism, as noted above, is a major feature of philosophic history which finds itself in direct conflict with the Christian explanation of the world. Both cynicism and agnosticism as a "moral posture," in White's words, emerge as a result of the success of the irony: doubt—epistemologically expressed in agnosticism or morally in cynicism—replaces certainty with the deflation of the Christian-world achieved by the skeptical tactic. The element of satire at work in irony as, what White calls, a "mode of emplotment," is certainly operative in Gibbon's narrative strategy.   Satire is an instrument of ridicule directed at conspicuous human weaknesses and displays of folly. Gibbon, with the assist of his spectacular erudition, often plays off of the "official" story of the apologists and recreates his own satirical version, one that is particularly compelling precisely because of the vulnerability of the official one. The facts are all there; much of them laid out by the apologists and church historians themselves, awaiting the moralist skeptic like Gibbon who turns them into weapons of ridicule. Gibbon's irony revels in the ambiguity and uncertainty of historical interpretation which works to the disadvantage of the apologist who writes with a brittle confidence that ignores or disdains ambiguity.

Irony thus is a fundamental element of philosophic history, which, at its best—both Hume and Gibbon tell us—entertains and instructs. The latter is more

---

[63]Lytton Strachey, *Portraits in Miniature and Other Essays* (New York: Harcourt, Brace, and Co., 1931), 161. In his chapter on Gibbon, Strachey writes: "Gibbon's style is probably the most exclusive in literature." He also quotes Samuel Coleridge on Gibbon: "Gibbon's style is detestable; but it is not the worst thing about him."

[64]Hayden White, *Tropics of Discourse: Essays in Cultural Criticism* (Baltimore: The Johns Hopkins University Press, 1978), 73-74.

important than the former, but unlikely to occur without it. Philosophic history's instructive purpose, as has been argued above, is moral: it provides the entertainment lacking in abstract, technical philosophy, and it serves to dramatize the instructive spectacle of virtuous and vicious people in action and the effects of that action on political and social institutions. And since political and religious authority lie, in part, in the actions and character of the founders of political and religious institutions, so then history, as a morally instructive discipline, also comes to play a role in establishing and dis-establishing the legitimacy of political regimes, and ultimately the authority of churches, prophets, saints and heroes, as well as that of kings and generals.

Irony, as a recent writer has remarked, echoing Gibbon, is not simply a matter of style, but a mode of thinking.[65] In the case of Hume and Gibbon, irony comes to express a distinctively moral aspect of the philosophical outlook which comprehends a tragic disparity between human aspiration and achievement, and hence the cynicism that frequently emerges from their writings.[66] The translation of philosophic observation into ironic commentary well serves the polemical intentions of the philosophic historian. This is illustrated in Hume's case in one of his most famous statements, near the end of the first *Enquiry*, in which he remarks on the role of reason in demonstrating the truths of religion. "Divinity or Theology, as it proves the existence of a Deity, and the immortality of souls, is composed partly of reasonings concerning particular, partly concerning general facts. It has a foundation in *reason*, so far as it is supported by experience. But its best and most solid foundation is *faith* and divine revelation." (*EHU*, 165, original italics)

Such a statement could easily be made by the most devout of Christians. Yet, from Hume, it is fully damning, and dramatically so, because we know "faith" and "revelation" to him are meaningless. Hume's qualifiers, "best" and "solid," two of the most positively value-charged terms one could think of, are ultimately, and cruelly in this case, attached to nothing. The type of ironic intent and achievement, is, as one writer has termed it, dismissive.[67] The epistemological result is doubt, or as termed above, agnosticism.

Near the end of "Of Miracles" Hume writes that "we may conclude that the *Christian Religion* not only was at first attended with miracles, but even at this day cannot be believed by any reasonable person without one." (*EHU*, 131, original italics) Isolated from the rest of the text, this conclusion may not discomfort the believer. Placed in the context of Hume's epistemological critique of miracles,

---

[65]D. C. Muecke, *The Compass of Irony* (London: Methuen, 1969), 10.

[66]For a detailed study of Hume's use of irony see John Valdimir Price, *The Ironic Hume* (Austin, TX: University of Texas Press, 1965).

[67]A. E. Dyson, *The Crazy Fabric: Essays in Irony* (London: Macmillan, 1965), 49.

however, the implications are stark and unpalatable: the heart of Christianity is a miraculous event, and yet no experientially based argument for belief in miracles can be formulated. The last clause of this sentence, that Christianity "cannot be believed by any reasonable person without one [a miracle]" amounts to a self-collapsing piece of irony: no reasonable person can be a Christian without believing in a miracle, but a belief in miracles has no reasonable support. Hume thus can speak the language of orthodoxy, but at the same time strike deeply into its heart.

Irony was Gibbon's principal weapon against orthodoxy. In his critique of Christianity in the *Decline and Fall*, Gibbon struggled, with varying success, to juggle his own methodological ideals of detachment and objectivity and empathetic engagement, an effort that was further complicated by the fact that the forces of orthodoxy were still strong enough to make open criticism of Christian orthodoxy somewhat perilous.[68] One of Gibbon's commentators, Harold Bond, has remarked that his ironic style was based on a conscious decision to approach the excesses of Christianity obliquely, fully understanding that he could not assault the "inner shrine of the temple of faith."[69] Against the forces of orthodoxy Gibbon responded by creating a work which consummately employs the art of irony. Gibbon credits Pascal as his model for the use of irony as a tool of deflation. "From the *Provincial Letters* of Pascal, which almost every year I have perused with new pleasure, I learned to manage the weapon of grave and temperate irony even on subjects of ecclesiastical solemnity." (*Memoirs*, 100) One of Gibbon's recent commentators, W. B. Carnochan, writes that: "Pascal taught Gibbon the art of seeming temperate; of mixing deference with doubt; of never meeting authority head-on or denying its legitimacy, but always subjecting it to the ruthlessness of insinuation."[70]

Gibbon's use of irony is noteworthy and remarkable because of the sheer enormity of its presence in the *Decline and Fall*.[71] Yet he is skillful enough to make the irony fresh and unpredictable throughout the entire work and hence effective in spite of its pervasiveness. The broader philosophical outlook behind the text's ironic permutations, as well as its polemical effectiveness, is all the more impressive in light of Gibbon's almost perverse ingenuity in making subtle though frequently startling applications of it. Writing of Christianity's most notable

---

[68]J. Norton, *A Bibliography of the Works of Edward Gibbon*, 84. Norton quotes Birkbeck Hill: "[i]f at times he [Gibbon] veiled his scepticism with an affectation of belief, part of the blame must be born by the law of the land which still held the threat of three years imprisonment over anyone who, having been educated in the Christian religion, should by writing, deny it to be true."

[69]Bond, *Literary Art of Edward Gibbon*, 120.

[70]W. B. Carnochan, *Gibbon's Solitude* (Stanford, CA: Stanford University Press, 1987), 86.

[71]Hayden White, *Metahistory* (Baltimore: The Johns Hopkins Press, 1973), 55, calls Gibbon's *Decline and Fall*, "the greatest achievement of sustained irony in the history of historical literature".

institutionalizer, Constantine, Gibbon states with apparent paradox that: "[a]s he gradually advanced in the knowledge of truth, he proportionably declined in the practice of virtue; and the same year of his reign in which he convened the council of Nice [actually Nicaea] was polluted by the execution, or rather murder, of his eldest son." (DF-20, II, 329) Thus, Constantine's elevated religious knowledge is ironically linked to a vicious (homicidal) character, and, in order to drive the point home, Gibbon provides a concrete, temporal linkage: the council of Nicaea, with its production of great theological formulas, is held *in the same year as* he had his son murdered—an ironic coincidence.   Gibbon does not have to state it, but the reader easily grasps the anti-theological perspective, and perhaps begins to share in Gibbon's massive feelings of revulsion in contemplating the disparity between the theological-political hero invented by the apologist and the actual man discovered by the philosophic historian. Gibbon's irony explodes the heroic myths of Constantine and undermines the official Christian story.

In Gibbon's footnotes lurk an additional element of polemically charged irony.[72] These notes compile a vast edifice of learning and knowledge that adds further interpretational complexity to the text of the *Decline and Fall*.[73] Gibbon uses his footnotes at appropriate places in the narrative as rhetorical and polemical devices.   They enable him to score points off of ironic twists in the text, thus effecting a double irony.[74] The actual narrative unfolds according to certain prescribed norms of appropriateness. The historian in his role as *entertainer* could not offend the eighteenth-century sensibilities of his reader.[75] The "triumph of vulgarity" is still two centuries away.[76] Yet the more critical purpose of history as *instruction* requires on occasion the divulgence of information that might offend

---

[72]Anthony Grafton, "The Footnote from De Thou to Ranke," *History and Theory: Studies in the Philosophy of History*, Theme Issue 33, *Proof and Persuasion in History* (1994): 54. "The most ironic footnotes ever written run underneath the text of Gibbon's *Decline and Fall* . . . . Gibbon's footnotes amuse and bemuse—as does the fact that he originally meant them to be endnotes, and moved them only when Hume and others complained."

[73]Burrow, *Gibbon*, 99-100. Also, Grafton, "The Footnote from De Thou to Ranke," 57, makes the important observation that the footnote, with its underlying rationale of support and evidence for the text, is a fundamental mark of modern history. "The presence of the footnotes is essential. They are the outward and visible signs of inward grace—the grace infused into history when it was transformed from an eloquent narrative created by·manipulating earlier chronicles into a critical discipline based on systematic scrutiny of original evidence and formal arguments for the preferability of one source to another."

[74]James D. Garrison, "Gibbon and the Treacherous Language of Panegyrics," *Eighteenth-Century Studies* 11, no. 1 (fall 1977): 52.

[75]My interpretation of Gibbon's use of footnotes differs significantly from Womersley, *The Transformation*, 94-95.

[76]Robert Pattison, *The Triumph of Vulgarity: Rock Music in the Mirror of Romanticism* (New York: Oxford University Press, 1987).

readers and overstep the boundaries of good taste.[77] The devil is truly in the details, and the footnotes provide the necessary specifics, the unsavory morsels, if you will, that fill out the picture and complete the reader's moral instruction. Gibbon's treatment of the Crusades late in the *Decline and Fall* is a case in point, and he makes an observation on the moral character of the Crusaders. Typically, with this sort of assessment, Gibbon deliberately creates a jarring contrast between the apologist's "official," idealized version of what the believers are supposed to be and how they actually are. Of the Crusaders he says: "[a] *speculative reasoner* might suppose that their faith had a strong and serious influence on their practice; and that the soldiers of the cross, the deliverers of the holy sepulchre, prepared themselves by a sober and virtuous life for the daily contemplation of martyrdom. *Experience* blows away this charitable illusion; and seldom does the history of profane war display such scenes of intemperance and prostitution as were exhibited under the walls of Antioch . . . . [T]he Christians were seduced by every temptation." (*DF-58*, VI , 314, italics added) Thus, Gibbon sets up the conclusions about the character of these crusaders that a "speculative reasoner" might draw and then uses "experience" as the disillusioner.[78] Gibbon takes his disillusioning activities, however, a step further with a brief footnote that instantiates his generalization and gives a dimension of particularity to the intemperance and intolerance alluded to in the text. This slender particular of information is one of a seemingly inexhaustible supply of historical details that Gibbon has at his disposal. "See the tragic and scandalous fate of an archdeacon of royal birth, who was slain by the Turks as he reposed in an orchard, playing at dice with a Syrian concubine." (*DF-58*, VI, 314, n.100) Almost every word of this short sentence condemns: slothfulness, gambling, prostitution by a sybaritic high level churchman with royal blood. The footnote, with its gossipy, bawdy tone, is available to the reader yet appropriately distanced from the narrative.[79] There is further malicious

---

[77]Grafton, "The Footnote from DeThou to Ranke," 54. "Like the toilet, the footnote enables one to deal with ugly tasks in private; like the toilet, it is tucked genteelly away—often, in recent years, not even at the bottom of the page but at the end of the book."

[78]See F. A. Hayek, *The Constitution of Liberty* (Chicago: University of Chicago Press, 1960), 24, where he speaks of "erroneous intellectualism," a concept of reason divorced from nature and experience. "The conception of man deliberately building his civilization stems from an erroneous intellectualism that regards human reason as something standing outside nature and possessed of knowledge and reasoning capacity independent of experience." While the object of Hayek's criticism here is secular utopianized thinking, particularly socialist types, this type of thinking also has religious manifestations, which are the objects of Hume's and Gibbon's disdain.

[79]In Dero A. Saunder's introduction to *The Portable Gibbon: the Decline and Fall of the Roman Empire*, ed. Dero A. Saunders (New York: Penguin, 1977), 15, reference is made to a joking remark by Philip Guedella that it was in his footnotes that Gibbon lived out his sex life.

irony in that the infidel "Turks" can easily be construed as an instrument of divine punishment as they slay the profligate churchman.

In his discussion of religious persecution in chapter twenty-one, Gibbon provides an account of Arianism with all its heretical contentiousness. The situation featured Athanasius advancing the orthodox trinitarian doctrine with all the intricate and profound distinctions present in theological controversy. Gibbon mentions Marcellus of Ancyra, a Sabellian and a friend of Anthanasius. "The life of Athanasius was consumed in irreconcilable opposition to the impious *madness* of the Arians; but he defended above twenty years the Sabellianism of Marcellus of Ancyra; and, when at last he was compelled to withdraw himself from his communion, he continued to mention, with an ambiguous smile, the venial errors of his respectable friend." (*DF-21*, II, 370, original italics) It would be difficult to find a more complex interplay of insinuations. The "ambiguous smile" of Anthanasius very likely draws a mischievous smile from the reader who attempts to sort out Athanasius's motives. Then in a footnote, Gibbon says: "[h]is [Marcellus's] work, in *one* book, of the unity of God, was answered in the *three* books, which are still extant, of Eusebius." (*DF-21*, II, 370, n.62, original italics) With this kind of "grace note" of ridicule, appended in order to trivialize the one-versus-three, theological controversy, Gibbon completes his insinuative, skeptical intentions without disrupting the narrative. The dismissive suggestion of the "three books answering the one" is that this controversy is largely a matter of insignificant verbiage.

In the same chapter and on the same topic, Gibbon records the death of Arius and notes that Arius's political triumph is (suspiciously) attended by his unsuspected demise ("[o]n the same day which had been fixed for the triumph of Arius, he expired"). (*DF-21*, II, 378) One would suspect, given the character of the contest, that Arius' theological enemies were, shall we say, materially involved. As Gibbon states: "[t]he strange and horrid circumstances of his death might excite a suspicion that the orthodox saints had contributed more efficaciously than by their prayers to deliver the church from the most formidable of her enemies." (*DF-21*, II, 378) Here Gibbon seems to be reciting the obvious, but then he adds a scatological footnote in which he says: "[t]hose who press the literal narrative of the death of Arius (his bowels burst out in a privy) must make their option between *poison* and a *miracle*." (*DF-21*, II, 378, n.83, original italics) Again, the "literal" details of the note are not really appropriate for the narrative body of the text. They are available for the reader with the courage, or stomach, to pursue them. Still, only the most credulous and naive can escape Gibbon's ironic intent, which is to scandalize theological politics with insinuations of the base motives of power and betrayal. In the text, Gibbon does, indeed, merely insinuate, but, unable to forbear, he uses the note to set up a cruel dilemma for the orthodox: Arius was poisoned (considering the motivational context and the suspicious circumstances of his death), *or* he miraculously (and conveniently) died by a most revolting sort of miracle.

These footnotes play an important didactic role in Gibbon's narrative. Essential to his goals of entertainment and moral instruction for his philosophic history, they are intended to heighten the reader's awareness of the dimensions of hypocrisy, fraud, and misuse of language. In *The Compass of Irony*, D. C. Muecke notes that "the first formal requirements of irony are that there should be a confrontation or juxtaposition of contradictory, incongruous, or otherwise incompatible elements, and that one should be seen as 'invalidating' the other."[80] Muecke adds that the ironist must always pretend, must feign an ignorance of these fatal juxtapositions.

A particularly artful juxtaposition is Gibbon's recreation of a scene of horror that centers on the Arian-Catholic dispute over the trinity (the Catholic Homoousion versus the Arian Homoiousion). "[T]he cruelties exercised by this Semi-Arian tyrant [Macedonius] in the support of the *Homoiousion*, exceeded the commission, and disgraced the reign, of Constantius. The sacraments of the church were administered to the reluctant victims, who denied the vocation, and abhorred the principles of Macedonius. The rites of baptism were conferred on women and children, who, for that purpose, had been torn from the arms of their friends and parents; the mouths of the communicants were held open, by a wooden engine, while the consecrated bread was forced down their throat; the breasts of tender virgins were either burnt with red-hot egg-shells or inhumanly compressed between sharp and heavy boards." (*DF-21*, II, 409) To the account of this gruesome and despicable scene Gibbon adds a footnote in which he says, "The principal assistants of Macedonius, in the work of persecution, were the two bishops of Nicomedia and Cyzicus, who were esteemed for their virtues, and especially for their charity. I cannot forbear reminding the reader that the difference between *Homoousion* and *Homoiousion* is almost invisible to the nicest theological eye." (*DF-21*, II, 409, n.157) How could the contrast Gibbon sets up be, at the same time, more subtle, yet more stark? Persecutors of the most cruel and odious type are esteemed for their virtue and love. Doctrinal distinctions admitting of the most arcane, esoteric, and, in Gibbon's view, trivial differences are contrasted with the most gruesome accounts of torture and horror. Gibbon, as he notes, simply cannot "forbear" reminding the reader that all the horrors he records are the result of a dispute over a diphthong.

---

[80]Muecke, *The Compass of Irony*, 29.

Julian the Apostate was one of the characters in the *Decline and Fall* that Gibbon admired most.   Nevertheless, Gibbon exposes Julian's own peculiar fanaticism. In describing his initiation into the Eleusinian mysteries he notes: "[a]s these ceremonies were performed in the depth of caverns, and in the silence of the night, and as the inviolable secret of the mysteries was preserved by the discretion of the initiated, I shall not presume to describe the horrid sounds and fiery apparitions, which were presented to the senses, or the imagination, of the credulous aspirant, till the visions of comfort and knowledge broke upon him in a blaze of celestial light." (*DF-23*, II 465) The footnotes adds: "[w]hen Julian, in a momentary sign of panic, made the sign of the cross, the dæmons instantly disappeared. Gregory supposes that they were frightened, but the [Eleusinian] priests declared that they were indignant. The reader, according to the measure of his faith, will determine this profound question." (*DF-23*, II, 465, n.24) Thus we have two opposing (and equally absurd) interpretations of an event that never happened. Gibbon pits the pagan against the Christian version, the effect being to reduce Christianity to the level of pagan superstition.

These examples begin to give a sense of Gibbon's creative genius as an ironist and also indicate to some extent the primary, skeptical use to which Gibbon puts his irony. As a philosophic historian, Gibbon aims to make impartial judgements about the conduct and character of those human beings who inhabit the past and influence the present. His irony furthers this purpose in its undermining of officially sanctioned predilections for interpreting the past. Throughout the *Decline and Fall*, irony remains a potent instrument of Gibbon's critique of Christianity, allowing him to attack orthodoxy in a way that makes its weaknesses and pretenses particularly conspicuous. The irony is closely linked to Gibbon's melancholy duty as a historian of religion. He uses it to expose the disparity between ideals and practice and subjects to scrutiny the limitations of the human condition.

The complex way that Edward Gibbon thus deals with religion throughout the *Decline and Fall* must be understood as the skeptical, anti-apologetic work of philosophic history. Philosophic history defines itself through its antagonism toward the institution of the church and its opposition to a theologically dominated view of history. This antagonism is developed with the instruments of irony and is manifest in artful insinuation. Through ironic insinuation, the moral character of religious figures is impeached. Philosophic history's anti-theological posture is rooted in a skeptically conditioned epistemology which casts doubt upon religious belief. Concern with impartiality, skepticism, and moralism are all interconnected elements of philosophic history. The emphasis on impartiality is an antidote to an ever-persistent human self-centeredness. Indeed, the conservatism of philosophic history turns on a view of human nature that assumes corruptibility and repudiates perfectibility. The skeptical perspective aims to subdue the hubris of the intellect. The philosophic historian, as moralist, focuses on fanaticism and superstition and hopes to illustrate the fragility of civilization and the value of freedom.

CHAPTER THREE

"OF MIRACLES" AT WORK
IN THE *DECLINE AND FALL*

I. Hume, Gibbon, and Miracles

A Galician priest was explaining to a peasant what miracles were.
'If I fell from that church tower and landed unhurt, what would you call
it?'
'An accident.'
'And if I fell again and was unhurt?'
'Another accident.'
'And if I did it a third time?'
'A habit.'

A story told by Lewis Namier to A. J. P. Taylor

Hume and Gibbon offended their Christian contemporaries because of what they made—in a largely insinuative, ironical way—of miracles. "Of Miracles" questions the credibility of witnesses to miracles, and chapter fifteen of the *Decline and Fall* ends with doubts about the historical accounts of the miracles of early Christianity. Donald Livingston's insightful observations on Hume's view of society and its roots in his historical consciousness help explain why "Of Miracles" provoked such passionate responses. "The social world, for Hume, is an order of passion and thought, and of the *reflective* passions and thoughts men have about that order. . . . The social world, then, will have some sort of narrative unity woven together by the temporally reflective imagination. People are held together not merely by passions unreflectively felt and tenselessly ordered, but by narrative associations, i.e., by the stories they tell about themselves. The legal, moral, social, political, aesthetic, and religious standards that constitute the moral world are the products of narrative associations of ideas, and so are part of some narrative unity. The moral world is a system of stories."[1]

The moral world is, indeed, a remarkable "system of stories," and "Of Miracles" calls into question the status of an important type of story—stories reflecting religious beliefs and ideals. More specifically, it deals with the credibility of certain kinds of religious story tellers—witnesses to miracles. The intent of Hume's essay was to make the literal truth of religious stories and beliefs—surrounded as they are by miracles—subject to doubt. "Of Miracles" strikes at the heart of the "stories" (the Christian story for one) which many people

---

[1]Livingston, *Hume's Philosophy of Common Life,* 218.

who read Hume reflected upon in creating their moral world and from which they derived their moral standards.[2] Since Christianity is conceived of as a miraculous intervention of the divine in human history that brings the message of hope and spiritual salvation, Hume's disparagement of the credibility of miraculous reports is not simply a philosophical exercise, but a profound critique of the Christian approach to organizing and interpreting moral experience. "Of Miracles" was, simply put, an attack on the story of Christianity.

To believe in reports of miracles is irrational: that is Hume's central point of the essay. The point is never lost on Gibbon who read "Of Miracles" and praised his Scottish mentor in the *Decline and Fall* for his anti-miracle polemics.[3] An essential part of Gibbon's Christian iconoclasm is featured in the skepticism he introduces into his historical treatment of miracles. Hume's philosophical skepticism becomes narratively interwoven by Gibbon into the historical picture introducing doubt about the moral story of Christianity. Throughout the *Decline and Fall* Gibbon considers claims for miracles, both Christian and non-Christian. Gibbon evinces a cool skepticism toward Muslim miracles that rebounds damagingly against Christian miracles. The skeptical way in which Gibbon deals with miracles throughout his narrative—raising doubts about the motives and character of those who attest to miracles (attacking the testifiers, if you will)—is one of his most persistent themes. To focus on Gibbon's treatment of miracles is to highlight the "philosophic" nature of his philosophic history with its own unique attack on the Christian story.

Much of the *Decline and Fall* grapples with the history of Christianity, and it is to *this* history that Gibbon applies the Humean skeptical approach from "Of Miracles." Christianity's early witnesses affirmed the reality of supernatural causality and the participation of the divine in the unfolding of the story. The Christian views all historical change and meaning through a theological perspective. Gibbon indirectly challenges this view with its basic assumption of God's entry into human affairs by impugning the *testimony* of those who affirmed the miraculous evidence of divine intervention. The narration of the *Decline and Fall* focuses not on the miracles witnessed but on the witnesses to them. The character and motives of the early Christians are what Gibbon questions. Credibility becomes the issue.[4]

---

[2]See Averil Cameron, *Christianity and the Rhetoric of Empire: The Development of Christian Discourse* (Berkeley, CA: University of California Press, 1991). In Chapter 3, entitled, "Stories People Want," Cameron describes Christianity as a religion with a story, a narrative. Cameron examines many of the apocryphal writings of the first two centuries and suggests that they help to flesh out the story of Jesus and the Apostles.

[3]See page 126 below.

[4]See, Bond, *Literary Art of Edward Gibbon*, 117. Bond writes that Gibbon's argumentation

Christian history is the story of heroes who act out the divine plan with miracles as evidence of supernatural direction. The originators of saint-biography and the founders of ecclesiastical history were, not surprisingly, Christians,[5] and *their* history dealt with the unfolding of events from a supernatural perspective. But for Gibbon this was a problem: the realm of the supernatural must be the province of the theologian, not the historian. In history dominated by theological assumptions he had little confidence. Which is perhaps why he opens his "infamous" chapter fifteen, "The Progress of the Christian Religion," with a dramatic, emblematic contrast between the *duty* of the historian and the *task* of the theologian, a piece often used as a vintage Gibbon epigram. "The *theologian* may indulge the *pleasing* task of describing Religion as she descended from Heaven, arrayed in her native purity. A more *melancholy* duty is *imposed* on the *historian*. He *must* discover the inevitable mixture of *error* and *corruption* which she contracted in a long residence upon earth, among a weak and degenerate race of beings." (*DF-15*, II, 2, italics added)

One cannot over stress the profundity of this distinction which echoes the theme of human nature's limitations—depravity even. Appreciating it is absolutely essential to an understanding of Gibbon's critique of Christianity and its implications for his treatment of miracles. The text is the prelude to Gibbon's skeptical version of Christianity's miraculous birth and early unfolding. The historian's work, Gibbon's work, so it seems, is to be an exercise in disillusionment, a "melancholy duty" that is "imposed" upon him, the historian of the Roman empire. The discoveries that he "must" make describe beings who are deeply flawed. Gibbon's "corruption" is discerned at two levels throughout the *Decline and Fall*: the unseemly *conduct* of human beings and its *rationalization* by interested observers. Human beings do evil deeds: others present sanitized accounts of them to the world. Evil endures and is compounded by apologists. The apologist, as noted, is the philosophic historian's *bête noire*. The theologian's task in contrast to the historian's is "pleasing," something that he "may indulge" himself in. "Indulge" is an important insinuative term and suggests the absence of

---

in chapter fifteen, loosely constructed, is really *ad hominem*. He does not attack Christianity directly, just its interpreters.

[5] Arnaldo Momigliano, *Essays in Ancient and Modern Historiography* (Middletown, CT: Wesleyan University Press, 1977), 114. Also see Arnaldo Momigliano, "Pagan and Christian Historiography in the Fourth Century A.D.," in *The Conflict Between Paganism and Christianity*, 88. "To put it briefly, the Christians invented ecclesiastical history and the biography of the saints, but did not try to christianize ordinary political history; and they influenced ordinary biography less than we would expect." Also, (92) "Eusebius made history positively and negatively by creating ecclesiastical history and by leaving political history alone. In a comparable manner another Christian invented the biography of the saints and left the biography of generals and politicians to the pagans. The inventor was Athanasius, whose life of St. Anthony was promptly made available in Latin by Euagrius."

the constraints of veracity and impartiality. The indulgence of the theologian, contemplating religion as a "heavenly" phenomenon, leads to the recreation of events as if by heavenly intervention, i.e., the invention of miracles. The historian's vocation by contrast drives him inevitably to investigate events with doubt and suspicion.

One significant aspect of human weakness discovered by the historian is closely associated with religion—the propensity for fanaticism.[6] Fanaticism was a troubling phenomenon for Gibbon because it unleashes strong passions that destroy the norms of self-restraint that make civilization possible such as honesty and promise-keeping. Fanaticism and mendacity have intimate ties. As a philosophic historian contemplating religion, Gibbon unearths the depressing incongruity of immaculate otherworldly preoccupations and shady this-worldly realities of human nature.[7] The "melancholy duty," of which Gibbon laments, involves the discovery of fraud and ambition in a particularly damaging context, namely within the history of the early church and in the conduct of Christian apologists. The writing of history turns out to be an activity of exposing and confronting the evidence of human corruption. This is particularly so in those social arenas, such as religion and politics, where the pious and self-righteous denial of its presence is usually a sign of its pervasiveness.

The invidious comparison that Gibbon sets up between theology and history seems to suggest that theology—at least the theology he encounters as a historian—corrupts history. Gibbon's disparagement of theology is *ad hominem*, attacking the motives and dispositions of the theologians who recast history in a theological perspective.[8] In performing the historian's melancholy duty, Gibbon produces a melancholy scene for Christian history. The historian-theologians operate by typical human motives—ambition, fanaticism, etc. Because the apologist makes *every* historical event testify to the truth of Christianity, apologetic history, i.e., theologically conceived history, is suspect.

Gibbon's interest in miracles was formative in his own personal religious experience. During his short and self-admittedly feckless career at Oxford, he did however read Conyers Middleton's *A Free Inquiry Into the Miraculous Powers, Which are Supposed to have Subsisted in the Christian Church from the Earliest*

---

[6]See Jay Newman, *Fanatics & Hypocrites* (Buffalo, NY: Prometheus Books, 1986), 30. "The term ['fanatic'] is derived from the classical Latin *fanaticus* meaning, 'of a temple,' and synonyms of the adjectival form are 'bigoted, intolerant, superstitious.'"

[7]A recent commentator on Gibbon has also noted Gibbon's contrast between theology and history: "[t]he historian needs the theologian, dreaming of purity, as he needs primitive Christianity for a backdrop to Christianity's human failings. The seemingly closed opposition of historian and theologian turns out to be open, an opposition of incommensurability." Carnochan, *Gibbon's Solitude*, 97.

[8]Bond, *Literary Art of Edward Gibbon*, 117.

Ages, Through Several Successive Centuries. Gibbon's encounter with Middleton was significant in precipitating his youthful, temporary conversion to Catholicism. (*Memoirs*, 84-85) Middleton's work posed a dilemma for Protestants. Many of them believed in the reality of the New Testament miracles, yet they also believed that the age of miracles had long ceased. Later miracles were, from the Protestant perspective, papist frauds. However, arguments used against later miracles could be employed against the earlier ones. Thus the dilemma: how is one to determine without complete arbitrariness when miracles ceased to occur? Gibbon's early twentieth-century biographer, D. M. Low, notes that the question of when miracles had ceased had been evaded by the English divines, but that there was a general agreement that miracles continued for about three centuries after Christ.[9] Gibbon, upon reading Middleton, took the Catholic way out of the dilemma; miracles had never ceased. (Ibid., 41)[10] Later, Gibbon recounts with a typical smugness of maturity reflecting upon the follies of youth: "I bewildered myself in the errors of the Church of Rome." (*Memoirs*, 84)[11]

Leslie Stephen states that "Gibbon's Catholicism, in fact, was nothing more than a temporary misapprehension of certain historical arguments: it was a conviction of the head, not of the heart; and as his knowledge widened and deepened, it spontaneously disappeared."[12] Nevertheless, it was, Stephen argues, the most critical passage in Gibbon's intellectual life. (Ibid., 446) Why? The experience immersed Gibbon in the polemics over miracles produced by the Protestant-Catholic split in Christianity. Each side was using miracle-related arguments against each other. The reading of Middleton fixed Gibbon's attention on the historical features of the problem and the argumentation. Gibbon recalls his adolescent struggle in the *Memoirs* and writes that upon reading Middleton: "I was unable to resist the weight of historical evidence, that within the same period, most of the leading doctrines of popery were already introduced in theory and practice: nor was my conclusion absurd, that *miracles are the test of truth*, and that the Church must be orthodox and pure, which was so often approved by the visible interposition of the deity." (*Memoirs*, 85, italics added) Thus, early in Gibbon's

---

[9]D. M. Low, *Edward Gibbon, 1737-1794* (London: Chatto and Windus, 1937), 41.

[10]Low writes: "[t]he English Divines had shirked the question of determining the exact date of cessation of miracles, but it was generally agreed that miracles had continued for some three centuries." Low also claims (42) that Middleton's work represented an advance by, "reducing a theological question to a matter of historical criticism."

[11]Low, *Edward Gibbon*, 44, notes that Gibbon's conversion to Catholicism was, technically, high treason. Both he and the priest who presided at his formal admission into the Church were liable to severe penalties.

[12]Stephen, *History of English Thought*, 1: 447.

intellectual development the connection was made between the reality of miracles and the truth of Christianity.

Doubts about Christian miracles had prompted Gibbon's religious rebellion which led to the casting off of his native Protestantism at an enormous cost. He was expelled from Oxford. His infuriated father threatened disinheritance and banished him for five years to a foreign land where, as he laments: "I . . . exchanged my elegant apartment in Magdalen College for a narrow, gloomy street, the most unfrequented of an unhandsome town." (*Memoirs*, 93)[13] In Lausanne Gibbon, under the tutelage of a benevolent Calvinist minister, M. Pavilliard, after fifteen months or so of gentle debate converted back to Protestantism. M. Pavilliard describes Gibbon as "a thin little figure, with a large head, disputing and arguing with the greatest ability, all the best arguments that had ever been used in favour of popery."[14] J. M. Robertson remarks of Gibbon's reconversion to Protestantism in Lausanne that Gibbon's intense study of the issues "must have conduced to make him feel that what began to look like the difference between Tweedledum and Tweedledee was not worth being miserable for."[15]

The *Decline and Fall*'s account of Rome's transformation from a classical to Christian culture is thus the work of a man whose own personal religious outlook underwent a series of remarkable changes: Protestant to Catholic; a reconversion back to Protestantism; and finally, deism. Gibbon's religious "conversions" had a bearing on the presentation of Christianity in the *Decline and Fall,* if only in focusing his attention on the historical dimensions of theological controversy. His religious career seems, quite remarkably, to be theologically emblematic of the bitter ideological struggle which engulfed Catholic and Protestant Christianity and the threat posed to Christianity generally by the rise of deism with its attack on revelation. The dynamics of conflict between eighteenth-century Catholicism and Protestantism turned on a contentious view of early church history and the authority of the church as evidenced by the power of its agents to perform miracles.[16] The Protestant rejection of the later miracles eschewed appeals to the miraculous as an apologetic weapon and moved Protestant thinking closer to a naturalistic view of history. Deism took the selective skepticism of Protestantism

---

[13]For an extensive discussion of Gibbon's conversions to and away from Catholicism see Edward Hutton, "The Conversion of Edward Gibbon," *The Nineteenth Century* 91, no. 661 (March 1932): 362-75.

[14]*The Encyclopedia Britannica*, 11 ed., s.v. "Gibbon."

[15]Robertson, *Gibbon*, 11-12.

[16]Owen Chadwick, "Gibbon and the Church Historians," in *Edward Gibbon and "The Decline and Fall of The Roman Empire'*, 219-20.

regarding miracles and made it universal and consistent by rejecting miracles altogether.[17]

---

[17]See Gellner, *Plough, Sword and Book*, 113, in a section called "Reformation to Enlightenment" where he argues that the Enlightenment is a logical continuation of the seeds of naturalism introduced by the Protestant Reformation. "The supposition that the Enlightenment is but a kind of continuation and completion of the Reformation is sometimes attacked as naive and over-intellectualist. Yet the logical connection is obviously there: the notion that it is legitimate to scrutinize the claims of a self-proclaimed sacred institution, by checking it against the independent testimony of scripture, would seem to lead naturally to the idea that everything, including scripture itself, can be scrutinized in the light of the independent testimony of 'Reason' or fact." Gibbon's approach to evaluating historical evidence shows a commitment to the independent testimony of fact as against any sacred self-proclamations. Also, Ernest Gellner, *Anthropology and Politics: Revolutions in the Sacred Grove* (Oxford: Blackwell, 1995), 41, defines a Protestant as one who "does not allow a segregated species of privileged cognitive specialists." Much of Gibbon's attack on Christianity is an attempt to undermine the credibility (via the imputation of natural motives of ambition, greed, etc.) of Christianity's cognitive specialists.

II. "Of Miracles" and the Writing of History

For no man is a witness to him that already believeth, and therefore
needs no witness; but to them that deny or doubt or have not heard it.

Thomas Hobbes

In early to mid-eighteenth-century England the question of miracles was a central philosophical preoccupation, and it was an enormously polemical issue with very high stakes. Deism's attack on revealed religion pushed the issue of miracles to the forefront. Isaac Newton, Robert Boyle, John Wilkins (founder of the Royal Society), and many leaders of the progressive Latitudinarians wrote about and argued for the reality of Christianity's miracles.[18]

That miracles were the subject of controversy for thinkers of the stature of Hume and Newton is hardly surprising. Confidence in the Christian world view, grounded as it was in a belief in the primacy of supernatural causality through miracles, was being gradually but steadily eroded by the growing explanatory efficacy of naturalism and its increasingly mechanized view of the world.[19] This in turn created a tension between two conflicting desires; the desire to preserve intact the Faith and all its accouterments, and the desire to pursue inquiry even when it threatened the Faith. As Gibbon himself points out, prior to the rise of modern science, miracles and prodigies are so commonplace, so much a part of the world view that one is reluctant to call them miracles. "The primitive Christians," Gibbon says, "perpetually trod on mystic ground, and their minds were exercised by the habits of believing the most extraordinary events." (*DF-15*, II, 33) This way of thinking, Gibbon suggests, is characteristic or typical of more primitive, pre-scientific people. Once a scientific, empirical perspective incorporates itself within a culture, even the most devout are less inclined to believe in miracles. "In modern times, a latent, and even involuntary, scepticism adheres to the most pious dispositions . . . . Accustomed long since to observe and to respect the invariable order of Nature, our reason, or at least our imagination, is not sufficiently prepared to sustain the visible action of the Deity." (*DF-15*, II, 33) Anthony Flew notes that the notion of a miracle only makes sense if there is a strong conception of a natural

---

[18]R. M. Burns, *The Great Debate on Miracles: From Joseph Glanville to David Hume,* (Lewisburg, PA: Bucknell University Press, 1981), 14.

[19]See E. J. Dijksterhuis, *The Mechanization of the World Picture: Pythagoras to Newton,* trans. C. Dikshoorn (Princeton, NJ: Princeton University Press, 1986), 495. "With the appearance of Newton's *Principia* the era of transition from ancient and medieval to classical science was concluded; the mechanization of the world-picture had in principle been accomplished; natural scientists had been furnished with an aim which they were to pursue for two centuries as the only conceivable one and which was to inspire them to great achievements."

order. "The inevitable tension between the ideas of rule and of exception thus gives concepts of the miraculous an inherent instability."[20]

In *The Great Debate on Miracles: From Joseph Glanville to David Hume*, R. M. Burns argues that the prominent thinkers writing in favor of miracles were not the religious conservatives but the scientific progressives of the late seventeenth and early eighteenth century such as Newton and Wilkins.[21] Burns makes this point so as to place Hume *in opposition* to the scientific progressives and castigate him as a destructive skeptic. Yet, the fact that scientist-believers, like Newton, were taking up the cudgel for miracles is powerful evidence of a growing awareness of dissonance between religion and natural science, and suggests that the scientific defenders of miracles felt compelled to defend miracles and somehow reconcile a mounting and troubling tension.[22]

By 1737 at age twenty-six, Hume had written an essay on miracles but was reticent about publishing it.[23] In 1748 "Of Miracles" appeared in the *Enquiry Concerning Human Understanding*. Hume knew the importance of miracles for the Christian world view. Miracles were claimed as evidence of the effects of divine intentions. Miraculous events, the processes of their documentation, and the significance attached to them as proof of the presence of the supernatural, all of these enter in some dramatic fashion into the history of Christianity. Considering the stature of those who defended miracles—Newton, Boyle, etc.—Hume's attack must be regarded as a major intellectual challenge of the time, and his skeptical treatment of miracles as the centerpiece of his critique of Christianity.[24]

---

[20]*Encyclopedia of Philosophy*, s.v. "Miracles."

[21]Burns, *Great Debate on Miracles*, Chapter one.

[22]See also James Noxon, *Hume's Philosophical Development* (Oxford: Clarendon Press, 1973), 54-67. Noxon points out how extensively Newton's natural philosophy was pushed in the eighteenth century into religious and moral areas.

[23]David Hume, *New Letters of David Hume*, ed. R. Kilbanski and E. C. Mossner (Oxford: Clarendon Press, 1954), 2. Also, see Burns, *Great Debate on Miracles*. In chapter six Burns argues, contrary to the prevailing view advanced by Kemp-Smith and others, that the work on miracles Hume mentions to Lord Kames in his 1737 letter is probably not what first appeared in 1748 as "Of Miracles." This later date is important to Burns because it supports his argument that "Of Miracles" is an unoriginal piece, a rehash of deistic arguments that Hume encountered in the late 1730s and 1740s. While Burns raises some interesting points, his argument is unconvincing. He ignores a very marked, life long habit of Hume's, that of reworking and editing his writings. This would explain away Burns' argument that the style "Of Miracles" is more elegant and mature than the Hume writings of 1937. Burns claims that Hume ignores points raised by those who argue a more moderate pro-miracle position.

[24]One of the most remarkable things about this short essay (twenty-two pages in the Selby-Bigge edition) is the voluminous response it has provoked. Unquestionably, it is one of Hume's most famous productions. From the initial publication over two hundred and forty years ago a continuous stream of books and articles have poured forth contending with, praising, or in someway commenting on Hume's efforts to discredit the testimony of miracles. Recently, we have Michael P. Levine, *Hume and*

So impressed with his own effort was he that at the beginning of "Of Miracles" Hume fails to stifle a boast. "I flatter myself, that I have discovered an argument of a like nature, which, if just, will, with the wise and learned, be an everlasting check to all kinds of superstitious delusion, and consequently, will be useful as long as the world endures. For so long, I presume, will the accounts of miracles and prodigies be found in all history, sacred and profane." (*EHU*, 110) Hume proudly signals what a momentous event he believes it is for the development of human critical capacities that he has "discovered" this type of argument for countering miraculous claims. Miracles as true events are established by human testimony, enter into the very core of religious history, and provide the grounds for religious belief. Therefore, a judicious approach to miracles is vital for any historian contemplating the historical unfolding of a religion. Historical religions, Christianity and Islam, for example, are not only immersed in miracles, but appeal to them as profound evidence for their truth.

Hume's boast also states his overriding motive for writing the essay: to provide, "an everlasting check to all kinds of superstitious delusion." To the extent then that a belief in miracles is a chief contributor to the progress and maintenance of superstition, an inclination or disposition to believe in miracles, Hume suggests, subverts common sense—which is inimical to superstition—and corrupts human understanding. Gibbon echoes this notion in an excoriating passage on the subject of monasticism. "The favourites of Heaven were accustomed to cure inveterate diseases with a touch, a word, or a distant message; and to expel the most obstinate dæmons from the souls, or bodies, which they possessed . . . . These extravagant tales, which display the fiction, without the genius, of poetry, have seriously affected the reason, the faith, and the morals of the Christians. Their credulity debased and vitiated the faculties of the mind; they corrupted the evidence of history; and superstition gradually extinguished the hostile light of philosophy and science." (*DF-37*, IV, 81)

Gibbon thought, as did Hume, that not only is the superstitious mentality richly nurtured by a belief in miracles, but that this mentality is also degenerative, corrupt, and extirpates human enterprises that seek the truth like history and philosophy. Here reverberates a common theme in the *Decline and Fall*; the alleged connection between the development of Christianity and the substantial growth of reports of miracles. Hume's interest in destroying the credibility of reports of miracles stems from a fear that miracles build the framework for superstition and that superstition

---

the *Problem of Miracles: A Solution* (Dordrecht: Kluwer Academic Publishers, 1989), and Francis J. Beckwith, *David Hume's Argument Against Miracles: A Critical Analysis* (Lanham, MD: University Press of America, 1989). Anthony Flew writes that: "Of Miracles" has probably provoked more polemic than anything else Hume ever wrote." Anthony Flew, *Hume's Philosophy of Belief: A Study of His 'First Inquiry'* (New York: Humanities Press, 1961), 171.

is inimical to the philosophical ideal of a dispassionate search for truth. The *Decline and Fall* creates a historical embodiment for that fear with its portrayal of Christianity as a growing phenomenon of credulity and superstition.[25]

The arguments of "Of Miracles," as Hume sees them, are a useful device to combat the delusive effects of superstition, a phenomenon he regards as morally degenerative and politically dangerous. Hume's primary, though not exclusive, antagonist in the writing of "Of Miracles" is, I believe, Roman Catholicism. Since Hume is nowhere explicit about this, the claim requires some justification.

Protestantism by Hume's time had for the most part ceased claims for the occurrence of miracles, while the Catholic Church had not. Miracles remained (and still remain) for Catholicism one of its apologetic and proselytizing tools: the authority of the Church rested in part on its participation in miraculous events. Hume responded in a letter to Hugh Blair to some criticisms of his "Of Miracles" by George Campbell in a manuscript, *Dissertation on Miracles*. Blair had passed the manuscript from Campbell to Hume. Hume ticks off a number of points of contention with Campbell. Of particular interest though is his comment about John Knox and Alexander Henderson, two of Scotland's early Calvinists and ferocious anti-Catholics. "I wonder the author does not perceive the reason why Mr John Knox and Mr Alexander Henderson did not work as many miracles as their brethren in other churches. Miracle-working was a Popish trick, and discarded with the other parts of that religion. Men must have new and opposite ways of establishing new and opposite follies." (*Letters*-H, I, 350). It is interesting to note Hume's remark that miracle-working, as a Popish trick was "discarded" with the rest of Catholicism. Certainly the tone of this remark suggests a strong linkage in Hume's mind between Catholicism and fraudulent miracles. The Protestant-Catholic polemics surrounding miracles has a history that reaches back to the closing decades of the seventeenth century when Protestant writers were attacking the Church of Rome, dismissing Catholic claims for miracles as religious fraud, and characterizing the miraculous as just so much Catholic chicanery and superstition.[26] Hume had perhaps imbibed some of the Calvinist aversion to popish miracles of his fellow Scots.

Hume viewed Catholicism primarily as a superstitious, priest-ridden religion, founded in fear and perpetuated by fraud and intimidation. Miracles play a major

---

[25]Jordan, *Gibbon and His Roman Empire*, 113, writes "[t]he miraculous tradition, Gibbon rightly thought, was essential to the triumph of Christianity. Miracles provided palpable proof of God's providence and gave justification to Christian intolerance. It is precisely here that Gibbon directed his attack. He wanted to discredit the miraculous tradition, but not merely theoretically, as David Hume had done. He wanted to show the historical absurdity of the tradition, and this could best be done, Gibbon believed, by writing a history of miracles."

[26]Burns, *Great Debate on Miracles*, 73.

part in this with the belief in them hinging on a high level of credulity and with the power that accrues to the priests that perform or recognize them. Superstitious Catholicism is contrasted with "enthusiastic" Protestantism which is animated less by fear than by a buoyant fanaticism. In his essay "Of Superstition and Enthusiasm" he writes: "[a] superstition is founded on fear, sorrow, and a depression of spirits, it represents the man to himself in such despicable colours, that he appears unworthy, in his own eyes, of approaching the divine presence, and naturally has recourse to any other person, whose sanctity of life, or, perhaps, impudence and cunning, have made him be supposed more favoured by the Divinity. To him the superstitious entrust their devotions: To his care they recommend their prayers, petitions, and sacrifices . . . . Hence the origin of Priests." (*Essays*, 75)

Superstitious, priestly religions are especially pernicious because of the incentives they create for the perpetuation of tyranny. Superstition in its crudest and most naked manifestation features beliefs which make the people who hold make them craven, fearful, credulous tools of a priestly, power-grasping class. "Superstition . . . steals in gradually and insensibly; renders men tame and submissive; is acceptable to the magistrate, and seems inoffensive to the people: Till at last the priest, having firmly established his authority, becomes the tyrant and disturber of human society, by his endless contentions, persecutions, and religious wars. How smoothly did the Romish church advance in her acquisition of power? But into what dismal convulsions did she throw all Europe, in order to maintain it?" (*Essays*, 78)

The "Romish church" is held up as a model of religious tyranny and oppression. By contrast, enthusiastic Protestant religions were more resistant to tyranny. Again, in "Of Superstition and Enthusiasm" Hume says: "[s]uperstition is an enemy to civil liberty, and enthusiasm a friend to it . . . . The *jansenists* are enthusiasts, and zealous promoters of the passionate devotion, and of the inward life; little influenced by authority; and, in a word, but half catholics. The consequences are exactly conformable to the foregoing reasoning. The *jesuits* are tyrants of the people, and the slaves of court: And the *jansenists* preserve alive the small sparks of the love of liberty, which are to be found in the French nation." (*Essays*, 78-79)

Protestantism's virtue from Hume's perspective was its rejection of religious authority, although this virtue has its vicious side. Hume hardly bothered to disguise his loathing for the fanaticism of Knox, Calvin and other early reformers. Protestantism's initial appearance with its radical challenge to the authority of the ancient church tore the social fabric of sixteenth- and seventeenth-century Europe to pieces. In his *History of Great Britain*, he rails against the Reformers. "But when the enraged and fanatical reformers took arms against the papal hierarchy, and threatened to rend from the church at once all her riches and authority; no wonder she was animated with equal zeal and ardor, in defense of such ancient and invaluable possessions." (*HGB*, 97)[27] But while Hume despised Knox and the other founders of Protestantism for their bigotry and fanaticism, he nevertheless viewed Protestantism historically as a favorable development in the progress of modern Europe insofar as it broke the ideological monopoly of the Catholic Church and ultimately undermined the power of the Catholic Church to maintain its *system* of superstition. Hume also viewed Protestantism in relative favor because with its less rigid ecclesiastical hierarchy it could be more easily co-opted and moderated by local and national forces. Protestantism, because of this feature, had become a collection of competing ideologies, hence weakening it politically and making it even less a force for superstition.

The breaking up of Protestantism into competing ideologies also had another advantage from Hume's perspective. It propelled a gradual movement toward deism, a complete rationalizing of religion. "Our sectaries, [the English Protestant dissenters of a century earlier] who were formerly such dangerous bigots, are now become very free reasoners; and the *quakers* seem to approach nearly the only regular body of *deists* in the universe, the *literati*, or the disciples of Confucius in China." (*Essays*, 78, original italics)

From the polemical standpoint therefore, it would seem then that the damage from "Of Miracles" would be greater for Catholicism and that Hume himself would see his efforts as delivering a greater blow to Catholicism, as a superstitious institution, than Protestantism. This in no way is meant to imply or suggest that Hume gave any preference to Protestant theology over Catholic. It is merely that Catholicism as a religious institution had more to lose than Protestantism from an attack on miracles because the credibility of the Catholic hierarchy and the power, prestige and authority that credibility conferred rested in part on belief in miracles. Nor should it be imagined that Hume's attack on miracles did not deeply offend Protestants. This work made him extremely unpopular with his countrymen some of whom denounced him as a dangerous infidel and wanted him excommunicated from the Scottish Kirk. (*Letters*-H, I, 246) Yet, it is worth noting that in 1870, one hundred and twenty years after Hume published the essay, the First Vatican Council pronounced an anathema on anyone who would deny that Christian miracles can be known with certainty. "If anyone shall say . . . that miracles can never be known for certain, or that the divine origin of the Christian religion cannot

---

[27]This was deleted from later additions of *The History of England.*

properly be proved by them: let him be cast out."[28] To whom would this apply more aptly and emphatically than Hume?

In his "Vindication," Gibbon too points to the lingering vested interest that the Catholic Church has in miracles. "About two hundred years ago, the Court of Rome discovered that the system which had been erected by ignorance must be defended and countenanced by the aid, or at least by the abuse, of science." (*EE*, 277) While the Church was under pressure to abandon the more incredible tales, Gibbon contemptuously dismisses the response as a corrupted concession to credulity. "The grosser legends of the middle ages were abandoned to contempt, but the supremacy and infallibility of two hundred Popes, the virtues of many thousand Saints, and the miracles which they either performed or related, have been laboriously consecrated in the Ecclesiastical Annals of Cardinal Baronius." (*EE*, 277)

Gibbon then compares the Cardinal Baronius with the Protestant Middleton. "A Theological Barometer might be formed, of which the Cardinal and our countryman Dr. Middleton should constitute the opposite and remote extremities, as the former sunk to the lowest degree of credulity, which was compatible with learning, and the latter rose to the highest pitch of scepticism, in any wise consistent with Religion." (*EE*, 277) Here then we get a sense of how Gibbon, with some similarity to Hume, conceived of Catholicism's institutional investment in the credulity surrounding belief in miracles.

The interest that Hume and Gibbon had in destroying the credibility of reports of miracles thus stemmed from an uneasiness that a belief in miracles creates the framework upon which superstition is built and that superstition is inimical both to the philosophical ideal of a dispassionate search for truth and to the political ideals of freedom and limited government. Their aim in undermining superstition was primarily to discredit superstitious institutions and ultimately to weaken the power of the church. Superstition was more virulent, Hume believed, the more systematic and entrenched it was. Philosophy and history are advanced by the discrediting of miracles: Hume attempted to make the philosophical advance with his essay; Gibbon's undermining of the miraculous perspective in the *Decline and Fall* was to be his historical advance.

---

[28]"*Si quis dixerit . . . aut miracula certo cognosci numquam posse nec iis divinam religionis christianae originem rite probari: anathema sit.*" Quoted from *Encyclopedia of Philosophy*, s.v. "Miracles."

III. "Of Miracles" at Work in the *Decline and Fall*

It is at best but a dangerous logic to drive men to the edge and precipice
of scepticism, in the hope that they will recoil in horror to the very
interior of credulity: possibly men may show their courage—they may
vanquish the argumentum ad terrorem—they may not find scepticism so
terrible. The last was Gibbon's case.

Walter Bagehot

In order to appreciate fully the significance of "Of Miracles" for Gibbon's critical
project in the *Decline and Fall*, it is necessary to focus briefly on three dimensions
of it: (1) its underlying empiricist assumptions and the implications for writing
history, (2) its rejection of the testimony for miracles on the basis of probability,
and (3) its focus on the passions and their effect on belief.[29]

Miracles and the writing of history

The eighteenth century witnessed enormous progress in developing canons for
assessing the credibility of historical narratives.[30] History had been the tool of
polemicists and apologists. For Hume the writing of history is, ideally, an
empirical discipline with all the constraints imposed by moral reasoning,
constraints that mean that the observations made by historians are entirely based
on the experience of the laws of nature. "It is experience only, which gives
authority to human testimony; and it is the same experience, which assures us of
the laws of nature." (*EHU*, 127) All "moral reasoning," that is, all reasoning which
deals with matters of fact and existence, Hume argues in the first *Enquiry*, is
ultimately, about cause and effect. (*EHU*, 35-36) As such, all moral reasoning is
founded on experience which is contingent and admits only of truths which are
probable. In Hume's theory of causality, no type of causal relation can ever be
established a priori. (*EHU*, 63) Causal claims are inherently probabilist and derive
their degree of certitude from the *experience* of the regularity with which effects
follow causes. (*EHU*, 73-79)

Moral reasoning, when applied to everyday experience or what Hume calls the
"reflections of common life," yields this probabilistic, fallible knowledge that is

---

[29] A short exposition is difficult because this piece has, as mentioned above, a long, and an
exceptionally voluminous and polemical history of interpretation. Also, the essay is intricately connected
with broader Humean philosophical themes.

[30] The influence of the seventeenth-century pyrrhonist skeptic, Pierre Bayle, on Hume and
Gibbon is well documented. For a discussion of Bayle's influence on Hume and British empiricism, see
Richard H. Popkin, *The High Road to Pyrrhonism* (San Diego, CA: Austin Hill Press, Inc., 1980). For
a discussion of Bayle's impact on Gibbon, see Jordan, *Gibbon and His Roman Empire*, 168-72.

subject to adjustment and correction. Distinguishing between "particular" and "general" facts, Hume says: "all deliberations in [practical] life regard the former; [i.e., particular facts] as also all disquisitions in *history*, chronology, geography and astronomy. The sciences, which treat of general facts, are politics, natural philosophy, physic, chemistry, &c. where the qualities, causes and effects of a whole species of objects are enquired into." (*EHU*, 164-165, italics added) We have thus a general typology of the empirical ("moral") sciences offered by Hume. This distinction between particular and general facts is conveniently overlooked by critics like J. B. Black who accuse Hume of a mechanistic, "repeating decimal" view of history.[31]

Where does theology fit in? Does it involve moral reasoning? Is it particular or general? Hume's response is to take up the posture of dismissive irony. "Divinity or Theology, as it proves the existence of a Deity, and the immortality of souls, is composed partly of reasonings concerning particular, partly concerning general facts. It has a foundation in *reason*, so far as it is supported by experience. But its best and most solid foundation is *faith* and divine revelation." (*EHU*, 165, original italics)

Theological topics can be reasoned about (reasoned in the sense of moral reasoning) to the extent that they have some experiential basis. Clearly, in Hume's view they do not: faith is the best foundation. He italicizes "faith" and "reason" to stress their exclusive, antithetical relation.

History, noted above, is a moral science, employing moral (causal) reasoning. The historian uses a complex form of causal reasoning which appeals to the collective experience of the behavior of both the moral and physical world. In creating true historical accounts, the historian draws upon the reports of others and weighs that testimony in light of causal laws, what Hume calls, laws of nature. This weighing process operates at two levels. The first deals with the actual content of the report itself. Is the report consistent? Does it describe events that conform to laws of nature, i.e., is the physical world in which the historical event occurs reported to behave in a way that is consistent with experience? Are people reported to behave in ways that are not simply peculiar or variant with experience, but in defiance of it? Such reports, Hume argues, the historian must dismiss. "Should a traveler, returning from a far country, bring us an account of men, wholly different from any with whom we were ever acquainted; men who were entirely divested of avarice, ambition, or revenge; who knew no pleasure but friendship, generosity, and public spirit; we would immediately, from these circumstances, detect the falsehood, and prove him a liar, with the same certainty

---

[31]Black, *Art of History*, 86, 89-94, 97-102.

as if he had stuffed his narration with stories of centaurs and dragons, miracles and prodigies." (*EHU*, 84)

The second level deals with the motivation of the person making the report and the circumstances surrounding the events related to the report. Here are causal relationships involving phenomena of human motivation and behavior. Certain types of behavior, e.g., lying, are linked to certain types of motives, e.g., personal gain, fear, jealousy, etc. For example, testimony about the conduct of someone by a person who hates him will be met with suspicion by the judicious historian because experience gives good reason to believe that strong emotional motivations, such as hatred, generally impair the inclination to be truthful.

Hume's theory of causality and its application to the "science" of history make it fair to say that for the historian, miracles are a priori out of court.[32] Without direct, immediate experience of God acting as a causal agent, the conditions for establishing a causal relationship (experiencing a cause-event follow by an effect-event) are ruled out a priori.[33] Donald Livingston writes that for Hume, God "has no direct causal relation to the historical world."[34] History is thus for Hume an empirical discipline with all the constraints imposed by moral reasoning, constraints that mean that the observations made by historians must be entirely based on the experience of the laws of nature. "It is experience only, which gives authority to human testimony; and it is the same experience, which assures us of the laws of nature." (*EHU*, 127) Hume's rationale for the exclusion of theology and divinity from the realm of moral reasoning provides the philosophical basis for Gibbon's sharp distinction between the task of the theologian and the historian as discussed above. The historian's purview is confined to common life experience—the "visible world," as Hume and Gibbon call it—with its conformity to laws of nature. Theology, insofar as it is based on revelation, operates in the "invisible world," a world of completely arbitrary occurrence where anything can and does happen. Exploration of such a world abandons the constraints that binds the historian. Gibbon's *Decline and Fall* explores Christian theological history in

---

[32]This is a controversial point of interpretation for "Of Miracles." Flew's widely read and highly regarded *Hume's Philosophy of Belief*, 176, argues that Hume "is not trying to prove a priori that any sort of describable event is inconceivable." However, Flew, I believe, is wrong here. Burns, in his *Great Debate On Miracles*, 143-148, points to a misplaced literalism in Flew's interpretation of key passages. More recently Levine, *Hume and the Problem of Miracles*, 18, argues, convincingly in my view, that Hume does indeed define miracles in such a way as to make them inexperienceable. "[A]ttempting to justify a belief in a miracle on the basis of testimony does involve one in a contradiction. The only way this belief, like any empirical belief, can be justified is on the basis of past experience. However, according to Hume, a miracle, by definition, is an event for which we neither have, nor can have, past experience."

[33]Levine, *Hume and the Problem of Miracles*, 33.

[34]Livingston, *Hume's Philosophy of Common Life*, 239.

order to demonstrate that the evolution of theological doctrine is a chaotic, groping affair with no possible appeal to stabilizing experiential determinants. Consider briefly these reflections on the "Theological History of the Doctrine of the Incarnation" in chapter forty-seven. "In the beginning of the fifth century, the *unity* of the *two natures* was the prevailing doctrine of the church. On all sides it was confessed that the mode of their co-existence could neither be represented by our ideas nor expressed by our language." (*DF-47*, V, 113, original italics) Here is a dilemma recreated for the early Christians in their attempts to discern the nature of Christ: the lack of ideas or language to articulate how Christ's nature is to be understood suggests that the problem is beyond common life experience. Nevertheless, a colossal theological dispute ensues. How are such questions resolved? Gibbon here employs a powerful imagery of lawlessness, chaos, and destruction. "The poverty of ideas and language tempted them to ransack art and nature for every possible comparison, and each comparison misled their fancy in the explanation of an incomparable mystery. In the polemic microscope an atom is enlarged to a monster, and each party was skillful to exaggerate the absurd or impious conclusions that might be extorted from the principles of their adversaries. To escape from each other, they wandered through many a dark and devious thicket, till they were astonished by the horrid phantoms of Cerinthus and Apollinaris, who guarded the opposite issues of the theological labyrinth. As soon as they beheld the twilight of sense and heresy, they started, measured back their steps, and were again involved in the gloom of impenetrable orthodoxy." (*DF-47*, V, 113-114)

Here then with grim, bleak overtones is an account of the theological quest unconstrained by experience. The "polemical microscope" is a compelling metaphor of distortion used to frame theological debate as a dangerous and perverse invention. The doctrine that emerges is a product of restless passion and unstable imagination. Gibbon's general characterization of the theological enterprise is one of complex futility with a twist of derangement.

The improbability of testimony for miracles

One of Hume's major interests in writing "Of Miracles" is as a propaedeutic for the writing of history. "[A]ccounts of miracles and prodigies," he says, "[will] be found in all history, sacred and profane." (*EHU*, 110) History is written for all sorts of motives, some of which are incompatible with truth-telling. Thus, history inevitably tends toward distortion. One only has to review the "history" emerging from the Soviet Union of the 1930s and 1940s featuring the "prodigies" of Stalin, transforming him into a near deity, all wise, all knowing, all powerful, to realize that Hume well understood how perennial is the human bent to distort history, particularly to make it serve the powerful.[35]   Since human beings are fallible creatures, their testimony must be presumed to have an element of unreliability. Historians must be skeptical.

Hume defines a miracle as "a violation of the laws of nature." (*EHU*, 114) A law of nature is established by "a firm and unalterable experience." (*EHU*, 114) A miracle would be an event that would contravene such a law, and defy experience. "Nothing is esteemed a miracle, if it ever happen in the common course of nature." (*EHU*, 115) In order to determine whether to believe the testimony to a miracle, one must weigh the probability that the miracle (the contravention of the law of nature) took place, against the probability that the testifier is either lying, mistaken or deluded. "[N]o testimony is sufficient to establish a miracle, unless the testimony be of such a kind, that its falsehood would be more miraculous, than the fact, which it endeavors to establish." (*EHU*, 115-116) Which is harder to believe, that the *report* of an event, which affirms the occurrence of an event completely contrary to our experience is false, or, that the report of this occurrence is true? Hume believes that the weighing of probabilities as a test to determine whether one can give credence to testimony which affirms the miraculous must always defeat a claim for the miraculous. "[We] may establish it as a maxim, that no human testimony can have such force as to prove a miracle, and make it a just foundation for any such system of religion." (*EHU*, 127) It is important to emphasize that Hume is saying nothing about whether or not miracles have or could ever occur. His concern is with the testimony about such events, and he is quite explicit here: no testimony could ever reasonably establish the occurrence of a miracle.

Hume, as we can see, was interested in miracles insofar as they were employed to provide the support or foundation of, as he says, "a system of religion." Christianity is an elaborate system, a comprehensive way of looking at and thinking about the world and the place of human beings in it. At the very foundation of this religion, the religion of many of his friends and countrymen, are reports of miracles (events contrary to their daily experience) reported by its founders, and Hume saw this as a profound dilemma.

---

[35]Joel Carmichael, *Stalin's Masterpiece: The Show Trials and Purges of the Thirties—The Consolidation of the Bolshevik Dictatorship* (London: Weidenfeld and Nicolson, 1976), 14. "Stalin's glorification went far beyond that of Marx and Engels, far beyond Lenin's. Though he fell just short of technical deification, he can fairly be compared with Muhammad and the Buddha." See also the Commission of the Central Committee of the C.P.S.U., *History of the Communist Party of the Soviet Union (Short Course)*, (New York: International Publishers, 1939), written under the personal direction of Stalin. Here we have a largely fabricated document that was passed off for years as the official history of the Soviet Union.

Gibbon too found the miraculous origins of the Church to be problematic as he posed the Humean test of probability to the accounts by the early Christian witnesses. "But how shall we excuse the supine inattention of the Pagan and philosophic world to those evidences which were presented by the hand of Omnipotence, not to their reason, but to their senses? During the age of Christ, of his apostles, and of their first disciples, the doctrine which they preached was confirmed by innumerable prodigies. The lame walked, the blind saw, the sick were healed, the dead were raised, demons were expelled, and the laws of Nature were frequently suspended for the benefit of the church." (DF-15, II, 74)

"Benefit" here reads two ways: as either the result of God's favor to the church—proof of its divine mission, or, as the fruit of a purely human ambition to make the church's claim authoritative. This passage harbors a major theme of the Decline and Fall, i.e., the unstable tension between the pursuit of religious ideals and the attempt to grasp the transcendental reality behind them, and the drive for power and domination as a ubiquitous feature of human society. The Decline and Fall captures, perhaps as well as any work, the human condition as a perpetual struggle between religious idealism and self-serving ambition. Idealism and ambition, Gibbon discovers, are frequently confounded, and his melancholy duty as a historian consists in sorting them out. The miracles attesting to the church's divine and miraculous foundations are reported by those who aim, in the voice of Gibbon's feigned naïveté, to "benefit" the church by their invention. So with its ironic twist we see a Hume-inspired dilemma: during the early times of the church either all of the pagan writers and historians (those individuals most likely to notice and record such extraordinary events) were asleep for some inexplicable reason and completely oblivious to these most marvelous happenings, or, the miracles were invented in order to vest the new religion with authority and make the church more powerful. Which, the reader must ask, is the more likely case? Gibbon's historiography gives no credibility to reports of miracles since, like Hume, he is driven to doubt the testimony affirming the occurrence of what is completely contrary to experience. Miracles might have a basis in faith, but they do not move the historian.

Related to the "improbability" argument is another point Hume makes in "Of Miracles" where he argues that the miraculous claims of rival religions cancel each other out. "[I]t is impossible the religions of ancient Rome, of Turkey, of Siam, and of China should, all of them, be established on any solid foundation. Every miracle, therefore, pretended to have been wrought in any of these religions (and all of them abound in miracles), as its direct scope is to establish the particular system to which it is attributed; so has it the same force, though more indirectly, to overthrow every other system." (EHU, 121) Miracles represent, so to speak, religions that are in competition for believers. And so religious apologists are in the business of discrediting each other. Near the end of the *Decline and Fall*, in an account of the siege of Constantinople, we have a historical dramatization of Hume's point. "The strength of the wall [of Constantinople] resisted an army of two hundred thousand Turks; their assaults were repelled by the sallies of the Greeks and their foreign mercenaries; the old resources of defence were opposed to the new engines of attack; and the enthusiasm of the dervish, who was snatched to heaven in visionary converse with Mahomet, was answered in the credulity of the Christians, who *beheld* the Virgin Mary, in a violet garment, walking on the rampart and animating their courage." (*DF-65*, VII, 81, original italics)

The juxtaposition of these two miracles as an integral part of the narrative brings off, with a definite comic tone, the canceling out effect spoken of by Hume. The first miracle is "answered" by a counter miracle. ('I'll see *your* miracle and raise you one.') Gibbon then adds one of his insidious notes to the text that completes the skeptical thrust of the whole story. "For this miraculous apparition, [of the Virgin] Cananus appeals to the Musulman saint; but who will bear testimony for Seid Bechar?" (*DF-65*, VII, 81, n.96) An interesting twist! The Christians' witness to the miracle is an opposed religionist. Yet, the dilemma of the credibility of witnesses relentlessly asserts itself.

Passions and Miracles

In the course of "Of Miracles" Hume shifts his focus from the weighing of conflictive evidence to a psychology of religious belief.[36] One of Hume's major philosophical concerns, indeed, is with the effects of *passion* on belief. Strong passions make certain kinds of belief (particularly beliefs which in turn stimulate more strong passions) irresistible. (*Treatise*, 271) "The passion of *surprise* and *wonder*, arising from miracles, being an agreeable emotion, gives a sensible tendency towards the beliefs of those events, from which it is derived." (*EHU*, 117, original italics) Hume claims the existence of a kind of dynamic reciprocity of passion and belief. Miracles and prodigies, being unique and awe inspiring, are exciting events to contemplate even, as Hume continues, if they are experienced vicariously through the related experience of others. "And this goes so far, that even those who cannot enjoy this pleasure immediately, nor can believe those miraculous events, of which they are informed, yet love to partake of the satisfaction at second hand or by rebound, and place a pride and delight in exciting

---

[36]Noxon, "Hume's Concerns with Religion," 76. Also, David Wooton, "Hume's 'Of Miracles': Probability and Irreligion," in *Studies in the Philosophy of the Scottish Enlightenment*, ed. M. A. Stewart (Oxford: Clarendon Press, 1990), 203, argues that Hume's "Of Miracles" is essentially an attack on the motives of miracle testifiers.

the admiration of others." (*EHU*, 117) This passion of "wonder" has a strong influence on what people are inclined to believe. When wonder combines with religious motivation, the reality of the objects of belief becomes questionable, hence the common perception of a religious zealot as lacking credibility. "But if the spirit of religion join itself to the love of wonder, there is an end of common sense; and human testimony, in these circumstances, loses all pretensions to authority." (*EHU*, 117) Hume moves the direction of his attack toward the believability or trustworthiness, if you will, of the testifier to miracles.[37]

The trustworthiness of the motives and character of a witness renders him or her believable. (Ibid., 46)[38] To the extent that one can affirm the motives and trust character of the witness one may quite reasonably believe that witness.[39] So motivation and character must be carefully considered. The historian works with generally accepted, experience-tested assumptions about the trustworthiness of testimony in which the motive for truth-telling may be in conflict with a either a motive of self-interest or with a strong passion. In his "Vindication" Gibbon says: "it *may* be sufficient to allege a clear and fundamental principle of historical as well as legal Criticism, that whenever we are destitute of the means of comparing the testimonies of the opposite parties, the evidence of *any* witness, however illustrious by his rank and titles, is justly to be *suspected* in his own cause." (*EE*, 298, original italics) Gibbon was responding to the charge that he was prejudiced against "respectable" early Christian witnesses. His accuser, it is suggested, had merely failed to apply a practical principle for verifying human testimony that is widely practiced. "It is unfortunate enough, that I should be engaged with adversaries, whom their habits of study and conversation appear to have left in total ignorance of the principles which universally regulate the opinions and practice of

---

[37]For a recent philosophical study of testimony focusing heavily on Hume, see C. A. J. Coady, *Testimony: A Philosophical Study* (Oxford: Clarendon Press, 1992).

[38]Coady writes: "[o]ur definition of testimony naturally concentrates upon the speaker or testifier, and what it is about his or her performance that constitutes it testimony, but a full understanding of testimony would be incomplete without some explication of the characteristic part played by the hearer. . . . When we believe testimony we believe what is said because we trust the witness."

[39]Consider the following example: Someone contemplating the purchase of a used car may encounter someone who shows them a car with 175,000 miles and says, 'this car, even though it has 175,000 miles is in excellent condition and will run well.' If the potential seller making this claim is an acquaintance of the potential buyer known by him to be highly attentive to the care and maintenance of his possessions, then it might be reasonable for the potential buyer to believe him, even though the claim in most circumstances would be questionable. If, however, the potential seller were a used car salesman, then it would be reasonable for him to reject the claim. Wooton, "Hume's 'Of Miracles': Probability and Irreligion," 218, provides this example. Hume's "Of Miracles" generally places those who make claims for the testimony of miracles in the later (used car salesman) category.

mankind." (*EE*, 298-299) The comparison between legal and historical criticism is remarkable. Both are grounded in common life experience.

Hume provides guidelines that apply to the historian's task of evaluating his sources. We must be suspicious of any historical testimony when:

(1) "[T]he witnesses contradict each other."
(2) "[W]hen they are but few, or of a doubtful character."
(3) "[W]hen they have an interest in what they affirm."
(4) "[W]hen they deliver their testimony with hesitation, or on the contrary, with too violent asservations." (*EHU*, 112-113)

These are basic, common sense principles for Hume. Ignoring them makes living a naive adventure and renders the historian incompetent. Placed in the context of evaluating the testimony of religious believers, the significance of these principles is obvious. Most religions are born in obscurity. Religious history is rife with faction and controversy, a veritable mill of claims and counterclaims. Believers frequently denounce the prophets of other religions as false, the miracles as frauds, and the beliefs as evil. Devout believers also cleave to their beliefs and values with passionate intensity. So, in evaluating the testimony surrounding the events of religious history, the level of suspicion must be extremely high. Gibbon, for example, notes quite agnostically of Muhammad, that he cannot really say with much confidence whether he was a fraud or a fanatic. "[A]t the distance of twelve centuries, I darkly contemplate his shade through a cloud of religious incense . . . ." (*DF-50*, V, 400) Religion by its volatile nature is a tricky matter for the historian because of the emotion surrounding it, the "interested" motives of believers, and the obscure status of its sources. As Hume notes, an "interested" witness or one who "violently" asservates is not fully credible. In order to determine if someone is a truth teller one needs to factor in the complex relationship of passions and motives. "A religionist," Hume writes, "may be an enthusiast, and imagine he sees what has no reality: he may know his narrative to be false, and yet persevere in it, with the best intentions in the world, for the sake of promoting so holy a cause." (*EHU*, 117-118) The fanaticism of the believer may be so powerful an influence that it erodes, in the religionist's mind, the barrier between reality and illusion. Or, a conflict of motivation between veracity and service to a cause may corrupt the testimony. These possibilities, Hume warns, must be considered in appraising a religionist's testimony.

Gibbon labors under the shadow of this warning and maintains a ready awareness of the complexities of motivation behind historical testimony: "[i]f the truth of any of those miracles [miracles of early Christianity] is appreciated by their apparent use and propriety, every age had unbelievers to convince, heretics to confute, and idolatrous nations to convert: and *sufficient motives might always be produced* to justify the interposition of Heaven." (*DF-15*, II, 32, italics added)

Miracles are important tools of religionists—instruments of conversion. The incentive to consider their foundation in reality may not be able to compete with the successes they promise the proselytizer. The historian of religion must consider the possibility that any religionist may be an enthusiast, and at best an unreliable, special pleading zealot; at worst, a mentally unstable fanatic. In setting the stage for his skeptical treatment of Christian miracles, Gibbon fashions a damning rendition of the Old Testament miracles. Making out Jewish miracles to be unbelievable corrodes Christian credibility. Its caustic, dismissive irony rivals Hume's "outrageous" passage in "Of Miracles" where he affirms that no "reasonable person" can believe in the Christian religion without a miracle.

> But the devout and even scrupulous attachment to the Mosaic religion, so conspicuous among the Jews who lived under the second temple, becomes still more surprising, if it is compared with the stubborn incredulity of their forefathers. When the law was given in thunder from Mount Sinai; when the tides of the ocean and the course of the planets were suspended for the convenience of the Israelites; and when temporal rewards and punishments were the immediate consequences of their piety or disobedience, they perpetually relapsed into rebellion against the visible majesty of their Divine King, placed the idols of the nations in the sanctuary of Jehovah, and imitated every fantastic ceremony that was practised in the tents of the Arabs, or in the cities of Phœnicia. As the protection of Heaven was deservedly withdrawn from the ungrateful race, their faith acquired a proportionable degree of vigour and purity. The contemporaries of Moses and Joshua had beheld with careless indifference the most amazing miracles. Under the pressure of every calamity, the belief of those miracles has preserved the Jews of a later period from the universal contagion of idolatry; and, in contradiction to every known principle of the human mind, that singular people seems to have yielded a stronger and more ready assent to the traditions of their remote ancestors than to the evidence of their own senses. (*DF-15*, II, 4-5)

Here, applied to the religion of the Jews, is an eloquent historically paraphrase of Hume's opening remark in "Of Miracles": "[o]ur evidence for the truth of the *Christian* religion is less than the evidence for the truth of our senses." (*EHU*, 109, original italics) This passage could be affirmed by the devout. Yet its implications could hardly be more damaging, particularly read with "Of Miracles" in mind. The Old Testament from which Gibbon masterfully paraphrases, describes a world totally (unbelievably?) different than that in which modern man lives, one in which the natural elements conform to the wishes of the people. The brunt of Gibbon's skepticism falls upon the *mentality* of the religionists, not the substance of their beliefs. This passage also brings to mind Hume's more prosaic criticisms of the Old Testament: "[u]pon reading this book [the Pentateuch], we find it full of prodigies and miracles. It gives an account of the state of the world and of human nature entirely different from the present . . . . I desire any one to lay his hand upon his heart, and after a serious consideration declare, whether he thinks that the falsehood of such a book, supported by such a testimony, would be more extraordinary and miraculous than all the miracles it relates." (*EHU*, 130)

Gibbon, having the advantage of a historical narrative in which to dramatize concretely the account, steps beyond Hume in setting up the striking and ludicrous contrast between the conduct of the Israelites of Mosaic times and their descendants. The former experienced first-hand amazing miracles and the direct and observable divine intervention in their lives and yet ignored it, while the latter exhibit a constancy of faith based on their beliefs in the miraculous testimony of their ancestors. All of this is to suggest the irrationality of belief in miracles and the primacy of the belief in intense religious emotion. Those in the latter group, Gibbon affirms, believe what is completely insupportable, i.e., their beliefs fly in the face of "every known principle of the human mind," and hence they are fanatics.

In his account of Muhammad in chapter fifty Gibbon says: "[t]he votaries of Mahomet are more assured than himself of his miraculous gifts, and their confidence and credulity increase as they are farther removed from the time and place of his spiritual exploits." (*DF-50*, V, 367) This is similar to the above mentioned phenomenon in chapter fifteen—the contrast of the intense faith of the progeny of the Children of Moses with the indifferent first-hand witnesses. The point is merely to show that belief in miracles has no evidential basis, that is, there is no evidence that can withstand criticism. The person who was actually supposed to have witnessed them directly acts with less confidence in them than the descendants of that person. Thus, with respect to miracles, there is a credulity factor that operates in a perverse manner of inversion: the further away, historically, from the actual occurrence of the miracle, the greater the belief in its reality.

Gibbon exploits this credulity factor in his account of the Legend of the Holy Lance, a miracle at Antioch during the first Crusade. The lance that had pierced the side of Jesus was suddenly "discovered", an event which served to inspire the weary, disenchanted Crusaders. Yet, even at the time of the supposed miracle, its authenticity was in question. "Some efforts were made by the Provincials to substitute a cross, a ring, or a tabernacle, in the place of the holy lance, which soon vanished in contempt and oblivion." (*DF-58*, VI, 318) In spite of its dismal career, however, it eventually ends up as a bona fide miracle. "Yet the revelation of Antioch is gravely asserted by succeeding historians; and such is the progress of credulity that miracles, most doubtful on the spot and at the moment, will be received with implicit faith at a convenient distance of time and space." (*DF-58*, VI, 318) Gibbon's reference to the "progress of credulity" points to the human propensity to believe what the passions dictate. The distance of time and space "conveniently" remove evidentiary obstacles.

The impeachment of Old Testament miracles and the fanaticism of the Jews mark a similar concern exhibited by Hume in "Of Miracles" with the role of the passions in belief. There is, for the affirmation of miracles, *always* a problem, it seems, lying in the makeup of the human personality with its intricate web of passion and motivation. The best intentioned people sometimes lie and are vulnerable to self-deception. Credulity and rationalization are inherent human weaknesses. The strong convictions aroused by religion and the high level of energy released by religious emotion, combined with the human proclivity to lie and misrepresent, inevitably make religiously-inspired testimony problematic.

IV. Miracles and the History of Christianity

Meanwhile the fat, phlegmatic little man polished his sarcasms, and sneered Christianity away with the most perfect unconsciousness that hot blooded revolutionaries were drawing strange lessons from his pages.

Leslie Stephen

The picture of Christianity emerging from the pages of the *Decline and Fall* is irremediably tragic and pessimistic—hence the historian's "melancholy duty." The aspirations of original Christianity, Gibbon seemed to believe, could never prevail. A religious movement over time inevitably absorbs all the assorted human malignancies. The susceptibility to overweening ambition, vanity, greed, duplicity, lust, and fanaticism remains always a part of the human condition. The philosophic historian cannot escape them. The *Decline and Fall* deals with the "progress" of Christianity—its corruption through institutionalization. Miracles cater to human weakness, to credulity, and ultimately play a major corruptive part in Gibbon's saga of spiritual decline. Gibbon's critique of miracles moves through three stages in the history of Christianity; its beginnings (the Apostolic period), its political institutionalization (Constantine), and its maturity (medieval).

The miraculous foundations of Christianity are based on the Apostolic *testimony*, and thus the historical basis of Christianity rests on the credibility of the Apostles. These Apostolic era accounts, however, are problematic. Hume argues in the *Natural History* that historical narratives passed across many generations are particularly vulnerable to a kind of degradation in truth value. "An historical fact, while it passes by oral tradition from eye-witnesses and contemporaries, is disguised in every successive narration, and may at last retain but very small, if any, resemblance of the original truth, on which it was founded. The frail memories of men, their love of exaggeration, their supine carelessness; these principles, if not corrected by books and writing, soon pervert the account of historical events, where argument or reasoning has little or no place; nor can ever recal the truth, which has once escaped those narrations." (*NHR*, 29)

The historical foundations of Christianity mark the point where Gibbon's narrative seems most to evince a Hume-like skepticism in the way in which it reviews miracles. In chapter fifteen, Gibbon strikes his first blow at the miraculous foundations of Christianity and wrestles historiographically with the whole issue of how to treat the testimony of miracles. Peter Gay remarks that chapters fifteen and sixteen "cost Gibbon immense effort and brought him more controversy than anything else he ever wrote. They are Gibbon's natural history of Christianity, the historian's counterpart to Hume's *Natural History of Religion.*"[40] The chapter opens with the observation that the origins of Christianity, with its attendant miracles, are immersed in historical obscurity and uncertainty. Long passages of time complicate the accounts and make them invulnerable to criticism. Here is an echo from "Of Miracles" where Hume says that during the infancy of new religions: "the wise and learned commonly esteem the matter too inconsiderable to deserve their attention or regard. And when afterward they would willingly detect the cheat, in order to undeceive the deluded multitude, the season is now past, and the records and witnesses, which might clear up the matter, have perished beyond recovery." (*EHU*, 126)

The historian of the church confronts an historiographical quagmire—with meager sources and unreliable witnesses. "The scanty and suspicious materials of ecclesiastical history seldom enable us to dispel the dark cloud that hangs over the first age of the church. The great law of impartiality too often obliges us to reveal the imperfections of the uninspired teachers and believers of the Gospel; and, to a careless observer, *their* faults may seem to cast a shade on the faith which they professed. But the scandal of the pious Christian, and the fallacious triumph of the Infidel, should cease as soon as they recollect not only *by whom*, but likewise *to whom*, the Divine Revelation was given." (*DF-15*, II, 1-2, original italics)

This passage reads as an oblique but cutting comment on the historiography of the early church. The material of ecclesiastical history is "scanty and suspicious." The first age of the church is shadowed by a "dark cloud;" the impartiality of the witnesses is in question. Gibbon's comment that the "scandal of the church should cease . . . as soon as they recollect not only by whom, but likewise to whom, the Divine revelation was given" is pure irony, and self-protective as well. Lots of unsavory characters in the *Decline and Fall* make claims to divine revelation, and Gibbon uses the vast array of charlatans, frauds, and mountebanks that populate his thousand years of history to make church history scandalous. In this passage we see almost all of Hume's points of suspicion raised; obscurity of sources, questions on the character of the witnesses, etc.

However, the end of chapter fifteen is where Gibbon delivers his most damaging blow against the miraculous foundations of Christianity by raising doubts about the reports of events surrounding the crucifixion of Christ. "Under the reign

---

[40]Gay, *Style in History*, 39. Also, chapters fifteen and sixteen of the *Decline and Fall* offended Joseph Priestley who attacked Gibbon in his *History of the Corruptions of Christianity* and attempted to engage Gibbon in public debate on Christianity. Gibbon politely declined and admonished Priestley to concentrate his energies on chemistry rather than religious polemics. "[G]ive me leave to convey to your ear the almost unanimous, and not offensive, wish of the philosophic world: that you would confine your talents and industry to those sciences in which real and useful improvements *can* be made." (*Letters-G*, II, 321, original italics).

of Tiberius, the whole earth, or at least a celebrated province of the Roman empire, was involved in a præternatural darkness of three hours. Even this miraculous event, which ought to have excited the wonder, the curiosity, and the devotion of mankind, passed without notice in an age of science and history. It happened during the lifetime of Seneca and the elder Pliny, who must have experienced the immediate effects, or received the earliest intelligence, of the prodigy. Each of these philosophers, in a laborious work, has recorded all the great phenomena of Nature, earthquakes, meteors, comets, and eclipses, which his indefatigable curiosity could collect. Both the one and the other have omitted to mention the greatest phenomenon to which the mortal eye has been witness since the creation of the globe." (*DF-15*, II, 74-75)

Gibbon here pits Christians against pagans historiographically. The leading naturalists of the time, who happened to be pagans, made no mention of this extraordinary event, the præternatural darkness. The reader is left to choose to believe in the miracle and be unable to explain the silence of the pagan naturalists, who would have had the strongest motives to report or speculate on such an important event, or, to doubt the happening of the event and conclude that the Christian witnesses were quite possibly deluded or lying. The stress Gibbon lays on the inexplicability of the silence of Pliny and Seneca suggests that the historian's verdict must be to question the testimony of the Christian witnesses. The central event of Christianity is plunged into historical doubt.

Christianity's long and illustrious tradition of miracles that reaches back to the events of Christ's life and death lives on the credibility of its founders who witnessed and reported these events. Gibbon here reconstructs for the reader a dilemma he encountered as a youth from reading Middleton. Considering the time period beginning with the birth of Christianity and vast multiplicity of miracles and ending with his own "miracle-free" modern times, when can we confidently say that miracles ceased? At the death of the Apostles? The conversion of the Roman Empire? "From the first of the fathers to the last of the popes, a succession of bishops, of saints, of martyrs, and of miracles is continued without interruption, and the progress of superstition was so gradual and almost imperceptible that we know not in what particular link we should break the chain of tradition." (*DF-15*, II, 32)

Thus precariously mounted on a skeptical slippery slope are the claims for Christianity's miraculous origins, the bottom of which is the tentative, agnostic view that there is no way to determine at what historical point we draw the line and say: before this time the reports of miracles are credible, afterwards they are not. The reader can draw the more far reaching conclusion that from the beginning none of the accounts can enjoy full credibility.[41]   In a footnote to this section Gibbon remarks that St. Bernard of Clairvaux reported many miraculous works by his friends, but none of his own. He then asks: "[i]n the long series of ecclesiastical history, does there exist a single instance of a saint asserting that he himself possessed the gift of miracles?" (DF-15, II, 32, n.83) Gibbon here makes no attempt to answer his own question and simply lets the reader draw the skeptical conclusion that not claiming the gift of miracles for oneself is a protective strategy which makes verification more difficult since one who never himself claims to work miracles can never be asked to perform more of them.

Miracles not only play a critical role at the birth of Christianity, they also enter into the political history of Christianity, its institutionalization by Constantine. Gibbon takes up the story of Constantine's Dream, the dream in which he was admonished by God to inscribe the monogram of the cross on the shields of his troops and his subsequent obedience which brought him the victory of the Milvian Bridge, and his Celestial Vision of the appearance of the cross in the sky prior to his battle against Maxentius. The discussion of these events is prefaced with some observations about Constantine's troops before the battle. "The enthusiasm which inspired the troops, and perhaps the emperor himself, had sharpened their swords, while it satisfied their conscience. They marched to battle with the full assurance that the same God, who had formerly opened a passage to the Israelites through the waters of Jordan, and had thrown down the walls of Jericho at the sound of the trumpets of Joshua, would display his visible majesty and power in the victory of Constantine." (DF-20, II, 317)

Gibbon's positioning of the term "enthusiasm" as an opener for the paragraph achieves a remarkable insinuative purpose. The term, in effect, with all its suggestiveness of inspiration and zealousness, covers the entirety of the following discussion with the shadows of fanaticism. The discussion of these miracles is set up by the reminder that the troops were expecting a miracle to occur. Their "enthusiasm," he seems to be suggesting, combined with, or maybe caused by, their identification with the miracle-working God of the Old Testament, provides an incentive to believe in miracles. Of Constantine, Gibbon throws in the word "perhaps" as a reminder that the motive of self-interest might be a factor to weigh, and hence a further impeachment of the account.

Immediately following these comments Gibbon adds: "[t]he evidence of ecclesiastical history is prepared to affirm that their expectations were justified by the conspicuous miracle to which the conversion of the first Christian emperor has

---

[41]"Gibbon's conversion [to Catholicism] depended on the conviction that there was no halfway house in matters of belief, that, in Patricia B. Craddock's words, 'either all miracles were false, or all were true'. " Carnochan, Gibbon's Solitude, 89.

been almost unanimously ascribed." (*DF-20*, II, 317) Ecclesiastical history will, indeed, affirm the truth of the miraculous events, but ecclesiastical history here means the corrupted non-critical history of the theologian, laden with vested interest, indulgent of the imagination. That this is Gibbon's meaning is obvious in the next sentence where he proposes to analyze these miraculous accounts and sort the historical from the marvellous aspects. "The real or imaginary cause of so important an event deserves and demands the attention of posterity; and I shall endeavor to form a just estimate of the famous vision of Constantine, by a distinct consideration of the *standard*, the *dream*, and the *celestial* sign; by separating the historical, natural, and the parts of this extraordinary story, which, in the composition of a specious argument, have been artfully confounded in one splendid and brittle mass." (*DF-20*, II, 317-318, original italics)

Here is one of Gibbon's eloquent methodological pauses. He notes, with a touch of self-consciousness ("I shall endeavor to form a just estimate . . .") that he is confronting an extraordinary creation of the imagination. This is the supreme challenge for the historian, requiring careful, serious work to sort out real events from the imaginary creations. The disjunction "real or imaginary" is the work of iconoclasm—just the presence of it has an undermining effect—and it is suggestive of the skeptical-Humean weighing-of-probabilities that the historian must undertake in considering accounts that are immersed in the miraculous.

Constantine's dream can be explained "naturally" in two possible ways. "[I]f the dream of Constantine is separately considered, it may be naturally explained either by the *policy* or the *enthusiasm* of the emperor." (*DF-20*, II, 321, italics added) Policy (ambition?) or enthusiasm (fanaticism?). The dream was either an invention to help motivate the troops ("one of those pious frauds"), or it was manufactured by passions, a product of "the anxiety of the approaching day." (*DF-20*, II, 321) Following the probabilistic method from "Of Miracles," Gibbon argues that the passions and motives of the characters sufficiently (i.e., "naturally") explain what likely happened.

The evidence for Constantine's vision of the cross in the sky rests primarily with the church historian, Eusebius in his *Life of Constantine*. However, the earlier *Ecclesiastical History* never mentions the vision. Gibbon adds in a note that "the silence of the same Eusebius, in his Ecclesiastical History, is deeply felt by those advocates for the miracle who are not absolutely callous." (*DF-20*, II, 323 n.48) Eusebius is unable to document the miracle even though he must have been aware that "the recent discovery of this marvellous anecdote would excite some surprise and distrust among the most pious of his readers." (*DF-20*, II, 323) Eusebius' only source is that of the testimony of Constantine himself many years after the event. The nineteenth-century historian Jacob Burckhardt concurs with Gibbon. "But the familiar miracle which Eusebius and those who copy him represent as taking place on the march against Maxentius must finally be eliminated from the pages of history. It has not even the value of a myth, indeed is not of popular origin, but was told to Eusebius by Constantine long afterwards, and by Eusebius written up with intentionally vague bombast. The Emperor indeed swore a great oath to the bishop that the thing was not imagined . . . but history cannot take an oath of Constantine the Great too seriously, because, among other things, he had his brother-in-law murdered despite assurances given under oath."[42]

In his "Vindication," Gibbon, who was attacked for supposedly misrepresenting Eusebius, says that the major issue regarding this ecclesiastical historian is "how far it appears from his words and actions that the learned Bishop of Cæsarea was averse to the use of fraud, when it was employed in the service of Religion." (EE, 255) In the Decline and Fall Gibbon writes off Eusebius who, by his own admission, discredits himself giving every indication that he is willing to use fraud to advance the faith.[43] "The gravest of the ecclesiastical historians, Eusebius himself, indirectly confesses that he has related whatever might redound to the glory, and that he has suppressed all that could tend to the disgrace, of religion." (DF-16, II, 144) Gibbon also attacks his character. "It is well known that he himself had been thrown into prison; and it was suggested that he had purchased his deliverance by some dishonourable compliance." (DF-16, II, 144, n.179)

None of the evidence, none of the testimony regarding the miraculous events surrounding Constantine adds up to anything that begins to withstand reasonable doubt. Then, to punctuate this general thrust of the critique, Gibbon adds a final note to this section in which he states that no advocates for the vision are able to find even a single sympathetic observer from fourth- and fifth-century sources to testify to the event. (DF-20, II, 324, n.52) Thus, the life of Constantine and the progress of Christianity in his time are reconstructed as events that feature the agencies of human nature; power, ambition, and the like, rather than supernatural causality.

The miracles of apostolic times and the period of Constantine possess something of a foundational status for Christianity. This accounts for the oblique,

---

[42]Jacob Burckhardt, The Age of Constantine the Great, trans. Moses Hadas (Berkeley, CA: University of California Press, 1949), 296.

[43]In his "Vindication" Gibbon has a long passage on the "Character and Credit of Eusebius" where he notes that: "I had acknowledged, and I still think, that his character was less tinctured with credulity than that of most of his contemporaries; but as his enemies must admit that he was sincere and earnest in the profession of Christianity, so the warmest of his admirers, or at least of his readers, must discern, and will probably applaud, the religious zeal which disgraces or adorns every page of his Ecclesiastical History." (EE, 299).

ironic way in which Gibbon deals with them. When Gibbon moves away from this period and further into medieval times, his critical posture towards miracles becomes less ironic and more open and straight forward. Here Gibbon directs his criticism at either non-Christian targets—Islam—or at Roman Catholic miracles. Gibbon's criticism at this point falls safely into line with Protestant polemics aimed at the Church of Rome.

Near the end of the *Decline and Fall* in a passage on the crumbling Eastern empire Gibbon says: "[b]ut in this abject distress the emperor and empire were still possessed of an ideal treasure, which drew its fantastic value from the superstition of the Christian world. The merit of the true cross was somewhat impaired by its frequent division; and a long captivity among the infidels might shed some suspicion on the fragments that were produced in the East and West." (*DF-61*, VI, 455)

The "ideal treasure" refers to the "authentic" crown of thorns. Gibbon constructs a somewhat convoluted account of how the crown of thorns gets sold to the King of France and how miracle-generating relics become objects of commercial exchange. A passage of utter scorn is then unleashed. "The success of this transaction tempted the Latin emperor to offer with the same generosity the remaining furniture of his chapel: a large and authentic portion of the true cross; the baby-linen of the Son of God; the lance, the spunge, and the chain, of his Passion; the rod of Moses; and part of the scull of St. John the Baptist. For the reception of these spiritual treasures, twenty thousand marks were expended by St. Louis on a stately foundation, the holy chapel of Paris, on which the muse of Boileau has bestowed a comic immortality." (*DF-61*, VI, 456-457)

Laden with contemptuous humor, here Gibbon captures the complete institutional corruption of Christianity. Its most precious relics are objects of commerce. Miracles have "progressed" over the course of 1,300 years, from the original miraculous entry of Christ into the world, his death and resurrection, to a trafficking in objects that have miraculous powers. Christianity, miraculous and wonderous in its birth, is thoroughly immersed in phoney miracles and ultimately corrupted by them. Some, like these latter ones are an inviting target for ridicule; others like the crucifixion and resurrection, are the foundation of the religion itself and can only be greeted with irony that shrouds them in doubt.

Gibbon finishes this account with some general observations about religious relics and human credulity. "The truth of such remote and ancient relics, which cannot be proved by any human testimony, must be admitted by those who believe in the miracles which they have performed. About the middle of the last age, an inveterate ulcer was touched and cured by an holy prickle of the holy crown: the prodigy is attested by the most pious and enlightened Christians of France; nor will the fact by easily disproved, except by those who are armed with a general antidote against religious credulity." (*DF-61*, VI, 457)

Of interest is that Gibbon cites a miraculous report that in contrast to many is affirmed, not by the ignorant and credulous, but by the "most pious and enlightened Christians of France." The "antidote" against the kind of "religious credulity" that grips even the most enlightened of Christians comes from Hume himself. In a footnote Gibbon writes: "Voltaire strives to invalidate the fact, but Hume . . . with more skill and success, seizes the battery, and turns the cannon against his enemies." (*DF-61*, VI, 457, n.67) Voltaire's critical skills cannot match Hume's. Gibbon has named Hume as the Anti-Miracle man. (Gibbon's citation is to a note that Hume appends to "Of Miracles.") In this note Hume discusses the "holy prickle" miracle performed, interestingly enough, on Pascal's niece. This miracle redounded to the favor of the Jansenists, confounded their Jesuit enemies, and allegedly helped save Port Royal. (*EHU*, 344-346) This particular miracle was a good one as it did not come from the heated imagination of ignorant peasants or soldiers and it was "scientifically" investigated and confirmed. "The queen-regent of France, who was extremely prejudiced against the Port-Royal, sent her own physician to examine the miracle, who returned an absolute convert. In short, the supernatural cure was so uncontestable, that it saved, for a time, that famous monastery from the ruin with which it was threatened by the Jesuits." (*EHU*, 346) Investigated by a trained physician, this miracle thus prevailed in the face of skepticism.

Where then is this "battery" of Hume's, Gibbon speaks of, that provides the "general antidote against religious credulity"? Hume in the note states: "[o]ur divines, who can build up a formidable castle from such despicable materials; what a prodigious fabric could they have reared from these [the Port Royal miracles] and many other circumstances, which I have not mentioned . . . . But if they be wise, they had better adopt the miracle, as being more worth, a thousand times, than all the rest of their collection. Besides, it may serve very much to their purpose. For that miracle was really performed by the touch of an authentic holy prickle of the holy thorn, which composed the holy crown, which, &c." (*EHU*, 346)

Hume strikes a relative comparison. The holy prickle miracle is well documented compared with some, but it is nevertheless an invention with a purpose. The thorn, the crown and all the connecting accouterments can be vested with miraculous powers. The general antidote comes, however, from the probability test of the "Of Miracles" where Hume says, "if the falsehood of . . . [someone claiming a miracle] would be more miraculous, than the event which he relates; then, and not till then, can he pretend to command my belief or opinion." (*EHU*, 116) Gibbon makes a summary allusion to this general antidote in his discussion of the miraculous powers of the primitive church in chapter fifteen of the *Decline and Fall*. "Our different sentiments on this subject [miracles] will be much less influenced by any particular arguments than by our habits of study and reflection; and above all, by the degree of the evidence which we have accustomed ourselves to require for the proof of a miraculous event." (*DF-15*, II, 31-32) So then the arguments for some miracles such as the holy prickle, may be, as Hume says, worth much more than others, but the experience from which the historian develops his critical habits and skeptical modes of reflection in the midst of a subject matter where so much vested interest is at stake requires the highest standard of evidence (unattainable in Hume's view). "The duty of an historian," says Gibbon, "does not call upon him to interpose his private judgment in this nice and important controversy; but he ought not to dissemble the difficulty of adopting such a theory as may reconcile the *interest* of *religion* with that of *reason* . . . ." (*DF-15*, II, 32, italics added) Back again to the melancholy duty. The credibility of reports of miracles tests the integrity of the historian. This is why miracles are so important to Hume and to Gibbon.

CHAPTER FOUR

THE DEMISE OF IMMORTALITY

I. Immortality—Going the Way of Miracles

And if Christ be not risen, then is our preaching vain, and your faith is also vain.

1st Corinthians, 15:14

Few men die convinced that it is their last hour; and there is no place where the deception of hope deludes us more.

Montaigne

The promise of personal immortality is Christianity's spiritual font of hope and inspiration. By Gibbon's own account the assurance of it greatly energized the Christians in their early battles against paganism. The reward of heaven and the threat of hell were also powerful proselytizing tools—instrumental in subverting the traditional pagan religions. The doctrine of personal immortality in the *Decline and Fall*'s history of Christianity is subject to a skeptical, caustic treatment similar to the account of miracles. Like Hume, Gibbon viewed the entire notion as a speculative matter about which nothing can be known. Gibbon was also unremittingly critical of how belief in immortality affects the conduct of believers, and he linked belief in immortality, as he did with belief in miracles, closely to fanaticism and superstition. Both miracles and the hope for immortality were casualties of the philosophic historian's critique of Christianity. Hume attacked the notions philosophically: Gibbon disparaged them in his history. Belief in miracles and hope for the afterlife, Gibbon insinuates, work on the minds of the believers in a similar fashion. Religious believers invent miracles to impress the doubters and waverers and to confront rival sectarians, and they create eternal paradises as a reward for correct belief and promise hell as the consequence of disbelief. Devout attachment to a belief in immortality, like a belief in the testimony of miracles, turns on the dynamics of the imagination and the passions. The Christian preoccupation with immortality is the work of hope and fear, stimulating a vision of a world beyond the grave.[1] Christianity emerged irremediably hostile to the

---

[1] Gibbon himself in a letter of grief to his friend Lord Sheffield over the death of his very dear Aunt Kitty alludes to the emotional force of hope in relation to the belief of immortality. "As I grew up, an intercourse of thirty years endeared her to me as the faithful friend and the agreable companion; you have seen with what freedom and confidence we lived together, and have often admired her character and conversation which could alike please the young and old. All this is now lost, finally irrecoverably lost! I will agree with Mylady that the immortality of the soul is, on some occasions, a very comfortable

traditional religions of the empire, and the antagonistic new believers, infused with hope for the rewards of the afterlife, became subversive agents of the political authority of the empire. (*DF-15*, II, 57-58) Gibbon's critique of immortality is yet another melancholy aspect of his attack on Christianity. The preoccupation with the prospect of the wondrous afterlife by early Christians actually seems to bring degeneration and corruption rather than amelioration. Immortality in the *Decline and Fall* goes the way of miracles as the spirituality of Christianity is confronted by the naturalism of the Enlightenment.

Of the five "secondary causes" for the success of Christianity argued by Gibbon in chapter fifteen, the "doctrine of the future life," and the "miraculous powers ascribed to the primitive church" are listed as causes two and three respectively. These are central elements of the Christian Faith and are tightly linked to each other. Christ's resurrection is both a vibrant symbol of the impotence of natural death and the central "historical" event for all believers, a guarantee of the Faith's miraculous triumph over spiritual and physical death and the promise of everlasting life. Belief in Christ's entry into the world as God-man is a historical-theological belief, and upon it rests all hope for the future.

While Gibbon subjects immortality as a Christian preoccupation to severe historical criticism, Hume attacks it philosophically. Hume's "Of a Particular Providence and of a Future State," which immediately follows "Of Miracles" in the first *Enquiry*, complements his study of miracles with a skeptical challenge to the notion of an afterlife. The two pieces combine to form a formidable critique of two of Christianity's life-giving doctrines.[2] "Of Miracles" looks backward and suggests that belief in the miraculous foundations of Christianity is irrational. "Of Particular Providence" looks forward and insinuates that the future envisioned by Christians for their souls is merely the imaginative product of wish and conjecture. "Of Miracles" attempts to strike down any rational basis for believing in miracles. "Of a Particular Providence" aims to show that belief in the afterlife is irrelevant to moral conduct. Hume also attacks notions closely associated with immortality such as heaven and hell in his essay, "Of the Immortality of the Soul," and he subjects the development of religious ideas such as immortality to a naturalistic critique in his *Natural History*.

The ways in which Hume and Gibbon write about death and the perspectives they offer on human mortality take their roots in pagan moralism and have important implications for their critique of Christianity. They held up the lives of

---

doctrine." (*Letters-G*, III, 46) The melancholy tone seems suggestive of Gibbon's disbelief.

    [2]Flew, *Hume's Philosophy of Belief*, 215, argues that the two essays are integrally connected and that "Of a Particular Providence" is particularly ambitious in its attempts to nullify the significance of natural religion for practical morality.

the pagan moralists and statesmen as models of moral distinction and pointed to their lack of concern with the future of their souls beyond the grave. "I desire to take my Catalogue of Virtues from *Cicero's Offices*, not from the *Whole Duty of Man*,"[3] writes Hume. (*Letters*-H, I, 34) Here Hume openly states his preference for pagan over Christian morality. "We are sufficiently acquainted," says Gibbon, "with the eminent persons who flourished in the age of Cicero, and of the first Caesars, with their actions, their characters, and their motives, to be assured that their conduct in this life was never regulated by any serious conviction of the rewards or punishments of a future state." (*DF-15*, II, 21-22) Gibbon's remarks are clearly intended to create an invidious comparison of the pagan ethical disposition with that of the Christian who is influenced profoundly by the expectations of what awaits after death.

Hume's affinity for pagan moralism, indifference to the afterlife, and antagonism toward traditional Christian moral teaching are particularly evident in his posthumously published essay, "Of Suicide." Hume was dissuaded by his friends from publishing this essay along with "Of the Immortality of the Soul." Hume's friends feared ecclesiastical proscription; there was even the possibility of official prosecution.[4] In "Of Suicide" Hume argues, against long established Christian teaching, for the morality of rational suicide. Hume's model here was Cato, who killed himself rather than submit to the tyranny of Julius Caesar. "In all cases, *Christians* and *Heathens* are precisely upon the same footing; and if *Cato* and *Brutus*, *Araria* and *Portia* acted heroically, those who now imitate their example ought to receive the same praises from posterity. The power of committing Suicide is regarded by *Pliny* as an advantage which men possess even above the deity himself." (*Essays*, 589 n.6, original italics) Immediately we see a problem from the Christian perspective with a limitation of God's power. Hume holds up these classical figures as heroic models and urges not merely the withdrawal of condemnation for emulators (Christian or otherwise) but actual approbation. Hume's essay was an affront to Christians not simply because of its advocacy of rational suicide and its denial of the inherent immorality of killing ones' self. Hume's view of suicide was embedded in a moral perspective that had been articulated and defended by pagan philosophers and moralists and had been repudiated by Christian theologians.[5] For the pagan philosophers suicide

---

[3]*The Whole Duty of Man*, published c.1658 was a Christian devotional manual that was widely used in England.

[4]For an account of the publication of these two essays, see the note attached to Hume's *Essays*, 577.

[5]See P. Russell, "Epigram, Pantheists, and Freethought in Hume's *Treatise*," 664, n.13. "The debate on suicide was itself firmly embedded in the wider controversy concerning Christian morality and metaphysics . . . ."

represented an assertion of freedom from fear and a repudiation of a life dictated by superstition and terror. "Philosophers of antiquity sought to free men from the fear of death, for, once freed from this fear, men would be beyond superstitious terrors and morbid preoccupations."[6] In a footnote in the same essay Hume says that "[i]t would be easy to prove, that Suicide is as lawful under the *christian* dispensation as it was to the heathens. There is not a single text of scripture, which prohibits it." (*Essays*, 588 n.6) This claim is ironic. Christian theologians had long argued against suicide, a fact of which Hume was well aware, and his withdrawal of the essay from publication suggests how little confidence he had in what he could "prove" in this regard.[7] The Christian and the pagan views of death were philosophically and morally unreconcilable.[8]

---

[6]Peter Gay, *The Enlightenment: An Interpretation. Vol. 2, The Science of Freedom* (New York: W. W. Norton, 1969), 85.

[7]See Hume's (1772) letter to William Strahan complaining of the pirating of these two ("Of Suicide" and "On the Immortality of the Soul") essays. "But there have other Copies got abroad; and from one of these, some rascally Bookseller is, it seems, printing this Edition." (*Letters-H*, II, 253-54)

[8]See Gay, *The Science of Freedom*, 89, on the subject of the philosophes attitude toward suicide. Hume's views, anti-Christian and based on an admiration for the heroic suicide of pagans, were widely shared by the Enlightenment writers. Gay also notes, with some irony, I suppose, that very few of the philosophes ever resorted to it. "Hume, like other philosophes, had defended man's right to suicide, aligning himself with the classical writers and making light of Christian prohibitions. Yet it is worth noting in passing that while the philosophes explored the subject of suicide at some length and approved of it on principle, none of them—with the unlikely exception of Condorcet, who in any event faced certain death—resorted to it, no matter what their private sufferings."

II. Immortality and Immorality

The idea of that dreary and endless melancholy, which the fancy naturally ascribes to their condition [i.e., the dead], arises altogether from our joining to the change which has been produced upon them, our own consciousness of that change, from our putting ourselves in their situation, and from our lodging, if I may be allowed to say so, our own living souls in their inanimated bodies, and thence conceiving what would be our emotions in this case. It is from this very illusion of the imagination, that the foresight of our own dissolution is so terrible to us, and that the idea of those circumstances, which undoubtedly can give us no pain when we are dead makes us miserable while we are alive.

Adam Smith

A preoccupation with the immortal soul and its future in the afterlife probably struck Hume as morbid and perverse. As a boy he had first hand experience with the lugubrious, death-absorbed Scottish divines.[9] In Scotland the attention paid to the afterlife was intense. Even the illustrious Frances Hutcheson had lamented: "[w]e are spirits carrying about with us frail decaying putrefying carcasses; that as yesterday were embryoes, and shall in a few days be earth and bones."[10] Hume rejected the notions of heaven and hell as places or states of eternal reward and punishment. Such notions were completely incongruous with his mixed view of human nature (human beings as a mixture of good and evil). Thus, Hume had departed from the Christian notion (or at least the Calvinist variant of it) that human beings were fully depraved or corrupt and *deserving* of eternal punishment.

Hume's deathbed found him no less preoccupied with religion than during the rest of his life, and from accounts of those last days we know of his complete philosophical indifference to the afterlife. His friend Adam Smith in a letter to William Strahan recounted that his final conversations with Hume were still laced with humor. Hume had feigned a conversation with the mythical Charon of Lucian's *Dialogues of the Dead*. Seeking a delay from Charon, Hume implored: "'[h]ave a little patience, good Charon, I have been endeavouring to open the eyes of the public. If I live a few years longer, I may have the satisfaction of seeing the downfall of some of the prevailing systems of superstition.'" (*Letters-H*, II, 451) But for Charon, this is just another excuse. "But Charon would then lose all

---

[9]Mossner, *Life of David Hume*, 33-34.

[10]Quoted from Richard B. Sher, "Professors of Virtue: The Social History of the Edinburgh Moral Philosophy Chair in the Eighteenth Century," in *Studies in the Philosophy of the Scottish Enlightenment*, ed. M. A. Stewart (Oxford: Clarendon Press, 1990), 96.

temper and decency," said Hume. " 'You loitering rogue, that will not happen these many hundred years. Do you fancy I will grant you a lease for so long a term? Get into the boat this instant, you lazy loitering rogue.' " (*Letters-H*, II, 451) This exchange, conjured up by Hume in his final days in order to entertain himself and his friends, conveys a pessimistic view of the obduracy of superstition and credulity as well as his stoical equanimity in the face of death.

Death, as Peter Gay notes, "was in the largest sense of the word a political issue in the eighteenth century. If there was a good pagan way to die, this threw doubts on some of the most cherished of Christian beliefs."[11] And so Hume's own death is a remarkable event. Not only does it cast some light on his view of immortality from the quite personal setting of his contemplation of his own demise, it also, as one scholar has recently pointed out, became the subject of a moral and philosophical controversy that touched on the basic relation of religion and morality. "The circumstances surrounding Hume's tranquil and very pagan death (probably from colon cancer) on August 25 [1776], as reported by his close friend Adam Smith, occasioned a controversy that continued for at least a decade and involved many of the leading writers of the age, including Smith and Gibbon, as well as Samuel Johnson, Edmund Burke, and James Boswell."[12]

Hume faced death, as Carnochan says, "like a witty, unrepentant, and philosophical highway man . . . ."[13] Peter Gay writes that Hume "had died as he had lived, with cool, ironic courage, as a complete pagan."[14] Hume, like Socrates, knew that he was shortly to die. His "My Life" was composed with his mortality closely in front of him. Indeed, his shift of tenses in the final paragraph after announcing in a most pedestrian fashion that he was dying ("I am, or rather was (for that is the style I must now use in speaking of myself, which emboldens me more to speak my sentiments")) is one of the truly remarkable speech acts in all of literature.[15] With one deft, ironic stroke of the pen Hume was already speaking from the grave and thus able to pose as the Impartial Spectator so prominently figured in his philosophy and history. Boswell visited Hume on his deathbed in order to question the irreligious philosopher on his views of immortality and his personal expectations for a future state.[16] Boswell reported that "I asked him [Hume] if it was not possible that there was a future state. He answered it was

---

[11]Gay, *The Science of Freedom*, 88.

[12]S. Miller, "Death of Hume," 30.

[13]Carnochan, *Gibbon's Solitude*, 164.

[14]Gay, *Science of Freedom*, 89.

[15]See Carnochan, *Gibbon's Solitude*, 138-9, for an extremely insightful interpretation of Hume's extraordinary remarks about his approaching death.

[16]For an account of Hume's death and Boswell's visit, see Mossner, *Life of David Hume*, Chapter 39, "Death Comes for the Philosopher."

possible that a piece of coal put upon the fire would not burn; and he added that it was a most unreasonable fancy that we should exist for ever. . . . I asked him if the thought of Annihilation never gave him any uneasiness. He said not the least; no more than the thought that he had not been, as Lucretius observes."[17] The approach of death apparently held little terror for Hume since he doubted that a future life with punishment or reward awaited him. His recollection of Lucretius in this context is further evidence of his affinity for the pagan view of death as annihilation.

Hume's passing appeared to cause consternation for Christians such as Boswell and Johnson. Hume not only lived and wrote as an anti-Christian philosopher, but even worse, he died as one. His pagan-philosopher's demise seemed to give support to his anti-Christian life's work. The serenity of his death was a kind of smug mockery in the face of Christian teachings of death's terrors for the unbelievers. But worse was the thought that Hume's equanimity had helped advance the cause of unbelief. "[W]hat Burke and Johnson mainly objected to in Hume was not his vain desire to appear serene as he lay dying. It was his unprincipled—to their minds—desire to strengthen the case for infidelity. Hume, they thought, had an agenda: he wanted his virtuous life and tranquil death to be proof positive that morality has nothing to do with religious faith."[18] Hume's offense in his pagan mode of dying was to raise doubts about the relation of religion to morality.[19]

Hume's disposition of skeptical indifference toward the afterlife in his dying moments has a full reflective articulation in his writings. "Of a Particular Providence" presents Hume's attempt to decouple moral conduct and the belief in immortality. The effort in this piece amounts to both a defense of pagan skeptical philosophy and an attack on Christian doctrine. Speaking for the pagan moralist,

---

[17]Quoted from Mossner, *Life of David Hume*, 597-608. Hume's death brought amazement and consternation to Boswell. After listening to Hume's tranquilly-expressed doubts of any future life possibilities, Boswell went away perplexed and disturbed by Hume's equanimity. Boswell reported his deathbed visit to the death-terrified Johnson and remarked of Hume's extraordinary cheerfulness and detachment on the brink of his own extinction. "When told by Boswell that Hume had professed to be 'quite easy at the thought of Annihilation—'He lied,' the moralist retorted." (606).

[18]S. Miller, "Death of Hume," 35.

[19]Gibbon, less prosaic in this matter than Hume, but no less stoical in the face of dissolution noted with a melancholy tinge in the concluding lines of his *Memoirs* that, "In old age, the consolation of hope is reserved for the tenderness of parents, who commence a new life in their children; the faith of enthusiasts who sing hallelujahs above the clouds; and the vanity of authors who presume the immorality of their name and writings." Here we catch a slight glimpse of Gibbon's own agnosticism with regard to the future life. "The present," he says, "is a fleeting moment, the past is no more; and our prospect of futurity is dark and doubtful." (*Memoirs*, 175-6) Gibbon appears to have shared Hume's philosophical indifference to the possibilities of an eternity of reward or suffering.

Hume argues that it isn't necessary for human morality to be bound to a cosmological order. Morality has its basis in human nature: no theological or transcendental grounding is requisite. "I am sensible, that, according to the past experience of mankind, friendship is the chief joy of human life, and moderation the only source of tranquillity and happiness. I never balance between the virtuous and the vicious course of life; but am sensible, that, to a well-disposed mind, every advantage is on the side of the former." (*EHU*, 140) No speculation beyond common life experience, Hume argues, no careful balancing between the advantages of virtue over vice are needed to justify virtuous conduct. He makes no appeal to the afterlife with its promise of punishment or reward. While this may have a ring of circularity or self-justification, Hume is quick to argue that an appeal to divine justice as a basis for morality has a circularity of its own. "And if you affirm, that, while a divine providence is allowed, and a supreme distributive justice in the universe, I ought to expect some more particular reward of the good, and punishment of the bad, beyond the ordinary course of events; I here find the same fallacy, which I have before endeavoured to detect." (*EHU*, 140) The "fallacy" to which Hume refers involves the extrapolation from the "ordinary course of events"—the everyday particular this-world experiences of human beings—to a being that makes these events and experiences part of a larger, more profound scheme. The assumption of the existence of a being who renders such a scheme of distributive justice is an assumption made in order to draw the conclusion. Reasoning concerning the nature of God moves from effects back to causes, and as a principle of such reasoning, Hume says: "[w]hen we infer any particular cause from an effect, we must proportion the one to the other, and can never be allowed to ascribe to the cause any qualities, but what are exactly sufficient to produce the effect." (*EHU*, 136) The hypothesis of divine justice has no appeal to experience. "You seem not to remember, that all your reasonings on this subject can only be drawn from effects to causes; and that every argument, deduced from causes to effects, must of necessity be a gross sophism; since it is impossible for you to know anything of the cause, but what you have antecedently, not inferred, but discovered to the full, in the effect." (*EHU*, 141)

Hume attempts to show that the doctrine of an afterlife in which people are subject to a divine justice rests on the insupportable assumption of a perfect God who renders it. The existence of any such God, so it is argued, cannot be philosophically demonstrated. Plainly put, the world as we contemplate it is full of disorder, discord, pain, suffering, and evil, and as such can only be a quite imperfect effect from which we can justly infer only an imperfect cause. None of this, Hume continues, is to suppose that vice is superior to virtue. Experience provides a solid and sufficient basis for preferring the latter to the former.

In his essay, "Of the Immortality of the Soul," Hume examines the doctrine of the afterlife in more detail and punches it full of holes. The opening of this essay mirrors the end of "Of Miracles" in its dismissive irony. "By the mere light of reason it seems difficult to prove the Immortality of the Soul. The arguments for it are commonly derived either from *metaphysical* topics, or *moral* or *physical*. But in reality, it is the gospel, and the gospel, alone, that has brought life and immortality to light." (*Essays*, 590) So, as it is with the miracles of Christianity, immortality's foundation for belief lies in its origins in the gospel, in a word, faith. No philosophical demonstration of it is possible. This is Hume's point right off the top.

The metaphysical arguments mentioned by Hume in favor of immortality treat the soul as a spiritual substance (antithetical to material substance). Yet, it all turns out to be verbiage. Spiritual like physical substance is something wholly unknown. "Matter, therefore, and spirit are at bottom equally unknown; and we cannot determine what qualities may inhere in the one or in the other." (*Essays*, 591) If we can't even know what the soul is then, quite obviously, we cannot know whether it is immortal or not.

The physical arguments based on natural analogies, Hume contends, work against any notion of immortality for the soul. The body gives every appearance of being a necessary condition for mental or spiritual existence, and the origin, development, and subsequent weakening of the mental aspects of life appear to be invariably linked to corresponding states of the body. The soul, perhaps, is an epiphenomenon of the body. "The weakness of the body and that of the mind in infancy are exactly proportioned; their vigor in manhood; their sympathetic disorder in sickness; their common gradual decay in old age. The step farther seems unavoidable; their common dissolution in death." (*Essays*, 596) Almost all natural systems die and pass out of existence. How is it that the soul of man is an exception? "All doctrines," Hume says, "are to be suspected, which are favoured by our passions. And the hopes and fears which give rise to this doctrine are very obvious." (*Essays*, 598) The doctrine, Hume concludes, is largely a product of the passions. Since a future of dissolution and personal extinction is for most of us an extremely melancholy prospect to contemplate, the notion that some part of the person survives beyond death is a doctrine with a vested emotive interest.

From a perspective that is critical of Christianity Hume's moral arguments against immortality are more interesting than the metaphysical or physical ones. The reason is that the moral perspective on immortality is integral to the traditional Christian world view. Christianity operates with the assumption that the soul, which is the essence of the human person, is divinely created, survives death, and faces judgment beyond the grave. From this assumption follow certain notions about the justice of God and his intentions to punish and reward individuals in the afterlife. Christian speculation about what kind of existence awaited people after the grave was part of a larger scheme that postulated reward and punishment in the form of eternal states to which human beings were consigned on the basis of their conduct and beliefs in this life.

Hume mounts two arguments against the Christian doctrine of eternal punishment or reward in the afterlife. First, it is completely uncharacteristic of the way human beings usually think about moral culpability and the way they normally administer reward and punishment. "Punishment", he says, "according to *our* conceptions, should bear some proportion to the offence." (*Essays*, 594, original italics.)   Eternal punishment completely violates this sense of proportion, particularly in considering what a vulnerable creature man is. "Why then eternal punishment for the temporary offences of so frail a creature as man?" (*Essays*, 594) But an even greater incongruity applies to these notions of eternal reward and punishment in that heaven and hell in their imaginative and conceptual forms represent extremes of good and evil for which the vast majority of human beings fall in between. "Heaven and hell suppose two distinct species of men, the good and the bad. But the greatest part of mankind float between vice and virtue." (*Essays*, 594)   In effect, from the everyday consideration of what most human beings are actually like, heaven and hell are not the kinds of places where we would want to send most of them. Heaven and hell as places where eternal reward and punishment are carried out make no sense against the backdrop of human frailty.

The second argument stems from Hume's view of the human passions and their impact on belief. As already noted with miracles: beliefs are enormously, perhaps predominately affected by strong feelings, particularly feelings of desire and aversion. Hume's above cited statement: "[a]ll doctrines are to be suspected, which are favoured by our passions," provides a negative guidepost for the evaluation of belief.   The philosopher and the historian must, therefore, be extremely suspicious of doctrines that have the objects of great hope and aversion at stake. Belief "chases" passion in the sense that it is generally the case that human beings are strongly inclined to rationalize what they want to believe. In the *Natural History* Hume drives a wedge between the psychology of religious belief and its justification (rational theology). Most people take up religious beliefs through a process that has little to do with the argumentation involved. "[T]he vulgar, in nations, which have embraced the doctrine of theism, still build it upon irrational and superstitious opinions, [and] . . . are never led into that opinion by any process of argument, but by a certain train of thinking, more suitable to their genius and capacity." (*NHR*, 51)   That any particular religious doctrine emerges and becomes prominent thus is a purely historical contingency to be explained by the various cultural forces at work.

The afterlife doctrine also is inexorably caught up with issues of ambition, self-interest, and power. Wielding spiritual knowledge of how to administer punishment and reward (being able to figure out the rules and how they work) confers an obvious advantage. "And those who foster them [i.e., beliefs in eternal punishment]; what is their motive? Only to gain a livelihood, and to acquire power and riches in this world. Their very zeal and industry, therefore, are an argument against them." (*Essays*, 593) We should be suspicious, Hume admonishes, of our own beliefs when they are grounded in strong passions, but we should also be skeptical of others' passionately held beliefs.

Immortality of the soul and the notion of a future state provide for the human imagination an infinite region of the unknown and with it an unlimited supply of terror and punishment that a capricious God may unleash. "Every image of vengeance, severity, cruelty, and malice must occur and augment the ghastliness and horror, which oppresses the amazed religionist." (*NHR*, 81) In addition, the fear of hell and of the being who may put one there creates an inner turmoil and conflict that further grieves and terrifies the believer. "The heart secretly detests such measures of cruel and implacable vengeance; but the judgment dares not but pronounce them perfect and adorable. And the *additional misery* of this inward struggle aggravates all the other terrors, by which these unhappy victims to superstition are forever haunted." (*NHR*, 83-84, italics added)

Hume poses a destructive dilemma for the advocate of divine justice. If, on the one hand, God's divine justice is said to be readily evident in the world, then our experience of justice is adequate and sufficient, and there is no need to suppose any remediation beyond what we currently experience. But, on the other hand, if it is asserted that there is no evidence of God's justice in what we currently observe, then an affirmation of some unfathomable or hidden version of it is merely a begging of the question. If one takes what Hume calls the "medium position"—that there is a partial justice in our current experience—one is left asserting that God's justice is merely what one presently observes. "[Y]ou have no reason to give it [i.e., justice] any particular extent, but only so far as you see it, *at present*, exert itself." (*EHU*, 142, original italics) Hume thus repudiated the future life doctrine as a piece of unfounded speculation. Also, hope for a future life reward or dread of eternal punishment, so far as he could determine from his observations—personally or historically—had not seemed to improve human conduct.

Hume had developed a sophisticated philosophical critique of the Christian notion of immortality, and on his death bed had acted like a stoical philosopher.

Gibbon in turn developed a historical critique of the conduct of individuals who seemed to be strongly motivated by the prospect of an afterlife. The afterlife doctrine was vital in the development of Christianity in its power to inspire hope. Gibbon knew this. The future life doctrine, as has been noted, was one of Gibbon's five secondary causes of the success of Christianity. Gibbon's critique affirmed that belief in an afterlife, like an affirmation of miracles, is a creation of the human passions and the imagination. Chapter fifteen of the *Decline and Fall* explains how the afterlife doctrine came to be invented. "Yet there were a few sages of Greece and Rome who had conceived a more exalted, and, in some respects, a juster idea of human nature; though it must be confessed that, in the sublime inquiry, their reason had been often guided by their imagination, and that their imagination had been prompted by their vanity." (*DF-15*, II, 21) All of this has very much the air of contingency: a few philosophers in their weaker, unconstrained moments succumb to their vanity and imagination. Imagination is simulated by vanity! Gibbon then describes just how the motive of vanity shapes the thinking on how the human soul comes to be viewed and what its illustrious and eternal career will be. "When they viewed with complacency the extent of their own mental powers when they exercised the various faculties of memory, of fancy, and of judgment, in the most profound speculations, or the most important labours, and when they reflected on the desire of fame, which transported them into future ages far beyond the bounds of death and of the grave; they were unwilling to confound themselves with the beasts of the field, or to suppose that a being, for whose dignity they entertained the most sincere admiration, could be limited to a spot of earth and to a few years of duration." (*DF-15*, II, 21)

Behind the quest for immortality is the melancholy prospect of the extinction of all things in death and the eternity of the grave. A "desire for fame" and an unwillingness to "confound themselves with the beasts of the field" in Gibbon's view account for the invention of an immortal soul, something separating human beings from all other natural creatures who appear merely to live a short time and die. Gibbon here highlights a tension between the *freedom of the imagination*, which fears extinction and conceives other realms of existence, and the *constraints of experience* out of which are drawn the morose comparisons of mortality between man and the other creatures. What remains from this is merely to lament quietly the brevity of human existence. This particular dramatization is illustrative of those recurring Humean-kinds of observations relative to the formation of belief: the resistance of the imagination to the fetters of sense experience and the active role of passion as a motivating force of belief. These philosophers, Gibbon adds, then "summoned to their aid the science, or rather the language, of Metaphysics." (*DF-15*, II, 21) Metaphysics cannot really be a science, as Gibbon with his skeptical jibe here tries to assert, because it operates in a realm of the imagination that cannot be corrected or modified by experience. The properties of the soul that the language of metaphysics creates are an object of wish. The soul possesses all those things denied to the body. "They soon discovered that, as none of the properties of matter will apply to the operations of the mind, the human soul must consequently be a substance distinct from the body, pure, simple, and spiritual, incapable of dissolution, and susceptible of a much higher degree of virtue and happiness after the release from its corporeal prison." (*DF-15*, II, 21) Here we have an echoing of Hume's viewpoint from "Of the Immortality of the Soul" where he says, "that by the mere light of reason it seems difficult to prove the Immortality of the Soul." Gibbon, like Hume, stresses the ultimate unknowability of one's destiny beyond the grave.

Gibbon also wrestles with the moral and practical aspects of the afterlife doctrine. A belief in personal immortality bears serious moral implications for the believer. The promise of a future beyond the grave means that one's conduct in this life is open to adjudication in the next and that existence is not merely transitory but in some way permanent. Since the soul is immortal, its future beyond death stretches limitlessly in comparison with its brief existence on this earth and hence the tendency to view this life entirely as a fleeting preparation for the next. Gibbon finds this disvaluing of the here-and-now a troubling feature of early Christian history and a corrosive element in the decline of the Roman empire. Christian preoccupation with the next world, he argued, led not only to neglect of this one but in some cases an outright contempt for it. "The ancient Christians were animated by a contempt for their present existence, and by a just confidence of immortality, of which the *doubtful* and *imperfect* faith of the modern ages cannot give us any adequate notion." (*DF-15*, II, 24, italics added) The text emits pure irony. The seeming invidious comparison of the modern age with its "doubtful and imperfect faith" against the genuine ancient forms is actually the reverse. Doubt and imperfection here reflect an appropriate and healthy skepticism. The "contempt" of the early Christians for their present existence, a feeling stimulated by an overweening confidence in their immortality, is a personal expression of a devalued estimation of what Gibbon calls the "visible world." The historian contemplates early Christianity with its growing preoccupation with an "invisible" unknowable world, observing the increasing investment of attention and energy into the unknowable and a concomitant loss of attachment to the known and experienced. This devalued "visible world" invidiously contrasted with the promised heavenly, spiritual world, the promise of which energized the early Christians. The heavenly world is the creation of the unshackled imagination in league with the passions. But there is more to this belief in an afterlife for Gibbon than just wish. Like Hume, Gibbon sees the Christian absorption with life after death as practically deleterious. This is certainly manifest in Gibbon's historical reconstruction of the events in which this doctrine was to have such a major role. "As the happiness of a *future* life is the great object of religion, we may hear, without surprise or scandal, that the introduction, or at least the abuse, of Christianity had some influence on the decline and fall of the Roman empire." (*DF-38*, IV, 175, italics added) The success of Christianity, its triumph over pagan religion, was due to "[t]he doctrine of a future life, improved by every additional circumstance which could give weight and efficacy to that important truth." (*DF-15*, II, 3) Moreover, understanding the next world, how it is set up, how one is to fare in it, is the work of the theological imagination—unconstrained by experience. The afterlife becomes a preoccupation surrounded by intense anticipation, uncertainty, and terror. "The Christian, who founded his belief much less on the fallacious arguments of reason than on the authority of tradition and the interpretation of scripture, expected it with terror and confidence, as a certain and approaching event; and, as his mind was perpetually filled with the solemn idea, he considered every disaster that happened to the empire as an infallible symptom of an expiring world." (*DF-15*, II, 28)

Here described by Gibbon is a quite different orientation toward daily existence, one in which fear and terror become a regular component of experience. The Christian lives with pressing eschatological convictions which guide his interpretation of natural events as confirmation of the natural world's end. The Christian in this regard differs remarkably from his pagan counterpart. In the *Decline and Fall* the conduct of the early Christians is scrutinized against a backdrop of classical pagan morality. Gibbon appeals to the classical moralists in an attempt to show the irrelevance of belief in an afterlife for good conduct. Classical moralists, like Cicero, were largely indifferent to the whole issue of the afterlife in stark contrast with the fanatical early Christians. "The writings of Cicero represent, in the most lively colours, the ignorance, the errors, and the uncertainty of the ancient philosophers, with regard to the immortality of the soul. When they are desirous of arming their disciples against the fear of death, they inculcate, as an obvious though melancholy position, that the fatal stroke of our dissolution releases us from the calamities of life, and that those can no longer suffer who no longer exist." (*DF-15*, II, 20-21)

The very idea of worrying about paybacks after death was greeted by the eminent pagans with scorn. "At the bar and in the senate of Rome the ablest orators were not apprehensive of giving offence to their hearers by exposing that doctrine as an idle and extravagant opinion, which was rejected with contempt by every man of a liberal education and understanding." (*DF-15*, II, 22) Gibbon thus sets up a profound contrast between the pagan view of death and the afterlife, steeped in indifference, and what would be the emerging Christian overriding preoccupation with it. Here we see a development of a Humean theme from the first *Enquiry*. Notions like immortality in Hume's view draw upon the imaginative resources of the human mind but are entirely conjectural and deal with objects that are beyond the range of human experience. Moreover, the sheer speculative nature of such notions as the soul and its eternal future, Hume argues, makes belief or disbelief in them of absolutely no practical or moral relevance. In "Of a Particular Providence" Hume, speaking hypothetically as Epicurus, says: "[i]f I can prove, from this very reasoning, that the question [of a future state] is entirely speculative, and that, when, in my philosophical disquisitions, I deny a providence and a future state, I undermine not the foundations of society, but advance principles, which they themselves, upon their own topics, if they argue consistently, must allow to be solid and satisfactory." (*EHU*, 135)

This is a dangerous subject matter—hence Hume's need to distance himself personally by having the pagan Epicurus make the completely defiant argument (defiant to Christianity, that is) that human goodness and morality can be uncoupled from a belief in an afterlife with all the associated rewards and punishments. "It seems . . . that you leave politics entirely out of the question, and never suppose, that a wise magistrate can justly be jealous of certain tenets of philosophy, such as those of Epicurus, which, denying a divine existence, and consequently a providence and a future state, seem to loosen, in a great measure, the ties of morality, and may be supposed, for that reason, pernicious to the peace of civil society." (*EHU*, 133-34) Unlike the Christians, the dominant view of the ancient pagan philosophers was that death was the end. Unconcerned with life after death, the pagan philosophers attached great value to virtuous living, friendship, and service to community.

An aspect of the divine justice surrounding the Christian doctrine of the afterlife is the eternal punishment of the non-believers. Recall that Hume rejects the Christian notions of heaven and hell as incompatible with a view of human beings as largely a mixture of good and evil. Gibbon, like Hume, raises this issue. In chapter fifteen he points to the eternal condemnation of the pagans of antiquity because of their disbelief. "The condemnation of the wisest and most virtuous of the Pagans, on account of their ignorance or disbelief of the divine truth, seems to offend the reason and the humanity of the present age." (*DF-15*, II, 28) Like Hume, Gibbon cannot make the notion of eternal punishment fit into common life observations about human nature with its frailty and its mixed qualities of goodness and evil. He refines his objection in an appended note. "And yet, whatever may be the language of individuals, it is still the public doctrine of all the Christian churches; nor can even our own refuse to admit the conclusions which must be drawn from the viiith and the xviiith of her Articles. The Jansenists, who have so diligently studied the works of the fathers, maintain this sentiment with distinguished zeal; and the learned M. de Tillemont never dismisses a virtuous emperor without pronouncing his damnation. Zuinglius is perhaps the only leader of a party who has ever adopted the milder sentiment, and he gave no less offence to the Lutherans than to the Catholics." (*DF-15*, II, 28, n.72) Belief in eternal damnation as a compensation for disbelief has, as Gibbon suggests, enormous staying power. Over the long centuries the Christian affinity for this doctrine is never even officially dislodged, and we witness the apologists condemning the pagans no matter how conventionally virtuous their lives may have been.

The afterlife doctrine, as Gibbon argues, was an enormously influential element in early Christianity. Why though had this idea, so attractive to the imagination, never taken hold in the popular pagan religions? Gibbon provides three reasons. First, the loose, mythopoeic character of the pagan religions was inadequate to provide the metaphysical framework sufficient to make arguments to support the doctrine. "The general system of their mythology was unsupported by any solid proofs; and the wisest among the Pagans had already disclaimed its usurped authority." (*DF-15*, II, 22) This is a similar observation to Hume's. "The pagan religion, therefore, seemed to vanish like a cloud, whenever one approached to it, and examined it piecemeal. It could never be ascertained by any fixt dogmas and principles." (*NHR*, 75) Second, the region of the afterlife had been the exclusive domain of the artists and poets. Their representations had no consistency and little approximation to any common life notions of reward and punishments. "The description of the infernal regions had been abandoned to the fancy of painters and of poets, who peopled them with so many phantoms and monsters, who dispensed their rewards and punishments with so little equity, that a solemn truth, the most congenial to the human heart, was oppressed and disgraced by the absurd mixture of the wildest fictions." (*DF-15*, II, 22)

Again, we find observations similar to those in the *Natural History* where Hume tries to show that the beliefs of pagan religionists had an affinity to stories or fables and hence there was little demand for logical consistency. The advent of scripture, as Hume notes, introduced the need for logical consistency. "Another cause, which rendered the ancient religions much looser than the modern, is, that the former were *traditional* and the latter are *scriptural*; and the tradition in the former was complex, contradictory, and, on many occasions, doubtful; so that it could not possibly be reduced to any standard and canon, or afford any determinate articles of faith. The stories of the gods were numberless like the popish legends; and tho' every one, almost, believed a part of these stories, yet no one could believe or know the whole: While at the same time, all must have acknowledged, that no one part stood on a better foundation than the rest." (*NHR*, 74-75) Scripture introduces the necessity of coherence and logical structure because it requires an interpretational apparatus to make it authoritative and prescriptive.

Third, and most important, the pagan religions were highly social religions whose ceremonies were directed toward concerns with this-life matters. "The providence of the gods, as it related to public communities rather than to private individuals, was principally displayed on the visible theatre of the present world. The petitions which were offered on the altars of Jupiter or Apollo expressed the anxiety of their worshipers for temporal happiness, and their ignorance or indifference concerning a future life." (*DF-15*, II, 22-23)

Thus, it was this concatenation of circumstances that made the Greek and Roman pagan religionists largely resistant or indifferent to the future life doctrine. Gibbon notes, however, that in non-Christian religions, those in India, Egypt, Assyria, and in Gaul, for example, one finds strong attachment to afterlife beliefs. How is it that *these* religions have such beliefs and the pagan classical religions did not? "[S]ince we cannot attribute such a difference to the superior knowledge of the barbarians, we must ascribe it to the influence of an established priesthood, which employed the motives of virtue as the instrument of ambition." (*DF-15*, II, 23)

Gibbon here articulates a variant of a widespread anti-clerical eighteenth-century theme: priests are manipulators who propagate ideas out of self-interest.[20] The future life doctrine prevails not because of its philosophical superiority but rather because of its imaginative power and political value. Belief in it confers power on those who interpret the ways of God. The truth-content of the doctrine in Gibbon's view is irrelevant to understanding why it becomes an important part of some religions.

Immortality is the pivotal element in a radical reversal of perspective in which the visible world becomes a transition to a completely different one. With this reversal of perspective, the entire question of the afterlife takes on a vast *practical* importance. It is this transformation of the afterlife-issue to practical significance that Gibbon finds troublesome. The *certainty* of an afterlife and the relegation of the visible world as a preparation for it, from the standpoint of the believer, impose a quite different order of values and different standards of conduct. Hence the overwhelming importance that the *belief* in an afterlife carries. "The assurance of

---

[20]See Peter Byrne, *Natural Religion and the Nature of Religion: The Legacy of Deism* (London: Routledge, 1989), 79-82. Byrne points out that the deists viewed the growth of the priesthood as an unqualified development of corruption within Christianity. The politics of the priesthood ruined the original pristine character of Christianity. Gibbon certainly speaks this way (ironically perhaps).

such a Millennium was carefully inculcated by a succession of fathers from Justin Martyr and Irenæus, who conversed with the immediate disciples of the apostles, down to Lactantius, who was preceptor to the son of Constantine." (*DF-15*, II, 26) The preoccupation with the next "invisible" (i.e., unknowable) world leads to the denigration of the visible world. Gibbon, in the unfolding of his pessimistic view of Christianity and the development of his thesis of Christianity's inevitable decline, establishes a close linkage between belief in miracles and belief in the afterlife as corrupt, uncivilized effects of fanatical religion. Thus in Hume's philosophy and Gibbon's history the Christian preoccupation with immortality comes under intense critical scrutiny. They both argue, using the pagan philosophers as their models, that belief in the afterlife is irrelevant to ethical conduct in this one. Hume's empirical philosophy rules out the possibility of demonstrating what the career of the soul should and will be. The theological framework built up around the whole notion of the afterlife and a supernatural reward system Gibbon views as a product of the passions. Moreover, the Christian concept of eternal reward and punishment runs counter to the common life experience of human beings. Gibbon rejected the afterlife preoccupations of the early Christians as an exercise in fanaticism. The concern for the afterlife corroded morals and contributed to the destruction of the Roman empire.

III. The Politics of Immortality

Then cometh the end, when he shall have delivered up the kingdom to God, even the Father; when he shall have put down all rule and all authority and power.

I. Corinthians 15:24

The Hume-Gibbon attack on Christianity purported to show that the early Christian preoccupation with heaven and hell had a deleterious effect on social relations and public morality precisely because of the devaluing of the visible world.   The afterlife-dismissive pagan philosophers were held up as moral counter-examples to the Christians, absorbed with their fate in the next world.   Hume uses the "atheistic" Epicurus to help him make this point.   Epicureans, though denying providence, participated in the religious rituals of Greek society, were model citizens, and were widely regarded as such.   "Epicurus lived at Athens to an advanced age, in peace and tranquillity: Epicureans were even admitted to receive the sacerdotal character, and to officiate at the altar, in the most sacred rites of the established religion." (*EHU*, 132) Skepticism involved no threat to public morality or to the state.   Indeed, the disbelieving Epicurus was allowed to participate respectfully with his fellow citizens in their religious rites.   Hume here speaks as Epicurus: "[y]our deliberations, which of right should be directed to questions of public good, and the interest of the commonwealth, are diverted to the disquisitions of speculative philosophy; and these magnificent, but perhaps fruitless enquiries, take place of your more familiar but more useful occupations.   But in so far as in me lies, I will prevent this abuse.   We shall not here dispute concerning the origin and government of worlds.   We shall only enquire how far such questions concern the public interest.   And if I can persuade you, that they are entirely indifferent to the peace of society and security of government, I hope that you will presently send us back to our schools, there to examine, at leisure, the questions the most sublime, but at the same time, the most speculative of all philosophy." (*EHU*, 134-35) This encapsulates Hume's view on the interrelation of speculative philosophy and morals and politics.   The "disquisitions of speculative philosophy," are, remarkably "magnificent but useless." Here is a variant on a persisting theme, the imagination unconstrained or reformed by human experience.   This imagination may be magnificent in many of its productions but is practically useless.   Hume nevertheless urges a complete freedom of philosophical speculation and at the same time denies that any harm to a society can result from speculative or conjectural controversy.   Speculation on the future of the soul, Hume would argue, may be philosophically interesting, but offers no demonstrable knowledge that could be morally or politically decisive. Out of the various possibilities for the destiny of the soul after death no possibility emerges which would be immoral to doubt or deny.

Yet, with the entry of Christianity upon the scene, coercion is introduced into philosophy. Coercion of belief in this speculative realm—the politicizing of the idea of immortality—leads to what I call the "politics of immortality." A politicized idea is an idea or set of ideas around which an institution or community focuses its instruments of power and coercion. That a just God *must* exist, that man is by nature depraved, that a "workers" state is the only just state; these are all ideas that have at some time or other been politicized, i.e., evidence or expression of disbelief in them has met with official punishment, sanction, or restriction.[21]

Christianity's great source of hope and inspiration, the doctrine of personal immortality, as Gibbon attempts to demonstrate in the *Decline and Fall*, also assumes important political as well as spiritual dimensions in the history of Christianity and the history of pagan Rome. A. D. Nock has written that, "[t]he central fact in the teachings of Jesus was not a novel doctrine of God or man but the heralding of the Kingdom."[22] A kingdom of course requires a king and the imposition of a certain kind of political order. Insofar as this kingdom is bound up with a community of believers who are beckoned by a future of immortality, the politics of immortality must come into consideration.

The politics of immortality plays a significant role in Gibbon's critique of early Christianity in the *Decline and Fall*. The enforcement of theological beliefs requires the erection of a power structure with a coercive apparatus and institutional paraphernalia administered by priests. "The memory of theological opinions cannot long be preserved without the artificial helps of priests, of temples, and of books." (*DF-28*, III, 218) From paganism to Christianity, the doctrine of immortality undergoes an important transformation: from being an entertaining, speculative possibility to an undoubtable truth with a belief-enforcement system. Immortality, reward, and punishment in an afterlife are entirely speculative notions that philosophers may entertain themselves with but are impossible to know with any certainty because they are beyond experience. But the preoccupation with these ideas by Christians, driven by passion, makes them into practical necessities around which the coercive. organs of the state converge. Once they enter the practical realm they become oppressive. Gibbon, like Hume, appeals to the

---

[21]For a modern example of a "scientific" idea (Lysenko's view of evolution) becoming politicized, see Zhores Medvedev, *The Rise and Fall of T. D. Lysenko* (New York: Columbia University Press, 1969).

[22]A. D. Nock, *Conversion: The Old and the New in Religion from Alexander the Great to Augustine of Hippo* (Oxford: Clarendon Press, 1933), 242.

example of Epicurus in order to set up his critique of the politics of immortality. "[T]he first lessons of Epicurus so strangely scandalized the pious ears of the Athenians that by his exile, and that of his antagonists, they silenced all vain disputes concerning the nature of the gods. But in the ensuing year they recalled the hasty decree, restored the liberty of the schools, and were convinced, by the experience of the ages, that *the moral character of philosophers is not affected by the diversity of their theological speculations.*" (*DF-42*, IV, 282, italics added) Christianity, so it seems by implication to Gibbon, completely exaggerates the practical importance of the afterlife and immortality and ends up politicizing these speculative ideas. The politics of immortality makes the business of caring for the immortal soul—its future in the afterlife—a matter of official concern and hence a matter of official coercion.

By converting the doctrine of immortality from a speculative notion into a profoundly moral preoccupation, and by the invention of a place of eternal torment for the unbelievers to inhabit, the early Christians moved against the moral order of pagan society. "But the primitive church, whose faith was of a much firmer consistence, delivered over, without hesitation, to eternal torture the far greater part of the human species." (*DF-15*, II, 28) There is a touch of irony here with the hint that with the modern church's diminution of the consistency of faith there has perhaps been an elevation of humanity. Gibbon then points out the destructiveness of this broad condemnatory view for normal human relations. "These rigid sentiments, which had been unknown to the ancient world, appear to have infused a spirit of bitterness into a system of love and harmony. The ties of blood and friendship were frequently torn asunder by the difference of religious faith; and the Christians, who, in this world, found themselves oppressed by the power of the Pagans, were sometimes seduced by resentment and spiritual pride to delight in the prospect of their future triumph." (*DF-15*, II, 28-29)

Out of this preoccupation with the fate of the soul in the next world comes divisiveness, rancor, and contention. "Faith, zeal, curiosity, and more earthly passions of malice and ambition kindled the flame of theological discord; the church, and even the state, were distracted by religion factions, whose conflicts were bloody, and always implacable." (*DF-38*, IV, 175) Thus, we see why the Christian creation of an afterlife and a concomitant system of eternal justice with its concept of hell becomes for Gibbon such a major event in the history of the decline of the empire.

The notions of hell and an infinitely powerful being who puts people there for an eternity of suffering because of their failure to worship him stimulate the development of a religious morality which relies primarily on the motivating force of fear and which encourages a fear-induced hypocritical conduct of adulation and devotion. The imaginative creation of a place or state of eternal damnation taken as a serious belief must vividly suggest what a large role the emotion of fear must play. Damnation of the soul as an unending, horrifyingly agonized form of existence had to be, to one who believed in its imminent possibility, the most torturous and fearful of experiences. Gibbon describes the enormous fear that seized the early Christians as they contemplated the future of their souls. "[The Christians] believed that the end of the world and the kingdom of heaven were at hand. The near approach of this wonderful event had been predicted by the apostles [and] . . . it was productive of the most salutary effects on the faith and practice of Christians, who lived in the awful expectation of that moment when the globe itself, and all the various race of mankind, should tremble at the appearance of their divine judge." (*DF-15*, II, 24-25)

Hume refers disparagingly to the "monkish virtue" behind the preoccupation with the fate of one's soul before a God who sends disbelievers in him to eternal torment. "Where the deity is represented as infinitely superior to mankind, this belief, tho' altogether just, is apt, when joined with superstitious terrors, to sink the human mind into the lowest submission and abasement, and to represent the monkish virtues of mortification, penance, humility and passive suffering, as the only qualities, which are acceptable to him." (*NHR*, 62)

Mortification, penance, and passive suffering are not "virtues" which Hume sees as in any way beneficial to human beings. They are a contrivance generated by fear and based on superstition. With belief in an afterlife necessary for the peace and order of civil society, theological and speculative notions like the nature of the soul and its future are transformed into practical problems and political preoccupations.

The politics of immortality, as it emerges in the *Decline and Fall*, amounts to a grand historical illustration of how the coercive apparatus that is normally associated with the workings of politics (politics involves coercing behavior) is intruded into the realm of philosophy, extirpating the freedom that is needed for philosophy to endure and prosper. In the first *Enquiry* Hume remarks about the importance that freedom has in making the philosophical enterprise possible. "Our conversion began with my admiring the singular good fortune of philosophy, which as *it requires entire liberty above all other privileges*, and chiefly flourishes from the free opposition of sentiments and argumentation, received its first birth in an age and country of freedom and toleration, and was never cramped, even in its most extravagant principles by any creeds, confessions, or penal statutes." (*EHU*, 133, italics added)

The politicalization of ideas, it would seem, is to be strenuously resisted if philosophy (i.e., critical thinking) is to endure. Gibbon stresses that the question

of a future life is beyond human experience, and he holds the doctrine up as a
perfect example of a speculative philosophic concern that has little practical import.
"A doctrine thus removed beyond the senses and the experience of mankind might
serve to amuse the leisure of a philosophic mind; or, in the silence of solitude, it
might sometimes impart a ray of comfort to desponding virtue; but the faint
impression which had been received in the schools was soon obliterated by the
commerce and business of active life." (*DF-15*, II, 21)

While a concern with life after death may have *some* minor relevancy to human
concerns, either in some detached speculative sense or in a melancholy, reflective
pause, for the bulk of mankind it has no experiential sustenance and hence cannot
stand up to human this-world concerns. The moral and practical significance of the
doctrine from Gibbon's perspective is minimal.

Thus, the future life doctrine lacked any philosophical foundation. It was a
purely "revealed" truth of religion. The aspiration to know what future lies beyond
the grave is vain and philosophically unattainable. "Since, therefore, the most
sublime efforts of philosophy can extend no farther than feebly to point out the
desire, the hope, or at most the probability, of a future state, there is nothing, except
a divine revelation, that can ascertain the existence, and describe the condition, of
the invisible country which is destined to receive the souls of men after their
separation from the body." (*DF-15*, II, 22)

Gibbon here echoes Hume's opening comments in "Of the Immortality of the
Soul"—"it is the gospel, and the gospel alone, that has brought life and immortality
to light." The "condition of the invisible country" is euphemistic language for a
completely unknowable world, the world beyond experience. Yet the Christian
theologians are absorbed with this question and pour their energies into elaborate
preparation for the unknowable.

In the *Decline and Fall* the doctrine of immortality becomes a key feature in
the church's elevation of superstition and its destruction of critical thinking. The
religious history of the Jews is Gibbon's initial entry point into the politics of
immortality. He seems intent here on showing that there is nothing inherently or
naturally important in the doctrine, and that the development of its significance for
the Jews was the outgrowth of ideological-religious conflict. His initial remarks
are ironic. The doctrine of immortality, given its truth, *should* have been a
prominent belief of the Jews. "We might naturally expect that a principle, so
essential to religion, would have been revealed in the clearest terms to the chosen
people of Palestine, and that it might safely have been intrusted to the hereditary
priesthood of Aaron." (*DF-15*, II, 23) Yet the Mosaic law neither mentions nor
treats the subject of immortality. Here then, indirectly expressed, is a damning
piece of information about this doctrine that is central to Christianity: it is, Gibbon

insinuates, historically insignificant. Gibbon then waxes even more sarcastic. "It is incumbent on us to adore the mysterious dispensations of Providence, when we discover that the doctrine of the immortality of the soul is omitted in the law of Moses." (*DF-15*, II, 23) Here is more tension between the "pleasing task" of the theologian who operates in a realm of mystery, and the "melancholy duty" of the historian who "discovers," in this case, the absence of this important doctrine. Gibbon also attaches a note to this text in which he obliquely mocks Bishop Warburton, Hume's lifelong nemesis. "The right reverend author of the *Divine Legation of Moses* assigns a very curious reason for the omission, and most ingeniously retorts it on the unbelievers." (*DF-15*, II, 23, n.59) This adds another dimension to Gibbon's repudiation of the politics of immortality by his insinuation of bigotry and rationalization on the part of modern apologists.

Gibbon observes that for a long period Jewish religious hopes were confined to this-world boundaries. "[I]t is darkly insinuated by the prophets, and during the long period which elapsed between the Egyptian and the Babylonian servitudes, the hopes as well as fears of the Jews appear to have been confined within the narrow compass of the present life." (*DF-15*, II, 23) The focus is on the passions—"hopes as well as fears"—when Gibbon attends to the issue of immortality. It is out of Judaism's latter sectarian rivalry of Sadducees and Pharisees that the practical importance of immortality as a religious belief emerges for the Jews. The Sadducees, aristocratic, tradition-bound, were attached to a literal view of the Mosaic law, and rejected the doctrine. The Pharisees, however, imported the doctrine ("they accepted, under the name of traditions, several speculative tenets from the philosophy or religion of the eastern nations") from the East and made it a critical element of their religious outlook. "[A]s the Pharisees, by the austerity of their manners, had drawn into their party the body of the Jewish people, the immortality of the soul became the prevailing sentiment of the synagogue, under the reign of the Asmonæan princes and pontiffs . . . . Their zeal, however, added nothing to its evidence, or even probability." (*DF-15*, II, 24)

The Pharisees, in effect, "politicized" the idea of immortality, or to use Gibbon's language, it became an instrument of their ambition. In order to politicize an idea, the evil consequences and dimensions of disbelief in that idea need to be creatively and dramatically portrayed so as to justify coercive action against those who express doubt in that idea. In a word, politicizing an idea involves criminalizing dissent from it. The harm resulting in disbelief is portrayed as so deleterious that the disbeliever deserves to be punished. With the politicalization of the future life doctrine by the Pharisees, no longer is immortality an open, speculative question but an incorporated element of an ideological movement. Once ensconced as a piece of ideology, it assumes a more immediate practical significance. The espousal of it is dictated because its value is primarily that of a mark of distinction from rival sectarians; one must affirm it in order to be an esteemed member of the espousing sect. Gone is the consideration of this idea as an abstract, philosophical question, it has now entered the domain of ideology.

Gibbon's short, concise account of the career of the future-life doctrine in Judaism is an opening gambit in a more expansive and harsh critique of its role in Christianity. He observes of the Pharisees, as cited above, that their "zeal [for the doctrine] however, added nothing to its evidence, or even probability"—a blunt reminder that the doctrine's appeal is primarily to the passions—and then Gibbon moves immediately to the Christian reception of the doctrine. "[A]nd it was still necessary that the doctrine of life and immortality, which had been dictated by nature, approved by reason, and received by superstition, should obtain the sanction of Divine truth from the authority and example of Christ." (*DF-15*, II, 24)

The afterlife doctrine, a product of Jewish sectarian zeal, becomes an essential element of Christian superstition, indeed, there is an element of necessity in this—"it was still *necessary* that the doctrine . . . *should* obtain the sanction of Divine truth," etc. Also, in the progression of the doctrine outlined by Gibbon— "dictated by nature, approved by reason, and received by superstition"—we can detect, in the most concise, adumbrated form, his conception of how religious belief establishes itself naturalistically. "Nature" here is of course ironically ambiguous but in this context is suggestive of human nature. Human nature is such that belief is "dictated" by the passions—belief, remember, chases passion. And even though beliefs are "approved by reason," without the corrective of common life experience, these beliefs become part of a body of superstition.

The Christians took from the Jews a preoccupation with the afterlife and made the concern for the soul a primary consideration. These same Christians then erected a massive ideational edifice that featured a dichotomous moral world of the saved and the damned with, respectively, the assignment of the widest extremes of reward and punishment. "Whilst the happiness and glory of a temporal reign were promised to the disciples of Christ, the most dreadful calamities were denounced against an unbelieving world. The edification of the new Jerusalem was to advance by equal steps with the destruction of the mystic Babylon . . . ." (*DF-15*, II, 27) Here then is the elevation of correct belief in an area that was once for the amusement of speculative philosophers. All believers in a sense become philosophers or theologians who seriously grapple with the truth and falsity of esoteric doctrinal matters. Gibbon quotes the pagan historian, Sozomen, who mocks the fourth-century Christians in Constantinople. "'This city . . . is full of mechanics and slaves, who are all of them profound theologians, and preach in the shops and in the streets. If you desire a man to change a piece of silver, he informs you wherein the Son differs from the Father . . . .'" (*DF-27*, III, 150) In contrast to the pagans, belief and disbelief relating to the content of doctrine are much more important to Christians.[23] Gibbon referring to the pagan religions, says "[t]he providence of the gods, as it related to public communities rather than to private individuals, was principally displayed on the visible theatre of the present world." (*DF-15*, II, 22) He is pointing out the primacy of ceremony for the pre-Christians and the essential social nature of the religion. Christianity elevates creed over ceremony, and with the dominance of creed emerges the overwhelming concern with the maintenance of orthodoxy and the punishment of heterodoxy and heresy. (Ibid., 31)[24]

"It is one measure of the difference between the pagan Emperors and their Christian successors," writes Robin Lane Fox, "that the former never had to devise and promote a deliberate religious policy for all their subjects."(Ibid., 593) The Christian emperors unlike their pagan predecessors, as Lane Fox seems to suggest, were confronted with a religion that claimed and demanded a universality of belief. For the pagan Emperors religion seemed to be part of a seamless social fabric. Its development was organic. Its primary expressions, as Gibbon notes, were found in ceremonial manifestations.[25] Gibbon's interpretation of the career of the doctrine of immortality in the history of Christianity fits into place with his general pessimistic reading of the institutionalization of Christianity. Christianity unfolds dramatically with the elaborate interplay of spirituality and ambition. The politics of immortality is one feature of this interplay and represents a betrayal of the ideal of freedom of thought as embraced by pagan philosophers. Late in the *Decline and Fall,* Gibbon says, the "philosophers of Athens and Rome enjoyed the blessings, and asserted the rights, of civil and religious freedom." (*DF-52*, VI, 35) The spirit of these pagan philosophers represents for Gibbon a measure by which to gauge the "progress" of Christianity as it descends into the world. This measurement is captured in its most vivid form with Gibbon's description of the character of the medieval Pope, just twenty-nine pages from the end of the *Decline and Fall.* "A

---

[23]Robin Lane Fox, *Pagans and Christians* (New York: Alfred A. Knopf, Inc., 1989), 31. Fox writes that the pagans put the greater emphasis on religious *acts* over *beliefs.*

[24]Lane Fox writes: "[t]o pagans, the Greek word *hairesis* meant a school of thought, not a false and pernicious doctrine. It applied to the teachings of different philosophical schools and sometimes to the medical schools too. Significantly, some pagans denied it to the Sceptics because they doubted everything and held no positive doctrine themselves: Sceptics, in turn opposed them, wanting to be a *hairesis*, like other schools. Among pagans, the opposite of 'heterodoxy' was not 'orthodoxy,' but 'homodoxy,' meaning agreement."

[25]Wilfred Cantwell Smith, *The Meaning and End of Religion: A New Approach to the Religious Traditions of Mankind* (New York: Macmillan, 1963), 180-81, argues that Christianity is perhaps of all the major religions the most absorbed with belief as a consciously formulated set of propositions, due primarily to the heavy intellectualist influence of Greek thought on Christianity.

Christian, a philosopher, and a patriot will be equally scandalized by the temporal kingdom of the clergy; and the local majesty of Rome, the remembrance of her consuls and triumphs, may seem to embitter the sense, and aggravate the shame, of her slavery." (*DF-70*, VII, 309)   The Christian, the philosopher, the patriot represent for Gibbon respectively the values of religion, philosophy, and civility. All three, under "the temporal kingdom of the clergy," have been diminished. Religion has decayed into superstition. Philosophy has been betrayed. Civility is lost.

Gibbon then draws the anti-philosophical portrait of the ecclesiastical prince. "The successful candidate is drawn from the church, and even the convent; from the mode of education and life the most adverse to reason, humanity, and freedom. In the trammels of servile faith, he has learnt to believe because it is absurd, to revere all that is contemptible, and to despise whatever might deserve the esteem of a rational being; to punish error as a crime, to reward mortification and celibacy as the first of virtues; to place the saints of the calendar above the heroes of Rome and the sages of Athens; and to consider the missal or the crucifix as more useful instruments than the plough or the loom." (*DF-70*, VII, 310)

Here described is the complete overthrow of classical values, a world turned upside down. Belief is now determined by absurdity. Servility supplants the ideal of freedom. The exaltation of the missal or crucifix (objects that fix human energies on the "invisible world") above or in place of "useful" instruments that help create food and clothing signifies for Gibbon the utter surrender of the human spirit to the enervation of superstition. The politics of immortality with its destruction of freedom of thought was an important part of growth of superstition and credulity that culminated in the eclipse of the values of reason, humanity, and freedom.

IV. Martyrdom and Worship of the Dead

*But because there is no natural knowledge of man's estate after death;
much less of the reward that is then to be given to breach of Faith; but
only a belief grounded upon other mens saying, that they know it
supernaturally, or that they know those, that knew them, that knew others,
that knew it supernaturally . . . .*

Thomas Hobbes

Out of the Christian preoccupation with the afterlife grew one of its most remarkable innovations—the worship of saints and relics. "The innumerable miracles of which the tombs of the martyrs were the perpetual theatre revealed to the pious believer the actual state and constitution of the invisible world; and his religious speculations appeared to be founded on the firm basis of fact and experience." (*DF-28*, III, 223) The linkage between miracles and the absorption with the afterlife is cast into a metaphor of theatrical production. Miracles and the setting of the martyrs' tombs form part of the "perpetual theatre" out of which a dramatic experience of the "invisible world" emerges. The tombs are the props which stimulate the imagination in its relentless quest to capture in detail the "actual state and constitution" of the next world. Gibbon then facetiously links "religious speculations" about the "constitution of the invisible world" to a "firm basis of fact and experience." Yet, this link, placed in the theatrical context of Christian eschatology, makes a certain kind of sense. "Whatever might be the condition of vulgar souls, in the long interval between the dissolution and the resurrection of their bodies, *it was evident* that the superior spirits of the saints and martyrs did not consume that portion of their existence in silent and inglorious sleep." (*DF-28*, III, 223, italics added) It was evident indeed! Those martyrs of the faith, passing from the visible to the invisible world, become active spiritual creatures, the agents of miracles. The entire workings of the afterlife become in themselves profoundly miraculous aspects of the Christian world.

Into the worship of saints and relics Gibbon writes another piece of the story of Christianity's corruption and its descent into superstition. "In the long period of twelve hundred years which elapsed between the reign of Constantine and the reformation of Luther the worship of saints and relics corrupted the pure and perfect simplicity of the Christian model; and some symptoms of degeneracy may be observed even in the first generations which adopted and cherished this pernicious innovation." (*DF-28*, III, 221)

This synopsis reiterates Gibbon's pessimistic view of Christianity and carries forward his theme of Christianity's spiritual corruption and decline. From a panoramic perspective the astute historian observes early on these "symptoms of degeneracy." The "pure and perfect simplicity of the Christian model" is illusory—a myth that is dispelled by historical scrutiny. The reader is subtly but grimly reminded of the inevitability of Christianity's corruption. Thus, when Gibbon focuses the historian's critical glance on the afterlife dimensions of Christian history—just as he does with miracles—the "weak and degenerate" nature of human beings emerges.

Given the Christian preoccupation with the afterlife and the eternal status of the soul, martyrdom becomes an understandable though amazing phenomenon. Since bodily death is not the end of existence, its terror for the true believer is radically diminished. Martyrdom is the greatest evidence of certainty that a creed can deliver. Since belief qua belief can never be coerced, the willingness of someone to die rather than to repudiate his belief publicly is an extraordinarily compelling phenomenon—hence the great affinity of many religions for martyrdom.

The suffering of the early Christians for their beliefs is one of Christianity's richest and most moving accounts. Tales of early Christian martyrdom abound, and because the almost "suicidal" behavior seems so completely contrary to the powerful human inclination for self-preservation, they can hardly fail to impress. "The Christians sometimes supplied by their voluntary declaration the want of an accuser, rudely disturbed the public service of Paganism, and, rushing in crowds round the tribunal of the magistrates, called upon them to pronounce and to inflict the sentence of law." (*DF-16*, II, 112) What is one to make of such enthusiasm for martyrdom? From the pagan perspective, the Christian who dies for the truth of his faith is an almost incomprehensible figure. "'Unhappy men!' exclaimed the proconsul Antonius to the Christians of Asia; 'unhappy men! if you are thus weary of your lives, is it so difficult for you to find ropes and precipices?'" (*DF-16*, II, 112) Gibbon himself understands the behavior of the early Christians as little more than a sort of dementia brought about by their "unnatural" devaluation of the current life in the questionable hope of attaining some future life reward. The motivational power of the hope for afterlife awards was, after its initial thrust, unsustainable. "But, although devotion had raised, and eloquence continued to inflame, this fever of the mind, it insensibly gave way to the more natural hopes and fears of the human heart, to the love of life, the apprehension of pain, and the horror of dissolution." (*DF-16*, II, 113) This marks the distinctive passage of Christianity from its early fanatical, anti-worldly beginnings to its ultimate institutional stage where ambition, power, honor and other this-worldly objects of human desire became a more conspicuous part of its history.

Related to the phenomenon of Christian martyrdom is the emergence within the church of the worship of relics. A belief in personal immortality, of course, radically changes one's view of death. Death becomes a state of sleep from which one awakens. The doctrine of the future state combined with the belief in resurrection gives the dead body something it never had before, a future. The Mosaic law had pronounced the grave to be an unclean place to be avoided by the living. With Christianity the bodies of the believers, particularly the martyrs and the saints, became objects of hope and veneration.[26]

Chapter twenty-eight of the *Decline and Fall* (one of the shortest but most vitriolic) describes the introduction of the worship of saints and relics. The target is more specifically Catholic than Protestant Christianity and hence Gibbon is more openly mocking and derisive. The initial description he provides is a quotation from a hostile, pagan observer. "The monks . . . are the authors of the new worship, which, in the place of one of those deities, who are conceived by the understanding, has substituted the meanest and most contemptible slaves. The heads, salted and pickled, of those infamous malefactors, who for the multitude of their crimes have suffered a just and ignominious death; their bodies, still marked by the impression of the lash, and the scars of those tortures which were inflicted by the sentence of the magistrate; such . . . are the gods which the earth produces in our days; such are the martyrs, the supreme arbitrators of our prayers and petitions to the Deity, whose tombs are now consecrated as the objects of the veneration of the people." (*DF-28*, III, 219)

Such is the incomprehensible "new worship" of relics and saints by Christians as construed by the Pagan sophist Eunapius, expressing the most outraged sense of defilement. Relic worship was a radical departure from the pagan and Jewish practices, as the sense of revulsion of this writer seems to suggest.[27]

Gibbon then provides a Humean interpretation of relic worship. In fact, he credits Hume in a footnote for his philosophical insights. "Mr. Hume . . . observes, like a philosopher, the natural flux and reflux of polytheism and theism." (*DF-28*, III, 225, n.92) The "flux and reflux" to which Gibbon refers comes directly from the *Natural History* where Hume argues that monotheism and polytheism rise from and fade into each other. "[T]he principles of religion have a kind of flux and reflux in the human mind, and . . . men have a natural tendency to rise from idolatry to theism, and to sink again from theism into idolatry." (*NHR*, 56-57) The flux-

---

[26]Lane Fox, *Pagans and Christians*, 447.

[27]See Peter Brown, *The Cult of the Saints: Its Rise and Function in Latin Christianity* (Chicago: University of Chicago Press, 1981), 2-3. Brown notes that the Christian practice of relic worship broke down previously established boundaries between the living and the dead. Bones, corpses, etc. began to be placed in areas where they never before would have been permitted.

reflux movement is guided by an unstable tension between the application of an abstract reasoning to causal relations and a kind of anthropomorphic reasoning. The search by human beings to understand what Hume calls, the "unknown causes" of all the various natural events, particularly those events which directly affect them, produces explanations in concrete, tangible, recognizable forms. "[T]he active imagination of men, uneasy in this abstract conception of objects, about which it is incessantly employed, begins to render them more particular, and to clothe them in shapes more suitable to its natural comprehension. It represents them to be sensible, intelligent beings, like mankind; actuated by love and hatred, and flexible by gifts and entreaties, by prayers and sacrifices." (*NHR*, 57)

Causal forces, it seems, become anthropomorphized. It is easy, perhaps natural, to make them into creatures resembling human beings. But the activity of worship gradually elevates the status of the gods to the point where they become entities with highly abstract, difficult-to-comprehend qualities like perfection, omnipotence, infinity, etc. Out of polytheism, or idolatry comes monotheism, i.e., one perfect, infinite, all powerful being. But for most people (the "vulgar" in Hume's parlance) intercessor-beings become necessary bridges to the perfect god and hence the invention of demi-gods, intercessors and the like. Here then is the reflux movement back to idolatry. One perfect god is beyond the comprehension of most. The intercessor beings, however, become increasingly earthy, and as Hume says, "at last destroy themselves, and by the vile representations, which they form of their deities, make the tide turn again toward theism." (*NHR*, 58)

Gibbon applies this flux-reflux notion of Hume's to the relic worship phenomenon with his own particular twist. First of all, Gibbon asks, how did all of this come about? How did all these martyrs of the Church reach this elevated status? "Without approving the malice, it is natural enough to share the surprise, of the Sophist, the spectator of a revolution which raised those obscure victims of the laws of Rome to the rank of celestial and invisible protectors of the Roman empire." (*DF-28*, III, 219) Gibbon in his own inimitable way then explains. The process initially began with the adoration of St. Peter and Paul whose bones were held at the Vatican ("the Vatican and the Ostian road were distinguished by the tombs, or rather by the *trophies,* of those spiritual heros."). (*DF-28*, III, 220, italics added) These were visited and adored by the Emperor who then resided in the new capital, Constantinople. Not to be outdone by the West, the Eastern empire unearthed and installed in Church of the Apostles the bodies of Saints Andrew, Luke, and Timothy as well as the ashes of Samuel, Israel's great judge and prophet. "The relics of Samuel were received by the people with the same joy and reverence which they would have shown to the living prophet; the highways, from Palestine to the gates of Constantinople, were filled with an uninterrupted procession." (*DF-28*, III, 220)

Success spawns imitation. A lucrative traffic for the remains of saints and martyrs was created. Gibbon in fact puts the discussion in the language of commerce. "The satisfactory experience that the relics of saints were more valuable than gold or precious stones stimulated the clergy to multiply the treasures of the church." (*DF-28*, III, 221). Relics thus worked enormously to the advantage of the church in providing the vulgar with visible objects to worship, and they became so popular that the bones of fictitious heros of the faith sprang up when necessary to meet popular demand. "To the invincible band of genuine and primitive martyrs, they added myriads of imaginary heroes, who had never existed except in the fancy of crafty or credulous legendaries . . . ." (*DF-28*, III, 221) The saints and martyrs became intermediary gods and acted as intercessors before the Almighty God on behalf of their particular votaries who maintained their shrines and worshiped their remains. Out of the monotheism of original Christianity with its adoration of an omniscient, omnipotent, infinite being came the massive proliferation of the saints and martyrs. From the flux of Christian theism came the reflux of polytheistic saint worship. "The imagination, which had been raised by a painful effort to the contemplation and worship of the Universal Cause, eagerly embraced such inferior objects of adoration as were more proportioned to its gross conceptions and imperfect faculties. The sublime and simple theology of the primitive Christians was gradually corrupted; and the monarchy of heaven, already clouded by metaphysical subtleties, was degraded by the introduction of a popular mythology, which tended to restore the reign of polytheism." (*DF-28*, III, 225)[28]

Gibbon was contemplating the movement of medieval Christianity toward a polytheist mode of belief aided by belief in miracles. "[T]he progress of superstition would have been much less rapid and victorious, if the faith of the people had not been assisted by the seasonable aid of visions and miracles." (*DF-28*, III, 221-22). The progress of Christianity was actually part of a cyclical movement which culminated in the gross superstition of medieval Christianity with its plethora of Gods. The rise of Protestantism with its rejection of saint worship represented a turning point in the cycle (recalling Hume, idolatry becomes so gross and crude that it eventually destroys itself) and initiated the movement back toward theism. Gibbon himself notes Luther's Reformation as the terminus point. (*DF-28*, III, 221)

---

[28]Also, see Brown, *Cult of the Saints*, 13-18. Brown also notes the link of Hume's *Natural History* to chapter twenty-eight of the *Decline and Fall*. Brown is quite critical of what he calls a two-tiered model of religious change by Hume in which the vulgar remain forever limited to popular superstition while reserving to the intellectual elite the possibility for growth and improvement.

The irony of the chapter is immense. The institutionalization of Christianity with the attendant "metaphysical subtleties" becomes from the perspective of the philosophic historian a phenomenon signaling a natural but inevitable corruption. Miracles, a preoccupation with the afterlife, worship of the dead, and the elevation of martyrs into saints are all central features of the history of Christianity and they play an important role in the decline of the empire. But Gibbon's history of Christianity is skeptical philosophic history. Just as Christian miracles are shown to be a manifestation of the credulity of human nature, so is immortality the work of human vanity.

CHAPTER FIVE

PERSECUTION, PLATONISM, AND THE VIRULENCE OF METAPHYSICS

I. The Persecution of Christianity

If there be found among you, within any of thy gates which the Lord thy God giveth thee, man or woman, that hath wrought wickedness in the sight of the Lord thy God, in transgressing his covenant. And hath gone and served other gods, and worshiped them, either the sun or moon, or any of the host of heaven, which I have not commanded. . . . Then shalt thou bring forth that man or that woman, which have committed that wicked thing, unto thy gates, even that man or that woman, and shalt stone them with stones, till they die.

Deuteronomy 17:2-5.

The history of Christianity affords ample opportunities for reflection on the nature of religious persecution. Christians endured it from the Roman state, fellow Christians, Jews, and pagan adversaries. In turn, Christians inflected it upon pagans, Jews, and heretics. Certainly, as moralists and as critics of Christianity, Hume and Gibbon occupied themselves with the phenomenon of religious persecution, particularly when Christians were the agents. They viewed it as eighteenth-century secular-oriented skeptics, disdainful of religious enthusiasm and in a vein of virtual rational incomprehensibility. Cruelty, fanaticism, arrogance were all elements that composed the mentality of religious fanatics. Hume wrote graphically of the religious persecution in sixteenth-century England and France that was a grisly feature of the Protestant-Catholic rupture of Christendom. Gibbon wove many twists and turns of Christian persecution into his narrative—it was a persistent, recurring element in his treatment of religion. The history of religion and the history of persecution seemed to be inexorably interwoven. His attention, however, was focused primarily on the unfolding of the history of Christian persecution: it is the Christian religion that triumphs over pagan Rome and imposes itself on the Western world.

Hume's most explicit formulations of his views on religious persecution are found in the *Dialogues* and the *Essays*. He also dwelt in some depth on the major events of Christian ignomy in his *History of England*—the Marian persecutions, the Saint Bartholemew's massacre, and other atrocities—and in his condemnation of them he is at his severest. "Human nature," writes Hume, "appears not, on any occasion, so detestable, and at the same time so absurd, as in these religious persecutions, which sink men below infernal spirits in wickedness, and below the beasts in folly." (*HE*, III, 341) Much of Hume's animus toward Christianity appears to arise from his historical emersion in the sectarian conflicts which led him to view Christianity as a bigoted, persecution-prone religion presided over by corrupt, manipulating priests and raging ministers.

Gibbon likewise featured the violent work of religious sectarians throughout the *Decline and Fall*. Indeed, the persecution associated with the history of Christianity is a quite salient characteristic and gives moral ammunition to critics of the Faith.[1] Within a relatively short time after their persecution by pagans, *Christians* became the perpetrators directing their persecuting energies not only toward the practitioners of the pagan religions they had rejected but toward fellow Christians who ventured into the paths of heterodoxy.[2]

In chapter sixteen of the *Decline and Fall* Gibbon continued his attack on Christianity. His observations were aimed at deflating the moral heroism of early Christianity—a display of his own animus toward what he viewed as the early development of a bigoted religion. Gibbon's account of the conduct of the Roman government toward the early Christians accused the apologists of grossly exaggerating both the nature and extent of the persecution suffered by the church. Even worse, Gibbon linked much of the martyrdom to the delusions of the fanatical Christians. The early persecution of Christianity, in effect, was in many instances a grudging but tempered reaction of the Roman state to seditious outbursts of religious fanaticism. What kind of people were these that, on occasion, even sought out persecution? "The behaviour of the Christians was too remarkable to escape the notice of the ancient philosophers; but they seem to have considered it with much less admiration than astonishment." (*DF-16*, II, 112) Gibbon appears to share the astonishment of the ancient philosophers. Religious zeal was, as it was with Hume, incomprehensible.

Gibbon concludes chapter sixteen by making an extremely invidious comparison of Hugo Grotius's claim for the Catholic persecution of Protestants in the Netherlands during the reign of Charles V against the claims of martyrdom by the early church apologists. "If we are obliged to submit our belief to the authority

---

[1]For a detailed historical study of persecution in Christianity, see E. S. P. Haynes, *Religious Persecution: A Study in Political Psychology* (London: Duckworth and Co., 1904). Wilbur Jordan's *The Development of Religious Toleration In England* 4 vols. (1932-1940; reprint, Gloucester, MA: Peter Smith, 1965) is a massive but splendid historical study dealing with the themes of religious persecution and religious toleration. Also see Scott L. Waugh and Peter D. Diehl, eds., *Christendom and Its Discontents: Exclusion, Persecution, and Rebellion, 1000-1500* (Cambridge: Cambridge University Press, 1996).

[2]G. C. Coulton, *Inquisition and Liberty* (Boston: Beacon Press, 1959), 15-16, writes that Constantine was more severe against heretical priests than against pagans.

of Grotius, it must be allowed that the number of Protestants who were executed in a single province and a single reign far exceeded that of the primitive martyrs in the space of three centuries and of the Roman empire." (*DF-16*, II, 148) By introducing this comparison of ancient-modern martyrdom as an issue of Grotius's credibility, Gibbon not only accuses the early church of hypocrisy and delusion in its claims of Roman persecution, he also strikes at the credibility of the early church apologists. Though Grotius himself is an interested party, and his "authority" is indeed a matter of question, Gibbon suggests that there are two reasons to believe that Grotius is a credible figure: his reputation for dispassion and great learning, and the fact that the technology of printing and communication would make it easier to dispute his exaggeration and mendacity. "In the Netherlands alone, more than one hundred thousand of the subjects Charles the Fifth are said to have suffered by the hand of the executioner; and this extraordinary number is attested by Grotius, a man of genius and learning, who preserved his moderation amidst the fury of contending sects, and who composed the annals of his own age and country, at a time when the invention of printing had facilitated the means of intelligence and increased the danger of detection." (*DF-16*, II, 148) Gibbon credits Grotius with the strength of character to resist the violent passions that fuel religious fanaticism, but Grotius is nevertheless suspect by his Protestant bias. Gibbon is rigorously following his norm of impartiality and will not fully credit *any* testimony from someone who has an interest in it other than the truth. In a footnote Gibbon adds, "Fra Paolo. . . reduces the number of Belgic martyrs to 50,000. In learning and moderation, Fra Paolo was not inferior to Grotius. The priority of time gives some advantage to the evidence of the former, which he loses on the other hand by the distance of Venice from the Netherlands." (*DF-16*, II, 148, n.187) So, it is still somewhat uncertain what numbers to believe. However suspect Grotius might be in his claims of persecution, the early church apologists emerge by comparison as wholly unbelievable. "[I]f Grotius should be convicted of exaggerating the merit and sufferings of the Reformers; we shall be naturally led to inquire what confidence can be placed in the doubtful and imperfect monuments of ancient credulity; what degree of credit can be assigned to a courtly bishop, and a passionate declaimer, who, under the protection of Constantine, enjoyed the exclusive privilege of recording the persecutions inflicted on the Christians by the vanquished rivals or disregarded predecessors of their gracious sovereign." (*DF-16*, II, 148) Just how much persecution did the early Christians endure? Gibbon's assault on the credibility of the early church apologists via Grotius badly spoils the moral authority that arises from a solidly established tradition of martyrdom. Even worse from a moral standpoint, the comparison Gibbon draws of Catholic persecution of

Protestants with the Roman persecution of Christians makes Christians appear especially sanguinary.

Chapter sixteen was sacrilege! Not only was the glorious martyrdom that imbued early Christianity with a deeply moving sense of spirituality and idealism derogated, Gibbon had unceremoniously turned the tables: the victim was transmogrified into the perpetrator. Christianity became Gibbon's model of a religion that persecutes[3]. Christians in a sense, suggests Gibbon, were even more deserving of condemnation in *their* persecution of others than the pagan persecutors because the pagans were reacting defensively to an assault on their long established traditions, whereas Christian action was an open and egregious violation of their professed principles of benevolence and humanity. "In the cruel reigns of Decius and Diocletian, Christianity had been proscribed, as a revolt from the ancient and hereditary religion of the empire; and the unjust suspicions which were entertained of a dark and dangerous faction were, in some measure, countenanced by the inseparable union and rapid conquests of the Catholic church. But the same excuses of fear and ignorance cannot be applied to the Christian emperors, who violated the precepts of humanity and the gospel." (*DF-28*, III, 215) Violating the "precepts of humanity and the gospel" were serious charges indeed, making the early Christians out to be profoundly hypocritical and outrageously cruel. Gibbon leveled them against those who had institutionalized Christianity. Persecution by the Church was a grim historical reality confronting the philosophic historian of Christianity, and it takes on a special significance in light of the role that philosophy itself plays in that history.

Gibbon's writing of religious history, specifically Christian history, thus, finds him at once revolted and fascinated with the violence and persecution in which it is immersed. His study of persecution adds still another melancholy dimension to his career as a philosophic historian. Just as he impugned the testimony of those who affirmed the miracles of Christianity, and just as he recreated the austere fanaticism of Christian afterlife preoccupations and impuned their uselessness, so

---

[3]See, H. A. Drake, "Lambs Into Lions: Explaining Early Christian Intolerance," *Past and Present* 153 (Nov. 1996): 3-34. Drake faults Gibbon for an unfair and unbalanced presentation of Christianity as an intolerant, persecuting religion. Gibbon, he argues, plays down pagan persecutors and fails to acknowledge that Christians also spoke for freedom of conscience and toleration. Because of Gibbon, Christianity has born the odium of being a persecuting religion. "Here then is the problem: if early Christians could speak for toleration as well as intolerance, it is no longer possible to account for the turn to coercion by a newly empowered Christianity in the fourth century with the premise that such coercion was a natural, logical, or inevitable outcome of predictions inherent in and unique to that faith." While I believe that Drake is correct in his assessment of Gibbon's bias toward pagan Rome and his animus toward the early Christians, in Gibbon's defense, it should be said that Gibbon did not, as Drake seems to suggest, hold Christianity to be uniquely intolerant. He argued that fanaticism is a pitfall for many forms of faith, particular for monotheistic forms such as Islam and Judaism, as well as Christianity.

then with some reluctance he also uncovered a long history of persecution beneath the Christian message of love and forgiveness. Gibbon with a somber tone invoking perhaps the specter of Tacitus with his suspicion of rationalizations might be tempted to utter that things are not always as they appear, and Christianity is not always what Christians have represented it to be. In a passing sarcastic remark about the accomplishments of Innocent III late in the *Decline and Fall*, Gibbon quips that "Innocent may boast of the two most signal triumphs over sense and humanity, the establishment of transubstantiation and the origin of the inquisition." (*DF-59*, VI, 369-70) Innocent for Gibbon is the embodiment of corrupted Christianity. He invented not only the doctrine of transubstantiation—a piece of theological nonsense—but put together the Inquisition, an institution representing the nadir (or the apex, depending upon your interpretation) of the Church's persecuting career. Innocent's spiritual contribution to mankind in Gibbon's cynical assessment is the vanquishment of common sense and a fettering of free thinking, and the institutionalization of cruelty.

Chapter fifteen of the *Decline and Fall* immersed the miraculous origins of Christianity in doubt. Chapter sixteen followed in its iconoclastic wake with a challenge to the Christian interpretation of the early years of the church's martyrdom. Gibbon's own version of Christian martyrdom was quite obviously intended to be the antidote to that of the apologists. Apologetic historians in their endeavors to create suitable martyrs and heroes understandably sought to obliterate or describe euphemistically those pieces of the historical picture which showed the members of their faith as perpetrators of violence and persecution, while at the same time they strove to highlight the events of their own victimization.

The motives of ambition and interest are predictably at work in apologetic history. Saint Augustine, as Gibbon noted, argues passionately for the righteousness of Christian persecution of the heretical Donatists. "By these severities, [persecuting measures taken against the Donatists by the emperor Honorius] which obtained the warmest approbation of St. Augustin, great numbers of Donatists were reconciled to the Catholic church; but the fanatics, who still persevered in their opposition, were provoked to madness and despair." (*DF-33*, III, 427) Interestingly, Gibbon here takes some pains in a footnote to point with tempered derision to St. Augustine's turnabout in his view of the persecution of heretics. "St. Augustin altered his opinion with regard to the proper treatment of heretics. His pathetic declaration of pity and indulgence for the Manicheans has been inserted by Mr. Locke among the choice specimens of his commonplace book. Another philosopher, the celebrated Bayle, has refuted, with superfluous diligence and ingenuity, the arguments by which the bishop of Hippo justified, in his old age, the persecution of the Donatists." (*DF-33*, III, 427, n.22) Gibbon's "in his old age," insinuates that Augustine's youthful Christianity was marred by insincerity or opportunism while the full maturation of his faith culminated in bigotry. In fact, Gibbon cannot seem to resist putting a gloss on Augustine that ultimately seems to make his apologetics for persecution an easy casualty of the Calvinism of Pierre Bayle[4] and renders the individual career of this great saint and theologian a larger symbol of the historical decline of Christianity itself.[5] As it matures, Christianity transforms itself into a rigid, persecuting ideology.

Gibbon's analysis of the ideological dimensions of Christian persecution employs an important demarcation of the boundaries between philosophy and religion that is articulated by Hume. Hume linked much of Christianity's intolerance to the metaphysical excrescence of Platonism that was absorbed by Christian theology. The antipathy to Plato was widely shared by Enlightenment thinkers, as Peter Gay points out. Plato was viewed as a mystic and closely linked to neoplatonic Christians such as Augustine.[6] Plato's philosophy drew heavy criticism from Hume for what he viewed as its flights of imagination and failure to be constrained by any common life experience. Consider this invidious comparison drawn by Hume of Plato with Plutarch. It gives some sense of how deeply Hume believed that Plato and Platonism had departed from direct, plain spoken, common sense thinking and writing. "I must confess that discourse of Plutarch, concerning the silence of the oracles, is in general of so odd a texture, and so unlike his other productions, that one is at a loss what judgment to form of it. It is written in dialogue, which is a method of composition that Plutarch commonly but little affects. The personages he introduces advance very wild, absurd, and contradictory opinions, more like the visionary systems or ravings of Plato than the plain sense of Plutarch." (*Essays*, 463, n.278)

---

[4]Bayle, as Richard Popkin notes, developed a defense of religious toleration that extended to Jews, Socinians, Catholics, even atheists—far beyond where Locke would go in his *Essay on Toleration. Encyclopedia of Philosophy*, s.v. "Pierre Bayle."

[5]See Peter Brown, *Augustine of Hippo: A Biography* (New York: Dorset Press, 1986), particularly chapter 21, "Disciplina" for a less harsh and probably fairer account of Augustine's conflict with the Donatists. Brown's Augustine is less hypocritical and opportunistic than Gibbon's. Brown points out that the Donatists were "ruthless in defending themselves. Converts to Catholicism among their clergy were, especially, treated without mercy. The bishop of Bagai was set upon and left for dead by the congregation he had deserted to become a Catholic. . . . Theory and practice had gone hand in hand to reinforce Augustine's change of mind." (233)

[6]Gay, *Rise of Modern Paganism*, 84-86. "Thus the philosophes slighted whatever contribution Aristotle may have made to the scientific method; they saw him mainly as the favorite of the Scholastics—a pagan who had trafficked with the enemy. Their treatment of Plato, which has long perplexed and annoyed students of the eighteenth century, was equally shabby."

Quite obviously, Hume had a low regard for Plato as a philosopher.[7] His philosophizing, Hume seemed to suggest, was unconstrained by experience. Ernest Gellner's account of the evolution of philosophical thought has two extremely important points about Platonism that are of relevance for Hume's own criticism of Plato. First: "[e]mpirical referentiality is spurned in pure Platonism. The Ideas stand in moral judgement over facts; facts do not, as with us, stand in cognitive judgement over Ideas."[8] The spurning of "empirical referentiality" is precisely what Hume complains of with Platonic philosophers. Hume gives ontological and epistemological priority to facts in the form of what he sees as immediate sense experience. This is the very heart of his philosophy, and Hume is thoroughly modern in this sense and is one of the "us" referred to by Gellner. Second: "[t]he profound paradox of Platonism proper is that it preached a return to, or a fortification of, the closed communally organized society: but it did so by means which themselves illustrated, highlighted, and sprang from that liberation from traditional ritualism and communalism. Plato represented dogmatism pursued by liberal means, an authoritarianism with a rational face." (Ibid., 84-85) Here then is a second aspect of Platonism that Hume rejects; its authoritarianism. Both philosophy and religion, as Hume viewed them, are valuable human creations, but can be subject to great abuse. Philosophy detached from the constraints of experience spins out speculative theories that are harmless as long as they do not become the objects of devout and passionate interest and are entertained in a reflective, hypothetical manner. Speculative systems come and go. They provide amusement, and properly understood, they stimulate the philosophical enterprise, particularly in demonstrating the limits of the human understanding and the tendency to overreach. Religion though when combined with speculative, or what Hume calls "metaphysical philosophy," is vulnerable to a vanity of the mind and takes on a kind of arrogance in what it can claim to be true. "Here indeed lies the justest and most plausible objection against a considerable part of metaphysics, that they are not properly a science; but arise either from the fruitless efforts of human vanity, which would penetrate into subjects utterly inaccessible to the understanding, or from the craft of popular superstitions, which, being unable to

---

[7]Marie A. Martin, "Hume on Human Excellence," *Hume Studies* 18, no. 2 (November 1992), 383-99, argues for an interpretation of Hume's ethics that aligns him with the classical ethical tradition. "For Hume is a virtue ethicist, albeit one in modern dress, who, poised between the ancients and moderns, self-consciously chose to align himself with the ancient tradition, asserting its superiority over the modern. (383) While there is some truth in this—certainly Hume had an affinity with classical moralists like Cicero—the claim is quite misleading in my view. Hume was very much in opposition to all aspects of platonic philosophy including its ethical rationalism.

[8]Gellner, *Plough, Sword and Book*, 75.

defend themselves on fair ground, raise these intangling brambles to cover and protect their weakness." (*EHU*, 11)

Two themes are much in evidence in Hume. Both, as we shall see, also attain prominence in the *Decline and Fall*. First, is the natural tendency of the mind to overreach itself which is expressed in the form of vanity. Metaphysics is the failure of self-restraint at the intellectual level, a manifestation of that vanity. Second, is the fecklessness of philosophy through the abuse of language. Hume's metaphor, "intangling brambles" refers primarily to the language of metaphysicians and theologians, a language that signifies nothing—as in Gibbon's above reference to the doctrine of transubstantiation—and that is used primarily for purposes of obfuscation.[9] The resort to meaningless and obfuscatory language is a complaint that Gibbon repeatedly directed at the Christian theologians in the *Decline and Fall*. Consider this comparison rendered by Gibbon between the philosophically sophisticated Greeks and the rustic Western Latins. "In every age the Greeks were proud of their superiority in profane and religious knowledge; they had first received the light of Christianity; they had pronounced the decrees of the seven general councils; they alone possessed the *language of Scripture and philosophy*; nor should the barbarians immersed in the darkness of the West, presume to argue on the high and mysterious questions of theological science. These barbarians despised, in their turn, the restless and subtle levity of the Orientals, the authors of every heresy; and blessed their own simplicity, which was content to hold the tradition of the apostolic church." (*DF-60*, VI, 381-82, italics added)

Here is a matchless piece of ironic contrast aimed at Greek vanity and pomposity. To the Greeks with all their civilized advantages, including a sophisticated philosophical language and their invention of "theological science," Gibbon attributes the decline of Christianity. They are the *real* barbarians, the conjurers of darkness. The "language of Scripture and philosophy" merely begets "heresy" and betrays the simplicity of Apostolic Christianity.

In Gibbon's history of Christian theology we see a perspective unfold that points to the mutual corruption of philosophy and religion. Monotheism, of which Christianity is a prime example, becomes persecuting because, in contrast to mutually tolerating, mythopoeic polytheistic religions, it wields the weapons to "prove" its exclusive truth. The more important it becomes that religious belief be literally true, the more so it would seem that erroneous belief be condemned and proscribed.

Christianity, Gibbon seems to suggest, was infected by the virus of rational system in its merger with Greek speculative philosophy, particularly neoplatonism.

---

[9]For a philosophical study of the obfuscating use of language, see G. A. Wells, *Belief and Make-Belief: Critical Reflections on the Sources of Credulity* (La Salle, IL: Open Court, 1991).

J. G. A. Pocock in writing of Gibbon's view of philosophy notes that: "[a]ncient philosophy, in the proper sense, is. . . a problem for Gibbon; since by 'philosophy' he means nothing more or less than a methodical skepticism which frees the mind for its proper concerns, he is obliged to recognize it only in Lucretius or Cicero, and to dismiss the whole Athenian and Alexandrian endeavor as metaphysics and *esprit de systéme*."[10]   A rational system of belief claims universality and imposes coercion.[11] Resistance implies an illegitimate rivalry and invites persecution.

Gibbon had done his own critique of the *esprit de systéme* in his first published work, *Essai sur l'étude de la littérature*.[12] In the *Essai* Gibbon attempts to distinguish an *esprit philosophique* which respects the discovery of facts and the particularities of the world from an *esprit de systéme* (an anti-philosophical approach), which makes the world of experience fit the procrustean bed. The anti-philosophical approach *"consist à se frayer des routes nouvelles, et á fronder toute opinion dominante, fut-elle de Socrate ou d'un inquisiteur Portugais, par la seule raison qu'elle est dominante."* (*MW*, IV, 58)[13] Note that Gibbon invokes the image of the Inquisition. The Inquisition is the instantiation of persecuting ideology. In the history of Christianity is also a story of the corruption of religion and the abuse of philosophy. Platonic metaphysics as it comes to be appropriated by Christian theology helps make Christianity a religion of persecutors.

---

[10]Pocock, "Gibbon's *Decline and Fall* and the World View of the Late Enlightenment," 144.

[11]See Gellner, *Plough, Sword and Book*, 75-76 who defines Platonism and explains its coercive features. "By generic Platonism I mean the kind of ideology that makes its appearance with the religious use of writing, and which is sustained by an organized clerisy. . . . Generic Platonism clearly delineates the Transcendent, and makes it morally and doctrinally authoritative without bounds, i.e., universalistic in its claims."

[12]Giuseppe Giarrizzo, "Toward the *Decline and Fall*: Gibbon's Other Historical Interests," in *Edward Gibbon and the Decline and Fall of the Roman Empire*, 235. "In February, 1761 Gibbon published the *Essai sur l'étude de la littérature*. The structure and methodological objectives of this work, which was written partly in Lausanne and partly in Buriton, are very complex. The chapters written in Lausanne deal with the polemic against '*l'esprit de système*' as distinct from the '*esprit philosophique*,' and here Gibbon espouses Montesquieu's thought. In England, however, after reading Hume's *Natural History of Religion* (1757), Gibbon wrote chapters 57 and 58 which deal with the pagan 'system.'"

[13]Giarrizzo, "Toward the *Decline and Fall*: Gibbon's Other Historical Interests," 236 writes that the *Essai*'s theme is "the historical erudition that rejects the '*esprit de système*,' when research and facts demonstrate the abstract and superficially all-embracing nature of the 'system' while at the same time attempting to liberate knowledge of the past—which is necessary to legitimize or modify the present—from the tenets of Pyrrhonism."

II. The Humean View of Religious Persecution

The Ecclesiastiques take from young men, the use of reason, by certain charms compounded of metaphysiques, and miracles, and traditions, and abused scripture, whereby they are good for nothing else, but to execute what they command them.

Thomas Hobbes

The key to understanding Hume's philosophical and moral grasp of religious persecution and Gibbon's analysis of religious persecution in his history lies in discerning how they came to view the relation of religion to philosophy. Philosophy's value to humanity is as a highly useful corrective discipline against the perennial human inclination to extend knowledge beyond its natural limitations. "Accurate and just reasoning is the only catholic remedy, fitted for all persons and all dispositions; and is alone able to subvert that abstruse philosophy and metaphysical jargon, which being mixed up with popular superstition, renders it in a manner impenetrable to careless reasoners, and gives it the air of science and wisdom." (*EHU*, 12-13) Again, the concern with the abuse of language—words that signify nothing intelligible and which are used primarily for obfuscation. Metaphysics, Hume charges, masquerades as knowledge. Both religion and philosophy, as enterprises of human pride and ambition, are easily corruptible. (Hume perhaps retained enough of his native Calvinism to impress upon him the *weakness* of the human frame.)

Philosophy at its best (best in the Humean sense) is rooted in what Livingston calls a "tensed and narrative structure,"[14] i.e., a historical framework. In his *History of England* Hume claims a highly instructive value for history. History he viewed as "the great mistress of wisdom, [as it] furnishes examples of all kinds; and every prudential, as well as moral precept, may be authorized by those events which her enlarged mirror is able to present to us." (*HE*, V, 275) This metaphor of the "enlarged mirror" illustrates the point that history expands the human perspective making it easier to transcend the particularities of time and place and entertain a broader moral point of view. History, properly written and presented, effects a *moral* enlargement. Hume also sees history as a potential corrective for the philosopher. History can help to constrain a natural human inclination to overreach itself. "Even philosophers," says Hume in his essay, "Of the Study of History," "are apt to bewilder themselves in the subtlety of their speculations. . . . [b]ut I think it a remark worthy the attention of the speculative, that the historians have been almost without exception, the true friends of virtue. . . ." (*Essays*, 567) A

---

[14]Livingston, *Hume's Philosophy of Common Life*, 5.

remarkable confession! It suggests a certain tentativeness of Hume toward philosophy itself, and also lends support to the view that history has an integral, even primary place in Hume's philosophy. Philosophers, Hume seems to suggest, without a historical, common life corrective will loose touch with the reality that they are trying to understand. As Livingston notes, "[t]he moral world (the world of human action) is the product of ideas associated narratively, and so has, ontologically, a narrative structure. Historical understanding, then, is internal to any understanding of the existences that populate the moral world."[15] The "bewildering" tendencies of philosophers may give birth to all sorts of absurdities: extreme philosophical skepticism and dogmatic philosophy both do this. Hume seems to see the "bewildering" tendencies of philosophy coming from linkages with theology inspired by religious zeal, a phenomenon of great interest to the philosophic historian. The corruption of religion and philosophy and the proper role of philosophy as a check against what Hume sees as an overreaching of reason are major preoccupations of his work. "Happy, if we can unite the boundaries of the different species of philosophy, by reconciling profound enquiry with clearness, and truth with novelty! And still more happy, if, reasoning in this easy manner, we can *undermine the foundations of an abstruse philosophy*, which seems to have hitherto served only as a *shelter to superstition*, and a *cover to absurdity and error!*" (*EHU*, 16, italics added)

On the boundaries of proper philosophy lies a major pitfall—superstition, which perhaps in some way resembles it, but operates in the service of obfuscation and culminates in confusion. Hume wants his philosophy to destroy metaphysically pretentious philosophy ("undermine the foundations of an abstruse philosophy") *in order to* expose the corrupted intellectual framework of superstitious religion.[16] Hume's attack on miraculous testimony as a prop of superstition is precisely such an application of his philosophy. So also is his skeptical treatment of the Christian afterlife doctrine with its elaborate speculation on the future of the soul.

In order to understand more completely Hume's view of the relationship between philosophy and religion, it is necessary to examine a seminal passage in the *Treatise* where he sets up a profound contrast between philosophy and superstition. This passage comes in the conclusion to Book I of the *Treatise* where Hume is

---

[15]Livingston, *Hume's Philosophy of Common Life*, 5. Also, Danford, *David Hume and the Problem of Reason*, 77, has a similar view. "[T]he full Humean philosophy-is best represented by the *History of England*, along with the *Essays* and the posthumous *Dialogues*."

[16]See P. Russell, "Epigram, Pantheists, and Freethought in Hume's *Treatise*, 660-61. Russell argues that the *Treatise* is fully anti-Christian in its intentions and that it was aimed specifically at the Christian rationalism of Samuel Clarke, an argument that would support my contention that Hume had a strong desire to refute claims for the rationality of Christianity. Moreover, Russell argues that Hume writes in a conscious spirit of free thinking that traces its pedigree back through the deists and anti-Christians such as John Toland and Anthony Collins to Hobbes and Spinoza.

wrestling with the question of the value of the whole philosophical enterprise. (Though the following quotation in the text is continuous, I divide it for purposes of explication)

(1) 'Tis certain, that *superstition* is much more bold in its systems and hypotheses than *philosophy*; and while the latter contents itself with assigning new causes and principles of the phenomena, which appear in the visible world, the former opens a world of its own, and presents us with scenes, and beings, and objects, which are altogether new.

(2) Since therefore 'tis almost impossible for the mind of man to rest, like those of beasts, in that narrow circle of objects, which are the subject of daily conversation and action, we ought only to deliberate concerning the choice of our guide, and ought to prefer that which is safest and most agreeable.

(3) And in this respect I make bold to recommend *philosophy*, and shall not scruple to give it the preference to *superstition* of every kind or denomination.

(4) For as *superstition* arises naturally and easily from the popular opinions of mankind, it seizes more strongly on the mind, and is often able to disturb us in the conduct of our lives and actions.

(5) *Philosophy* on the contrary, if just, can present us only with mild and moderate sentiments; and if false and extravagant, its opinions are merely the objects of a cold and general speculation, and seldom go so far as to interrupt the course of our natural propensities. The Cynics are an extraordinary instance of philosophers, who from reasonings purely philosophical ran into as great extravagancies of conduct as any *Monk* or *Dervise* that ever was in the world. Generally speaking, the *errors in religion are dangerous; those in philosophy only ridiculous.* (*Treatise*, 271-72, italics added)

Note the first sentence in segment (1) and the last sentence in segment (5). Hume begins with a contrast of *philosophy* and *superstition* by virtue of their self-imposed limitations, and ends with an invidious comparison of *philosophy* and *religion* with respect to the practical consequences that errors in these activities give rise. Superstition is a corrupted form of religion. It is limitless in its projections, unconstrained, driven by the restlessness of the imagination, the natural quest for novelty, for new "scenes, and beings, and objects." Philosophy is distinguished by its self-discipline. Philosophy's self-defined domain, by contrast, is the "visible world" where philosophy's explanations are thus confined. Hume's boundaries for what we can legitimately claim to know are the parameters of our sense experience, the "visible world" and its observable, somewhat predictable phenomena. "Visible-invisible world" is a an image frequently resorted to by both Hume and Gibbon to create a stark contrast between useful and futile pursuits of the human intellect.

Segment (2) at first glance seems completely wrong. Constraining the mind of man to only what is "safest" and "agreeable" appears to be a dreary fetter to human thought and would seem to impoverish the imagination. Yet Hume in segment (3) gives philosophy a categorical recommendation over superstition. He provides the justification in (4) and (5). Segments (4) and (5) provide the practical contrast between philosophy and superstition. The errors of religion Hume says are "dangerous"; philosophy's mistakes and excesses are, at worst, merely objects of ridicule.

Religious and philosophical beliefs, Hume is arguing, have profound effects on behavior. The advantages of philosophy as a guide for conduct are related to the kinds of sentiments that philosophical speculation produces—"mild and moderate"—an effect due directly to the self-imposed, somewhat skeptical limitations of philosophy's activity to the visible world. The reason why superstition is dangerous, and philosophy is not, is because the invisible world of superstition remains forever unfathomable, unpredictable, terror-ridden; all those things which give rise to and stimulate the extreme sorts of passions such as intense fear, foreboding, and melancholy. Such passions in turn lead to extremes in human behavior and often to the undoing of fragile, self-imposed norms of self-restraint. The loosening of self-restraint in turn damages the community and spoils the work of civilization itself.

It is important, however, to note that Hume qualifies his recommendation of philosophy. Philosophy, "if just," Hume says, presents us with "mild and moderate sentiments." Philosophy too is corruptible. In one of his essays Hume writes: "[t]heories of abstract philosophy, systems of profound theology, have prevailed during one age: In a successive period, these have been universally exploded: their absurdity has been detected." (*Essays*, 242) The kind of philosophy Hume is speaking of is that which is disconnected from historical understanding. Philosophy understood in this way passes in and out like fashions, and the preference for one over another has less to do with the discovery of truth than with the vagaries of passion and inclination.

Hume as mentioned above links the persecution in the history of Christianity to its *esprit de systéme*, that is, its appropriation of dogmatic philosophy expressed by ancient philosophers such as Plato. In this essay, "The Rise and Progress of the Arts and Sciences," Hume writes: "I have sometimes been inclined to think, that interruptions in the periods of learning, were they not attended with such a destruction of ancient books, and the records of history, would be rather favourable to the arts and sciences, by breaking the progress of authority, and dethroning the tyrannical usurpers over human reason." (*Essays*, 123)

This is a rather intriguing remark. Rebellion against intellectual authority *might not* be such a bad thing if it did not involve the actual destruction of the intellectual records. The gain would be the relinquishment of dogmatism. As an example, Hume cites the dogmatism of the ancient sects. "Consider the blind submission of the ancient philosophers to the several masters in each school, and you will be convinced, that little good could be expected from a hundred centuries of such a servile philosophy." (*Essays*, 123) These ancient schools represent for Hume philosophy working at a dead end, philosophy corrupted. That their absolute authority could never be completely reestablished was in Hume's view a happy circumstance. "Upon the revival of learning, those sects of Stoics and Epicureans, Platonists and Pythagoricians, could never regain any credit or authority; and, at the same time, by the example of their fall, kept men from submitting, with such blind deference, to those new sects, which have attempted to gain an ascendant over them." (*Essays*, 123)

It is important for Hume, it seems, that intellectual authority be tentative and provisional. The circumstances surrounding the incorporation of philosophy into Christianity in Hume's view resulted in the kind of "blind deference" he so much deplored and in the destruction of free, critical thinking. The occurrence of Christianity's appropriation of philosophy was also used by Hume as evidence for his broader thesis regarding the rise of monotheism and the growth of intolerance. Monotheistic and polytheistic religions offer interesting comparisons with regard to the whole issue of persecution. With the rise of monotheism is a concomitant intolerance largely absent from polytheistic religions. "The intolerance of almost all religions, which have maintained the unity of God, is as remarkable as the contrary principle in polytheists." (*NHR*, 60)

What then are the roots of intolerance in monotheistic religion? In his book *Conversion*, A. D. Nock points out that the pagan religions of Rome were without theology. "Except in the late phase of paganism, when the success of Christianity had put it on the defensive and caused it to fight for its existence, there was no traditional religion which was an entity with a theology and an organization."[17] Polytheistic religions, theologically unsophisticated and intellectually primitive as they were, admitted of the happy circumstance of being mutually tolerant. "[I]dolatry is attendant with this evident advantage, that, by limiting the powers and function of its deities, it naturally admits of the gods of other sects and nations to a share of divinity, and renders all the various deities, as well as rites, ceremonies,

---

[17]Nock, *Conversion*, 10.

or traditions, compatible with each other." (*NHR*, 59) No small advantage! The willingness to extend a "share of divinity" for another's gods, like most forms of sharing, promotes concord and cooperation. The advantage of polytheism is that its "divinity" is an *unlimited* good, like air, infinitely divisible and shareable. The *History of England* dwells at length on the *incompatibility* of religious beliefs, rites, and ceremonies and of their potential for sectarian violence, civil discord, and religious wars of persecution and extermination.

Theism in contrast with polytheism "is opposite in both its advantages and disadvantages." (*NHR*, 59) The ideas of theism are incomparably richer, its tone more serious, its ideals more worthy of emulation. "As that system supposes one sole deity, the perfection of reason and goodness, it should, if justly prosecuted, banish everything frivolous, unreasonable, or inhuman from religious worship, and set before men that most illustrious example, as well as the most commanding motives of justice and benevolence." (*NHR*, 59)

In his rhapsodic essay, "The Platonist," Hume, speaking as *the* representative Platonic philosopher writes: "[w]here is the adoration due to infinite perfection, whence everything good and valuable is derived? Where is the gratitude, owing to thy creator, who called thee forth from nothing, who placed thee in all these relations to thy fellow-creatures, and requiring thee to fulfil the duty of each relation, forbids thee to neglect what thou owest to himself, the most perfect being, to whom thou art connected by the closest tye?" (*Essays*, 157) Here with deliberate irony is Hume's presentation of the Platonist admonishing the adoration of an infinitely perfect God. How is this "closest tye" to be understood? This perfect, unified God is a philosophically sophisticated concept, and theism, insofar as it appropriates this refined notion of the deity, assumes this high level of sophisticated understanding.

However, theism's advantage—its theological sophistication, its elevated, enriched idea of God, its unification of perfect attributes in a single being—is also the cause of its disadvantage to human affairs. Theism exacts a unity of faith and practice, which, Hume says, "furnishes designing men with a pretext for representing their adversaries as prophane, and the subjects of divine as well as human vengeance." (*NHR*, 59) The unification efforts of faith render the different sects implacable enemies and fire the engines of intolerance and repression. Unity of faith is also inconvenient in that it provides a strong rationale (a "pretext") for power seeking individuals ("designing men") to elevate the ruthlessness of their quests for power. It is not, as Hume would admit, that seeking power in itself is opprobrious; it is rather that the profanation of one's political opponents serves to exaggerate differences as well as to make one's adversaries irremediably hostile.

Later in the *Natural History* Hume adds two additional points to consider with regard to the disadvantage of theism. (1) "But where theism forms the fundamental principle of any popular religion, that tenet is so conformable to sound reason, that *philosophy is apt to incorporate itself with such a system of theology.*" (*NHR*, 65, italics added) (2) "Upon the whole, the greatest and most observable difference betwixt a *traditional, mythological* religion, and a *systematical, scholastic* one, are two: The former is often more reasonable, as consisting only of a multitude of stories, which, however groundless, imply no express absurdity and demonstrative contradiction; and sits also so easy and light on men's minds, that tho' it may be as universally received, it makes no such deep impression on the affections and understanding." (*NHR*, 80-81, original italics)

In (2) Hume argues that traditional and mythologically oriented religionists are not cognizant of or concerned with the specific truth claims of their religious ideologies. Nor are they worried about the logical implications—should they care to draw them—of their theological tenets. Pagan religion was mythical and poetic, not amenable to logical or systematic analysis. "The pagan religion, therefore, seemed to vanish like a cloud, whenever one approached to it, and examined it piecemeal. It could never be ascertained by any fixed dogmas and principles." (*NHR*, 75) The traditional character of polytheistic religion unifies people ("that tho' it may be universally received"), but because its objects of veneration and worship are not objects of specific truth claims, the polytheist is not incensed by the dogmas of a rival religionists, or is at least tolerant with regard to the gods of another religionist.

The incorporation of philosophy into religion noted by Hume in (1) occurs because theistic religionists aspire for their ideology a "reasonability" and coherency beyond that which the "multitude of stories" furnishes the polytheist. In contrast to the mythical character of polytheism, theists strive for a literal and systematic explanation of the world. Schopenhauer, like Hume, recognized the profound contrast between religion mythopoeically construed and logically construed and wrote: "[b]ut the bad thing about all religions is that, instead of being able to confess their allegorical nature, they have to conceal it; accordingly, they parade their doctrine in all seriousness as true *sensu proprio*, and the absurdities form an essential part of these doctrines, you have the great mischief of a continual fraud. And, what is worse, the day arrives when they are no longer true, *sensu proprio*, and then there is the end of them; so that in that respect, it would be better to admit their allegorical nature at once."[18]

---

[18]Arthur Schopenhauer, "The Christian System," in *The Pessimist's Handbook: A Collection of Popular Essays*, trans. T. Bailey Saunders, ed. Hazel E. Barnes (Lincoln, NE.: University of Nebraska Press, 1964), 311-12.

Philosophy abets the *sensu proprio* endeavor with all its "great mischief" by providing the tools for making religious discourse logically coercive. In so doing philosophy becomes co-opted by religion, pressed into combative service, perverted by its association into an activity which seeks to criminalize doubt. "[P]hilosophy will soon find herself very unequally yoked with her new associate; and instead of regulating each principle, as they advance together, she is at every turn perverted to serve the purposes of superstition." (*NHR*, 65) The "purposes of superstition" include the various but predictable manifestations of corrupted human ambition, vanity, and venality. As evidence Hume, and latter Gibbon, appealed to church history ("Ecclesiastical history sufficiently confirms these reflections") which displays an endless, amoeba-like multiplication of conflicting and disputatious theologies, inherently unresolvable, forever embroiled in hostile contest.

In Hume's approach to persecution therefore, we find a tension between two kinds of religion, mythopoeic, generally polytheistic religions, and philosophical, monotheistic religions. Philosophical religions are those that have acquired the tools of logic and argumentation, and they inevitably make their religious doctrine more intellectually sophisticated, more compelling. One of the ironies of philosophical religion is that its increased intellectual sophistication is accompanied by a decrease in its toleration of different religious entities. Philosophical religionists are neither more nor less emotional than mythopoeic religionists, it is just that the tools of philosophy come to focus on the objects of belief as exclusive. Thus, philosophy assists the emotive ideals of religion with an argumentative apparatus with which to attempt the coercion of belief. Theology becomes disputatious, confrontational, preoccupied with establishing its doctrinal superiority. But since belief is based on custom, and religious belief is linked more closely to emotion and imagination, the *logically* coercive force that philosophy lends to religion is illusory. What philosophy brings to religion is a kind of arrogance of reason, one which translates into what Hume describes as persecuting zeal.

Speaking specifically of Christianity and its link with philosophy, Hume, in one of his essays on politics, notes that Christianity came into being at a time when philosophical systems were already developed and ready for incorporation. "[A]s philosophy was widely spread over the world, at the time when Christianity arose, the teachers of the new sect were obliged to form a system of speculative opinions; to divide, with some accuracy, their articles of faith; and to explain, comment, confute, and defend with all the subtilty of argument and science." (*Essays*, 62)

Here then is a historical link between Christianity and philosophy. The result is sectarianism, factionalism, and persecution. "Hence naturally arose keenness in dispute, when the Christian religion came to be split into new divisions and heresies: And this keenness assisted the priests in their policy, of begetting a mutual hatred and antipathy among their deluded followers." (*Essays*, 62-63)   This sectarianism characterizing the philosophy-inspired Christianity stands in stark contrast to religions arising in more "barbarous" times without the benefit of metaphysical systems such as Platonism to inspire and guide dispute. "Religions, that arise in ages totally ignorant and barbarous, consist mostly of traditional tales and fictions, which may be different in every sect, without being contrary to each other; and even when they are contrary, everyone adheres to the tradition of his own set, without much reasoning or disputation." (*Essays*, 62) Philosophy badly serves religion by lending it the logical and rhetorical tools by which it transforms itself from a mythopoeic representation of socially unifying ideas and values into an ideology which claims to offer a literally true, objective system of belief. The monopoly of truth by religion has the effect of making exclusive adherence to a given system of belief an item of primary consideration. The logical corollary of exclusive belief is heresy, a condemnatory form of disbelief which supplies the warrant for "righteous" persecution. In Hume's theory of religious persecution then we see a couple of notions at work. First, is the tension between philosophy in its healthy, uncorrupted sense as a corrective to the natural imaginative tendencies of the human mind to overreach itself and find knowledge beyond experience, and superstition, which is corrupted religion, a system of thought ruled by an unconstrained imagination. Hume highlights this tension, as we have seen in the *Treatise,* where he dichotomizes true philosophy, a discipline that exercises constraint upon the imagination, and superstition which eagerly rides it wherever it will go. Second, is the mutual corruption of philosophy and religion manifest in the emergence of intolerant, persecuting monotheistic religions like Christianity. Philosophy loses its detachment and becomes completely absorbed into the vast reaches of religious emotion. Religion becomes focused on the truth-value of its beliefs and correct belief in turn becomes the most important aspect of religion.

So Hume's theory of religious persecution focuses on a tension between philosophy as a freedom pursuing enterprise—self-disciplined, skeptical, and restrained in its knowledge claims—and philosophy as an agent of perverted religion, superstition. Corrupted philosophy serves the persecuting zeal of religionists. In Gibbon's *Decline and Fall* we find the historical unfolding of this corruptive process.

III. Religious Persecution in the *Decline and Fall*

Some paradox of our nature leads us, when once we have made our fellow man the objects of our interest, to go on to make them the objects of our pity, then of our wisdom, ultimately of our coercion.

Lionell Trilling

The persecuting zeal of Christians is an object of intense and considerable scrutiny in the *Decline and Fall*. Gibbon's portrait of persecuting Christians is a major part of his reputation as an anti-Christian writer.[19] Rome's transformation from a classical to a Christian culture featured a colossal struggle between the tradition-based mythopoeic polytheistic religions and monotheistic Christianity. The dynamics of persecution were a big part of the contest and the explanation of how it happened involved coming to grips with the unique nature of monotheistic, i.e., philosophic, religions. Gibbon cites Hume in a footnote where he credits him with the observation of the intolerant nature of philosophical religions. "Mr. Hume, in the Natural History of Religion, sagaciously remarks that the most refined and philosophic sects are constantly the most intolerant." (*DF-8*, I, 219, n.29) This citation comes early in Gibbon's work where he is discussing Persian religion under the monarchy of Artaxerxes, yet it marks an important reference point when Gibbon discusses the role of Christianity in the decline of the empire. Gibbon thus is very aware of Hume's thesis on monotheism and intolerance, and the mutual corruption of philosophy and religion. The "Vindication" provides an important distinction between religious persecution justified by ancient polytheists and pagan philosophers, and the rationale for modern religious persecution. "I must lament that I have not been successful in the explanation of a very simple notion of the spirit both of philosophy and of polytheism, which I have repeatedly inculcated. The arguments which assert the rights of conscience are not inconclusive in themselves, but the understanding of the Greeks and Romans was fortified against their evidence by an invincible prejudice." (*EE*, 284)

Note that Gibbon like Hume is grappling with the interaction of "philosophy" and religion, i.e, "polytheistic religion." What becomes apparent is that, in contrast with the modern mind, religious thinking is removed from the logical rigor of philosophical speculation. The religious "rights of conscience" as argued by modern philosophers seem to be clear and obvious. "When we listen to the voice of Bayle, of Locke, and of genuine reason, in favour of religious toleration, we shall easily perceive that our most forcible appeal is made to our mutual feelings." (*EE*, 284) The argumentation, Gibbon notes, is based on the most elemental notions of

---

[19]McCloy. *Gibbon's Antagonism to Christianity*, 19-20.

consistency and mutuality. "If the Jew were allowed to argue with the Inquisitor, he would request that for a moment they might exchange their different situations, and might safely ask his Catholic Tyrant, whether the fear of death would compel *him* to enter the synagogue, to receive the mark of circumcision, and to partake of the paschal lamb." (*EE*, 284, original italics) This dramatic piece of role reversal helps Gibbon draw the obvious conclusion. "As soon as the case of persecution was brought home to the breast of the Inquisitor, he must have found some difficulty in suppressing the dictates of natural equity, which would insinuate to his conscience, that he could have no right to inflict those punishments which, under similar circumstances, he would esteem it as his duty to encounter." (*EE*, 284-85)

Yet, there is an "invincible prejudice" on the part of the pagan Greeks and Romans that makes this appeal to mutuality of treatment in matters of conscious incomprehensible. "But this argument could not reach the understanding of a Polytheist, or of an ancient Philosopher. The former was ready, whenever he was summoned, or indeed without being summoned, to fall prostrate before the altars of any Gods who were adored in any part of the world, and to admit a vague persuasion of the *truth* and divinity of the most different modes of religion. The Philosopher, who considered them, at least in their literal sense, as equally *false* and absurd, was not ashamed to disguise his sentiments, and to frame his actions according to the laws of his country, which imposed the same obligation on the philosophers and the people." (*EE*, 285, original italics) Gibbon's point is that in the historical context of pagan religion the truth and falsity of the doctrines are irrelevant. Religion does not need philosophy to defend it doctrines. The pagan religionist will worship "any" god while the pagan philosopher will dissimulate his opinion and follow the customs. This custom-based view of religious belief has significant implications for persecution. "When Pliny declared, that whatever was the opinion of the Christians, their obstinacy deserved punishment, the absurd cruelty of Pliny was excused in his own eye, by the consciousness that, in the situation of the Christians, he would not have refused the religious compliance which he exacted. I shall not repeat, that the Pagan worship was a matter, not of *opinion*, but of *custom*; that the toleration of the Romans was confined to nations or families who followed the practice of their ancestors; and that in the first ages of Christianity their persecution of the individuals who departed from the established religion was neither moderated by pure reason, nor inflamed by exclusive zeal." (*EE*, 285, original italics) Ancient religious persecution was not, as Gibbon notes, motivated by passionate conviction of the doctrinal truth. Pliny urged persecution of the Christians not because he believed that Christianity was a false religion but because they violated the customs.

The *Decline and Fall* provides an extensive, detailed study of the tension between the polytheistic, relatively non-persecuting state religions of pagan Rome, rooted in custom, and the rising monotheistic persecuting Christianity described by Hume that was energized by the philosophical quest for universal truth. Gibbon supplies a precise historical description of this process in the fourth-century struggle between paganism and Christianity. Speaking of St. Ambrose, he says: "[i]n this controversy, Ambrose condescends to speak the language of a philosopher. . . . He justly derides the absurd reverence for [pagan] antiquity which could only tend to discourage the improvements of art and replunge the human race into their original barbarism. From thence gradually arising to a more lofty and theological tone, he pronounces that Christianity alone is the doctrine of truth and salvation, and that every mode of Polytheism conducts its deluded votaries, through the paths of error, to the abyss of eternal perdition." (*DF-28*, III, 203-4) Here, heavily embedded in irony, is the description of Christianity's corruption with Ambrose's movement from the "language of the philosopher" with its legitimate criticism of the superstitious excesses of paganism to the more "lofty and theological tone" with all of its implications for heretical belief and righteous persecution. The threat of *eternal* perdition (the damnation of the immortal soul) provides the justification for persecution.

Chapter twenty-one of the *Decline and Fall* is where Gibbon draws out the tension between Christianity and paganism. Early in this chapter Gibbon pauses (a personal intercession in the narrative) to insinuate that what he, as a historian, is about to do involves what will probably be an unpleasant disclosure. "The historian may therefore be permitted respectfully to withdraw the veil of sanctuary; and to deduce the progress of reason and faith, of error and passion, from the school of Plato to the decline and fall of the empire." (*DF-21*, II, 355) This quotation is vintage Gibbon with its mocking imagery. *Who* has given the historian the permission to "withdraw the veil of sanctuary?" *Why* should it be done? The "veil of sanctuary" becomes another image of corruption. The work of the historian's melancholy duty is further revealed with the discovery that comes from the withdrawal of the veil. Gibbon positions the "school of Plato" in a chronology of decline so as perhaps to give the impression that Platonism is a precipitate factor in the empire's decline. The word "respectfully" is a tip off, another of the many ironic clues for the reader. The irony lies in the ambiguity. Is the respect directed toward the principles of faith or toward the act of disclosure? Moreover, Gibbon's coupling of "reason and faith" and "error and passion" completes a complex and major piece of ironic insinuation. Reason and faith represent a conjunction of incompatible notions for Gibbon who here reverberates Hume's own famous ironic conclusion in his essay "Of Miracles" where he says that "whoever is moved by faith to assent to [the truth of the Christian religion] is conscious of a continued miracle in his own person which subverts all the principles of understanding." To the extent that faith progresses, Gibbon insinuates, reason declines. Gibbon's irony is indeed an echo of Hume's ironic impeachment of miracles with all its troublesome implications for revealed religion.

Error and passion are merely the natural, unavoidable aspects of religion as it develops, a reminder that religion is dominated by passion and subject to all sorts of unpredictable, and sometimes unsavory contingencies in its various manifestations. Again, here is more irony in that error and passion nourish and feed off of each other and give rise to the most grandiose yet absurd ideational edifices. This coupling recalls Hume's *Treatise* contrast of the superstitious preoccupations with the "invisible world" and the strong and conduct-disturbing passions it begets with the "mild and moderate sentiments" of philosophy. Errors of religion, Hume reminds us, are dangerous. What Gibbon as a philosophic historian points out is that the passionate beliefs in the reality of invisible objects set in process a career of fanaticism. The historian cannot help but discover that the greatest zealots (those with the most profound conviction in their beliefs) are the most exclusive. Of the fourth-century fanatical Rogation sect Gibbon says: "[e]ven the imperceptible sect of the Rogatians could affirm, without a blush, that, when Christ should descend to judge the earth, he would find his true religion preserved only in a few nameless villages of the Cæsarean Mauritania." (*DF-21*, II, 355) The language stresses the anonymity of this group of backwater fanatics—"the imperceptible sect," "a few nameless villages"—whose fanaticism is so immense that it is blind to the stupid, ridiculous pretension.

We find thus Gibbon converting Hume's general philosophical thesis into a direct application. Moreover, this application involves a particular view of the merger of Platonic philosophy with Christianity. Recall that speculative, abstruse philosophy removed from common life experience is what Hume views as a potentially pernicious source for superstition. The following is Gibbon's account in chapter twenty-one of the marriage of Christianity and Platonism. First, we have Gibbon's description of the pagan Platonist philosophers themselves. "A chosen society of philosophers, men of a liberal education and curious disposition, might silently meditate, and temperately discuss. . . the abstruse questions of metaphysical science. The lofty speculations which neither convinced the understanding, nor agitated the passions, of the Platonists themselves were carelessly overlooked by the idle, the busy, and even the studious part of mankind." (*DF-21*, II, 361)

Note the emphasis is placed, not on the content of the philosophic doctrine, but the manners, demeanor, and character of the philosophers: silent, temperate, curious, dispassionate. Philosophy, properly conducted, is a kind of esoteric, "speculative" entertainment tempered by a discipline of the passions. But danger lurks! This group is elite, "chosen," in Gibbon's words. The Platonic philosopher, guiding the interplay of imagination and reason, possesses something of great power. Because philosophy, properly practiced involves a discipline of the passions, it arouses only those "mild and moderate sentiments" of which Hume speaks. But consider now Gibbon's unhappy description of Christianity's discovery of Platonism. "But after the *Logos* had been revealed as the sacred object of the faith, the hope, and the religious worship of the Christians, the mysterious system was embraced by a numerous and increasing multitude in every province of the Roman world. . . . A theology, which it was incumbent to believe, which it was impious to doubt, and which it might be dangerous, even fatal to mistake, became the familiar topic of private mediation and popular discourse. The cold indifference of philosophy was inflamed by the fervent spirit of devotion." (*DF-21*, II, 361-62, original italics)

Thus the link is made between the religious passions and the speculative ambitions of Platonic philosophy. Both philosophy and Christianity lose. Philosophy is transformed from metaphysical amusement into a deadly serious enterprise which adds an unwarranted certainty to the strong emotion associated with religious belief. Philosophy loses its detachment and impartiality, and Christianity, imbued with a false arrogance of reason, loses its humility and criminalizes doubt. Errors in corrupted religion are *dangerous*, as Hume has noted: here, as Gibbon suggests, mistakes in the Platonized Christian theology may even be *fatal*! "The familiar study of the Platonic system, a vain and argumentative disposition, a copious and flexible idiom, supplied the clergy and the people of the East with an inexhaustible flow of words and distinctions; and, in the midst of their fierce contentions, they easily forgot the doubt which is recommended by philosophy, and the submission which is enjoined by religion." (*DF-21*, II, 374)

An "inexhaustible flow of words and distinctions," here is a variation of the Humean complaint of obfuscation and the abuse of language. The temperate Platonist philosopher is transmogrified into the fanatical Christian theologian. In his account of the Reformation Gibbon also works over this theme of the corruption of religion by the logomachy brought by philosophy. "Transubstantiation, the invisible change of the bread and wine into the body and blood of Christ, is a tenet that may defy the power of argument and pleasantry; but instead of consulting the evidence of their senses, of their sight, their feeling, and their taste, the first Protestants were entangled in their own scruples, and awed by the words of Jesus in the institution of the sacrament." (*DF-54*, VI, 131)

Gibbon views the doctrine of transubstantiation as the product of a thoroughly corrupted philosophical enterprise having no rational or amusing features (it defies "the power of argument and pleasantry") and involving a complete departure from all constraints of experience-"sight," "feeling," etc. Gibbon then pits the Catholic doctrine of transubstantiation against the Calvinist doctrine of predestination. "But the loss of one mystery was amply compensated by the stupendous doctrines of original sin, redemption, faith, grace, and predestination, which have been strained from the epistles of St. Paul." (*DF-54*, VI, 131-32) No theological advance is detected by Gibbon. One absurdity merely gives way to another—one pernicious "mystery" displaces another. Gibbon is harshly ironic here. The language of the Gospel in service to the unconstrained imagination is capable of yielding an infinite assortment of incomprehensible theories. "These subtle questions had most assuredly been prepared by the fathers and schoolmen; but the final improvement and popular use may be attributed to the first reformers, who enforced them as the absolute and essential terms of salvation. Hitherto the weight of supernatural belief inclines against the Protestant; and many a sober Christian would rather admit that a wafer is God, than that God is a cruel and capricious tyrant." (*DF-54*, VI, 132) The theological polemics of the Reformers bring the debate of these theological issues to their culminating absurdity ("the final improvement"). In the war of absurdities the Catholics "win" in this particular battle: it is easier to accept God as a wafer than as a benevolent God who acts like a cruel despot.

Hume in the *Natural History* describes how philosophy becomes co-opted and ultimately corrupted by religion. First of all, the logical and rhetorical tools of philosophy, quite naturally, place a high value on consistency. As Hume says, "speculative reasoners naturally carry on their assent, and embrace a theory, which has been instilled into them by their earliest education, and which also possesses some degree of consistency and uniformity." (*NHR*, 65) But when the quest for system and uniformity is extended to objects of the invisible world, i.e., objects of the superstitious imagination, no limitations exist to check these ideas (the invisible world, recall for Hume, presents scenes "altogether new"). Consistency and uniformity prevail against the evidence of the experienced world. But theories and doctrines that are in opposition to common world experience yield absurdity. What begins as a quest to provide a consistent interpretation of some facet of existence ends in incoherence. "And thus a system becomes more absurd in the end, merely from its being reasonable and philosophical in the beginning." (*NHR*, 66) What occurs then is the emergence of a multiplicity of theologies (some of them mutually hostile) whose advocates at once declare their own unique truth and condemn their rivals. Since none of the theologies is rooted in the shared experience of the common world, and since each has created its own invisible world, no accommodation is possible. Force or chance determines who prevails. "When a controversy is started, some people pretend always with certainty to foretell the issue. Which ever opinion, say they, is most contrary to plain sense is sure to prevail. . . . Any one, it is pretended, that has but learning enough of this kind to know the definition of *Arian, Pelagian, Erastian, Socinian, Sabellian, Eutychian, Nestorian, Monothelite,* etc. not to mention *Protestant,* whose fate is yet uncertain, will be convinced of the truth of this observation." (*NHR*, 65-66) All of these sects cited by Hume were variants of "true" Christianity.

Gibbon draws a similar point in showing how Platonic philosophy was co-opted by Christian theologians. Gibbon's historical context is the Christian theological battle over the doctrine of the trinity, a conflict he calls "an abuse of philosophy." The following is Gibbon's short, extremely critical account of Plato's philosophical theology. What is particularly remarkable about this critique is its empirical basis. Like Hume, Gibbon argues that philosophy loses its moorings whenever it attempts to extend itself beyond the "visible world," the world of our sense experience. "But, as soon as we presume to reason of infinite substance, of spiritual generation; as often as we deduce any positive conclusions from a negative idea, we are involved in darkness, perplexity, and in inevitable contradiction. As these difficulties arise from the nature of the subject, they oppress, with the same insuperable weight, the philosophic and theological disputant . . . . " (*DF-21*, II, 361)

The overreaching of the imagination culminates in "darkness" and "perplexity." Gibbon accuses the later Platonists of abandoning legitimate "visible world" enterprises for unproductive logomachy. "The knowledge that is suited to our situation and powers, the whole compass of moral, natural, and mathematical sciences, was neglected by the new Platonists, whilst they exhausted their strength in the verbal disputes of metaphysics [and] attempted to explore the secrets of the invisible world." (*DF-13*, I, 423) Gibbon's critique is pervaded with a tone of mitigated skepticism. "The genius of Plato . . . had ventured to explore the mysterious nature of the Deity. When he had elevated his mind to the sublime contemplation of the first self-existent, necessary cause of the universe, the Athenian sage was incapable of conceiving *how* the simple unity of his essence could admit the infinite variety of distinct and successive ideas which compose the model of the intellectual world; *how* a Being purely incorporeal could execute that perfect model, and mould with a plastic hand the rude and independent chaos. The vain hope of extricating himself from these difficulties, which must ever oppress the feeble powers of the human mind, might induce Plato to consider the divine nature under the threefold modification: of the first cause, the reason or *Logos*, and the soul or spirit of the universe. His poetical imagination sometimes fixed and animated these metaphysical abstractions: the three *archical* or original principles were represented in the Platonic system of three Gods, united with each other by a mysterious and ineffable generation; and the Logos was particularly considered under the more accessible character of the Son of an Eternal Father, and the Creator and Governor of the world." (*DF-21*, II, 355-56, original italics)   Gibbon's skeptical critique of Plato's poetic construction of the three Gods, connected in a fully mysterious, unfathomable fashion sets up the historical discussion of the whole trinitarian controversy, for it is Plato's tri-theism that builds the philosophical mills for the theological grist. Plato provided a technical language which the theologians used as building blocks for their systems. "The respectable name of Plato was used by the orthodox, and abused by the heretics as the common support of truth and error: the authority of his skilful commentators, and the science of dialectics, were to justify the remote consequence of his opinions, and to supply the discreet silence of the inspired writers." (*DF-21*, II, 360)

With this single sentence in a way typical of his elusive style, Gibbon touches on all the problematic features of a Platonic-Christian marriage. Plato is both "used and abused" by the orthodox and heretics respectively. The outcome is both truth and error. Platonism's "common support" of truth and error, orthodoxy and heresy, one concludes, must vitiate it since a system that proves everything, proves nothing. That this is Gibbon's intent becomes obvious shortly when he describes the trinitarian controversy of the fourth century in a way that makes it impossible to distinguish orthodoxy from heresy, truth from error.   Gibbon follows the controversy moving from the Ebionites to Arius to Sabellius. Its progress, as he notes, is illusory. "Thus, after revolving round the theological circle, we are surprised to find that the Sabellian ends where the Ebionite had begun; and that the incomprehensible mystery which excites our adoration eludes our enquiry." (*DF-21*, II, 367) Without an experiential anchor, theologizing merely spins itself out in meaningless circles.

Gibbon's gloss that the "authority of Plato's skillful commentators and the science of dialectics were used to justify the remote consequences of his opinions" seems to suggest that this remote distance was full of corruption and arbitrariness, particularly since truth and error emerge from Plato. That Platonism is used "to supply the discreet silence of the inspired writers" completes Gibbon's impeachment of the Christianity's co-option of it. "Discreet", after all, is another one of those carefully chosen, pivotal words with a double meaning that enables Gibbon to prosecute his case with safety.

Because Greek was more philosophically subtle and sophisticated than Latin, the trinitarian controversy was slower to take hold in the West where the technical distinctions were absent from the language. "The poverty and stubbornness of [the Latin's] native tongue was not always capable of affording just equivalents for the Greek terms, for the technical words of the Platonic philosophy, which had been consecrated by the gospel or by the church to express the mysteries of the Christian faith; and a verbal defect might introduce into the Latin theology a long train of error or perplexity." (*DF-21*, II, 374) Gibbon sees this as an advantage and refers to the "happy ignorance of the Gallican church" of the Nicene creed.

While Christianity absorbed Platonic metaphysics, it nevertheless failed to be philosophical in an impartial and critical sense because of two specific reasons—passion and institutional authority. Once philosophical speculation became tied to the future of the immortal soul, it assumed serious practical dimensions. "These speculations, instead of being treated as the amusement of a vacant hour, became the most serious business of the present, and the most useful preparation for a future life." (*DF-21*, II, 361-62) One's fate in the eternal future-world comes to hinge on belief, that is, on correct belief. Hence belief becomes highly charged with emotion because so much is at stake with the truth and falsity of the belief. "The cold indifference of philosophy was inflamed by the fervent spirit of devotion." (*DF-21*, II, 362)

On the one side then, philosophy becomes infused with religious zeal and emotion; on the other, the intellectual freedom necessary for philosophy to thrive becomes crushed by the institutional authority of the Church. "The devotion of individuals was the first circumstance which distinguished the Christians from the Platonists; the second was the authority of the church. The disciples of philosophy asserted the rights of intellectual freedom, and their respect for the sentiments of their teachers was a liberal and voluntary tribute, which they offered to superior reason. But the Christians formed a numerous and disciplined society; and the jurisdiction of their laws and magistrates was strictly exercised over the minds of the faithful. The loose wanderings of the imagination were gradually confined by creeds and confessions; the freedom of private judgment submitted to the public wisdom of synods; the authority of a theologian was determined by his ecclesiastical rank; and the episcopal successors of the apostles inflicted the censures of the church on those who deviated from the orthodox belief." (*DF-21*, II, 363)

Platonism, we are left to conclude, failed to advance the truth of Christianity, and indeed its long range effect was to politicize it. "A metaphysical argument became the cause or pretence of political contests; the subtleties of the Platonic school were used as badges of popular factions, and the distance which separated their respective tenets was enlarged or magnified by the acrimony of dispute . . . . After the edict of toleration had restored peace and leisure to the Christians, the trinitarian controversy was revived in the ancient seat of Platonism, the learned, the opulent, the tumultuous city of Alexandria; and the flames of religious discord was rapidly communicated from the schools to the clergy, the people, the provinces, and the East." (*DF-21*, II, 363-64)

Thus we see Gibbon's description of the effects of Platonic philosophy on Christianity. Stripped away from Platonism is the detachment, the dispassion of the philosopher. Christianity becomes a coercive ideology; more precisely, it becomes a loose conglomeration of competing sub-sects. From the mutually tolerating pagan polytheistic religions and the civic concord they afforded we now find the rapid communication of the "flames of religious discord." Christianity's career of persecution is set.

CHAPTER SIX

MONKISH VIRTUES AND CONVENTIONAL MORALITY: THE MORAL CRITIQUE OF RELIGION

I. Morality and the Useful and Agreeable

It is easy to discern that some sects have rather followed truth, others utility; whereby the latter have gained credit. It is the bane of our condition that often what appears to our imagination as most true does not appear to it as most useful for our life.

Montaigne

The Hume-Gibbon attack on Christianity directed its most open hostility toward the monks. Monasticism was, of course, a manifestation of Roman Catholicism, which was more available to direct attack by writers from Protestant countries. Monasticism for Hume and Gibbon was the undistilled, superstitious essence of the Church of Rome. In the monks they saw the rejection of the moral virtues practiced by the pagan philosophers and statesmen they so much admired. Monasticism had spurned the natural world and rejected the virtues that were supposed to improve life within it. Hume's revulsion with monasticism is connected with the importance he attaches to usefulness as the foundation of moral value,[1] and the monks represented for him a pathological rejection of the useful.

---

[1] The basis for all morality, Hume argues in the first *Enquiry*, is utility. His use of the term "utility" and the subsequent significance of it in Hume's moral and political philosophy need some explanation lest the attribution of "utilitarianism" to Hume be confused with the narrower, more popular constructivist utilitarianism of Bentham and his followers. "Utility" for Hume is a "means"-term referring primarily to the *usefulness* something has, its *potential* to yield value. This is in contrast to the Benthamite meaning where utility becomes an "end"-term, i.e., is seen to be a *measure* of satisfaction. The importance of the distinction lies in its implications for the necessity of rule-governed activity. Rules have utility in the Humean sense, i.e., they are useful. They are also necessary because human interaction is so complex that it is impossible always to predict the outcomes. Rules are means, tested by experience, to guide decision-making in the face of relative ignorance. Their usefulness is attested by their long-term tendency to yield good over evil. The Benthamite conception of utility as a measure of satisfaction requires that rules justify themselves by virtue of the *known* good or evil that results from following them. The problem with this, as F. A. Hayek points out, is that it overlooks the crucial factor of relative human ignorance. "Bentham's conception of a calculus of pleasure and pain by which the greatest happiness of the greatest number is to be determined presupposes that all the particular individual effects of any one action can be known by the acting person. Pursued to its logical conclusion it leads to a particularistic or 'act' utilitarianism which dispenses with rules altogether and judges each individual action according to the utility of its known effects." Bentham's hedonic calculus operates, in effect, with the assumption of

The notion of usefulness, Hume argues, persists throughout the spectrum of cross cultural experience. "The epithets *social, good-natured, humane, merciful, grateful, friendly, generous, beneficent,* or their equivalents, are known in all languages, and universally express the highest merit, which *human nature* is capable of attaining." (*EPM*, 176, original italics) Scrutiny of common life practices shows that qualities of character and personality which are perceived as both useful and agreeable, both to the possessor as well as others, command universal approbation. Honesty, wit, courage, resourcefulness; qualities such as these are universally acclaimed, as are their opposites disdained. Religious beliefs, attitudes, and practices are measured by Hume against these standards of usefulness and agreeableness. Moreover, it is religion as it is actually practiced, not an idealized version of it, that Hume considers. "True religion," says Hume, "I allow, has no such pernicious Consequences [endless disputes, quarrels, factions, persecutions, and civil commotions]: But we must treat of Religion, as it has commonly been found in the World." (*DNR*, 256) Hume's dichotomy, "true religion" (idealized, philosophically refined religion) versus religion discovered historically, i.e., "commonly found in the world" expresses, ironically, what is an essentially disapprobative view of the effects of religion on human society. True religion is a philosopher's elixir: religion as it is practiced seems to be widely corrupt.[2] This at least is Hume's judgment as a philosophical historian. In the *History of England* Hume makes a rather broad generalization about the intolerance of religionists. "It seems to be almost a general rule, that in all religions, except the true, no man will suffer martyrdom who would not also inflict it willingly on all that differ from him." (*HE*, III, 340) Since persecution is such a major feature of religious history, true, i.e., philosophically refined religion, can hardly be said to exist.

Utility, characterized by Hume as the property of usefulness and agreeableness, is what people everywhere and at all times approbate. It is a universal standard, a standard, incidentally, employed by the philosophic historian who attempts to achieve the moral point of view. Hume calls this a "common life"

---

omniscience, a condition, quite obviously impossible to realize in common life experience. The problem thus with Bentham's formulation, Hayek notes, is that it "never grasped the significance of rules as an adaptation to this inescapable ignorance of most of the particular circumstances which determine the effects of our actions, and thus disregarded the whole phenomenon of rule guided action." Hume's recognition of the dimensions of human ignorance and its significance for human action, and his view of human nature as flawed, make rules and rule-governed activity an extremely important element of his moral and social perspective. Rules are what make social life possible. See F. A. Hayek, *Law, Legislation and Liberty,* vol. 2, *The Mirage of Social Justice* (Chicago: University of Chicago Press, 1976), 2: 19-20.

[2]Gaskin, *Hume's Philosophy of Religion,* 193-95, for a discussion of the Humean perspective on the socially and morally corruptive aspects of religion.

observation. Recall his remark in the first *Enquiry* that "philosophical decisions are nothing but the reflections of common life, methodized and corrected." In questions of morals, general opinions, i.e., widespread, common sense opinions, born out in the practice of tradition, carry more weight than the refined theories of philosophers or theologians. These reflections of common life represent an evolved, collective wisdom developed out of the practices which human beings engage in, with varied levels of success, to make their lives easier and happier. Hayek, writing of Hume's moral theory, says that Hume "demonstrates that our moral beliefs are neither natural in the sense of innate, nor a deliberate invention of human reason, but an 'artifact' in the special sense in which he introduces this term, that is, a *product of cultural evolution*, as we would call it."[3] The value of those qualities that effect useful and agreeable consequences are a basic part of human experience. Again, this is confirmed by common life experience. "In common life, we may observe, that the circumstance of utility is always appealed to; nor is it supposed, that a greater eulogy can be given to any man than, to display his usefulness to the public, and enumerate the services, which he has performed to mankind and society." (*EPM*, 212)

Utility, as Hume explains, breaks out into four more specific categories: qualities *useful* to *others*, e.g., honor, kindness; qualities *useful* to the *person himself*, e.g., diligence; qualities *agreeable* to *others*, e.g., wit, good manners; and qualities *agreeable* to the *person himself*, e.g., serenity and equanimity. (*EPM*, 269-70, original italics) It is the tendency of these and such like qualities to promote the states of being valued everywhere that makes these qualities universally esteemed and their opposites objects of general abhorrence. The human frame is so constituted such that these qualities have a natural appeal. Moral virtue holds a certain basic kind of attraction for human beings as fitting and appropriate. "The social virtues must, therefore, be allowed to have a natural beauty and amiableness, which, at first, antecedent to all precept or education, recommends them to the esteem of uninstructed mankind, and engages their affections." (*EPM*, 214)

Both Hume and Gibbon employ what I call a "spectrum of utility," used to evaluate historical personages on the basis of the useful and agreeable as discussed above. This spectrum is their moral gauge for the rendering of that disinterested, impartial perspective that is the unique, morally-corrective contribution of the philosophic historian. Against this spectrum (an array of virtues and vices) the qualities of character of an historical figure are compared and made relative to some concrete standards of achievement. Consider first this analysis of the Spanish-Austrian Emperor, Philip II by Hume in the *History of England*. "When

---

[3]F. A. Hayek, "The Legal and Political Philosophy of David Hume," in *Studies in Philosophy, Politics and Economics* (Chicago: University of Chicago Press, 1967) 111, italics added.

the dominions of the house of Austria devolved on Philip II, all Europe was struck with terror, lest the power of a family, which had been raised by fortune, should now be carried to an immeasurable height, by the wisdom and conduct of this monarch. But never were apprehensions found in the event to be more groundless. Slow without prudence, ambitious without enterprise, false without deceiving anybody, and refined without any true judgment; such was the character of Philip . . . ." (*HE*, IV, 222-23)

Hume assesses those qualities of character in Philip that might be relevant in judging him as a leader in light of some standards of usefulness or agreeableness. Each of these morally neutral qualitites (slowness, ambition, dissimulation, refinement) however, is disapprobatively qualified, e.g., refinement *without* "any true judgment." In spite of expectations, none of Philip's qualities of character can be mined for anything that might distinguish in any way a person who gets things done or is very attractive. On the utility spectrum Philip is an unmitigated failure, an extreme case for Hume who sees most people as a mix of good and evil.

Consider now Gibbon's assessment of the third-century Emperor, Carinus. "He was soft, yet cruel; devoted to pleasure, but destitute of taste; and, though exquisitely susceptible of vanity, indifferent to public esteem." (*DF-12*, I, 368) The contrasts here are somewhat sharper and more acidic than Hume's, but the stylistic parallelism is quite remarkable, not just in the ironic contrast in which a quality of character that a reader would *expect* to be qualified approbatively gets reverse treatment (we would be more likely to expect something like, "he was soft, but determined," etc.), but in its relative use of standards of utility. Gibbon, like Hume, is making a moral assessment of a historical figure based on a disinterested judgment of utility. These limitations of both Philip and Carinus in most other people might admit of usefulness: pleasure should be accompanied by taste; ambition needs enterprise. What is at work in both character evaluations is the application of these measures of usefulness and agreeableness in order to determine what sort of moral judgment—framed in an appropriate historically contextualized perspective—to make of these men.

The utility-based notion of morality is closely linked to what Hume calls a "convention," and thus we use the term "conventional morality."[4] A "convention" in this sense represents a transgenerational, evolutionary working-out of commonly accepted ways for dealing with the problems and limitations presented by having to live in human society. Language (analogous in Hume's sense to morality in this

---

[4]There is an extensive literature on the concept of convention in Hume. In addition to the treatment of it in Livingston, *Hume's Philosophy of Common life*, see William C. Charron, "Convention, Games of Strategy, and Hume's Philosophy of Law and Government," *American Philosophical Quarterly* 17 no. 4 (October 1980): 327-34.

context) is a good example of a convention, a means, if you will, gradually created and evolving, that enables human beings to communicate with, understand each other and advance their mutual interests. Morality, analogously, allows people to impose upon themselves rule-determined standards of behavior and expectations of mutually beneficial conduct. Hayek, as noted above, writes that Hume conceives of human morality as a "product of cultural evolution." Moral standards for him "are an outcome of the practical experience of mankind, and the sole consideration in the slow test of time is the utility each moral rule can demonstrate towards promoting human welfare."[5] Conventional morality may in fact contain religious elements or sanctions, but what makes something a convention is that it is widely and usually gradually accepted as binding and comes to be so because of its overall long range usefulness. In both Hume and Gibbon there is a profound respect and attachment to conventional morality, representing as it does an accumulated, tried and tested wisdom.[6] In contrast to Hume's and Gibbon's conventional morality, which is based on utility, is the religious morality of Christianity. Christian morality is a major target of the attack. It operates with notions about what is right and wrong for human beings based at least in some way upon beliefs of what kind of being God is and what his expectations are for mortal beings.[7] This indeed is the major dilemma for Christian morality: it appears to revolve around a persistently disputable or contentious conception of what God is supposed to be and what he is supposed to approbate. The history of Christianity, as Hume and Gibbon read it, reveals a salient and enduring conflict over the determination of genuine Christian belief. So the criticism is the very practical one that with the basis of morality observed to be so historically fissionable and so much in contention, solid and lasting agreement on the rules that are supposed to issue from it is elusive at best, unattainable at worst.

Hume attacks Christian morality in the *Natural History*, Sections XIII and XIV, and in Part 12 of the *Dialogues*. The *Natural History* begins with the following critical observation about the practice of religion: "[h]ere I cannot forbear observing a fact, which may be worth the attention of those, who make human nature the object of their enquiry. It is certain, that, in every religion, however sublime the verbal definition, which it gives of its divinity, many of the

---

[5]Hayek, "Legal and Political Philosophy of David Hume," 111.

[6]Livingston, *Hume's Philosophy of Common Life*, 4, writes: "[t]he concept of convention is, perhaps, the most important in Hume's philosophy. A Humean convention is not the result of conscious agreement but is arrived at over time as the unintended result of man's involvement with the world and with his fellows."

[7]This definition is in no way intended to deny a wide range of theological ethical theorizing within Christianity. See Vernon J. Bourke, *History of Ethics* (Garden City, NY: Doubleday, 1968), for an explication of Christian ethical theorizing in a historical context.

votaries, perhaps the greatest number, will still seek the divine favour, not by virtue and good morals, which alone can be acceptable to a perfect being, but either by frivolous observances, by intemperate zeal, by rapturous extasies, or by the belief of mysterious opinions." (*NHR*, 86-87)

Religions have a tendency, Hume alleges, to invent these various incidental or "frivolous" devices for courting favor with God. These devices may include all sorts of rituals, arcane beliefs, or very emphatic or dramatic asseverations of belief. Hume thus describes what might be called a kind of "devotional industry" which produces unique techniques and practices designed to arouse and intensify religious feelings, or, as we might want to call them, religiously emotive intensifiers. These intensifiers, Hume charges, have the unfortunate, and perhaps unintended effect of introducing hypocrisy into moral conduct. The devotional industry trades in morally specious and superfluous standards of conduct. High concentrations of energy become required to *show* the intensity of one's belief. Such energies devoted to the display of devotion displace those that might be invested in simply trying to be virtuous, and hence Hume's ironic observation that the more seemingly religious and devout people appear to be, the more dubious their real virtue becomes.[8] "And when we have to do with a Man, who makes a great Profession of Religion and Devotion; has this any other Effect upon several, who pass for prudent, than to put them on their Guard, lest they be cheated and deceiv'd by him?" (*DNR*, 253)

Those qualities that would make a person commendable and a particularly valuable member of almost any society are, from the standpoint of the religious votary, Hume argues, insufficient to please the gods. Not only that, Hume adds, religious practitioners for whatever reason create pressure for the invention of additional moral rituals, beliefs or observances, even where there might be no encouragement for it on the part of the clergy. "[I]f we should suppose, what seldom happens, that a popular religion were found, in which it was expressly declared, that nothing but morality could gain the divine favour; if an order of priests were instituted to inculcate this opinion, in daily sermons, and with all the arts of persuasion; yet so inveterate are the people's prejudices, that for want of some other superstition, they would make the very attendance on these sermons the

---

[8]See Letwin, *The Pursuit of Certainty*, Chapter 2, "The Kirk," for interesting speculation on Hume's personal experience with Scottish Calvinism and his likely reaction against what he saw as the extreme hypocrisy generated by religious emotionalism: (24) "[f]rom the emphasis in his adult invective, it seems likely that the taint of hypocrisy in religious enthusiasm first inspired him to doubt. There is an echo of a personal experience and excuse, a suggestion that he began by disliking the flavour of his own devotion in the line: 'Men dare not avow, even to their own hearts, the doubts which they entertain on such subjects. They make a merit of implicit faith; and disguise to themselves their real infidelity, by the strongest asseverations and the most positive bigotry.'"

essentials of religion, rather than place them in virtue and good morals." (*NHR*, 87-88)

These remarks support a certain sardonic tone of incomprehensibility and betray Hume's general pessimism. Even in the face of a hypothetical deterring clergy who would encourage morality solely because of its usefulness, the devout religionist would not only make the ritual of attendance into a virtue, but the supreme one at that! Utility gets shunted aside for the ritual. The devotional industry, Hume suggests, is a largely useless but inherent aspect of religion. And so Hume sees a destructive dynamism operating in many religions—and certainly Christianity—that simply takes them off of a course of moral conduct compatible with the principles of human nature and into perniciously artificial devotional practices.

From the standpoint of the moral philosopher or philosophic historian looking at human conduct and attempting to comprehend the motivational dynamics at work in this kind of situation, it is difficult, at least initially, to understand ("one may be at some loss to account for it") how this could be the case. Why, Hume notes, don't religious believers simply attribute those most useful of traits of character, virtue and honesty, to the gods as the most valuable qualities any creature could possess? "Why not make all religion, or the chief part of it, to consist in these attainments?" (*NHR*, 88) From the perspective of what Hume calls "natural reason" this makes perfect sense. Virtue and honesty are universally lauded as the most important qualities for success in life and for society to function well. When considering these things apart from religion no one denies it. "[T]here is no *man* so stupid, as that, judging by his natural reason, he would not esteem virtue and honesty the most valuable qualities, which any person could possess." (*NHR*, 88, original italics)

What makes this evasion of "natural reason" even more puzzling is that these contrived, superstitious practices are even more involved, troublesome, and tortuous than the practice of conventional morality. Hume cites the fasting practices of the Turks during Ramadan ("the poor wretches, for many days, often in the hottest months of the year, and in some of the hottest climates of the world, remain without eating or drinking") and notes that these and other such penances "must be more severe than the practice of any moral duty, even to the most vicious and depraved of mankind." (*NHR*, 88)

The "moral" behavior of religious believers in these seeming incomprehensible modes, however, becomes intelligible, Hume argues, when it is seen how much connected this religious conduct is to the religious emotion of supernatural terror and the elevated levels of uncertainty generated by this cosmic fear. Fear in the context of supernatural forces explains why religious behavior takes the shape that it does. Hume, recall, in the *Dialogues* states that extreme fear is the dominate emotion in religion. "[I]t must be acknowledg'd, that, as Terror is the primary Principle of Religion, it is the Passion, which always predominates in it." (*DNR*, 259) The gods are powerful, invisible, and to a large extent, unknowable. Man's relationship to them is thus immersed in the uncertainty (due to this unknowability) of being able to discern what would suffice to please or appease the gods. The attitude that arises is shaped by a profound sense of fear due to this unremedial uncertainty and sense of powerlessness relative to the gods. "The primary religion of mankind arises chiefly from an anxious fear of future events; and what ideas will naturally be entertained of invisible, unknown powers, while men lie under dismal apprehensions of any kind, may easily be conceived. Every image of vengeance, severity, cruelty, and malice must occur and augment the ghastliness and horror, which oppresses the amazed religionist." (*NHR*, 81)

Fear and uncertainty create the setting and establish the backdrop out of which the rules and practices of religious morality are formed. The distinguishing feature of these rules and practices is their total lack of relevance to any practical purposes or any applicability to conventional human enterprises. To the moral philosopher like Hume the most obvious question is: what possible usefulness do any of these things have? The answer is none, but it is their sheer practical irrelevance that commends these rules. "And any practice recommended to him [the religionist], which either serves to no purpose in life, or offers the strongest violence to his natural inclinations; that practice he will the more readily embrace, on account of those very circumstances which should make him absolutely reject it. It seems the more purely religious, that it proceeds from no mixture or any other motive or consideration." (*NHR*, 90) Hume thus sets up religious morality as distinct, even antithetical, to conventional morality which is based upon certain inclinations he views as natural to human beings.[9] The morality developing out of the natural inclinations is the morality of the ancient philosophers which is linked to the nature of man rather than to God. With this morality, Hume argues, it is relatively easy to achieve conformity. "The duties, which a man performs as friend or parent, seem merely owing to his benefactor or children; nor can he be wanting to these

---

[9]For a provocative interpretation of Hume's naturalism see Wind, *Hume and the Heroic Portrait*. Although the discussion is primarily in the area of aesthetics, the implication for religion is significant insofar as it emphasizes Hume's repudiation of artificiality, i.e., excess in theorizing and emotion, as a perversion: (7) "[i]n his ethics, while applying his critique of the imagination to the extremes of enthusiasm and superstition, Hume still gave natural feeling its proper place; but in his theory of knowledge imagination is not only exposed in its excesses, but constantly shown to be playing its tricks in the most simple acts of the understanding." Wind argues that Hume's philosophical skepticism performs a regulative function that attempts to undermine excess, both emotional and intellectual, and maintain what is "natural."

duties, without breaking thro' all the ties of nature and morality." (*NHR*, 89) Even the harder virtues of self-restraint and self-command are understood by most to be necessary for the advancement of sociability and the stability of public life. One could hardly expect to be a respected member of a community without employing some basic notions of duty and responsibility. "Even with regard to the virtues, which are more austere, and more founded on reflection, such as public spirit, filial duty, temperance, or integrity; the moral obligation, in our apprehension, removes all pretense to religious merit; and the virtuous conduct is esteemed no more than what we owe to society and to ourselves." (*NHR*, 89)

The shortcoming of conventional morality for the religious believer is, ironically, that it is too easy, too much in accord with his or her general constitution and nature. The observance of conventional rules does not impose a level of self-denial sufficient to impress a jealous or diffident god. The believer's *fear* of the gods requires more of him, more in the sense of something that will thoroughly abase him, something wholly sufficient to show his fear-inspired deference. "In restoring a loan, or paying a debt, his divinity is no way beholden to him; because these acts of justice are what he was bound to perform, and what many would have performed, were there no god in the universe. But if he fast a day, or give himself a sound whipping; this has a direct reference, in his opinion, to the service of God. No other motive could engage him to such austerities. By these distinguished marks of devotion, he has now acquired the divine favour; and may expect, in recompence, protection and safety in this world, and eternal happiness in the next." (*NHR*, 90)

Such is the *quid pro quo* relation of fear-based religious worship. The strong-god/weak-man relationship turns on the hopes for the exchange of future life rewards for self-abnegation, mortification, self-denial, and abasement in this life. Uncertain of what the Almighty God might want from him, his fear dictates his own rituals of effacement and appeasement. Doing one's duty in the sense of conforming to social norms—being honest, upright, loyal, kind, etc.—does not avail because the motives for performance exist independently of the consideration of God's existence ("what many would have performed, were there no god in the universe").

The morality of the monks (with its extreme posture of self-denial) sets itself in an untenable opposition to human inclinations: it pushes human beings toward fakery or hypocrisy or fanaticism. "[T]he very diverting of the Attention, the raising up a new and frivolous Species of Merit, the preposterous Distribution, which it makes of Praise and Blame; must have the most pernicious Consequences, and weaken extremely Men's Attachment to the natural Motives of Justice and Humanity." (*DNR*, 254) Religious morality gives rise to hypocrisy because the devotional requirements and the observances have no natural affinity for things pleasing or affirming in the human personality. The contrived character of religious moral concepts creates the need for feigned piety and for shows of zeal. "Many religious Exercises are enter'd into with seeming Fervor, where the Heart, at the time, feels cold and languid: a Habit of Dissimulation is by degrees contracted: and Fraud and Falsehood become the predominant Principle. Hence the Reason of that vulgar Observation, that the highest Zeal in Religion and the deepest Hypocrisy, so far from being inconsistent, are often or commonly united in the same individual Character." (*DNR*, 254)

Here is one of Hume's "common life" observations: the strong corollary relationship drawn between religiosity and hypocrisy. The two are so frequently and ordinarily observed by ordinary people, the "vulgar," that this is a kind of folk wisdom. Hume is thus very emphatic in this contrast between his utility-based conventional morality and religious morality which operates largely out of the fears created by the imagination. Hume equates monasticism with the very worst, the most extreme features of religious morality; fanaticism, emotionalism, self-denigration, false, abject humility. Its effects are inimical to the civilized values of self-restraint, moderation, and the enjoyment of the refinements of human achievements.

II. Monkish Morals

Whatever merit a man may have thought there would be in making himself miserable, no such notion seems ever to have occurred to any of them, that it may be a merit, much less a duty, to make others miserable: although it should seem, that if a certain quantity of misery were a thing so desirable, it would not matter much whether it were brought up by each man himself, or by one man upon another.

Jeremy Bentham

The poor man's son, whom heaven in its anger has visited with ambition, when he begins to look around him, admires the condition of the rich.

Adam Smith

Gibbon's harsh judgments of Roman-empire Christians are related to what he sees as their departure from social norms based upon the useful and agreeable. Of the early Christians, "it was not in *this* world that the primitive Christians were desirous of making themselves either agreeable or useful." (*DF-15*, II, 37, original italics) So indeed in *this* world, the Christians of the *Decline and Fall* frequently emerged from Gibbon's description as disagreeable and useless. Here is the crux of Gibbon's Humean criticism: the linking of moral worth to belief in God and the preoccupation with pleasing *Him* shifts the emphasis on goodness away from man as a natural creature to man as a supernatural being. The very nature of human beings—the non-supernatural aspects of it anyway—becomes morally irrelevant, and likewise, serious concern with improving it.[10]

The tragedy of Rome's collapse, a great civilization driven to ruin, was in Gibbon's own words the work of barbarism and religion. Christianity played a major role in the collapse, and while Gibbon's history of Christianity does produce Christian heroes, he discovers his nemesis in the monk, the abject enemy of civilization. Monks are in Gibbon's estimation effete barbarians. The Christian monk in his epic tragedy is pitted against the pagan philosopher. The former triumphed. The latter, however, commanded Gibbon's admiration. The monk represents Christianity in its most extreme posture of otherworldliness, and Gibbon excoriates him for repudiating those virtues that are linked to success in this world. Monasticism was manifestation for Gibbon of Christianity at its worst, a turning-on-its-head of the virtues that invigorated and sustained Greek and Roman civilization. "The clergy successfully preached the doctrine of patience and

---

[10]R. N. Parkinson, *Edward Gibbon* (New York: Twayne, 1973), 108, comments on the influence of Hume's notion of the useful and agreeable on Gibbon.

pusillanimity; the active virtues of society were discouraged; and the last remains of the military spirit were buried in the cloister . . . ." (*DF-38*, IV, 175)The monk is the embodiment of the credulity and superstition that engulfed the classical world. The monk represents the ultimate and consummate perversion of morality by otherworld preoccupations. Of the rapid expansion of monasticism in the fourth and fifth centuries Gibbon intoned with open derision. "Every mode of religious worship which had been practiced by the saints, every mysterious doctrine which they believed, was fortified by the sanction of divine revelation, and all the manly virtues were oppressed by the *servile and pusillanimous reign of the monks*." (*DF-37*, IV, 81, italics added) Courage and all the other "manly" virtues went into a slide with the rise of monasticism. Cowardice and servility were the products of mystery and divine revelation—the enervating effects of a "denatured" religion.

What Gibbon ironically refers to as the "pusillanimous reign of the monks" in chapter thirty-seven is discussed in the "Origin, Progress, and Effects of the Monastic Life," one of the most vitriolic, acerbic, and unrestrained sections of the entire *Decline and Fall*. Gibbon seemed unable either to temper his utter disdain for the early Christian monks (at one point he calls them "insects"), or to moderate his revulsion with their conduct, which "embraced a life of misery, as the price of eternal happiness." (*DF-37*, IV, 63) The "manly virtues" that the monks had oppressed with their craven, superstitious, and otherworldly ways were, in Gibbon's view, precisely those that had made the Roman empire the pinnacle of civilization. Gibbon's hostility to monasticism waxed so intense because it was the monks who had cultivated those "virtues" antithetical to those of classical Rome. "Manly virtue" was an expression that Hume also had used as a counterpoise to the self-abnegating practices of monastic life. Again we see the stylistic and philosophical parallels. "Whatever weakens or disorders the internal frame promotes the interests of superstition: And nothing is more destructive to them than a *manly, steddy virtue*, which either preserves us from disastrous, melancholy accidents, or teaches us to bear them." (*NHR*, 91, italics added) Here, by implication, we have the superstition-promoting Christian monk put against the steady and virtuous pagan philosopher.[11] Gibbon's disgust with monasticism and the language he used to denounce it mirror that of Hume. In his conclusion to the second *Enquiry* Hume held up "monkish virtues" as the product of deluded superstition. "Celibacy, fasting, penance, mortification, self-denial, humility, silence, solitude, and the whole train of monkish virtues; for what reason are they everywhere rejected by men of sense, but because they serve to no manner of

---

[11]Pocock, "Gibbon's *Decline and Fall and the World View of the Late Enlightenment*," 144, says: "[i]n Voltaire and Hume, as well as in Gibbon, we find an avowed preference for Greco-Roman polytheism as permitting philosophy to develop independently of the gods . . . ."

purpose; neither advance a man's fortune in the world, nor render him a more valuable member of society; neither qualify him for the entertainment of company, nor increase his power of self-enjoyment?" (*EPM*, 270) Hume's rejection of the "whole train of monkish virtues" goes back to his repudiation of a morality rooted in notions of what God is like and what kind of worship he expects from man. He could comprehend no value in it. No amusement or profit seems to come from it. Neither does it appear to him to have advanced human sociability nor stimulated the enjoyment of life's better moments.

For Gibbon the conduct of the monks was anti-social and their "virtue" inimical to everything which makes life happy and human existence bearable in the face of all of its contingencies and uncertainties. "The preachers recommended the practice of the social duties; but they exalted the perfection of monastic virtue, which is *painful* to the individual and *useless* to mankind." (*DF-20*, II, 346, italics added) To the superstitious monks Gibbon counterpoised the superstitious Julian. Julian the Apostate was one of the historical characters Gibbon most admired. While flawed with gross pagan superstition, he nevertheless stands out as an exemplar of classical Roman "manly virtue." "These sleeping or waking visions, the ordinary effects of abstinence and fanaticism, would almost degrade the emperor [Julian] to the level of an Egyptian monk. But the useless lives of [monks] Antony or Pachomius were consumed in these vain occupations. Julian could break from the dream of superstition to arm himself for battle; and, after vanquishing in the field the enemies of Rome, he calmly retired into his tent, to dictate the wise and salutary laws of an empire, or to indulge his genius in the elegant pursuits of literature and philosophy." (*DF-23*, II, 466)

Julian's superstition, unlike that of the monks, was attenuated and had not completely enervated his useful and admirable qualities like courage and curiosity. The monks were utterly and hopelessly sunken in their useless "occupations." In contrast with the Apostate Emperor Julian, we have the Christian Emperor, Theodosius the Younger, whom Gibbon described as "chaste, temperate, liberal, and merciful." Yet, the effects of superstition nullified the value of these qualities. "[T]hese qualities, which can only deserve the name of virtues when they are supported by courage and regulated by discretion, were seldom beneficial, and they sometimes proved mischievous, to mankind." (*DF-32*, III, 409) Theodosius's admirable qualities of character were almost never put to any good effects because he was simply too immersed in stultifying superstition. "His mind, enervated by a royal education, was oppressed and degraded by abject superstition; he fasted, he sung psalms, he blindly accepted the miracles and doctrines with which his faith was continually nourished. Theodosius devoutly worshiped the dead and living saints of the Catholic church; and he once refused to eat, till an insolent monk, who had cast an excommunication on his sovereign, condescended to heal the spiritual wound which he had inflicted." (*DF-32*, III, 409)

Julian and Theodosius the Younger, separated by about one hundred years, standout as a remarkable contrast of the impact of religious superstition on the character and as another invidious comparison of Christian monasticism with Roman pagan virtue. Gibbon could not pass up the opportunity to lament the scene of this "insolent monk" exalting in his superstition-based authority over a credulous sovereign, a gross violation of a proper and appropriate social order. In chapter fifteen, in a section in which he deals with the morality of the early Christians, Gibbon articulates a short, but concise Humean basis for assessing Christian morals.

There are two very natural propensities which we may distinguish in the most virtuous and liberal dispositions, the *love of pleasure* and the *love of action*. If the former be refined by art and learning, improved by the charms of social intercourse, and corrected by a just regard to economy, to health, and to reputation, it is productive of the greatest part of the happiness of private life. The love of action is a principle of a much stronger and more doubtful nature. It often leads to anger, to ambition, and to revenge; but, when it is guided by the sense of propriety and benevolence, it becomes the parent of every virtue; and, if those virtues are accompanied with equal abilities, a family, a state, or an empire may be indebted for their safety and prosperity to the undaunted courage of a single man. To the love of pleasure we may therefore ascribe most of the *agreeable*, to the love of action we may attribute most of the *useful* and respectable, qualifications. The character in which both the one and the other should be united and harmonized would seem to constitute the most perfect idea of human nature. The insensible and inactive disposition, which should be supposed alike destitute of both, would be rejected, by the common consent of mankind, as utterly incapable of procuring any happiness to the individual, or any public benefit to the world. (*DF-15*, II, 37, italics added)[12]

---

[12]See Hume's essay, "Of Refinement in the Arts," where he descants upon the proper mixture of "action, pleasure, and indolence" and defends "moderate" luxury. "In times when industry and the arts flourish, men are kept in perpetual occupation, and enjoy, as their reward, the occupation itself, as well as those pleasures which are the fruit of their labour. The mind acquires new vigour; enlarges its powers and faculties; and by an assiduity in honest industry, both satisfies its natural appetites, and prevents the growth of unnatural ones, which commonly spring up when nourished by ease and idleness. Banish those arts from society, you deprive men both of action and of pleasure; and leaving nothing but indolence in their place, you even destroy the relish of indolence, which is never agreeable, but when it succeeds to

Here, with its roots in the useful and agreeable and a delimitation of the basis of public and private virtues, is a succinct but fundamental view of moral conduct at odds with that practiced by the Christians of the Roman empire. Within human nature itself lies the originative impulses for positive human achievement. Gibbon distinguishes two "natural propensities" (the desire for pleasure and the yearning for action) which give rise to the creation of "dispositions," which in turn results in certain states of character. Like the philosophers of Greece, Gibbon deduces his morals from the nature of man, not God. The love of pleasure, properly tempered and refined, brings private happiness (the ghost of Epicurus at work), while the love of action, properly directed, achieves great social good. Both of these propensities are neutral from a moral perspective. An undisciplined love of pleasure may be one's personal undoing, just as unprincipled ambition may destroy one's social or political position. Moreover, love of action is powerful, unstable, and hence a more volatile propensity than the love of pleasure as it is guided by violent passions and may lead to destructiveness. In a word, the voluptuary may, relatively speaking, corrupt only himself, while from the corruption of the will-to-power ensues violence, tyranny, and oppression. It is the linkage of these two propensities to the *useful* and the *agreeable* that brings them into alignment with moral approbation. The contemplation of someone indulging in *refined* pleasures arouses an agreeable (morally approbated) feeling ("The insensible . . . disposition would be rejected, by the common consent of mankind, as utterly incapable of procuring any happiness to the individual"). Properly directed action may produce, as Gibbon suggests, the most highly commendable public benefactor, someone whose ambition leads to accomplishments or deeds of great usefulness to society.

The monastic life is one of Gibbon's major topics in chapter thirty-seven of the *Decline and Fall*. The measure of monasticism is the useful and the agreeable. "[T]he Ascetics, who obeyed and abused the rigid precepts of the gospel, were inspired by the savage enthusiasm which represents man as a criminal and God as a tyrant." (*DF-37*, IV, 62) The violent passions ("savage enthusiasm") had already corrupted the perspective of the "Ascetics" who viewed their own natures as abased and degraded. "They seriously renounced the business, and the pleasure, of the age; abjured the use of wine, of flesh, and of marriage; chastised their body, mortified their affections, and embraced a life of misery, as the price of eternal happiness." (*DF-37*, IV, 63) The ways of the monks are nearly incomprehensible to Gibbon.[13] Guided by their man-criminal/God-tyrant perspective of the divine-

---

labour, and recruits the spirits, exhausted by too much application and fatigue." (*Essays*, 270)

[13]Likewise Hume in his essay "Of Refinement in the Arts," Hume opens with the following observation. "I have, indeed, heard of a monk abroad, who, because the windows of his cell opened upon a noble prospect, made a *convenant with his eyes* never to turn that way, or receive so sensual a

creature relationship, the entirety of their conduct operated as a quid pro quo: perpetual, self-inflicted misery in this world in exchange for a substantial payoff in the next. "Pleasure and guilt," Gibbon says, "are synonymous terms in the language of the monks; and they had discovered, by experience, that rigid fasts and abstemious diet are the most effectual preservatives against the impure desires of the flesh." (*DF-37*, IV, 72) Since in Gibbon's view pleasure is one of the most basic of human inclinations and is the basis for human fulfillment and happiness, the equation of pleasure and guilt must bring about the most disastrous practical consequences. The useful and the agreeable as standards of approbation and their linkage to certain qualities of character gave way to different kinds of preoccupations, ones that spelled destruction for the Roman empire. Monasteries were sanctuaries of escape in a doubt-ridden age. They abetted cowardice and resignation and helped to undermine the empire. "The subjects of Rome, whose persons and fortunes were made responsible for unequal and exorbitant tributes, retired from the oppression of the Imperial government; and the pusillanimous youth preferred the penance of a monastic, to the dangers of a military, life. The affrighted provincials, of every rank, who fled before the Barbarians, found shelter and subsistence; whole legions were buried in these religious sanctuaries; and the same cause, which relieved the distress of individuals, impaired the strength and fortitude of the empire." (*DF-37*, IV, 69)[14]

Such is Gibbon's imagery of death, debasement, and decline. While the monasteries provided physical sanctuaries, the moral character of monasticism with its obsession with the afterlife and its rewards wreaked of passivity, servility, even cowardice. Gibbon added here a footnote where he says: "[t]he emperors attempted to support the obligation of public and private duties; but the feeble dykes were swept away by the torrent of superstition . . . ." (*DF-37*, IV, 69-70, n.32) The martial norms that had supported the sense of duty ("public" or "private") were enervated by the gross superstition that accompanied the growth of monasticism. The monastic life, in complete defiance of natural human inclinations for rest, comfort, sociability, and happiness, cultivated misery. "Even sleep, the last refuge of the unhappy, was rigorously measured . . . . In this

---

gratification. And such is the crime of drinking champagne or burgundy, preferably to small beer or porter." (*Essays*, 268-69, original italics) Hume can never resist an opportunity to heap abuse upon an asceticism that is beyond his comprehension.

[14]"Do not any longer love this world or its military service, for Scripture's authority attests that whoever is a friend of this world is an enemy of God. He who is a soldier with the sword is the servant of death, and when he sheds his own blood or that of another, this is the reward for his service." This is the admonition of the late fourth- and early fifth-century Paulinus, Bishop of Nola. Quoted from Grant, *The Fall of the Roman Empire*, 187. Grant concurs with Gibbon's analysis of the deleterious impact of Christian otherworldliness on political and military vitality of the Roman Empire.

comfortless state, superstition still pursued and tormented her wretched votaries."
(*DF-37*, IV, 77) Added to the deliberately created physical wretchedness was the
unfathomable terror of eternal damnation, an outgrowth of the preoccupation with
the afterlife.   "[A]nd while they considered each natural impulse as an
unpardonable sin, they perpetually trembled on the edge of a flaming and
bottomless abyss." (*DF-37*, IV, 77) Monasticism had conjured up a terror-laden
interpretive scheme of the world based on a complete repudiation of human nature
and all its attendant inclinations. This scheme of the world, permeated as it was by
relentless apprehension and unappeasable guilt, engendered a paralysis of the kind
of conduct that Gibbon had associated with classical civilization, a conduct of
achievement, resulting in law, roads, art, and philosophy.

Monasticism, immersed in otherworldliness and self-abnegation, brought in
its "spiritual" wake the destruction of the detached, critical thought characteristic
of the high-minded classical philosophers so admired by Gibbon. "The freedom
of the mind, the source of every generous and rational sentiment, was destroyed by
the habits of credulity and submission; and the monk, contracting the vices of a
slave, devoutly followed the faith and passions of his ecclesiastical tyrant." (*DF-
37*, IV, 71) Gibbon's language is permeated with the sense of freedom's loss.
Slavery, tyranny, blind submission are all tragically associated with the ascendancy
of monasticism.

One of the curious historical features of monasticism is that the rigorous
asceticism of the founders, because of its very rejection of the natural make up of
human beings, becomes unsustainable over the long run. Nature itself functions
as a corrective to the extremes of behavior that violent passions will generate. "But
the human character, however it may be exalted or depressed by a temporary
enthusiasm, will return, by degrees to its proper and natural level, and will resume
those passions that seem the most adapted to its present condition." (*DF-15*, II, 41)
Only the most ferocious and intrepid fanaticism could overcome the hedonic and
felicitous tendencies built into the human frame. As a consequence, monastic
asceticism gave way over time to the kind of degeneracy that came from an
institution committed to unattainable standards.   "But their discipline was
corrupted by prosperity: they gradually assumed the pride of wealth, and at last
indulged the luxury of expense. Their public luxury might be excused by the
magnificence of religious worship and the decent motive of erecting durable
habitations for an immortal society. But every age of the church has accused the
licentiousness of the degenerate monks; who no longer remembered the object of
their institution, embraced the vain and sensual pleasures of the world which they
had renounced, and scandalously abused the riches which had been acquired by the
austere virtues of their founders. Their natural descent from such painful and

dangerous virtue to the common vices of humanity will not, perhaps, excite much grief or indignation in the mind of a philosopher." (*DF-37*, IV, 75-76)

The moral philosopher, as Gibbon seems to suggest at the end of this quotation, would not be at all surprised at this turn about. Why? The descent from "painful and dangerous virtue to the common vices of humanity" is quite predictable. Once the initial fanaticism of the founders dissipates, only lip service to the impossible and unnatural ideals remains. The monks discover pleasure but without the refinement of "art and learning," without improvement by the "charm of social intercourse," without "the correction by a just economy," without any of the improving, correcting activities needed to make the character of the pleasure seeker agreeable or useful. Ironically, the attempt to deny pleasure, with its origins in the body, gives way to the extremes of licentiousness.[15]

So while Christianity's intense preoccupation with otherworldly objects and its repudiation of the pleasures associated with the body are in the long run unsustainable, and ultimately mocked by the ironic appearance of licentiousness, so also, the love of action is irrepressible. "The primitive Christians were dead to the business and pleasures of the world; but their love of action, which could never be entirely extinguished, soon revived, and found a new occupation in the government of the church." (*DF-15*, II, 41-42) This observation, applied by Gibbon to the progress of Christianity from its initial ascetic origins to its political instantiation, pertains as well to the progress of monasticism. The accumulation of wealth belies the renunciation of the world. Monasticism, like other *human* institutions, became focused on all the typical accouterments of power and wealth, and administered to the designs of its most ambitious members. "The popular monks, whose reputation was connected with the fame and success of the order, assiduously laboured to multiply the number of their fellow-captives. They insinuated themselves into noble and opulent families; and the specious arts of flattery and seduction were employed to secure those proselytes who might bestow wealth or dignity on the monastic profession." (*DF-37*, IV, 68)

Gibbon, like Hume, believed that monkish morality, a morality which bases itself on pleasing a divine being, gives rise to a devotional industry with stultifying effects on the natural virtues. The Crusades from Gibbon's perspective were a social phenomenon especially revealing of the various superstitious extremes and fanatical absurdities of medieval, monk-ridden Christianity. In the Crusades the philosophic historian could find the most conspicuous examples of monastic excess. For Gibbon these excess were to be exhibited as a part of the entertainment and instruction of his history. It was at this time particularly that the devotional

---

[15]"The more men refine upon pleasure," writes Hume, "the less will they indulge in excess of any kind; because nothing is more destructive to true pleasure than such excesses." (*Essays*, 271)

industry was most productive. "As the manners of the Christians were relaxed, their discipline of penance was enforced; and, with the multiplication of sins, the remedies were multiplied." (*DF-58*, VI, 278) Gibbon then described the invention of the *penitentials*, a kind of theological jurisprudence involving an elaborate, highly differentiated scheme of sins and corresponding penalties. "In this dangerous estimate of crimes and punishments, each case was supposed, each difference was remarked, by the experience or penetration of the monks; some sins are enumerated which innocence could not have suspected, and others which reason cannot believe; and the more ordinary offenses of fornication and adultery, of perjury and sacrilege, or rapine and murder, were expiated by a penance which, according to the various circumstances, was prolonged from forty days to seven years." (*DF-58*, VI, 279)

All of this is material which feeds Gibbon's animus and enlivens his cynicism. Already we see the absurdity at work. The "experience or penetration of the monks," is, of course, sarcastic: no rhyme or reason seems to apply to their enumeration of sins, and the wide ranging penalties for serious crimes suggests extensive corruption. Gibbon's description of the discipline of penance, it would appear, amounts to a *reductio ad absurdum* argument that shows how this elaborate invention of sins and the administration of penalties for them were completely inimical to the well being and the stability of the society, or the reform of malefactors or the execution of justice. "But the rigid execution of these laws would have depopulated the palace, the camp, and the city; the barbarians of the West believed and trembled; but nature often rebelled against principle; and the magistrate laboured with effect to enforce the jurisdiction of the priest." (*DF-58*, VI, 279) Thus the absurdity: laws are *supposed* to make society more safe and stable. But in this case, executing the laws *destroys* society. The observation that "nature often rebelled against principle" again applies the basic Humean philosophical principle: "philosophical decisions," says Hume, "are nothing but the reflections of common life, methodized and corrected." It also echoes Hume's warning about philosophers who "reverse the whole course of nature, as to render this life merely a passage to something further." The departure of theorizing from the correctives grounded in common life experience yields absurdity. The practical consequence is the rebellion of nature against uncorrected, unmethodized principle.

Another aspect of the absurdity was that the multiplication of sins at this time had manufactured such a vast and pervasive dimension of immorality within even the ranges of normal, routine human conduct, that the most ordinary person with all of the predictable human frailties and weaknesses could easily incur massive penalties. "[E]ach act was separately numbered; and in those times of anarchy and vice, a modest sinner might easily incur a debt of three hundred years." (*DF-58*, VI,

279) Punishment for sin was exacted in the form of money (for those who had it) and in flagellation (for those who did not). "That whosoever cannot pay with his purse must pay with his body; and the practice of flagellation was adopted by the monks, a cheap, though painful, equivalent." (*DF-58*, VI, 280) The call to recover the Holy Lands provided, in the form of a call to service, another means for the atonement of sin. "In the council of Clermont, that Pope proclaimed a plenary indulgence to those who should enlist under the banner of the cross: the absolution of *all* their sins, and a full receipt for *all* that might be due of canonical penance." (*DF-58*, VI, 280, original italics)

The implication for all of this, Gibbon points out, is even more absurdity. "At the voice of their pastor, the robber, the incendiary, the homicide, arose by thousands to redeem their souls, by repeating on the infidels the same deeds which they had exercised against their Christian brethren; and the terms of atonement were eagerly embraced by offenders of every rank and denomination. None were pure; none were exempt from the guilt and penalty of sin; and those who were the least amenable to the justice of God and the church were the best entitled to the temporal and eternal recompense of their pious courage." (*DF-58*, VI, 280-81)

Note how the narrative resorts to an immediate and grotesque linkage of the pastor's "voice" to "the robber," "the incendiary," "the homicide." This religious calling raises up the criminal dregs of society. We see the pathetic outcome of a moral system in which the most benighted and culpable (rapists, murders, thieves) are the most advantaged, the most favored in the dispensation of justice. Evil motives and deeds are merely redirected against non-believers. Gibbon thus recreated for us a spectacle of all that is the worst in human conduct: institutional greed and corruption, hypocrisy, and barbarism. In his description of the conduct of the Crusaders at the siege of Antioch, Gibbon again holds up the antimony of abstracted moral principle versus common life experience. "In the eventful period of the siege and defense of Antioch, the crusaders were, alternately, exalted by victory or sunk in despair; either swelled with plenty or emaciated with hunger. A *speculative reasoner* might suppose that their faith had a strong and serious influence on their practice; and that the soldiers of the cross, the deliverers of the holy sepulchre, prepared themselves by a sober and virtuous life for the daily contemplation of martyrdom. *Experience blows away this charitable illusion*; and seldom does the history of profane war display such scenes of intemperance and prostitution as were exhibited under the walls of Antioch." (*DF-58*, VI, 314, italics added)

"Speculative" reasoning is blown away by historical experience. Here we have a direct application of Hume's philosophical method to history. Hume in fact in one of his essays says that: "[t]heories of abstract philosophy, systems of profound theology, have prevailed during one age: In a successive period, these have been *universally exploded*: their absurdity has been detected: Other theories and systems have supplied their place, which again gave place to their successors . . . ." (*Essays*, 242, italics added) Hume is talking about historical experience used to correct and methodize speculative reasoning. Note even the similarity of "demolition" imagery in the language: Gibbon speaks of how experience "blows away" the illusions of speculation; while Hume talks about systems of theology being "exploded" by the experience of passing time. We also have historical confirmation of two of Hume's observations in the *Dialogues* regarding the effects of superstitious morality on human conduct: "[t]hus the Motives of vulgar Superstition have no great Influence on general Conduct; nor is their Operation very favourable to Morality in the Instances, where they predominate;" (*DNR*, 255) and, "the Terrors of Religion commonly prevail above its Comforts." (*DNR*, 257)

Monasticism thus represented for Hume and Gibbon both the culmination point of Christianity's corruption by otherworldly preoccupations and the counterpoint to a morality based on human nature and derived from common life experience centering on enterprises that are useful and agreeable. Gibbon's characterization of monasticism with its repudiation of classical virtue was another element of his harsh moral critique of Christianity and its role in the decline and fall of the Roman empire.

From both Hume and Gibbon thus, with poignant emotion, emerged a most profound contrast drawn between a conventional morality rooted in human nature and justified by utility, and a theological morality which rests upon conceptions of God and His notions about what is appropriate behavior for human beings. Theological morality retains a disposition for promoting hostility and contention because no non-coercive means are apparent or available to resolve conflict or disagreement over the theological or doctrinal principles which ground the morality. Theological morality, in effect, is *anti-conventional* in the sense that it can appeal to no common experience that provides for a "convening" process out of which mutually agreed upon rules or norms might be established.

CHAPTER SEVEN

POLITICS AND FANATICISM

*And thus is religion also panic when enthusiasm of any kind gets
up, as oft, on melancholy occasions, it will do.*

Shaftesbury

The work of religious fanatics figured prominently in Gibbon's history of Christianity's ascendancy in the Roman empire and in Hume's account of the Reformation in England and Scotland. Religious fanaticism was indeed a subject which greatly challenged them as philosophic historians. There was a certain inexplicability about it, yet they were required to find both entertainment and moral instruction in a phenomenon that closely followed the career of Christianity itself. "Fanatics," Hume writes, "may suppose, *that dominion is founded on grace*, and *that saints alone inherit the earth*; but the civil magistrate very justly puts these sublime theorists on the same footing with common robbers, and teaches them by the severest discipline, that a rule, which, in speculation, may seem the most advantageous to society, may yet be found, in practice, totally pernicious and destructive." (*EPM*, 193, original italics) Hume pits the religious fanatic (the purveyor of speculative ideals) against the magistrate (the representative of the social order) and sides with the magistrate. Hume was referring here to the seventeenth-century English Puritans who toppled Charles I from the throne at the conclusion of a bloody civil war and then beheaded him as a traitor. "That there were *religious* fanatics of this kind in England, during the civil wars, we learn from history; though it is probable, that the obvious *tendency* of these principles excited such horror in mankind, as soon obliged the dangerous enthusiast to renounce, or at least conceal their tenets. Perhaps the *levellers*, who claimed an equal distribution of property, were a kind of *political* fanatics, which arose from the religious species, and more openly avowed their pretensions; as carrying a more plausible appearance, of being practicable in themselves, as well as useful to human society." (*EPM*, 193, original italics)[1] Hume links religious and political fanaticism. They are not tight, firmly distinguishable categories; they fade into each other. Religion and politics would seem to have a large region of

---

[1]Compare Hume's censorious remarks about the Levellers with those of Norman Cohn, *The Pursuit of the Millennium* (Fairlawn, NJ: Essential Books, Inc. 1957), who spends much of the book discussing the antinomian effects of religious enthusiasm in medieval Christianity. See 226-36 for his discussion of the levelling Bohemian Taborites of the fifteenth century. "Unfortunately for their social experiment, the Taborite revolutionaries were so preoccupied with common ownership that they altogether ignored the need to produce." (230) These "men of the Law of God" believed themselves entitled to plunder the rich. In the Spring of 1420 the Taborites proclaimed the abolition of all feudal bonds. They then began plundering the lands of the peasants.

interpenetration. The avowal of economic equality by Hume's Levellers, though wearing the face of utility and seemingly of a purely political nature, is ultimately grounded in speculative religious idealism.

The key issue here for Hume, aside from the pure irrationality of the speculative principle upon which the Levellers' claims are based, is the problem of justifying political power, a problem, one might say, of plausibility, particularly when religion enters the scene. Power, Hume says, is the most coveted of all possessions. (*Essays*, 498) For this most coveted of goods there is an intense competition, one which historical study demonstrates is often ferocious and destructive. One important piece of that competition for power is the process of justifying the claim for its possession, establishing a rationale, so to speak, that makes the claim believable or acceptable.[2] The more convincing that rationale is, the more *plausible* it seems, the less pure force needs to come into play to secure or maintain that power. Those who govern must be perceived in some way to be entitled to the allegiance of those who are governed. Hume makes this observation in "Of the First Principles of Government." "Nothing appears more surprizing to those, who consider human affairs with a philosophical eye, than the easiness with which the many are governed by the few; and the implicit submission, with which men resign their own sentiments and passions to those of their rulers. When we enquire by what means this wonder is effected, we shall find, that as Force is always on the side of the governed, the governors have nothing to support them but opinion." (*Essays*, 32)   Although government readily coerces through its enforcement of the law, its authority rests ultimately on its acceptance (the *opinion* of legitimacy) by those who are governed.

Religion is an important source for establishing rationales to justify power; and herein lies the plausibility problem. No universal religion exists or ever existed. Religious systems have limited plausibility; that is a basic and uncontestable fact as evidenced by the vast multiplicity of them, their high level of mutually exclusivity, and their long history of competition and conflict. And, in a society where a new or a variant religion arises to challenge an established one, such as in the seventeenth-century England Hume describes, the challengers must resort to force in order to compensate for the lack of plausibility, while the challenged exert the force of resistance. Since the overthrow or displacement of one religion by another is never for Hume a matter of reason—rival sectarians don't *argue*

---

[2] See Peter Drucker, *The End of Economic Man: A Study of the New Totalitarianism* (New York: John Day Co., 1939), 14. "For the last two thousand years, ever since Aristotle, the justification of power and authority has been the central problem of European political thought and of European political history. And since Europe became Christian there has never been any other approach to this problem than that of seeking justification in the benefit which the exercise of power confers upon its subjects—be it the salvation of their souls, the 'good life,' or the highest standard of living for the greatest number."

themselves into ascendency—sectarian confrontation or doctrinal contention almost always precedes with some dimension of force or power which is accompanied by strong emotion. The strong emotion often associated with sectarian strife is advantageous from the perspective of its possessor because its strengthens the resolve of the sectarian, making it possible to face hardship, opposition, and even persecution. This emotion makes its possessor more likely both to endure and resort to force. Religious fanaticism is almost always historically connected with force: wars, rebellions, pogroms, inquisitions, all of these are linked in some way to religious fanaticism. As Hume notes above, the magistrate, encountering religionists such as the Levellers who are about redistributing property, regards them merely as criminals, as "common robbers" even though their notions or theories may be quite "sublime." Religious fanaticism from the perspective of Hume is an abuse of religion, one in which religion becomes an instrument of confrontation and coercion.

The Levellers, as noted above, had attempted to repudiate the traditional rules of property. These fanatics, Hume argues, were basing their repudiation on a principle that would not survive a practical test. Their principle of allocation (what might be called the "moral merit" principle) was philosophically appealing but historically ignorant. The most obvious allocation principle for material goods, Hume says, that would occur to a "creature, possessed of reason, but unacquainted with human nature . . . would be, to assign the largest possessions to the most extensive virtue, and give every one the power of doing good, proportioned to his inclination." (*EPM*, 192-193) This is the "sublimity" which is the basis for Hume's sarcastic reference. This moral merit principle is obvious, appealing, and commendable, but would have to be seen as unworkable by someone who had observed human beings in action, someone with historical experience and insight. What, indeed, is wrong with such a principle? "In a perfect theocracy, where a being, infinitely intelligent, governs by particular volitions, this rule would certainly have place, and might serve to the wisest purposes: But were mankind to execute such a law; so great is the uncertainty of merit, both from its natural obscurity, and from the self-conceit of each individual, that no determinate rule of conduct would ever result from it; and the total dissolution of society must be the immediate consequence." (*EPM*, 193)

Hume links the moral merit principle to theological utopianism and thus attempts to deflate it. The principle does not work because natural human egoism and the subjective (and naturally disputatious) character of moral merit make the allocation forever contentious. Every allocation decision requires a perspective and an impartial distance beyond the capacity of imperfect creatures who generally tend to favor themselves and those with whom they are close. "We are naturally partial," Hume says, "to ourselves and to our friends . . . ." (*EPM*, 188) Allocating social goods according to a pure moral merit principle can never get around this problem of naturally partiality. What is necessary is some allocation principle that pushes toward a general acceptance even among naturally partial, self-regarding human beings. *"What is a man's property?* Anything which it is lawful for him, and for him alone, to use. *But what rule have we, by which we can distinguish these objects?* Here we must have recourse to statutes, customs, precedents, analogies, and a hundred other circumstances; some of which are constant and inflexible, some variable and arbitrary. But the ultimate point, in which they all professedly terminate, is the interest and happiness of human society." (*EPM*, 197-98, original italics)

Hume makes a point against considering notions like property and possession too abstractly and apart from the established practices. What is important is that notions of property have their ultimate basis in utility and mutual self-interest. His appeal again is to reflections on common life and the correcting and methodizing work of such observations. Religious merit or merit derived from religious ideals as principles of allocation do not work if everyone does not share the religious beliefs. Even a unanimity of religious belief may not suffice, since the co-religionists still must agree on how to interpret and apply the beliefs. Allocating things of value is a thorny, perennial problem for naturally partial human beings.

The program of the fanatical Levellers, Hume argues, would lead to tyranny. This is the basis for Hume's characterization of their principles as "totally pernicious and destructive." These principles are attractive to the imagination but incompatible with human nature. They would aggravate rather than remediate partiality. "But besides, that so much authority [to enforce full equality of distribution] must soon degenerate into tyranny, and be exerted with great partialities . . . ." (*EPM*, 194)[3] Hume makes the link between fanaticism and tyranny, and the kind of fanaticism that Hume had focused upon historically was religious, and particularly Christian. Thus one can say that the significance of fanaticism in Christianity for the development of political institutions in the West is paramount in the work of Hume.

---

[3]See Robert Nisbet, *Twilight of Authority* (New York: Oxford University Press, 1975), 202. Nisbet makes, in my view, a very profound observation about equality as a political ideal. The observation would seem to support Hume's critique of the Levellers' program and his observation that the notion is ultimately of a religious or utopian nature. Equality "resembles some of the religious ideals or passions which offer, just by virtue of the impossibility of ever giving them adequate representation in the actual world, almost unlimited potentialities for continuous onslaught against institutions." Equality as an ideal, Nisbet argues, is unmanageable. "Equality has a built-in revolutionary force lacking in such ideas as justice or liberty. For once the ideal of equality becomes uppermost it can become insatiable in its demands."

Gibbon's fanatics were the early Christians of the empire who rejected the pagan gods and subverted the Roman government. Christianity, Gibbon argues, contributed to the dissolution of the Roman empire, and while the originative forces of the Christian challenge to the Roman empire were religious, its victory was established by political power as well as religious. "Of all our passions and appetites," says Gibbon, "the love of power is of the most imperious and unsociable nature, since the pride of one man requires the submission of the multitude. In the tumult of civil discord the laws of society lose their force, and their place is seldom supplied by those of humanity." (*DF-4*, I, 93) Like Hume, Gibbon argues that the struggle for power, more than any other contest, brings the natural egoism of human beings into direct conflict.

The dynamics that Gibbon presents in Christianity's early challenge to the Roman state are analogous in many ways to Hume's account of the Puritan revolution: fanatical believers confront an established order they view as morally bankrupt and challenge its legitimacy, i.e., its authority to subject them to its rules and demand their allegiance. Frank Manual writes that "Hume's chronicle of the evil contagion of enthusiasm in his history of the Stuarts had a profound influence on Gibbon's world-historical view."[4] So within the history of Christianity there is for Hume and Gibbon an entertaining and instructive history of fanaticism. Three themes help to explicate this history, all dealing, in the case of Hume, with seventeenth-century Puritans; with Gibbon, the early Christians: (1) religious fanaticism and the destruction of conventional morality; (2) the social effects of otherworldliness, and (3) religious fanaticism and the emergence of tyranny.

Religious Fanaticism and the Destruction of Conventional Morality

Puritanism fueled itself with a hatred of Catholicism and ancient traditions that smacked in any way of popery. Aversion to popery by Hume's account brought the Puritan-dominated House of Commons into open conflict with Charles I and ultimately led to his tragic downfall. "The distempered imaginations of men were agitated with a continual dread of popery, with a horror against prelacy, with an antipathy to ceremonies and the liturgy, and with a violent affection for whatever was most opposite to these objects of aversion." (*HE*, V, 102) Two descriptive features in Hume's narrative stand out. First, is the characterization of the enormous intensity of emotion—"continual dread," "horror," and "violent affection." Religious passions of the most extreme kind were at work in pushing the participants in the story into the sanguinary civil war. This intensity and extremity of emotion are clearly reflected in Hume's language. Second, is the dimension of pathology connected with the mentality of the Puritans, which Hume

---

[4]Frank Manuel, "Edward Gibbon: 'Historien-Philosophe,'" 174.

designates with the epithet "distempered imaginations." Hume distrusted intense emotion, particularly religious emotion, because it was connected by the imagination to the unfathomable, "invisible" world. Hume viewed much of the history of this period as a kind of collective insanity or dementia fueled by raging religious emotion. Those seized by this religious dementia were engaged in the repudiation of conventional modes of moral and ethical behaviour. Adherents of the latter were at a disadvantage because of *their* relative lack of a zeal in comparison with that of their enthusiastic rivals. Conventional norms of behavior by their very nature are supported by milder emotions or sentiments.

The effect of a conflict such as this, a conflict, if you will, of two normative orders, resulted in conflagration—civil war. "The fanatical spirit let loose, confounded all regard to ease, safety, interest; and dissolved every moral and civil obligation." (*HE*, V, 102) The loss, the damage described is stark. This religious conflict unleashed forces that destroyed much of the old order and its norms. "Ease," "safety," "interest," these were all made possible in Hume's perspective by long-established norms of self-restraint, and they all became casualties of the religious conflict that arose from Charles's conflict with his Puritan subjects. Hume is particularly critical in this context of the conduct of the Puritans. Their fanaticism, he argues, "liberated" them from the constraints of conventional morality. Because they conceived of themselves as agents of a divine cause they believed they were free from the established norms and rules which govern most people.[5] Consider Hume's description of the character of Harry Vane, one of the Puritan leaders of the Republican party. "Vane was noted, in all civil transactions, for temper, insinuation, address, and a profound judgment; in all religious speculations, for folly and extravagance. He was a perfect enthusiast; and fancying that he was certainly favoured with inspiration, he deemed himself, to speak in the language of the times, to be a *man above ordinances*, and, by reason of his perfection, to be unlimited and unrestrained by any rules which govern inferior morals." (*HE*, V, 413, original italics)

Vane stands out as a kind of split personality—a characterization in keeping with Hume's view of the process as an episode of mass psychosis. Deep judgment, wisdom, and decorum reside with folly, extravagance, and arrogance. In his religious convictions Vane was gripped by a fanaticism which destroyed his judgment and made him arrogant and contemptuous of the rules of conventional morality—a "man above ordinances." "These whimsies, mingling with pride, had

---

[5]Max Weber, *The Sociology of Religion*, trans. Ephriam Fischoff (Boston: Beacon Press, 1993), 202. Weber writes of the great sense of spiritual superiority the Puritans possessed once their conviction of grace was set. "Predestination provides the individual who has found religious grace with the highest possible degree of certainty of salvation, once he has attained assurance that he belongs to the very limited aristocracy of salvation who are the elect."

so corrupted his excellent understanding, that sometimes he thought himself the person deputed to reign on earth for a thousand years over the whole congregation of the faithful." (*HE*, V, 413) Vane in Hume's judgment was thoroughly spoiled by this immense moral superiority and arrogance, the product of his religious dementia. In such an antinomian society full of men above ordinances, who imagine themselves to be perfect and unfettered by rules, the possibilities for anarchy and tyranny are considerably enlarged. This was precisely the effect of the civil war and the regicide of Charles I. "The confusions which overspread England after the murder of Charles I. proceeded as well from the spirit of refinement and innovation which agitated the ruling party, as from the dissolution of all that authority, both civil and ecclesiastical, by which the nation had ever been accustomed to be governed." (*HE*, V, 280) The Puritan "innovations" in religion helped to usher in a chaos that destroyed the bonds of authority, authority generations in the making. Now, "[e]very man had framed the model of a republic; and however new it was, or fantastical, he was eager in recommending it to his fellow-citizens, or even imposing it by force upon them." (*HE*, V, 280) All sorts of novel ideas or "models" of the best kind of society were abundant, but since opinion was so varied and divided, such models were merely points for contention and dispute. The destruction of political authority was a casualty of the demise of religious authority. "Every man had adjusted a system of religion, which, being derived from no traditional authority, was peculiar to himself; and being founded on supposed inspiration, not on any principles of human reason, had no means, besides cant and low rhetoric, by which it could recommend itself to others." (*HE*, V, 280)

With the dismantling of "traditional authority" came the onset of a kind of religious solipsism. Each particular religious faction recognized no authority beyond itself and advanced its own "inspired" principles for the organization of society and the distribution of goods. The Levellers advocated a system of communism. "The levellers insisted on an equal distribution of power and property, and disclaimed all dependence and subordination." (*HE*, V, 280) The chiliastic Fifth Monarchy men wanted to destroy human government altogether. "The millenarians or fifth monarchy men required, that government itself be abolished, and all human powers be laid in the dust, in order to pave the way for the dominion of Christ, whose second coming they suddenly expected." (*HE*, V, 280) The Antinomians believed they completely transcended the boundaries of law and morality. "The Antinomians even insisted, that the obligations of morality and natural law were suspended, and that the elect, guided by an internal principle more perfect and divine, were superior to the *beggarly elements* of justice and humanity." (*HE*, V, 280, original italics) Such then were the competing sects with their "inspired" views of how society ought to be organized. But the overall effects, Hume says, were that the "bands of society were everywhere loosened; and the irregular passions of men were encouraged by speculative principles still more unsocial and irregular." (*HE*, V, 281)

This loosening of the bands of society by religious factionalism culminated with the elevation of the usurper and regicide, Oliver Cromwell, as Head of the Protectorate. Cromwell by Hume's account was an artful but fanatical tyrant. "The murder of the king, the most atrocious of all his actions, was to him covered under a mighty cloud of republican and fanatical illusions; and it is not impossible but he might believe it, as many others did, the most meritorious action that he could perform." (*HE*, V, 392) Here is Hume's equation of religious fanaticism with moral perversion: an act of evil is reconstructed as an act of merit. While Hume pays tribute to Cromwell's courage and political abilities, he nevertheless considered his elevation to power a national tragedy. The *political* circumstances that brought about the civil war, the regicide and the Protectorate could have been peacefully resolved if the possibilities for amelioration had not been destroyed by *religious* factionalism. "It is true, had the king been able to support government, and at the same time to abstain from all invasion of national privileges, it seems not probable that the puritans ever could have acquired such authority as to overturn the whole constitution: yet so entire was the subjection into which Charles was now fallen, that had not the wound been poisoned by the infusion of theological hatred, it must have admitted of an easy remedy." (*HE*, V, 22)

The Puritan revolution was a strange and unforgettable event for Hume. In it he saw the worst of Christianity manifest in a fanaticism that transformed normally decent people into arrogant and reckless anarchists. The noxious vapors of religious enthusiasm that the Puritans had inhaled seemed to release them completely from the usual norms of self-restraint. "Among the generality of men, educated in regular civilized societies, the sentiments of shame, duty, honour, have considerable authority, and serve to counterbalance and direct the motives derived from private advantage." (*HE*, V, 220) The humanizing force of these civilizing conventions are, as Hume suggests, of value in tilting human beings back away from egoistic, self-seeking inclinations that make them fundamentally unsociable and combative. The fanaticism of the Puritans had the effect of undoing all of this beneficial work. "[B]ut, by the predominancy of enthusiasm among the parliamentary forces, these salutary principles lost their credit, and were regarded as mere human inventions, yea, moral institutions, fitter for heathens than for Christians. The saint, resigned over to superior guidance, was at full liberty to gratify all his appetites, disguised under the appearance of pious zeal. And, besides the strange corruptions engendered by this spirit, it eluded and loosened all the ties of morality, and gave entire scope, and even sanction, to the selfishness and ambition which naturally adhere to the human mind." (*HE*, V, 220) This is probably Hume's most clarion expression of his view that religious fanaticism destroys conventional morality and the sorts of valuable things conventional morality makes possible. It also makes clear an underlying Humean assumption about civilization itself, namely that the values that gradually emerge from the process of civilization are the work of self-restraint against the background of perennial human weakness.

Gibbon's narration, like Hume's, features the clash of religious fanaticism with conventional morality but went beyond Hume's minimal account of the actual theological disputes and delved deeply into the rich polemical history of Christian theology and doctrine. With all of its inimitable ironic twists and turns the story of theological warfare in extensive detail enlivens the *Decline and Fall* and affords a kind of dark amusement. In chapter twenty-one it is the Arian controversy over the nature of the Trinity. In chapter forty-seven Gibbon recreates the tumult and clamor over the Incarnation doctrine, and in chapter forty-nine the reader becomes immersed in the raucous iconoclast controversy in the Eastern church. Roy Porter writes that "Gibbon the philosophical historian made religious belief itself into a historical problem."[6] This was a Humean epistemological legacy, and Gibbon's approach to showing just how much of a historical problem religious belief was amounted to an extensive exploration of the permutation of theological doctrine, the multiplication of sects, and the bearing of sectarian fission on the moral conduct of the disputants.[7] Gibbon seemed intent on recapturing the actual unfolding of the controversies and how they ultimately are incorporated into sects which divide and subdivide.[8] The absurdity that persistently surfaces in the narrative is the correlation between intense, passionate, otherworldly belief, and civil war, cruelty, persecution, hypocrisy, and destruction. Again, we see Gibbon pursuing his "melancholy duty" as a historian—here, as a historian of theological doctrine. The religious passions of the early Christians with their precipitous work and extreme direction were a problem. "The desire of perfection became the ruling passion of their soul; and it is well known that, while reason embraces a cold mediocrity, our passions hurry us, with rapid violence, over the space which lies

---

[6]Porter, *Edward Gibbon: Making History*, 118.

[7]Craddock, *Edward Gibbon: Luminous Historian*, 212, notes that in chapter forty-seven Gibbon seems to be saying that religious questions are never really decided by anything but power or force."

[8]See Lionel Gossman, *The Empire Unpossess'd: An Essay on Gibbon's 'Decline and Fall.'* Cambridge: Cambridge University Press, 1981, 26, where he writes: "[o]ne of the least attractive aspects of Christianity, for instance, and a sign, for Gibbon, of the lack of credibility, is its continual division of itself into innumerable sects."

between the most opposite extremes." (*DF-15*, II, 35) Gibbon's criticism of the early Christians is suggested by the imagery of "hurry" and the "rapid violence." Chapter forty-seven chronicles a wild and bitter two hundred and fifty year religious war. This chapter's overriding purpose seems to be to capture the whole odd business of doctrinal dispute as a petty yet bloody affair to, in Gibbon's words, "represent the ecclesiastical and political schism of the Oriental sects, and to introduce their clamourous or sanguinary contests by a modest inquiry into the doctrines of the primitive church." (*DF-47*, V, 103) Note the curious balance Gibbon strikes with his antithesis: "*their* [the barbarian's] clamourous or sanguinary contests" held up to "*his* [the philosophic historian's] modest inquiry" into them. Here Gibbon is eager to recreate the degenerate spectacle of endlessly dividing, mutually persecuting sects, the effects as always, "clamourous" and "sanguinary"—barbarians at work. The theological topic that generated this two hundred and fifty year war was the nature of the incarnation. "I have already observed that the disputes of the Trinity were succeeded by those of the Incarnation: alike scandalous to the church, alike pernicious to the state, still more minute in their origin, still more durable in their effects." (*DF-47*, V, 103) Compact as this statement is, it aptly summarizes Gibbon's major points of contention. Religion is diminished. The state crumbles. The evil effects are long term and not to be undone, and the cause of it all is a fanatical preoccupation with "minute" points of doctrine that are inherently unresolvable. This description with its intense focus on the relationship between controversy over doctrinal minutia and political violence is striking in its resemblance in tone to Hume's summary analysis of the causes of the conflict between Charles I and the Puritan Parliament. "[T]he grievances which tended chiefly to inflame the Parliament and nation, especially the latter, were the surplice, the rails placed about the altar, the bows exacted on approaching it, the liturgy, the breach of the sabbath, embroidered copes, lawn sleeves, the use of the ring in marriage, and of the cross in baptism." Such then are the doctrinal *causes* of the conflict, trivial in Hume's estimate to the extreme. Here now are the *effects*—massive and destructive. "On account of these, were the popular leaders content to throw the government into such violent convulsions; and, to the disgrace of that age and of this island, it must be acknowledged that the disorders in Scotland entirely, and those in England mostly, proceeded from so mean and contemptible an origin." (*HE*, V, 22)

Christianity's early conflict with pagan Rome in Gibbon's controversial reconstruction of it pits the otherworldly-absorbed fanatical early Christians against the conservative pagan Roman state. Chapter sixteen of the *Decline and Fall*, "The conduct of the Roman Government towards the Christians, from the Reign of Nero to that of Constantine," opens in a fashion that parallels in both tone and method the proceeding chapter. Gibbon had launched chapter fifteen with an ironic posturing which, as we have seen, barely dissimulated his intention to cast doubt on the credibility of the earliest historians of the church. Chapter sixteen, likewise ironic, poses deliberately troubling questions about the character and personality of the early Christians. While chapter fifteen raised doubts about the historical truth of early Christianity, chapter sixteen posed questions about the ethical conduct of the early Christians. Given the high moral character of the early Christians, and given the generally tolerant policy toward religion, how account for the Roman government's persecution of them? "If we seriously consider the purity of the Christian religion, the sanctity of its moral precepts, and the innocent as well as austere lives of the greater number of those who, during the first ages, embraced the faith of the gospel . . . and [i]f . . . we recollect the universal toleration of Polytheism, as it was invariably maintained by the faith of the people, the incredulity of philosophers, and the policy of the Roman senate and emperors, we are at a loss to discover what new offence the Christians had committed, what new provocation could exasperate the mild indifference of antiquity, and what new motives could urge the Roman princes, who beheld, without concern, a thousand forms of religion subsisting in peace under their gentle sway, to inflict a severe punishment on any part of their subjects, who had chosen for themselves a singular, but an inoffensive, mode of faith and worship." (*DF-16*, II, 76)

So Gibbon begins this chapter with the *ironic* confession: we are "at a loss" to explain what the early Christians could have done to provoke the wrath of the usually "indifferent" Roman governors and the persecution that issued from it. But this piece of irony is merely a gambit used to camouflage an attack. What follows is a piece of flagrant iconoclasm. Christians brought about their own persecution because of their fanaticism and their emphatic and visible rejection of the traditions of the society in which they lived. "It has already been observed that the religious concord of the world was principally supported by the implicit assent and reverence which the nations of antiquity expressed for their respective traditions and ceremonies." Gibbon thus affirms the integration of this traditional pagan religion with social morality and then points to the consequences of an attack on them. "It might therefore be expected that they would unite with indignation against any sect of people which should separate itself from the communion of mankind, and, claiming the exclusive possession of divine knowledge, should disdain every form of worship, except its own, as impious and idolatrous. The rights of toleration were held by mutual indulgence; they were justly forfeited by a refusal of the accustomed tribute." (*DF-16*, II, 77)

Because of their separatism, their zeal, and their intolerance, the early Christians, Gibbon argues, forfeited the toleration that was extended to other sects.

Mutual toleration rested on reciprocity and the Christians were, with their "exclusive possession of divine knowledge," unwilling to tolerate non-Christians. Gibbon's early Christians, like Hume's Puritans, were gloomily focused on the "invisible world" and like them, to the puzzlement and contempt of onlookers, rejected the pleasures and felicities of the visible world. "Their gloomy and austere aspect, their abhorrence of the common business and pleasures of life, and their frequent predictions of impending calamities, inspired the Pagans with apprehension of some danger which would arise from the new sect, the more alarming as it was the more obscure." (*DF-16*, II, 84) Gibbon then quotes Pliny, who upon observing these dour, calamity inspired Christians comments that, "'[w]hatever . . . may be the principle of their conduct, their inflexible obstinacy appeared deserving of punishment.'" (*DF-16*, II, 84) Gibbon's disapprobation for the early Christians grew out of his revulsion with their repudiation of the social order and their determination, based upon a supreme confidence in divine inspiration, to cast aside the centuries of tradition. "By embracing the faith of the Gospel, the Christians incurred the supposed guilt of an unnatural and unpardonable offence. They dissolved the sacred ties of custom and education, violated the religious institutions of their country, and presumptuously despised whatever their fathers had believed as true, or had reverenced as sacred . . . . Every Christian rejected with contempt the superstitions of his family, his city, and his province." (*DF-16*, II, 80) Thus, the Christians became implacable enemies of the existing social order, contemptuous of all its customs, values, and institutions.

It is easy to see why this chapter so aggrieved Christian readers, both in Gibbon's own and in later generations. Yet, given his Humean view of religious belief as an essentially irrational enterprise, Gibbon's judgment is understandable. Since religious belief cannot be based on reason, i.e., since religious doctrines cannot be proved or demonstrated, the willingness of members of parvenu sects to reject and condemn venerable religious traditions constitutes an act of supreme arrogance as well as danger. Gibbon viewed religious traditions as conventions like other cultural artifacts such as language, law, and art. They emerge from long term collaborative efforts and represent in institutionalized form accepted ways of interpreting experience. Conventions provide commonality, draw people together, and mediate differences. While traditions inevitably change, both Hume and Gibbon argue that gradual transformation is almost always preferable to drastic change because the traditions and institutions undergoing change contain much of tried and tested value which fanaticism tends to destroy. Fanatical challenges and confrontations provoke reaction which in turn escalates conflict. Thus, either the reactionaries prevail and repress even constructive change, or the fanatics win and implement their own special programs of repression and reigns of terror.

The Social Effects of Otherworldliness

The religion of the seventeenth-century Puritans was lugubrious and almost entirely otherworldly in its preoccupations and in its disdain for comfort and refinement. At one point in his narrative Hume says: "[t]he gloomy enthusiasm which prevailed among the parliamentary party is surely the most curious spectacle presented by any history; and the most instructive, as well as entertaining, to a philosophical mind." (*HE*, V, 427) A "curious spectacle" indeed! Hume seems to find it difficult to comprehend, yet perhaps for that very reason the spectacle is of value both as a philosophical curiosity insofar as it unveils a further complexity of human nature, and as a piece of entertainment. One of the social effects of this otherworldly Puritan religiosity was a severity and a hostility toward anything and everything that was pleasurable. "All recreations were, in a manner, suspended by the rigid severity of the presbyterians and independents. Horse races and cock-matches were prohibited as the greatest enormities. Even bear-baiting was esteemed heathenish and unchristian: the sport of it, not the inhumanity, gave offense." (*HE*, V, 427) The reader must understand that it was the *enjoyment* involved in gruesome spectacles like bear-baiting that the Puritans could not abide. But this severity extended much wider than just to sport and general merriment. "It must, however, be confessed, that the wretched fanaticism which so much infected the parliamentary party was no less destructive of taste and science, than of all law and order. Gaiety and wit were proscribed; human learning despised; freedom of inquiry detested; cant and hypocrisy alone encouraged." (*HE*, V, 436)

The theology of the Puritans when carried into practice, Hume believed, had plunged England into anarchy. Its corrosive effects seeped into every corner of social existence. "In every discourse or conversion, this mode of religion entered; in all business it had a share; every elegant pleasure of amusement it utterly annihilated." (*HE*, V, 69). Note the pervasiveness of this new religious mentality and its effect of universal diminishment of sociability and enjoyment. It, Hume seems to suggest, amounts to of a kind of social pathology. "[M]any vices or corruptions of mind it promoted; even diseases and bodily distempers were not totally exempted from it; and it became requisite, we are told, for all physicians to be expert in the spiritual profession, and, by theological considerations, to allay those religious terrors with which their patients were so generally haunted." (*HE*, V, 69) Even the tools of learning, Hume adds, were turned into the service of fanaticism. "Learning itself, which tends so much to enlarge the mind and humanize the temper, rather served on this occasion to exalt that epidemical frenzy which prevailed." (*HE*, V, 69)

In a society that is in the grip of an "epidemical frenzy"—Hume is resorting here to medical imagery—fervor and the high emotional agitation are signs of inspiration, evidence of devotion, proof of true belief. Powerful incentives come into play to encourage hyperbolic expressions of religious emotion whether it is genuinely felt or not. Since correct belief is what becomes highly valued, and since what one really believes can, if desired, always be held private, *expressions* of sincerity become extremely important, an irony in itself because of the close connection between strong asseveration of belief and insincerity. Where asseveration reigns supreme, hypocrisy takes on particularly large dimensions. Indeed, it seems to be an almost natural, predictable outgrowth of a society with a powerfully sanctioned official ideology.[9]

This elevation of hypocrisy brought about by the ascendancy of the Puritans and their own particular brand of religiosity was another part of the destructive impact of the religious fanaticism. "[S]o congenial to the human mind," says Hume, "are religious sentiments, that it is impossible to counterfeit long these holy fervours, without feeling some share of the assumed warmth; and, on the other hand, so precarious and temporary, from the frailty of human nature, is the operation of these spiritual views, that the religious ecstasies, if constantly employed, must often be counterfeit, and must be warped by those more familiar motives of interest and ambition which insensibly gain upon the mind." (*HE*, V, 526, n.D)

Here is a shrewd and extraordinarily devastating observation about some interesting characteristics of religious emotion. While intense religious emotion is to some extent self-authenticating (even going through the motions will stimulate some "share of assumed warmth"), the psychological-emotional makeup of human beings is such that it is impossible to sustain it continuously or frequently without some degree of insincerity. Even worse is that the insincerity or hypocrisy is shaped by myriad human interests; as Hume says, it becomes "warped," and predictably so, by less "spiritual" interests such as ambition, etc. Intense religiosity, the kind Hume associated with his seventeenth-century Puritans, with its usual festering hypocrisy, it would seem, moves relentlessly toward self-delusion and rationalization. This is precisely what Hume claims happened to the Puritan leaders of the revolt against Charles I. "This indeed seems the key to most of the celebrated characters of that age. Equally full of fraud and of ardour, these pious patriots talked perpetually of seeking the Lord, yet still pursued their own purposes; and have left a memorable lesson to posterity, how delusive, how

---

[9]The Soviet Union, especially under Stalin, is history's most conspicuous, most extreme example of this phenomena. See Leonard Schapiro, *The Communist Party of the Soviet Union*, 2nd ed. (New York: Random House, 1971), 477. Schapiro writes: "[n]o one understood better than Stalin that the true object of propaganda is neither to convince nor even to persuade, but to produce a uniform pattern of public utterance in which the first trace of unorthodox thought immediately reveals itself as a jarring dissonance."

destructive, that principle is by which they were animated." (*HE*, V, 526, n.D)
Hume's explanation, ("key to the characters" of this period) is the religious
fanaticism at work with its volatile combination of deceit and zealotry ("fraud and
ardour").

The Anglican Church, Hume argues, was quite justified in its retention of
certain of the ancient Catholic rites and ceremonies. Interestingly, Hume sees these
Catholic vestiges to be an especially valuable antidote to Puritan asceticism. The
ceremonies help link the religious ideas of the worshipers to the sensible world.
They humanize, so to speak, the religion. The Puritans, with their disdain of pomp
and ceremony, had moved God to the level of an incomprehensible abstraction.[10]
The emotions associated with contemplating such a removed and inaccessible being
were of the most extreme ranging from the holy despair to mystic ecsticy. "Laud
and his associates, by reviving a few primitive institutions of this nature, corrected
the error of the first reformers, and presented to the affrightened and astonished
mind, some sensible, exterior observances, which might occupy it during the its
religious exercises, and abate the violence of its disappointed efforts." (*HE*, V,
186) Laud's efforts, Hume suggests, were entirely appropriate and beneficial. The
rites and ceremonies were more likely to give worshipers some sense of what they
aspired to, a sense of the divine. Hume then adds: "[t]he thought, no longer bent
on that divine and mysterious essence so superior to the narrow capacities of
mankind, was able, by means of the new model of devotion, to relax itself in the
contemplation of pictures, postures, vestments, buildings; and all the fine arts
which minister to religion thereby received additional encouragement." (*HE*, V,
186) A quite remarkable observation: it shows another dimension of Hume's
pervasive naturalism when dealing with religion. The perspective here is one
almost entirely of social utility. Hume holds up this "new model of devotion" that
represents a kind of useful compromise between the extremes of Puritan
enthusiasm, with its moral severity and asceticism, and Catholic superstition with
its passivity and resignation. Such a model with its reliance on the products of
human genius and inventiveness serves religion well and makes it an instrument of
traditional needs and interests. Operating underneath this observation are Hume's
moral notions of the useful and the agreeable and a support for religion which is
normatively conservative and traditional, religion rooted in custom.

---

[10]See Max Weber, *The Sociology of Religion*, 203. Weber, writing of the Puritans observes:
"[e]very consistent doctrine of predestined grace inevitably implied a radical and ultimate devaluation of
all magical, sacramental, and institutional distributions of grace, in view of god's sovereign will, a
devaluation that actually occurred wherever the doctrine of predestination appeared in its full purity and
maintained its strength. By far the strongest such devaluation of magical and institutional grace occurred
in Puritanism."

Like the *History of England*, the *Decline and Fall* attempts to capture for the reader a sense of how turbulent, unpredictable, and chaotic societies are that confront religious fanatics and sectaries. In chapter eight, fairly early in the work, Gibbon writes: "[e]very mode of religion, to make a deep and lasting impression on the human mind, must exercise our obedience by enjoining practices of devotion, for which we can assign no reason; and must acquire our esteem, by inculcating moral duties analogous to the dictates of our own hearts." (*DF-8*, I, 216) Religious morality must somehow be aligned with the principles of human nature, if, as Gibbon says, it is to have an enduring impact. And, the "practices of devotion" arise not because of any specific rationale ("we can assign no reason"), but, it seems the implication would be, through habits, long standing traditions or conventions that give those practices an authority. Gibbon, like Hume, endorses religion that is rooted in custom. Gibbon's generalization here about how religion comes to have a grip on the human personality derives from a view of religion which sees it as a secondary rather than primary principle in human nature. This is a view that Hume states explicitly in the *Natural History*, a work that particularly impressed Gibbon. Hume says: "[t]he first religious principles must be secondary; such as may easily be perverted by various accidents and causes, and whose operation too, in some cases, may, by an extraordinary concurrence of circumstances, be altogether prevented." (*NHR*, 25-26) Gibbon's generalization also amounts to a kind of paraphrase of Hume's claim about the secondary status of religious principles. Religion can be, as Hume notes, "perverted" by all sorts of "accidents and causes."

Gibbon viewed the otherworldly focus of the early Christians with its repudiation of qualities that would make this world useful and agreeable as a perversion of religion insofar as the moral duties it attempted to inculcate were harshly ascetic and in conflict with what he saw as the general tendencies in human nature reflected in an approbation of the useful and agreeable. A nineteenth century historian, E. G. Hardy in a study of the interaction of the early Christians and the Roman government, writes that the early Christian converts were the anti-social nihilists of the time and were drawn to the faith because of its socially levelling tendencies and because the belief in an immediate coming of the Savior and the end of the world brought a predictable disregard for such institutions as the family, the community, and the traditional cults.[11] This is close to Gibbon's own view, and Gibbon in fact sees the anticipation of the end of this world as a rationale for actually attacking its institutions and eroding its customs. "Whilst the happiness and glory of a temporal reign were promised to the disciples of Christ,

---

[11]E. G. Hardy, *Christianity and the Roman Government: A Study in Imperial Administration* (London: Longmans, Green and Co., 1894), 46.

the most dreadful calamities were denounced against an unbelieving world. The edification of the new Jerusalem was to advance by equal steps with the destruction of the mystic Babylon; and, as long as the emperors who reigned before Constantine persisted in the profession of idolatry, the epithet of Babylon was applied to the city and to the empire of Rome." (*DF-15*, II, 27)

Certainly, no one who possessed such an apocalyptic view of the social-political order could be seen as anything but an enemy of it. Every achievement associated with the old order could not but be an object of aversion. Gibbon, for effect, quotes Tertullian who relishes the thought of contemplating the eternal torment of the luminaries of the pagan world. "How shall I admire, how laugh, how rejoice, how exult, when I behold so many proud monarchs, and fancied gods, groaning in the lowest abyss of darkness; so many magistrates, who persecuted the name of the Lord, liquefying in fiercer fires than they ever kindled against the Christians; so many sage philosophers blushing in red hot flames, with their deluded scholars; so many celebrated poets trembling before the tribunal, not of Minos, but of Christ; so many tragedians, more tuneful in the expression of their own sufferings; so many dancers___!" (*DF-15*, II, 29) Gibbon's lengthy citation of Tertullian certainly goes a long way in demonstrating how far the otherworldly fanaticism was carried by some of the devout and how much of a complete repudiation of every value was intended by it.

In chapter twenty-eight of the *Decline and Fall*, the "Final Destruction of Paganism," Gibbon attempts an assessment of the ruins of paganism. Like Hume, Gibbon believed that the external *forms* of religious worship, the rites, ceremonies, and the like, are extremely important in determining the emotive character of the religion. And, like Hume, he argues that religions whose rites and ceremonies work through symbols and images to connect worshipers to the visible, sensible world are an advantage in that as they make it less remote and abstract. "The popular modes of religion that propose any visible and material objects of worship have the advantage of adapting and familiarizing themselves to the senses of mankind . . . ." (*DF-28*, III, 213) But there is a disadvantage Gibbon points out with "material objects of worship" particularly in religions where these objects function as idols. "[B]ut this advantage is counterbalanced by the various and inevitable accidents to which the faith of the idolater is exposed. It is scarcely possible that, in every disposition of mind, he should preserve his implicit reverence for the idols or the relics which the naked eye and the profane hand are unable to distinguish from the most common productions of art or nature; and, if, in the hour of danger, their secret and miraculous virtue does not operate for their own preservation, he scorns the vain apologies of his priest, and justly derides the object, and the folly, of his superstitious attachment." (*DF-28*, III, 213)

Superstition is built on tradition, and when it is challenged by an intolerant rival sect the impotence of the idols is relatively easy to observe. The Christian assault on Roman idolatry in Gibbon's words, "dissolved the ancient fabric of Roman superstition, which was supported by the opinions and habits of eleven hundred years." (*DF-28*, III, 200-201) The dissolving of this "ancient fabric" also involved the destruction of the pagan temples and all the artifacts associated with the old religion. Theodosius had ordered his agents: "to shut the temples, to seize or destroy the instruments of idolatry, to abolish the privileges of the priests, and to confiscate the consecrated property for the benefit of the emperor of the church, or of the army. Here the desolation might have stopped, and the naked edifices, which were no longer employed in the service of idolatry, might have been protected from the destructive rage of fanaticism. Many of those temples were the most splendid and beautiful monuments of Grecian architecture . . . . [A]s long as they subsisted, the Pagans fondly cherished the secret hope that an auspicious revolution, a second Julian, might again restore the altars of the gods . . . ." (*DF-28*, III, 206-207) Gibbon evokes the imagery of barbarism and destruction. Religious fanaticism had undone the arts of civilization.

So, the English Puritans and the early Christians emerge from the pages of Hume and Gibbon as fanatical sectaries focused on the invisible, spiritual world in which they soon expect to reside. This otherworldliness and its concomitant rejection of the laws, the traditions, and the institutions, made them enemies of the social order.

Religious Fanaticism and the Emergence of Tyranny: Cromwell and Constantine
The emergence of tyranny remains as the last point of comparison that deals with religious fanaticism in Hume's Puritans and Gibbon's early Christians. This comparison pushes two tyrants to the fore, Cromwell and Constantine. Each was a major religious-political figure for Hume and Gibbon, respectively, and each one was in command of events that were major historical turning points or watersheds. Cromwell represents the political triumph of Puritan religious ideology over the old "Catholic" order, and Constantine presided over the political institutionalization of Christianity itself. Beyond that, the careers of both Cromwell and Constantine stand out as spectacular historical examples of religious fanaticism conjoined with the quest for political power. Religious idealism, founded so much in passion, is highly corruptible by the human interests of political ambition. Of Constantine Gibbon intones with his theme of decay: "[h]is unworthy favourites, enriched by the boundless liberality of their master, usurped with impunity the privilege of rapine and corruption. A secret but universal decay was felt in every part of the public administration, and the emperor himself, though he still retained the

obedience, gradually lost the esteem, of his subjects." (*DF-28*, II, 216-17) Obedience was stripped of esteem. Constantine's moral authority completely evaporates under the venality of his minions. Constantine was a very powerful Christian ruler, and a very corrupt one.

Religiosity, particularly when manifest in dramatic gestures and strong emotions, works to dissimulate motives of power and gain. Recall Hume's remarks (quoted above) that frequently employed religious ecstasies are often insincere, and "must be warped by those more familiar motives of interest and ambition which insensibly gain upon the mind." The mixture of interest and ambition with religious enthusiasm was conspicuous with the Puritan leaders, who, "equally full of fraud and of ardour . . . talked perpetually of seeking the Lord, yet still pursued their own purposes." Cromwell and Constantine were world historical figures who were consummate in their fullness of "fraud and ardour." They pose profound interpretive challenges to the impartial and skeptical philosophic historian precisely because of the difficulty in sorting out and making sense of the religious and political motivations. A course must be negotiated between the self-serving panegyrists and the cynical detractors. Gibbon, echoing Hume's "fraud and ardour" assessment of the Puritans, says, speaking of Constantine, that: "[i]n an age of religious fervour, the most artful statesmen are observed to feel some part of the enthusiasm which they inspire; and the most orthodox saints assume the dangerous privilege of defending the cause of truth by the arms of deceit and falsehood." (*DF-20*, II, 325) Gibbon alludes to the circumstances of the co-mingling of religiosity and power.

In his essay, "Of the Independency of Parliament," Hume writes: "[i]t is, therefore, a just *political* maxim, *that every man must be supposed a knave:* Though at the same time, it appears somewhat strange, that a maxim should be true in *politics*, which is false in *fact*. But to satisfy us on this head, we may consider, that men are generally more honest in their private than in their public capacity, and will go greater lengths to serve a party, than when their own private interest is alone concerned." (*Essays*, 42-43, original italics) Hume believed that human beings are normally more honest, decent, and law abiding as private individuals than as members of political parties or groups. Power is more likely to secrete its corruptive juices when the person who seeks and acquires power is a sectarian. "Honour is a great check upon mankind: But where a considerable body of men act together, this check is, in a great measure, removed; since a man is sure to be approved of by his own party, for what promotes the common interest; and he soon learns to despise the clamours of adversaries." (*Essays*, 43) Politics is always vulnerable to the dangers of sectarianism. Sects, particularly if they are of the fanatical kind—political or religious—are thus capable of undermining the rules of justice and the political authority that makes institutions serve a wider interest. The distinction Hume makes between the honesty of people pursuing their private, as opposed to party interests, is especially relevant to major political historical figures like Cromwell and Constantine since they were not only great political and military figures but also great (legendary in the case of Constantine) religious leaders.[12]   In fact, the respective historical studies of Hume and Gibbon on Cromwell and Constantine represent in large part an attempt to determine the level of knavery in their careers.

Cromwell's character, by Hume's account, was a most difficult one to comprehend. "[N]o human mind," Hume exclaims, "ever contained so strange a mixture of sagacity and absurdity, as that of this extraordinary personage." (*HE*, V, 360-361) Cromwell's sagacity resided in his substantial native political cunning and powerful, forceful personality; the absurdity in the bombast of his religious fanaticism and in the bumptious quality of his manners and deportment. Throughout Hume's account of Cromwell's rise to power and the course of his career as Lord Protector these extreme cleavages in his character and personality emerge making him a highly enigmatic figure. "The same warmth of temper which made Cromwell a frantic enthusiast, rendered him the most dangerous of hypocrites . . . ." (*HE*, V, 307) Cromwell is an extreme personage—a frantic enthusiast and a dangerous hypocrite. Even with Cromwell's religious conversion, his extremism is transferred from debauchery to devotion. Before the "spirit of the reformation seized him," as Hume so figuratively describes his conversion, Cromwell was a gambling, carousing, philanderer. Into his religious life he brought the same extreme passionate intensity that he had previously devoted to vice. "The same vehemence of temper which had transported him into the extremes of pleasure now distinguished his religious habits." (*HE*, V, 335) Given the seeming complete mediocrity of Cromwell's early career and his undistinguished qualities, his rise to greatness was quite astonishing. "His person was ungraceful, his dress slovenly, his voice untenable, his elocution homely, tedious, obscure, and embarrassed." (*HE*, V, 336) Even when he came to power there was a certain inexplicability about how it could have all happened. "All Europe stood astonished to see a nation so turbulent and unruly, who, for some doubtful encroachments on their privileges, had dethroned and murdered an excellent prince, descended from a long line of monarchs, now at last subdued and reduced to slavery by one, who, a few years

---

[12]Michael Grant, *Constantine the Great: The Man and His Times* (New York: Charles Scribner's Sons, 1993), 226-7 writes: "[i]t is a mocking travesty of justice to call such a murderer Constantine the Great. Or, perhaps not: for what does Greatness mean? Constantine was, as we have seen, a superlative military commander, and a first-rate organizer. He was also an utterly ruthless man, whose ruthlessness extended to the execution of his nearest kin, and who believed that he had God behind him in everything he did."

before, was no better than a private gentleman, whose name was not known in the nation, and who was little regarded even in that low sphere to which he had always been confined." (*HE*, V, 338)

Cromwell's intentions, Hume alleges throughout his account of him, were to subvert the laws and to attain unlimited power. This is a constant and unrelenting theme. Hume attempts to show that Cromwell was the perfect example of a religious fanatic who was skillful in manipulating people and events in a quest for power. "Hating monarchy, while a subject; despising liberty, while a citizen; though he retained for a time all orders of men under a seeming obedience to the Parliament, he was secretly paving the way, by artifice and courage, to his own unlimited authority." (*HE*, V, 282) Through his considerable political capacities, his military successes, and his religious zeal, Cromwell was able to create the basis for a military dictatorship. "From low commands he rose with great rapidity to be really the first, though in appearance only the second in the army. By fraud and violence he soon rendered himself the first in the state." (*HE*, V, 338)

Cromwell's career as Protector is the tale of a tyrant masquerading behind the religious enthusiasm of the sect which he came to dominate. After dissolving the "Barebones" Parliament, Cromwell was declared Protector by the army, his own instrument of power. The Protector, as Hume describes it, was a virtual and complete military dictator. "The protector was appointed supreme magistrate of the commonwealth; in his name was all justice to be administered; from him were all magistracy and honours derived; he had the power of pardoning all crimes, excepting murder and treason; to him the benefit of all forfeitures devolved. The right of peace, war, and alliance, rested in him; but in these particulars he was to act by the advice and with the consent of his council . . . . The protector was to enjoy his office during life, and on his death the place was immediately to be supplied by the council. This was the instrument of government enacted by the council of officers, and solemnly sworn to by Oliver Cromwell. The council of state, named by the instrument, were fifteen men entirely devoted to the protector, and, by reason of the opposition among themselves in party and principles, not likely ever to combine against him." (*HE*, V, 344-45) This nearly unlimited power, which Hume says more resembled the "maxims of eastern tyranny" than "the legal manner of European nations," conjoined with Cromwell's autocratic ambitions, were sufficient to make the Commonwealth under Cromwell's relatively short reign a dismal historical interlude of despotism. "[T]he pretence of liberty and a popular election was but a new artifice of this great deceiver, in order to lay asleep the deluded nation, and give himself leisure to rivet their chains more securely upon them . . . . [H]is imperious character, which had betrayed itself in so many incidents, could never seriously submit to legal limitations; nor would the very image of popular government be longer upheld . . . ." (*HE*, V, 350)

Hume's language here is, ironically, almost theological. His reference to Cromwell as "the great deceiver," a favorite Puritan appellation for Satan, and his riveting of chains has a distinct tone of theological evil. History, as both Hume and Gibbon frequently remind us, is to entertain and to give moral instruction. What instruction does the reader gain from Hume's account of Cromwell's reign? First, is the fragility of the fruits of civilization and their vulnerability to fanaticism. Gifted demagogues, even ones who *seem* initially to be undistinguished, can subvert long standing traditions and laws. Society is held together by conventions which themselves are based upon shared opinions. This commonality of opinion when disrupted by fanaticism and sectarianism dissolves into anarchy and creates or enlarges the opportunities for tyrants. Second, out of the destruction of conventions tyranny often emerges. The rupture of the conventions—those tacit agreements that help regulate conduct and restrain overreaching—makes the direct and open application of power more necessary and favors individuals like Cromwell who are adroit at manipulation. The breakdown of these *impersonal* customs makes the *personal* characteristics of those contending for power more important and hence increases the vulnerability to the emergence of a tyrant.

Constantine, like Cromwell, is characterized as a man of unlimited ambition. "The boundless ambition, which, from the moment of his accepting the purple at York, appears as the ruling passion of his soul . . . ." (*DF-18*, II, 215)[13] And, like Cromwell, this relentless ambition, though cloaked in religiosity, culminates in tyranny. "[A]n impartial narrative of the executions, or rather murders, which sullied the declining age of Constantine, will suggest to our most candid thoughts the idea of a prince who could sacrifice without reluctance the laws of justice and the feelings of nature to the dictates either of his passions or of his interest."(*DF-18*, II, 217) Gibbon begins this severe pronouncement with the reiteration of his impartiality and moves with hesitation from execution to murder—Constantine's career was immersed in criminality.

Around the life of Constantine Gibbon does indeed weave his recurring, pervasive theme of Christianity's degeneracy through political institutionalization. Gibbon develops this theme by focusing on the course of Constantine's career and its movement into the depths of tyranny. Consider though the striking contrast Gibbon draws between Constantine and Augustus. "In the life of Augustus, we

---

[13]Grant, *Constantine the Great*, 107. "[A]s Gibbon rightly discerned, Constantine was also unlimitedly, ruthlessly ambitious. Highly emotional and religious (or superstitious, for his religious views were in a bit of a muddle), and didactically devoted to lecturing all and sundry, he was dedicated to his own personal success, and despotically determined at all cost to achieve it . . . ."

behold the tyrant of the republic converted, almost by imperceptible degrees, into the father of his country and of human kind. In that of Constantine, we may contemplate a hero, who had so long inspired his subjects with love and his enemies with terror, degenerating into a cruel and dissolute monarch, corrupted by his fortune, or raised by conquest above the necessity of dissimulation." (*DF-18*, II, 216)

Two tyrants pass under historical scrutiny—the pagan Augustus and the Christian Constantine. Augustus, considered initially, is the betrayer of the Republic—his "vast ambition," as Gibbon says in an earlier passage, had levelled "[e]very barrier of the Roman constitution." (*DF-3*, I, 65) Yet his own person becomes upon historical scrutiny ("by imperceptible degrees") enlarged to the highest level of acclaim—"father of his country" and more—the highest symbol of benevolence. Constantine, however, though he begins his reign as a hero, moves through a course of degeneracy and corruption and culminates his public life in cruelty and dissolution. Constantine's own character and career is Christianity's decline personified. Born with great promise and hope, his progress in the world with all its temptations of power and glory slides pathetically into the depths of corruption.

Gibbon's contrast between Augustus and Constantine helps him make another major point about Christianity and paganism, namely that the Christian apologists' claims for Christianity's vast moral superiority over paganism are belied by the gross hypocrisy of its moral heros. The circumstances of Augustus' tyranny are a matter of straight-forward political interpretation. Augustus carries out a crafty, willful usurpation. His career is the story of a wily despot breaking down the institutions of limited government. "But unless public liberty is protected by intrepid and vigilant guardians, the authority of so formidable a magistrate will soon degenerate into despotism." (*DF-3*, I, 65) The events surrounding Constantine are more complicated because of the mixture of the elements of otherworldly religion and worldly power. The assessments—pro or con—of Constantine, as Gibbon points out in chapter eighteen, turn entirely on the religious perspective. "By the grateful zeal of the Christians, the deliverer of the church has been decorated with every attribute of a hero, and even of a saint; while the discontent of the vanquished party has compared Constantine to the most abhorred of those tyrants, who, by their vice and weakness, dishonoured the Imperial purple." (*DF-18*, II, 214) The verdict on Constantine is the verdict on Christianity.

Constantine, as Gibbon surmises, was corrupted by Christianity, and the real story of his conduct as emperor is an embarrassment to Christian moralists. "The sublime theory of the gospel had made a much fainter impression on the heart than on the understanding of Constantine himself. He pursued the great object of his ambition through the dark and bloody paths of war and policy; and, after the victory, he abandoned himself, without moderation, to the abuse of his fortune." (*DF-20*, II, 329) Gibbon zeroes in on Constantine's ambition and opportunism ("a much fainter impression on the heart than on the understanding . . . ."). Constantine was not deterred, at least by his understanding of the gospel, from his excesses. Yet Gibbon adds that his Christian growth was accompanied by his moral decline. "As he gradually advanced in the knowledge of truth, he proportionably declined in the practice of virtue; and the same year of his reign in which he convened the council of Nice [i.e., Nicaea] was polluted by the execution, or rather murder, or his eldest son." (*DF-20*, II, 329) Again we see some hesitation on Gibbon's part, as if he must overcome some initial reluctance in saying it—"execution," no . . . its actually "murder." Gibbon though presses on and makes Constantine's Christianity even more of a problem. "At the time of the death of Crispus [Constantine's son], the emperor could no longer hesitate in the choice of a religion; he could no longer be ignorant that the church was possessed of an infallible remedy, though he chose to defer the application of it, till the approach of death had removed the temptation and danger of a relapse." (*DF-20*, II, 329-30) Though punishment for the murder of his son awaits in the next world, his baptism and confession are the "remedy" for escape. "The bishops, whom he summoned in his last illness to the palace of Nicomedia, were edified by the fervour with which he requested and received the sacrament of baptism, by the solemn protestation that the remainder of his life should be worthy of a disciple of Christ, and by his humble refusal to wear the imperial purple after he had been clothed in the white garment of a neophyte. The example and reputation of Constantine seemed to countenance the delay of baptism. Future tyrants were encouraged to believe that the innocent blood which they might shed in a long reign would instantly be washed away in the waters of regeneration; and the abuse of religion dangerously undermined the foundations of moral virtue." (*DF-20*, II, 330)

Not only is Constantine's grotesque hypocrisy cynically depicted here in these layers of unctuous prose, but his conduct, as Gibbon has it, is instructive for tyrants in the generations to come. Moral constraints, ironically, are loosened by this otherworldly view of punishment and atonement. Moral hypocrisy and religious fanaticism are complements of each another. Constantine emerges as the archetype religious hypocrite and moral libertine. Christianity practiced this way destroys the moral order. Gibbon's condemnation is unequivocal.

The careers of Cromwell and Constantine are vintage pieces of philosophic history. The accounts are entertaining: they reveal complex personalities of influential figures stripped of panegyrics, playing large, dramatic roles in the world historical theater. Cromwell and Constantine capture the totality of human aspiration as they are both spiritual and political heroes, though badly tainted. And, the stories of their careers give full display of the dimensions of human frailty and the depths of fallibility. Thus, we have moral instruction at work. Philosophic history, recall, entertains and instructs. The lives of tyrants, Hume and Gibbon seem to suggest, have something important to teach us about human nature and the depths of its corruptibility. This corruptibility is with a considerable gloomy irony manifested in spiritual aspirations, and this perhaps is the lesson. Religion is a human creation attendant with all of the human frailties, one of which is a passionate, rationalizing self-centeredness. The purity of aspiration is rare. The saint dissimulates. The hero is corrupt. Religion and ambition are often discovered by the philosophic historian in an insidious commingling. This is why the duty of the historian is so melancholy.

CHAPTER EIGHT

THE PRIEST AND THE PRINCE: CO-OPTING THE CHURCH

I. The Ambitious Clergy

James II, 1685: "Is it not the custom in Spain for the king to consult with his confessor?"
Spanish Ambassador, Ronquillo: "Yes, and it is for that very reason our affairs succeed so ill."

The Hume-Gibbon attack on Christianity brought to bear harsh criticism of a church which used its political power to crush its spiritual rivals. Pagan Rome was relatively tolerant of diverse religious practices—a favorable circumstance for the advancement of the freedom of thought in the view of Hume and Gibbon—and the predominately civic character of the theologically primitive polytheistic cults seemed to appeal to both of these philosophic historians. Hume's *Natural History* and Gibbon's *Decline and Fall* link the phenomena of religious intolerance and chauvinism inexorably to the growth and development of the monotheistic doctrines that emerged in Judaism, Christianity, and Islam. In the history of Christianity, as Hume and Gibbon present it, the political development of the church, with a jealously protected body of doctrinal truth and with its increasing power and influence, puts into play a highly visible but unstable tension between the aspirations of otherworldly spirituality and this-worldly ambition. In the history of Christianity we observe the development of a class of spiritual professionals (the clergy) who balance their spiritual designs with their rivalry for material goods, including political power. In the church Hume and Gibbon saw a slavish and uncritical devotion to orthodoxy and a vested interest in the elevation of superstition.

In contrast to Christianity with its devotion to the truth of its teachings and its abhorrence of false belief, the religions of the Roman world, Gibbon writes in chapter two of the *Decline and Fall*, were considered by the vulgar to be true, by the philosophers to be false, and by the magistrate to be useful—useful to the state. Gibbon's social distinction relative to the perception of religious truth have been interpreted by one recent commentator as a recognition of the supreme value of the magistrate as *the* mediator and arbitrator of religious value in the society.[1] Roman political policy toward religion was conservative, i.e., religious innovation though

---

[1]Gossman, *The Empire Unpossess'd*, 69.

grudgingly tolerated was officially discouraged.[2] But the state was willing to tolerate theological and ritualistic variations and permutations as long as they were not perceived to threaten the authority of the state. (Ibid., 79)[3] Charles Norris Cochrane captures this politically conservative disposition of Roman state power toward religion with the comment that "the Romans, with the ingrained contempt of the 'man of action' for the intelligentsia, apprehended much more danger from the introduction of religious novelty than from the confused babble of the schools."[4] The Roman government tolerated a certain amount of rebelliousness from the Jews but not the Christians, Gibbon notes, because the Jews were a separate political entity.[5] "The difference between them is simple and obvious; but, according to the sentiments of antiquity, it was of the highest importance. The Jews were a *nation*; the Christians were a *sect*; and, if it was natural for every community to respect the sacred institutions of their neighbors, it was incumbent on them to persevere in those of their ancestors." (*DF-16*, II, 80, original italics)

Official Roman religious persecution, such as it was, was political and practical, while medieval Christian persecution was fully ideological and hence tended to be more pervasive.[6] Gibbon labors this point in chapter sixteen where he draws invidious comparisons between the zealous persecution of modern Christians such as Charles V and Louis XIV and the more pragmatically oriented pagan Romans who, "[a]s they were actuated, not by the furious zeal of bigots, but by the temperate policy of legislators, contempt must often have relaxed, and humanity must frequently have suspended, the execution of those laws which they enacted against the humble and obscure followers of Christ." (*DF-16*, II, 87) The safety

---

[2]W. H. C. Frend, *Martyrdom and Persecution in the Early Church: A Study of a Conflict from the Maccabees to Donatus* (Garden City, NY: Doubleday, 1967), 86. "Roman religion like the religion of the peoples Rome conquered was one of acts based on ancestral usage. The complex of ideas defined in such phrases as 'disciplina publica', 'mores nostri', or 'leges veteres', formed a barrier against the foreign cults, and equally against Judaism and Christianity. Except in dire emergencies, acceptance by the Senate took a long time, and even then, the cult might not be recognized with the *pomerium* of the city of Rome."

[3]Frend writes: "Roman religion was therefore less a matter of personal devotion than of national cult."

[4]Cochrane, *Christianity and Classical Culture*, 102.

[5]For a study of Imperial Roman reaction to Jewish resistance see Martin Goodman, *The Ruling Class of Judaea: The Origins of the Jewish Revolt Against Rome A.D. 66-70* (Cambridge: Cambridge University Press, 1987), particularly Chapter four, "Problems Facing the Ruling Class: Religious Ideology."

[6]Simeon L. Guterman, *Religious Toleration and Persecution in Ancient Rome* (reprint; 1951, Westport, CT: Greenwood Press, 1971), 15.

of the state not the honor of the gods was the first concern of the Roman government.[7]

This concord of religious and civic aspirations in the ancient world was a salient feature of social life, one which was used as a basis for the criticism of Christianity by Hume and Gibbon. Hume notes in one of his essays that in the ancient world the "magistrate embraced the religion of the people, and entering, cordially into the care of sacred matters, naturally acquired an authority in them, and united the ecclesiastical with the civil power." (*Essays*, 61) This unity of ecclesiastical and civil power was advantageous compared with the separate religious and secular authority that arose in Christianity and had led to ecclesiastical tyranny in Scotland and Spain, civil war in England, and full scale international conflict in the devastating Thirty Years' War in seventeenth-century Europe. On the Christian priests and the clergy Hume heaped copious blame as makers of political turbulence, agents of mischief, and abusers of power. "But [in] the *Christian* religion . . . the priesthood was allowed to engross all the authority in the new sect. So bad a use did they make of this power, even in those early times, that the primitive persecutions may, perhaps, *in part*, be ascribed to the violence instilled by them into their followers. And the same principles of priestly government continuing, after Christianity became the established religion, they have engendered a spirit of persecution, which has ever since been the poison of human society, and the source of the most inveterate factions in every government." (*Essays*, 61-62, original italics)

This is strong language for the usually mild and moderate Hume. He links the "spirit of persecution" directly to the professional clergy in the official Christian establishment. Their work, he argues, injects a poisoning of human relations through the relentless factionalization that arises from a preoccupation with ideological conformity. The happier alternative is modeled in pagan Rome where civic-religious functions were intertwined. It was unwise, it seemed, to have the sacerdotal order as a rival for political power with the secular order. The history of Christianity provided overwhelming evidence in making this argument. The political and social stability of the pagan Roman institutions established the point of contrast.

Christianity was not unique as a religion corrupted by an ambitious sacerdotal order. Gibbon early in the *Decline and Fall* blamed the corruption of Zoroastrianism on overreaching priests. "Had Zoroaster, in all his institutions, invariably supported this exalted character, his name would deserve a place with

---

[7]Hardy, *Christianity and the Roman Government*, 4. Hardy here says: "[t]he Roman religion was essentially and before all things a national religion: its object was primarily not the honour of the gods but the safety of the state, of which the good will of the gods was supposed to be the necessary condition."

those of Numa and Confucius, and his system would be justly entitled to all the applause which it has pleased some of our divines, and even some of our philosophers, to bestow on it." (*DF-8*, I, 218) Gibbon with this sentence sets up the reader for a debunking: we cannot trust the theologians ("our divines") to write religious history. The "applause" they have bestowed on Zoroastrianism is undeserved. "But in that motley composition, dictated by reason and passion, by enthusiasm and by selfish motives, some useful and sublime truths were disgraced by a mixture of the most abject and dangerous superstition. The Magi, or sacerdotal order, were extremely numerous, since, as we have already seen, fourscore thousand of them were convened in a general council." (*DF-8*, I, 218)

Note Gibbon's conjunctions here: "reason and passion," "enthusiasm and . . . selfish motives," "useful and sublime truths." With a great economy of expression they help him express what a remarkable mixture of human designs and capacities the work of religion is and, again, how unstable and volatile it is. Given all the complex forces at work in the human personality, it would seem, it is difficult to predict just how something as enigmatic as religion turns out. The agents of this sacerdotal order focused their ambition on the acquisition of property. Gibbon quotes from the Zoroastrian divine institution of tithes: "[t]hough your good works . . . exceed in number the leaves of the trees, the drops of rain, the stars in the heaven, or the sands on the sea-shore, they will be unprofitable to you, unless they are accepted by the *destour*, or priest. To obtain the acceptation of this guide to salvation, you must faithfully pay him *tithes* of all you possess, of your goods, of your lands, and of your money. If the destour be satisfied, your soul will escape hell tortures; you will secure praise in this world and happiness in the next." (*DF-8*, I, 218-19, original italics)

The terms of exchange are clear and unambiguous. The price of the *spiritual* guidance and preparation for the next world is *material* goods of this one; land, money, etc. The relation of power is absolute. The *destour* determines to his own satisfaction the adequacy of the exchange. This absolute power leads predictably to oppression and persecution. Like the Christianity that Gibbon traced in its struggle for political power and material gain under the guise of spiritual ideals, the Persian religion became fratricidal and persecutory. "The sword of Aristotle (such was the name given by the Orientals to the polytheism and philosophy of the Greeks) was easily broken: the flames of persecution soon reached the more stubborn Jews and Christians; nor did they spare the heretics of their own nation and religion." (*DF-8*, I, 219-20)

Gibbon had discovered his own melancholy truth, that the history of institutional religion is an entertaining spectacle of a never ending struggle for power. The history of Christianity is particularly illustrative of this generalization.

The church represents Christianity in its institutionalized form—ideals and aspirations, if you will, instantiated in social practice—and Gibbon presented the history of that institution largely as a framework of power and ambition.

II. Erastianism

*And the end which the Pope had in multiplying sermons, was no other but
to prop and enlarge his own authority over all Christian kings and State.*

Thomas Hobbes

The admiration of Hume and Gibbon for the civically oriented pagan religions was
the foundation for what I characterize as their Erastian view of church and state.
Erastianism owes its name to Thomas Erastus, 1524-1583, a follower of Zwingli.
Erastianism includes, among other things, the doctrine that the church should be
politically subordinate to the state. "Erastus's entire system was never accepted nor
promoted by any sect, but his theories on Church-State relations had great influence
in Germany and England in the 17th century. The Presbyterians rejected them, but
England's Established Church had an Erastian group. The Presbyterians used, the
term 'Erastian' as an unfavorable epithet for their opponents in the Westminister
Assembly in 1643."[8] The disdain that Hume and Gibbon held for enthusiastic
religions coupled with their fear of a clergy dominated state would have inclined
them to favor the Erastian-leaning Anglicans over the Presbyterians. Erastianism
was inspired in part by the fear of a persecuting clergy and a freedom-stifling
theocracy.[9]

Hume's and Gibbon's view of Roman Catholicism as a priestly religion,
replete with driving aspirations for power and gain, helped condition the formation
of their Erastian perspective of church-state relations, as will become evident.
Also, this Erastianism was a product of their antipathy toward the dogmatic
theology characteristic of medieval Catholicism. Theology of this sort dealt
prescriptively and authoritatively with the "invisible" world, the world of the
imagination. The violent disagreements that the theological imagination had always
seemed so ready and able to conjure up appeared to be resolvable only by force.
Theologians, indirectly perhaps, were agents of civil war and sedition and so
reducing their political power and influence was good policy.

---

[8]*The New Catholic Encyclopedia*, s.v. "Erastianism." Note also that Erastianism is not
exclusive in its insistence on subordination of the church to the state. The Byzantine practice of
"Caesaropapism" would make the church an ideological instrument of the emperor, although it is doubtful
that complete domination or subordination of the church to the Byzantine rulers ever took place. "The
Byzantine emperors have often been accused of 'Caesaropapism'. It is now generally agreed that the term
is not apt. No emperor before or after Justinian exercised such unlimited authority over his church." D.
M. Nicol, "Byzantine Political Thought," in *The Cambridge History of Medieval Political Thought, c.
350—c. 1450*, ed. J. H. Burns (Cambridge: Cambridge University Press, 1988), 67-68.

[9]*Dictionary of the History of Ideas: Studies of Selected Pivotal Ideas*, s.v. "Religious
Toleration."

Hume's account of the ascendancy of Puritanism and its challenge to Anglican-Catholic theology and ecclesiology looms large in his history, and his interpretation of these events filters through a predictably cynical view of the political aspirations of the Roman Catholic church. Protestantism, while no less bigoted than Romanism, lacked its monolithic character, and hence was institutionally more limited in the tyranny it could potentially muster. "But where superstition has raised a church to such an exorbitant height as that of Rome, persecution is less the result of bigotry in the priests than of a necessary policy. . .." (*HE*, III, 387) This is a remarkable observation and with it Hume suggests that ambition and political power are the primary considerations with the religious ideology playing merely a fronting role. Protestantism with its attack on the Roman Catholic hierarchy, its emphasis on the scriptures, and its repudiation of celibacy and monasticism, was from Hume's standpoint a long term advantage because it freed Christianity somewhat from the intrusiveness and oppressiveness of institutional control and rendered it a more private, free-thinking religion. "[O]ur sectaries, [English Protestants] who were formerly such dangerous bigots, are now become very free reasoners; and the *quakers* seem to approach nearly the only regular body of *deists* in the universe . . . ." (*Essays*, 78, original italics) It was easier, in effect, to make a deist out of a Quaker than a Catholic, the advantage being that deists had never persecuted anyone and were not interested in coercing religious uniformity. The path away from creedal Christianity toward philosophical theism was for Hume the proper course.

Gibbon took a similar view of the Protestant Reformation. With it, he says, "[t]he chain of authority was broken, which restrains the bigot from thinking as he pleases, and the slave from speaking as he thinks; the popes, fathers, and councils were no longer the supreme and infallible judges of the world; and each Christian was taught to acknowledge no law but the scriptures, no interpreter but his own conscience." (*DF-54*, VI, 132-33) Gibbon then is quick to add that this was not the intention of Luther, Calvin, and the other Reformers. "This freedom, however, was the consequence, rather than the design, of the Reformation." (*DF-54*, VI, 132-3)

The gradual emergence of religious freedom from the Protestant Reformation came unintendedly, as Gibbon pointed out. The Reformers were as persecutory in disposition as their papists adversaries. "The pious or personal animosity of Calvin proscribed in Servetus the guilt of his own rebellion; and the flames of Smithfield, in which he was afterwards consumed, had been kindled for the Anabaptists by the zeal of Cranmer." (*DF-54*, VI, 133) Incidentally, Gibbon adds a footnote where he excoriates Calvin. "I am more deeply scandalized at the single execution of Servetus, than at the hecatombs which have blazed in the auto da Fès of Spain and Portugal." (*DF-54*, VI, 133, n.43) Calvin, Gibbon added, should have known and done better. In the Servetus affair, he was motivated by personal hatred, and he betrayed a private correspondence of Servetus. "The zeal of Calvin seems to have been envenomed by personal malice, and perhaps envy. He accused his adversary before their common enemies, the judges of Vienna, and betrayed, for his destruction, the sacred trust of a private correspondence." (*DF-54*, VI, 133, n.43) Calvin's betrayal and destruction of Servetus was from Gibbon's perspective the vindictive work of an ecclesiastical tyrant who acted from the basest of motives. "In his passage through Geneva, Servetus was an harmless stranger, who neither preached, nor printed, nor made proselytes." (*DF-54*, VI, 133, n.43)[10]

Religious freedom had begun to emerge in Europe because the political power of the Protestant clergy was diminished. "The nature of the tiger," says Gibbon, "was the same, but he was gradually deprived of his teeth and fangs." (*DF-54*, VI, 133) The ferocious persecutory spirit of Protestantism waned because its principal spokesmen and theorists had become private citizens. Again, the less temporal power the theologians possess the better. "A spiritual and temporal kingdom was possessed by the Roman pontiff; the Protestant doctors were subjects of an humble rank, without revenue or jurisdiction. *His* decrees were consecrated by the antiquity of the Catholic church; *their* arguments and disputes were submitted to the people; and their appeal to private judgment was accepted, beyond their wishes, by curiosity and enthusiasm." (*DF-54*, VI, 133, original italics) Gibbon clearly approbates the political outcome of the Reformation with its resulting fragmentation of political power in the hands of the clergy. *Individual* ministers were less menacing than the *collective* power of the papacy.

Hume described this progress of the Reformation in England whereby the temporal powers of Catholicism were wrestled away from the church by ambitious and avaricious English monarchs. The ambition of these monarchs helped England eventually, to use Gibbon's expression, deprive the tiger of its teeth and fangs. Much of Hume's qualified admiration for Henry VIII was due to Henry's successful battles with Rome and his the nationalizing of the church. Henry was

---

[10]Gibbon's harsh censure of Calvin seems particularly interesting in light of Lord Acton's "Protestant Theory of Persecution," in *Essays on Freedom and Power*, ed. Gertrude Himmelfarb (Gloucester, MA: Peter Smith, 1972), 113-40. Acton makes a distinction between Catholic and Protestant persecution. Catholic persecution, he argues, begins with a concern with social unity as well as doctrinal unity and persecutes for extra-theological values as well as doctrinal. Protestants persecuted for theological error. Acton holds Calvin up as the most intolerant and extreme of the persecutory Reformers. "His system was not founded on existing facts; it had no roots in history, but was purely ideal, speculative, and therefore more consistent and inflexible than any other." (134) Acton's comments on Calvin's destruction of Servetus sound similar to Gibbon's. "The circumstances of the condemnation of Servetus make it the most perfect and characteristic example of abstract intolerance of the reformers. Servetus was guilty of no political crime; he was not an inhabitant of Geneva, and was on the point of leaving it, and nothing immoral could be attributed to him." (138)

able to deflate the spiritual authority of Catholicism and put the papacy on the political defensive. "The abolition of the ancient religion [under Henry] much contributed to the regular execution of justice. While the Catholic superstition subsisted, there was no possibility of punishing any crime in the clergy: the church would not permit the magistrate to try the offences of her members, and she could not herself inflict any civil penalties upon them. But Henry restrained these pernicious immunities . . . . The farther progress of the reformation removed all distinction between the clergy and other subjects; and also abolished the privileges of sanctuaries." (*HE*, III, 222-23)   The "ancient religion" (Catholicism) was sufficiently powerful to exempt its own officials from the laws (rules of justice). It existed de facto as a separate, autonomous political entity. Henry's success, as Hume notes, made a more "regular execution of justice" possible by eliminating the immunity of the clergy from the laws.

Hume's *History of England* creates a set of profound contrasts in its treatment of the Tudor queens, Mary and Elizabeth, particularly with respect to religious policy, and it argues indirectly for Erastianism. The short, miserable, persecutory reign of "Bloody" Catholic Mary marks a pathetic prelude to the crafty, pragmatic Anglican Elizabeth. Of Mary, "she possessed all the qualities fitted to compose a bigot; and her extreme ignorance rendered her utterly incapable of doubt in her own belief, or of indulgence to the opinions of others." (*HE*, III, 309) Mary's obsession was the restoration of Catholicism to England. It was to be done by coercion. "It was determined to let loose the laws in their full vigor against the reformed religion; and England was soon filled with scenes of horror, which have ever since rendered the Catholic religion the object of general detestation, and which proved that no human depravity can equal revenge and cruelty covered with the mantle of religion." (*HE*, III, 339)

What follows then is a graphic description of the persecution unleashed by Mary and her government ministers in their designs to extirpate the Protestant faith and effect a spiritual reconciliation of England with Rome. While horrifying in the extremes of its violence, Hume points out that the policy of persecution nevertheless failed. It reversed the intended effect and inflamed English resentment toward Catholicism. "Each martyrdom, therefore, was equivalent to a hundred sermons against popery; and men either avoided such horrid spectacles, or returned from them full of a violent, though secret, indignation against the persecutors." (*HE*, III, 343) Mary's religious policy brought about her ruin. She plunged the country into the depths of fratricidal religious division and hatred and fatally injured the cause of Catholicism in England. Weakening England internally and abroad, she earned herself the loathing of her subjects and actually set the stage for a strengthening of the state church by her successor.

By contrast, Elizabeth was determined to uphold the progress of the Reformation in England, but her inclinations and disposition, unlike those of her immediate predecessor, Mary, were guided, as Hume insinuates, more by practical and political than by religious considerations. "The education of Elizabeth, as well as her interest, led her to favour the reformation; and she remained not long in suspense with regard to the party which she should embrace. But though determined in her own mind, she resolved to proceed by gradual and secure steps, and not to imitate the example of Mary, in encouraging the bigots of her party to make immediately a violent invasion on the established religion." (*HE*, III, 375)

Elizabeth was well aware that Mary's persecutions had rendered the church of Rome odious to her subjects. Moreover, the marriage of Elizabeth's mother to Henry had been denounced by two Popes, so she knew that the Papacy would use the issue of legitimacy to make her compliant and England a tool of Vatican diplomacy and interest. (*HE*, III, 374) Elizabeth, astute in her comprehension of the decline of Rome's moral and political authority, and confident of her political abilities, resolved to pursue her own as well as the political fortunes of her country with a religious course embarked upon by her father, a path that was independent of the Roman pontiff. Elizabeth, Hume points out, saw through the impotent facade of official papal rhetoric. "[T]he curses and execrations of the Romish church, when not seconded by military force, were, in the present age, more an object of ridicule than of terror, and had now as little influence in this world as in the next." (*HE*, III, 374) From this observation it is obvious how much Hume was inclined to look at institutionalized religion in terms of ambition, force, and power.

Hume also notes that Elizabeth took care in the pursuance of her religious policy to advance the Protestants who were the "most calm and moderate of the party." (*HE*, III, 376) Elizabeth in contrast to Mary was more interested in political stability than religious orthodoxy. Her primary consideration relative to religious policy was in the reconciliation of her subjects to the religion of their ancestors. Thus while removing the church from the political control of Rome, she nevertheless sought to preserve its ancient, Catholic ceremonies. This gradualist type of approach had the advantages of making the state religion with its ties to the past more acceptable to her Catholic subjects and effecting *their* allegiance. She was able to pursue the Reformation without alienating her Catholic subjects. "The forms and ceremonies still preserved in the English liturgy, as they bore some resemblance to the ancient service, tended farther to reconcile the Catholics to the established religion . . . ." (*HE*, III, 382)

Elizabeth's long and illustrious reign as Hume interprets it owed its success to her astute religious policy and her willingness to make religion an instrument of political expediency. She placed her own person at the center of a state church that practiced the traditional and venerable ceremonies. In so doing she thus established her own political-religious position as the titular head of the English church, the legitimate purveyor of the prevailing ideology, and coerced—gently by the standards of those times—non-conformists, both Puritans and Catholics. Elizabeth by Hume's account was only looking for as much religious conformity as she needed to maintain her power and carry out her policies. The comparison between Mary's reign and its political-religious policies inspired by a theological or doctrinal aim (in Mary's case the belief of her subjects in Catholicism) and Elizabeth's reign, which placed secular-political over doctrinal-religious goals, enabled Hume to establish one of his central claims. The claim is that political policy dictated by otherworldly, religious ideology only works in a society controlled by priests who have a vested interest in perpetuating the ideology. Once the ideological monopoly is broken, as it had been in Mary's England where Protestantism had raised itself as a major competitor to the older, more established Catholicism, the ideological competition that was unleashed became the spark for the ensuing religious conflict. The Thirty Years' War was another example of the devastation wrought by competing religious ideologies. The ideological justifications provided by the competing powers amount to contradictory claims about the value and truth of the ideology and thus make the contenders irremediably hostile to each other—hence the ferocity of conflict. Mary's otherworldly policy was divisive and its practical effect was to plunge the country into sectarian warfare. Elizabeth's policy was reconciliatory both in terms of its end and its execution. It attempted to find a moderate center around which to draw in potentially hostile, extremist parties: the retention of the ancient ceremonies would attract Catholics; the rejection of Rome would placate anti-Romanist Protestants, and it would have the added advantage of removing the meddlesome foreign influence of the Vatican.

Thus Hume's account of the reigns of two most powerful Tudor monarchs, Henry VIII and Elizabeth, provided historical support for an Erastian view of church and state. Hume's generalizations about the nature of the clerical profession—most of them disapprobative—make the great importance he attaches to subordinating the church to the state even more understandable. His observations about the clergy are scattered throughout his writings, but there are two places, one in the *History of England* and one in the *Essays*, where he is explicit about the clergy as a *profession*, particularly with regard to considerations of ambition and self-interest. In the *History*, referring to the notions of useful and agreeable discussed in chapter six, Hume distinguishes between two kinds of productive activities: (1) those which are useful and/or agreeable to society as a whole as well as to particular individuals ("[m]ost of the arts and professions in a state are of such a nature that, while they promote the interest of the society, they are also useful or agreeable to some individuals"), and (2) those which are useful to society in general but not to any specific individual ("[b]ut there are also some callings, which, though useful, and even necessary in a state, bring no particular advantage or pleasure to any individual"). (*HE*, III, 24-25)

Of the first type of activity—useful to society and to individuals—Hume says that it is to everyone's advantage for these to be as little regulated by the state as possible. "The artisans, finding their profits to rise by the favour of their customers, increase as much as possible, their skill and industry; and as matters are not disturbed by any injudicious tampering, the commodity is always sure to be at all times proportioned to the demand." (*HE*, III, 24) The regulation of productive goods and services, Hume seems to suggest here, is best left to market forces in what we would call the "private sector."[11]

Of the second category of activities, those "though useful [but which] bring no particular advantage or pleasure to any individual," Hume calls for careful government regulation. "It [the magistrate] must give them public encouragement, in order to [maintain] their subsistence; and it must provide against that negligence to which they will naturally be subject, either by annexing peculiar honors to the profession by establishing a long subordination of ranks and a strict dependence, or by some other expedient." (*HE*, III, 25) Hume is speaking of what we would call the "public sector." Here we have the institutions of public finance, public health, defense, police protection, the courts, in short, all those "public needs" the state is called upon to supply. "The persons employed in the finances, armies, fleets, and magistracy, are instances of this order of men." (*HE*, III, 25) The primary motivation for individuals in these callings is not profit—as in the private sector—but honor, rank, distinction. The state supplies the salary and carefully regulates the conduct of these individuals. The clerical profession, Hume argues, aims at the public benefit, and hence should be set up as a public sector profession. "It may naturally be thought, at first sight, that the ecclesiastics belong to the first class, and that their encouragement, as well as that of lawyers and physicians, may safely be entrusted to the liberality of individuals who are attached to their doctrines, and who find benefit or consolation from their spiritual ministry and assistance . . . . But if we consider the matter more closely, we shall find that this *interested diligence* of the clergy is what every wise legislator will study to prevent." (*HE*, III, 25, italics added)

---

[11]For a discussion on Hume's substantial contribution to the development of eighteenth century political economy, see Eugene Rotwein's lengthy "Introduction" to *David Hume: Writings on Economics* (Madison, WI: University of Wisconsin Press, 1955).

This "interested diligence," as Hume calls it, is a source of great political turbulence, dislocation, and instability, as the reign of Mary and as the activities of the latter Puritans demonstrate.   Interested diligence typically becomes an instrument of intolerance and sectarian violence.   "Each ghostly practitioner, in order to render himself more precious and sacred in the eyes of his retainers, will inspire them with the most violent abhorrence of all other sects . . . . No regard will be paid to truth, morals, or decency, in the doctrines inculcated." (*HE*, III, 25) Apparently, Hume did not trust the market as a device for regulating the commerce of religious ideas since the actual competition historically had shown itself to be so fierce, destructive and devoid of self-restraining rules that it ruined the competitors.   In his essay, "Idea of a Perfect Commonwealth," where Hume sketches out what he believes would be the best kind of government, he is clearly Erastian in his proposed arrangement for the role of the clergy.   "The magistrates name rectors or ministers to all the parishes.   The Presbyterian government is established; and the highest ecclesiastical court is an assembly or synod of all the presbyters of the county.   The magistrates may take any cause from this court, and determine it themselves.   The magistrates may try, and depose or suspend any presbyter." (*Essays*, 520)   Short and succinct, this is the extent of Hume's remarks on church-state relations in the entire essay, yet it makes it obvious that Hume thinks it necessary that the church be politically subordinate to the state.

Hume thus recommends that the clergy be put on the state payroll.   This reduces their need to compete for followers by eliminating one of the incentives—the financial one—that gives rise to aggressive proselytizing.   "[T]he most decent and advantageous composition which he [the magistrate] can make with the spiritual guides, is to bribe their indolence, by assigning state salaries to their profession, and rendering it superfluous for them to be farther active, than merely to prevent their flock from straying in the quest of new pastures." (*HE*, III, 26)

Bribing the indolence of the clergy, in effect, making them state employees, achieves two important objectives.   First, as noted above, it separates their source of livelihood from success in proselytizing.   The clergy does not have to be in the business of constantly trying to secure new converts in order to maintain themselves.   This produces the benefit of a reduced zealotry, which has the beneficial effect of shrinking the devotional industry which manufactures hypocritical and morally superfluous standards of conduct.   "[T]ho Superstition or Enthusiasm shou'd not put itself in direct Opposition to Morality," they nevertheless through their frivolous rites and ceremonies must "weaken extremely Men's Attachment to the natural Motives of Justice and Humanity." (*DNR*, 254)

In a lengthy footnote to his essay, "Of National Characters," Hume makes some observations about the nature of the clergy and how their interest in perpetuating the devotional industry as a means to their own spiritual aggrandizement has a particularly deleterious impact on their characters and personalities. "It must, therefore, happen, that clergymen, being drawn from the common mass of mankind, as people are to other employments, by the views of profit, the greater part, though no atheists or free-thinkers, will find it necessary, on particular occasions, to feign more devotion than they are, at that time, possessed of, and to maintain the appearance of fervor and seriousness, even when jaded with the exercises of their religion, or when they have their minds engaged in the common occupations of life. They must not, like the rest of the world, give scope to their natural movements and sentiments: They must set a guard over their looks and words and actions: And in order to support the veneration paid them by the multitude, they must not only keep a remarkable reserve, but must promote the spirit of superstition, by a continued grimace and hypocrisy. This dissimulation often destroys the candor and ingenuity of their temper, and makes an irreparable breach in their character." (*Essays*, 199-200, n.3)

Again we see one of Hume's favorite themes in the discussion of religion—the predictability of hypocrisy that grows out of a religion that focuses heavily on the invisible world. Here though is a complete and prosaic demystification of the priestly-ministerial profession. The clergy, in spite of the trappings of sanctity, are nevertheless human beings and are motivated by the same sorts of things as their fellow man; power, reputation, status, and material gain. Yet the otherworldly preoccupations that define their calling, and the affected demeanor ("the continued grimace") that serves to remind the world of the otherworldly character of their calling stultify the personality and corrupt the character. A whole range of "normal" emotions and conduct are unavailable to the clergy since an indulgence in them would reveal their ascendancy and undermine the official importance of the devotions, etc. Pretense must be manufactured in order to overcome the disparity between what would be a natural inability on the part of most people to maintain preoccupations so contrary to human inclinations.

Those rare individuals, Hume adds, who are completely sincere and single minded in their devotion are no less vicious than the religious hypocrite. "If by chance any of them be possessed of a temper more susceptible of devotion than usual, so that he has but little occasion for hypocrisy to support the character of his profession; it is so natural for him to over-rate this advantage, and to think that it atones for every violation of morality, that frequently he is not more virtuous than the hypocrite." (*Essays*, 200, n.3) The church as a profession presents major problems for Hume: its otherworldly preoccupations and the various ceremonies and rituals that are invented and purveyed to convey these preoccupations, on the one hand, turn the practitioners into hypocrites. On the other hand, too much sincerity of attachment to the religious calling results in an arrogance which discards the demands of conventional morality. The minister must try to weave a difficult course between the poles of hypocrisy and fanaticism. There seems to be, from Hume's perspective, an artificiality and impracticability about the whole profession that makes it very difficult for its practitioners to uphold normal standards of virtue and decency.

There is a second important objective that putting the clergy on the payroll achieves. It makes the state the organizational foundation for the church and eliminates the competition for allegiance between the church and state. A universal or transnational church, such as the Roman Catholic church of his time, Hume saw as positioning its clergy in a conflict of political interest. "The supreme head of the church was a foreign potentate, guided by interests always different from those of the community, sometimes contrary to them." (*HE*, III, 26) Moreover, this contrary "interest" is heavily committed to maintaining—even by force—a complete uniformity of religious practice, a circumstance frequently attended by credulity, subservience, and persecution.

The cynical, anti-Catholic tone of Hume's writings sprang from his historically-based dread of Catholic political ambitions. As for Protestant and Catholic theological doctrines, they were equally absurd to him. Catholicism was an object of antipathy because its theology and inclination for persecution emerged from a transnational church and thus remained more autonomous and formidable. In the essay, "Of the Protestant Succession," Hume notes that the main problem with the Stuarts was with their religion. "The disadvantages of recalling the abdicated family consist chiefly in their religion, which is more prejudicial to society than that established amongst us, is contrary to it, and affords no toleration, or peace, or security to any other communion." (*Essays*, 506) The intolerance of Catholicism, Hume thought, was more structurally entrenched than Protestantism and, because of its independent clergy, more potentially seditious. "The Roman Catholic religion, with its train of priests and friers, is more expensive than ours: Even though unaccompanied with its natural attendants of inquisitors, and stakes, and gibbets, it is less tolerating: And not content with dividing the sacerdotal from the regal office (which must be prejudicial to any state), it bestows the former on a foreigner, who has always a separate interest from that of the public, and may often have an opposite one." (*Essays*, 510) Hume viewed and judged Catholicism as an institution primarily guided by considerations of power.

Hume's Erastianism with its caustic, anti-Catholic emphasis has an entirely non-theological, utilitarian foundation. The political-religious ambitions evidenced in medieval and early modern European history—violent and disruptive in their expression—were what made him so critical of the Roman Catholic church and so antipathic toward its clergy. Hume's Erastianism also played off of his skepticism toward theology. Since Hume believed that the specialized knowledge that theologians claimed to possess was not really knowledge at all (as evidenced by the frequent appeal to force in order to resolve differences), it was better that they be maintained in subordinate positions of power or influence.

The advantage of a state church, at least from the Humean eighteenth-century perspective on medieval ecclesiastical history, was that it was most likely to mediate between the extremes of a tyranny brought by a separate self-seeking clergy like that of the Catholics on the one hand, and a religious-political anarchy like that of the Puritans on the other. Papists and Puritans represented the political culmination of spiritual extremes: Christianity seemed to lurch, politically, between the control of ecclesiastical tyrants and anarchist zealots.

In Gibbon's work there is an Erastian perspective similar both in the tone and in the rationale it advances to Hume's. The Erastian perspective that emerges in the *Decline and Fall* reflects a melancholy disillusionment with Christianity that is rooted in his view of human nature as highly imperfect and corruptible. The Erastianism surfaces early in chapter two where Gibbon seems to take some satisfaction in pointing to a link between the relatively healthy political order in the period of the Antonines and a generally tolerant religious policy. In fact, Gibbon's description of the tolerant Antonines in chapter two is a fairly obvious attempt to set up the stark contrast to later chapters where he argues that official Christian intolerance helped destroy the empire. Gibbon attempts to establish a connection between general political conditions and the character of religious life. "The policy of the emperors and the senate, as far as it concerned religion, was happily seconded by the reflections of the enlightened, and by the habits of the superstitious, part of their subjects. The various modes of worship which prevailed in the Roman world were all considered by the people as *equally true*; by the philosopher as *equally false*; and by the magistrate as *equally useful*. And thus toleration produced not only mutual indulgence, but even religious concord." (*DF-2*, I, 31, italics added)

Gibbon notes the happy convergence of support from both those who make religion an object of critical philosophical reflection ("the enlightened") and those for whom religion is simply taken as a natural part of their everyday experience. Both from the theoretical and the practical perspective of the Romans, religious toleration was advantageous. Gibbon has succinctly summarized the three modalities of perspective on religion during the age of the Antonines. One would not expect, at least in the abstract, to see these three all of a harmonious piece—truth, falsity, and utility. However, Gibbon, via historical contextualization, puts them all felicitously together with the outcome being "religious concord." This harmony is to stand in contrast to the raging religious conflict that is to come latter. To the people, all the religions were equally true: hence religious toleration. To the philosophers, they were equally false: also, religious toleration. To the magistrates, the religions were equally useful. From a political perspective truth and falsity in religion, it seems, are irrelevant. Here then is Gibbon's skepticism with regard to religious doctrine: what matters is its socially cohesive function. The *content* of the belief seems to be less important than the *general congruence* of assent to the belief and the conserving, stabilizing effects it brings. Doctrinally, Gibbon remains agnostic.

This felicitous observation also suggests a rich dimension of complexity in the way in which Gibbon himself views the interplay of politics and religion. All three of these modalities in fact are Humean in perspective and give distinctive shape to his perspective on church-state relations. Because the various modes of pagan worship were largely devoid of theological or doctrinal elements, the devotees had no particular inclination to resent whatever beliefs might be expressed by rival religionists: hence, the "equally true" regard by the people for all religions. "The superstition of the people was not embittered by any mixture of theological rancour; nor was it confined by the chains of any speculative systems. The devout polytheist, though fondly attached to his national rites, admitted with implicit faith the different religions of the earth." (*DF-2*, I, 32) Note that Gibbon speaks of philosophical speculation as a problem for religion. The "chains" he speaks of are metaphors for the loss of freedom brought by philosophical religion. Gibbon cites the *Natural History* and Hume's observations on the tolerating nature of polytheists. "There is not any writer who describes in so lively a manner as Herodotus the true genius of Polytheism. The best commentary may be found in Mr. Hume's Natural History of Religion; and the best contrast in Bossuet's Universal History." (*DF-2*, I, 32, n.4)

Philosophers were "instructed in every school to despise the religion of the multitude," (hence the "equally false" regard of the philosophers for all religions). Yet they were respectful of the religious traditions and willing to submit to the rites and ceremonies because of their venerability. "Viewing with a smile of pity and indulgence the various errors of the vulgar, they diligently practiced the ceremonies of their fathers, devoutly frequented the temples of the gods; and, sometimes condescending to act a part on the theatre of superstition, they concealed the sentiments of an Atheist under the sacerdotal robes." (*DF-2*, I, 34) Here again Gibbon echoes Hume. "Did ever one make it a point of honour to speak truth to children or madmen? If the thing were worthy [of] being treated gravely, I should tell him, that the Pythian oracle, with approbation of Xenophon, advised every one to worship the gods—'for the good of the state.'" (*Letters*-H, I, 439)[12] This element of respect by the skeptical, disbelieving philosopher for the religious traditions of his own society is extremely important for Gibbon. The established religion of a society, like its laws, language, art, and other cultural expressions has important cohesive and unifying qualities. These atheists in sacerdotal robes placed high value on the religion of their ancestors because their fellow citizens valued it. In the *Natural History* Hume attempts to make the same point as Gibbon with his observations about the conduct of Cicero. "[W]hatever sceptical liberties that great man [i.e., Cicero] might use, in his writings or in philosophical conversation; he yet avoided, in the common conduct of life, the imputation of deism and profaneness. Even in his own family, and to his wife, *Terentia*, whom he highly trusted, he was willing to appear a devout religionist . . . ." (*NHR*, 73, original italics) Irreligion equates with disrespect and incivility. Hume appeals to common life experience to defend reverence for the established customs. Much later in the *Decline and Fall* Gibbon describes the sacrilegious conduct of the libertine Michael III, son of Theodora, a ninth-century Byzantine Emperor. "But the most extraordinary feature in the character of Michael is the profane mockery of the religion of his country. The superstition of the Greeks might, indeed, excite the smile of a philosopher; but his smile would have been rational and temperate, and he must have condemned the ignorant folly of a youth who insulted the objects of public veneration." (*DF-48*, V, 214) The skeptical smile of the philosopher is a reoccurring image in the *Decline and Fall*, and Gibbon in a manifestation of his conservative temperament here invokes it and effects the striking contrast of the philosopher whose temperate demeanor embodies discipline, moderation, and respect to the mindless degradation and abuse of tradition.

Since the philosophers are also magistrates, the third and final modality (all religions are "equally useful") falls into place. The philosopher-magistrates "encouraged the public festivals which humanize the manners of the people. They managed the arts of divination as a convenient instrument of policy; and they respected, as the firmest bond of society, the useful persuasion that, either in this or in a future life, the crime of perjury is most assuredly punished by the avenging gods." (*DF-2*, I, 35) Religion, morality, law are part of a whole fabric. The magistrate, who also plays the role of priest, encourages respect for the law, truth telling, and humanization of manners, activities that help stabilize society. Since

---

[12]See Brown, *Cult of the Saints*, 13-18, where Brown, in criticism of Hume, attributes to him a two-tiered model of religious change in which the "vulgar" remain intellectually as well as culturally limited, while a philosophical elite move through the processes of intellectual and cultural growth. Brown links this two-tiered model in Hume's *Natural History* to chapter twenty-eight of the *Decline and Fall*. That two-tiered model is evident here in Hume's letter as well in chapter two of the *Decline and Fall*.

the roles of the philosopher and the magistrate were combined in the same person there was no separate order of people, no separate clerical class with a vested interest in promoting an exclusive adherence to a particular ideology. "It is not easy," wrote Gibbon, "to conceive from what motives a spirit of persecution could introduce itself into the Roman councils. The magistrates could not be actuated by a blind though honest bigotry, since the magistrates were themselves philosophers; and the schools of Athens had given laws to the senate. They could not be impelled by ambition or avarice, as the temporal and ecclesiastical powers were united in the same hands." (*DF-2*, I, 34)

One of Christianity's most important innovations—of crucial import to Gibbon's account of Rome's decline—is its creation of a politically powerful sacerdotal order. "The progress of the ecclesiastical authority gave birth to the memorable distinction of the laity and of the clergy, which had been unknown to the Greeks and Romans." (*DF-15*, II, 49) This order, as noted above, did not exist in pagan Rome. Christianity came into the world as an otherworldly, apocalyptic religion. Indeed, the intense otherworldly focus of the earliest Christians played a large part in undermining the Roman traditional cults. The otherworldliness gave way to ambition, and ultimately to the institutionalization of the church. The church's gradual accretion of political power distinctively marks its inevitable corruption. The clergy, Gibbon notes in a passage reminiscent of Hume's own demystifying observations, were "a celebrated order of men which has furnished the most important, though not always the most edifying, subjects for modern history." (*DF-15*, II, 50) Here are the themes, ironically understated, of hypocrisy and corruption. "[The clergy] were destitute of any temporal force, and they were for a long time discouraged and oppressed, rather than assisted, by the civil magistrate; but they had acquired, and they employed within their own society, the two most efficacious instruments of government, rewards and punishments: the former derived from the pious liberality, the latter from the devout apprehensions, of the faithful." (*DF-15*, II, 50)

At the beginning of chapter thirty-seven on the "Origin, Progress, and Effects of the Monastic Life," Gibbon reviews his account of Christianity: "[t]he indissoluble connexion of civil and ecclesiastical affairs has compelled and encouraged me to relate the *progress*, the *persecutions*, the *establishment*, the *divisions*, the *final triumph*, and the *gradual corruption* of Christianity." (*DF-37*, IV, 62, italics added) Here set out are the separate stages of Christianity from its initial entry into the world, its "progress," its institutionalization and, ultimately, its "gradual corruption." Christianity's "final triumph" is the vanquishment of paganism and its extirpation of Christian heresy, particularly Arianism. Christianity's triumph, was in short, a military-political victory and with it follows its gradual corruption. The irony is quite apparent: Christianity's triumph in *this* world—the world it had initially repudiated—is its means of ruin.

Christianity's political victory so announced, it seems, has a hollow ring. The gradual accretion of political power that was to build an institutional church and make it a temporal as well as spiritual force also created the conditions for the extinction of freedom. The final destruction of paganism brought the end of religious toleration and the systematization of persecution. To the clergy, primarily, Gibbon attributes the instigation of persecution. "The Christians, more especially the clergy, had impatiently supported the prudent delays of Constantine and the equal toleration of the elder Valentinian; nor could they deem their conquest perfect or secure, as long as their adversaries were permitted to exist." (*DF-28*, III, 198) These words begin the chapter and would seem to be an attempt to recreate this period as a sinister prelude to disaster. Equal toleration was merely an irritating expedient for the Christians. They were resolved to exterminate their adversaries. "The influence which Ambrose and his brethren had acquired over the youth of Gratian and the piety of Theodosius was employed to infuse the maxims of persecution into the breasts of their Imperial proselytes. Two specious principles of religious jurisprudence were established, from whence they deduced a direct and rigorous conclusion against the subjects of the empire who still adhered to the ceremonies of their ancestors: *that* the magistrate is, in some measure, guilty of the crimes which he neglects to prohibit or to punish; and, *that* the idolatrous worship of fabulous deities and real demons is the most abominable crime against the supreme majesty of the Creator." (*DF-28*, III, 198, original italics)

Here we see the religious policy of Trajan and the Antonines, the policy Gibbon notes in chapter two that over the ages worked so well, stood on its head. The magistrate waits upon the priest! Otherworldly doctrinal concerns dominate temporal political ones. The most abominable of crimes are manifestations of disbelief, and the magistrate himself shares that culpability in proportion to his deficit of zeal in persecuting non-believers. No longer is the principle of government "wise, simple, and beneficent," as it was under the Antonines where the religious policy was crafted to further the temporal good of the society. Rather, the elevation to power of the sacerdotal order leads to all the various sorts of irreconcilable conflicts that typically arise when religious belief becomes an object of coercion, dictated by the enforcers of a speculative system. The Christianization of the Roman empire is in part an elaborate account of the separation of the sacerdotal from the magisterial order and the development of its political power. With the Antonines the "magistrates were themselves philosophers." But the institutionalization of Christianity cleaved the political world into conflictive realms with temporal and spiritual leaders locked in a perpetual power struggle. We have a description of the humiliation of the emperor John Paleaologus by Urban V, a vivid illustration of the power of the sacerdotal order, enriched with Gibbon's carefully measured sarcasm.

> [Paleaologus] was the first of the Byzantine princes who had ever visited the unknown regions of the West, yet in them alone he could seek consolation or relief; and with less violation of his dignity he might appear in the sacred college than at the Ottoman *Porte* . . . . In this suppliant visit, the emperor of Constantinople, whose vanity was lost in his distress, gave more than could be expected of empty sounds and formal submissions. A previous trial was imposed; and, in the presence of four cardinals, he acknowledged, as a true Catholic, the supremacy of the pope and the double procession of the Holy Ghost. After this purification, he was introduced to a public audience in the church of St. Peter: Urban, in the midst of the cardinals, was seated on his throne; the Greek monarch, after three genuflexions, devoutly kissed the feet, the hands, and at length the mouth of the holy father, who celebrated high mass in his presence, allowed him to lead the bridle of his mule, and treated him with a sumptuous banquet in the Vatican. (*DF-66*, VII, 93)

Christianity has triumphed politically, but Gibbon's account of this political triumph, which moves across the historical expanse covered by the *Decline and Fall*, equates that victory with the destruction of freedom and with the spiritual destruction of Christianity itself. There is more irony here which lies in the inevitability of the corruption of the simple message of the founder of Christianity. "Ambition is a weed of quick and early vegetation in the vineyard of Christ." (*DF-69*, VII, 248) This evocative image of inevitable decay and desolation which appears near the end of the *Decline and Fall* is a tragic recasting of Gibbon's infamous remark at the beginning of chapter fifteen comparing the theologian who describes religion, "descended from Heaven, arrayed in her native purity," with the historian who studies its corruption among a "weak and degenerate race of beings." Strategically placed throughout the *Decline and Fall* are references to the corruption of Christianity. "The meekness and resignation which had distinguished the primitive disciples of the gospel was the object of the applause rather than of the imitation of their successors. The Christians, who had now possessed about forty years the civil and ecclesiastical government of the empire, had contracted the insolent vices of prosperity, and the habit of believing that the saints alone were entitled to reign over the earth." (*DF-23*, II, 502)

Only a short time, about a generation or so of possession of political power, is sufficient to show Christianity markedly departed from the ideals of its founder. Worth emphasizing here though is the timetable that emerges from the discussion suggested by Gibbon's careful mention of the "forty years" after which the disparity between practice and ideal became obvious.   The corruption of Christianity in its "native purity" seems to march inexorably to a schedule of deterioration. The effects of natural human failings on religion, religion as it is found in this world, as Hume might say, are discovered by the historian. In the very next chapter, after a discussion of the luxury and ambition of Damasus, Bishop of Rome, Gibbon pauses and observes: "[t]his lively picture of wealth and luxury of the popes in the fourth century becomes the more curious as it represents the intermediate degree between the humble poverty of the apostolic fisherman and the royal state of a temporal prince whose dominions extend from the confines of Naples to the banks of the Po." (*DF-25*, III, 33) Again, we note the timetable of moral deterioration. We see here the beginning ("humble poverty of apostolic fishermen"), the implication being that Christianity in its originative and pristine state eschewed power and wealth, but that these were bound to become the preoccupations of the clergy and inevitably draw them into arrogance and corruption. Next, the intermediate point, is the already corrupted activity of the clergy. Finally, we have Christianity in its finished, institutionalized form, its leaders utterly indistinguishable from anyone else in their unfettered worldly ambition. Gibbon also captures the inexorability of the decline later in chapter forty-nine. "In the long night of superstition, the Christians had wandered far away from the simplicity of the gospel; nor was it easy for them to discern the clue, and tread back the mazes, of the labyrinth. The worship of images was inseparably blended, at least to a pious fancy, with the Cross, the Virgin, the saints, and their relics; the holy ground was involved in a cloud of miracles and visions; and the nerves of the mind, curiosity and scepticism, were benumbed by the habits of obedience and belief." (*DF-49*, V, 270)

The tone is dark and lamenting. Christianity's history unfolds, figuratively, in a "long night."   The moral simplicity of early Christianity, it seems, is irrecoverable. Gibbon is again at work practicing the historian's melancholy duty of tracing the progress of religion in a "weak and degenerate race of beings." Finally, Gibbon compares the early and medieval church, attempting to draw the invidious contrast of freedom and tyranny. "In the primitive church, a voluntary and open confession prepared the work of atonement. In the middle ages the bishops and priests interrogated the criminal; compelled him to account for his thoughts, words, and actions; and prescribed the terms of his reconciliation with God." (*DF-58*, VI, 278) Belief has become the object of political coercion in the medieval church. Religion has been transformed from a free, open, collaborative enterprise aimed at moral reparation into a despotic, coercive ideology.

For Gibbon, the simplicity of original Christianity with all of its basic virtues, I believe, could never prevail and could never be recovered. His view of Christianity is irremediably pessimistic. A religious movement over time must inevitably absorb all the assorted human malignancies. Ambition, greed, vanity, duplicity, lust are all woven into imperfect human nature. For the philosophic historian they are inescapable. These defects cannot be eradicated. Human beings cannot be perfected. Christianity in Gibbon's account had two flaws that were both complementary and fatal to its spiritually pristine aspirations. First, its otherworldly ideology devalued human nature rendering it something to be fatuously and hypocritically repudiated rather than something to be understood with all its limitations. Second, the elevation of creed led to the criminalizing of doubt. Belief and the experience that contradicted that belief existed side by side. Inevitably, a vast disparity had to emerge between the *Christian doctrines* that urged a rejection of all worldly objects of human desire and affection and actual *human conduct* that could not resist the pursuit of all of these things. Experience told one story: the creed affirmed the opposite, yet it was criminal to doubt the creed.

Nowhere in the *Decline and Fall* does this discomforting disparity between otherworldly ideology and actual human experience resonate more fully than in chapter sixty-nine just two chapters from the end of the entire work where Gibbon returns to Rome after following the course of nine hundred years of Byzantine history and its tragic culmination in the destruction of Constantinople by the Turks in 1453. The Rome, however, to which Gibbon now returns is the twelfth-century city of decadent Popes not the heart of a powerful empire. Its greatness is only a gray shadow. "[N]or could Rome, in the twelfth century, produce an antiquary to explain, or a legislator to restore, the harmony and proportions of the ancient model." (*DF-69*, VII, 234) Gibbon's prose at the beginning of the chapter betrays hints of compulsion. *This* Rome is one to which he with great reluctance must return as the historian of the empire to wrap up his account and to finish his story. "The name of Rome must yet command our involuntary respect; the climate (whatsoever may be its influence) was no longer the same; the purity of blood had been contaminated through a thousand channels; but the venerable aspect of her ruins, and the memory of past greatness, rekindled a spark of the national character. The darkness of the middle ages exhibits some scenes not unworthy of our notice. Nor shall I dismiss the present work till I have reviewed the state and revolutions of the Roman city, which acquiesced under the absolute dominion of the Popes about the same time that Constantinople was enslaved by the Turkish arms." (*DF-*

69, VII, 219) Gibbon's tone and phrasing ("some scenes not unworthy of our notice") here evince a kind of grim resolve. His account needs to be closed out with a picture of the corruption and venality. This is the most depressing comparison imaginable.

The temporal power of the Popes compared with the power of the pagan Roman emperors becomes the major theme of this chapter. Gibbon here quotes at length from Hume's *History of England*. "'Though the name and authority of the court of Rome were so terrible in the remote countries of Europe, which were sunk in profound ignorance, and were entirely unacquainted with its character and conduct, the pope was so little revered at home that his inveterate enemies surrounded the gates of Rome itself and even controlled his government in that city; and the ambassadors, who, from a distant extremity of Europe, carried to him the humble, or rather abject, submissions of the greatest potentate of the age, found the utmost difficulty to make their way to him and to throw themselves at this feet.'" (*DF-69*, VII, 225)

Much rides on this striking observation of incongruity in the Pope's authority. First, we have the suggestion of corruption. The religious authority propping up the Pope, it would seem, was a facade that could only hold up to contemplation from afar. Those observing the activities of the Vatican from close range could, as Hume notes, bear it little reverence. Second, is the very dimension of the incongruity itself. How could one person at the same time be so powerful as to hold sway over distant potentates yet be at the disposal of his local enemies? Religious as well as political authority was in an advanced stage of deterioration.

The focus on this greed and corruption is not merely to expose the hypocrisy of a decadent church and the betrayal of spiritual ideals to lust and ambition. Gibbon, as he quotes Hume, also is attempting to make a case for his Erastian view of church and state by showing that a political order controlled by clerics provides none of the stabilizing benefits that one expects from good governments. "Under the first Christian princes, the chair of St. Peter was disputed by the votes, the venality, the violence, of a popular election; the sanctuaries of Rome were polluted with blood; and, from the third to the twelfth century, the church was distracted by the mischief of frequent schisms. As long as the final appeal was determined by the civil magistrate, these mischiefs were transient and local." (*DF-69*, VII, 248-49)

So while Vatican politics was always corrupt, as long as final authority for resolution was in civil hands the disruptive consequences were manageable and not far flung. "But, after the emperors had been divested of their prerogatives, after a maxim had been established that the vicar of Christ is amenable to no earthly tribunal, each vacancy of the holy see might involve Christendom in controversy and war. The claims of the cardinals and inferior clergy, of the nobles and people, were vague and litigious; the freedom of choice was over-ruled by the tumults of a city that no longer owned or obeyed a superior." (*DF-69*, VII, 249) Here is the ultimate irony: the complete political triumph of Christianity is attended with the disintegration of freedom. The authority of the church exerts no effect. All is in tumult.

Unbounded by temporal authority, clerical aspirations to power rested upon otherworldly sorts of claims that were inherently unresolvable without the use of force. Since political authority, as we have noted, comes out of opinion, the great disadvantage of religionists fighting for power is that the justification for their claims to power are based on theological arguments that no appeal to experience can resolve. Agreement in religion is harder to come by, it would seem at least from a historical purview, than in most other aspects of life. Because religious differences cannot be settled by rational argument or appeal to experience, they must be bounded by tradition and temporal authority. An appeal to a religious principle or idea which has not been set in some accepted tradition merely invites contention. Hume says that: "the empire of all religious faith over the understanding is wavering and uncertain, subject to all varieties of humour, and dependent on the present incidents, which strike the imagination." (*NHR*, 76) The metaphor (the "empire" of "religious faith") employed by Hume is political, and the image evoked is social instability and uncertainty. The primary usefulness of government lies in its capacity to encourage rule-governed behavior. Imperfect though the rules and their application may be, they provide the advantage of allowing individuals to predict each other's behavior and thus to plan their activities, carry out their designs, and enjoy some level of security. The shifting and volatile nature of religious emotion and the extreme difficulty in establishing agreement on religious ideas makes religious principle a particularly difficult element on which to build government. The Rome of the twelfth century, Gibbon reports, "continually presented the aspect of war and discord; the churches and palaces were fortified and assaulted by the factions and families . . . ." (*DF-69*, VII, 228) Quoting Bernard of Clairvaux: "'Who is ignorant . . . of the vanity and arrogance of the Romans? a nation nursed in sedition, cruel, untractable, and scorning to obey, unless they are too feeble to resist . . . . Lofty in promise, poor in execution: adulation and calumny, perfidy and treason, are the familiar arts of their policy.'" (*DF-69*, VII, 228)

One of the legacies of Hume and Gibbon is the profundity of their observations and reflections on the shaping of the state by the church. Anti-apologetic and iconoclastic, their historical recreation of institutionalized Christianity turns the spotlight on fanatical, highly energized religionists engaged in a fierce and often violent competition for political power. Hume and Gibbon argue that the inherently unresolvable nature the claims of religious ideologies—directed as they are to the otherworld—immerses their adherents in continual controversy and contention, and makes their resolution possible only through force. From temporal interests both Hume and Gibbon would seem to agree, it is easier to create the kinds of political institutions that support the "arts of cooperation" and result in useful human endeavors. Gibbon's Erastianism is built upon the broader Humean philosophical backdrop which views religious belief as determined primarily by emotion rather than reasoning or experience.

CHAPTER NINE

NATURALIZING RELIGION: SUPERSTITION, ENTHUSIASM, AND RELIGIOUS CONDUCT

I. The *Natural History of Religion*
and Religious Naturalism

Radical criticism of religion is by intent scientific criticism.

Leo Strauss

In 1757 Bishop William Warburton, Hume's implacable enemy, obtained a manuscript copy of Hume's *Four Dissertations*. The first was a piece that was eventually published as *The Natural History of Religion*. He then wrote to Andrew Millar, Hume's friend and publisher, in order to persuade him to suppress the work. "Sir," he wrote, "I supposed you would be glad to know what sort of book it is which you are about to publish with Hume's name and yours to it. The design of the first essay is the very same with all Lord Bolingbroke's, to establish *naturalism*, a species of atheism . . . ."[1] Hume disdained Warburton as a bully: petulant, insolent, and abusive. (*Letters-H*, II, 244)[2] Even so, the bully Bishop clearly understood what Hume was about in the *Natural History*. A naturalistic account was indeed Hume's overriding design in writing this work.[3] Published in 1757, the *Natural History* was probably written between 1749 and 1751, around the same period Hume was also working on the posthumously published *Dialogues Concerning Natural Religion*.[4] The *Dialogues* in fact attack the much vaunted design argument for the existence of God. The existence of a perfectly designed

---

[1]Wayne Colver, "Note on the Text," in *NHR*, 9, original italics.

[2]Stephen, *History of English Thought*, 1: 1, notes that Warburton and Johnson were successive dictators of eighteenth-century England's literary world. Also, Gibbon's *Critical Observations on the Sixth Book of the Aeneid* was an early, anonymously published work attacking Warburton's allegorical interpretation of Virgil's *Aeneid*.

[3]Immanuel Kant referred to his first *Critique* as effecting a Copernican revolution in philosophy, reversing the understanding of the conceptual structure of thinking relative to the knower and the known. Hume never wrote of his own work in any such way, but he initiated a type of "Copernican revolution" of his own, one that reversed the order of thinking about ethics and religion. One of the major effects of Hume's philosophical writings was to naturalize the study of religion. See Sterling P. Lamprecht, "Naturalism and Religion," in *Naturalism and the Human Spirit*, ed. Yervant H. Krikorian (New York: Columbia University Press, 1944), 18, for a discussion of naturalism and religion. Lamprecht defines naturalism as: "a philosophical position, empirical in method, that regards everything that exists or occurs to be conditioned in its existence or occurrence by causal factors within one all-encompassing system of nature, however 'spiritual' or purposeful or rational some of these things and events may be in their functions and values prove to be." Such a definition would apply to Hume and Gibbon.

[4]Colver, "Note On Text," *NHR*, 7.

universe implies the existence of a Perfect Designer: this was the eighteenth-
century bulwark against atheism and the conceptual linchpin of natural religion. [5]
Hume's *Dialogues*, however, were damaging. As Norman Kemp Smith proclaims
in his own "Introduction" to the *Dialogues*: "[t]he argument from design is,
[Hume] suggests, the 'religious hypothesis' *par excellence*, yet is not defensible."[6]
Though Hume, as Kemp Smith goes on to suggest, had resorted to writing in the
dialogue form so as to dissimulate his iconoclastic intentions, he nevertheless
decided to delay the publication of the *Dialogues* until after his death knowing that
it would greatly offend Christians and that the outcry from his critics would be
shrill.[7]

The step from interpreting our experience to a comprehension of the
supernatural powers behind that experience, while an inviting one to take, is in
Hume's view unsurmountable. "Were a man to abstract from every thing which he
knows or has seen," Hume says in the *Dialogues*, "he wou'd be altogether
incapable, merely from his own Ideas, to determine what kind of scene the
Universe must be, or to give the Preference to one State or Situation of things
above another." (*DNR*, 165) *The Natural History* (much admired and occasionally
cited by Gibbon)[8] complements the *Dialogues* as a complete and formidable
critique of natural religion.[9] While the *Dialogues* strike at the design argument and
attempt to undermine the theological framework of natural religion and hence the
rational justification for religious belief, the *Natural History* examines religious
belief from the perspective of its origins in human experience. This work marks
the culmination of Hume's quest for a causal explanation of religious thinking and
considers religious experience as a *natural* rather than a *supernatural* phenomenon.
Bishop Warburton, as noted, had denounced the naturalism of Hume's *Natural
History*. He quite rightly apprehended that the book's message, taken seriously,
would lead to the erosion of Christianity's moral and intellectual authority. Though
the *Natural History* begins with the sufficiently vague declamation that "religion

---

[5]Redwood, *Reason, Ridicule and Religion*, 70.

[6]Norman Kemp Smith, "Hume's Arguments Against Miracles, And His Criticism of the
Argument From Design, in the '*Enquiry*,'" introduction to *Dialogues Concerning Natural Religion*, by
David Hume, ed. Norman Kemp Smith (Indianapolis, IN: Bobbs-Merrill, 1947), 56.

[7]See John Vladimir Price, "David Hume's 'Dialogues Concerning Religion,' Composition and
Publication," in *DNR*, 105-128, for a detailed account of the posthumous history of Hume's *Dialogues*.
This account also provides detail on Adam Smith's reluctance to get the *Dialogues* published. Smith had
been directed by Hume's will to get them into print.

[8]There are twenty-nine citations to all of Hume's works in the *Decline and Fall*.

[9]Gibbon did not read the *Dialogues* until 1776 or 1777 when they were lent to him in
manuscript copy by Hume's publisher William Strahan. Therefore, the first two volumes of the *Decline
and Fall* were published before Gibbon absorbed this work. See Craddock, *Edward Gibbon: Luminous
Historian*, 87

is of the utmost of importance," Hume also adds that the "first religious principles must be secondary; such as may easily be perverted by various accidents and causes, and whose operation too, in some cases, may, by an extraordinary concurrence of circumstances, be altogether prevented." (*NHR*, 25-26) With this right-hand-giveth, left-hand-taketh-away statement, religious belief, it is suggested, important as it is, must be something shaped by chance and contingency. So much for divine destiny. Systems of religious belief are distinguishable and comparable according to the "various accidents and causes" from which they are derived. The effect of Hume's naturalism from the perspective of Warburton was to draw Christianity down, down, that is, to a level of comparison with other religions.[10]

The *Natural History* with its naturalistic perspective would also make an attempt at comparative religion: the attempted comparisons were mainly of a historical nature between the polytheistic religions of primitive groups and the monotheistic religions of civilized people. The work could also be read as a speculative study in the evolution of abstract theorizing. Hume was curious about how abstract and spiritual notions peculiar to religious thinking originated in intellectually unsophisticated people. The link drawn between monotheism and cultural development is an important part of his effort to establish a cultural interpretation of religious belief that sees religious ideas evolving in their sophistication and complexity in a manner analogous to other kinds of cultural productions. "We may as reasonably imagine, that men inhabited palaces before huts and cottages, or studied geometry before agriculture; as assert that the deity appeared to them a pure spirit, omniscient, omnipotent, and omnipresent, before he was apprehended to be a powerful, tho' limited being, with human passions and appetites, limbs and organs." (*NHR*, 27)

Hume challenged what I term, the "doctrine of monotheistic predominance," which holds that a monotheistic view of the world is an obvious and immediate belief for anyone to embrace upon reflecting upon their experience. This doctrine was a legacy of the great deistic thinkers and rationalist-oriented Christians like Locke and Toland—one that Hume was intent on demolishing. Monotheism, Hume argues, is a product of philosophy, and philosophy is an activity associated only with intellectually sophisticated, civilized peoples.[11] "'Tis a matter of fact

---

[10]Byrne, *Natural Religion and the Nature of Religion,* 111, writes that deism was on the cusp of a modernist perspective on religion. The deists were coming to have a strong sense of the humanity of religion.

[11]Gaskin, *Hume's Philosophy of Religion,* 184-185, writes that the basic thesis of Hume's *Natural History of Religion,* now quite acceptable to the twentieth-century reader, that primitive religion was polytheistic, was a radical step for Hume. Arguing against Locke and company, Hume wanted to show that their view that monotheism was an obvious and natural belief for all men made the howling assumption that primitive people and the vulgar were capable of a rational contemplation far beyond them.

uncontestable, that about 1700 years ago all mankind were idolaters." (*NHR*, 26) Religion, however, though secondary in its principles, is ancient. Religious ideas have their causal origins as emotive responses to interaction with the world, not as the consequence of a rational contemplation of it. Religion was in its originative phases the work of fear not the abstract fruit of contemplative construction or the results of a sophisticated cognitive process. The earliest gods were powerful but limited vengeful beings which men feared and attempted to appease. Early religion was thus the outgrowth of action taken by human beings as they attempted to cope with indeterminate fears that arose from their daily confrontation with a hostile and unpredictable world.

The *Natural History* is more radical in its implications for religion than anything else Hume wrote.[12] In it Hume takes the innovative approach of formulating a *psychology* of religious belief independent of theology. The reductivism is apparent. It was to Warburton anyway. Hume is more attentive to the mind of the believer than the content of the belief. Religion thus comes under critical scrutiny from two directions in Hume's *Dialogues* and his *Natural History*: first, theological and religious truth claims are disputed on logical and evidentiary grounds; second, religious belief and practice are conceived of and explained as human inventions, the products of the imagination and the passions.[13]

An important feature of Hume's religious naturalism is the conspicuous role played by the passions in determining religious belief and behavior, and so the concern with passion becomes paramount in grappling with the nature and significance of religious belief and conduct, particularly for Christians. The way Hume views the interactions of the passions with religious belief has serious implications for the rational basis of Christian belief and for religiously motivated conduct. Passions infuse belief with energy and move believers to act on those beliefs. Loaded with power and volatility, passion-infused beliefs have the potential to light the destructive fires of misery-creating conflict and ruin humanity's most intelligent, noble, and best laid plans. "All doctrines," writes Hume in an essay, "are to be suspected, which are favoured by our passions." (*Essays*, 598) Because of the practical myopia engendered by the violent passions, human society requires for its endurance the creation of passion-bridling norms of self-restraint which place some self-correcting checks on what our feelings may

---

[12]Keith E. Yandell, "Hume on Religious Belief," in *Hume, A Re-evaluation*, 111, argues that *The Natural History of Religion* contains the most explicit and straightforward statement of Hume's views on religion. "I suggest that *The Natural History of Religion* contains the key to Hume's position, and that the *Dialogues* must be read in the light of the *Natural History*. Or, to be more accurate, *The Natural History* expresses straightforwardly theses which the *Dialogues* express only by implication."

[13]See M. Jamie Ferreira, Hume's *Natural History*: Religion and 'Explanation,'" *Journal of the History of Philosophy* 33, no. 4 (1995), 596.

lead us to do. All beliefs insofar as they give rise to human action do so by virtue of the passions aroused in the believer, passions that are in some way associated with the objects of belief. Hume says that "[o]bjects have absolutely no worth or value in themselves. They derive their worth merely from the passions." (*Essays*, 166) Abstract religious ideas, argues Hume, need to be in some way connected to the sensible world in order to have some sustaining efficacy. "To render the passion of continuance, we must find some method of affecting the senses and imagination, and must embrace some *historical*, as well as *philosophical* account of the divinity. Popular superstition and observances are even found to be of use in this particular." (*Essays*, 167, original italics) So also opines Gibbon: "[e]very mode of religion, to make a deep and lasting impression on the human mind, must exercise our obedience by enjoining practices of devotion, for which we can assign no reason; and must acquire our esteem, by inculcating moral duties analogous to the dictates of our own hearts." (*DF-8*, I, 216-17)

Religious naturalism, particularly in the context of eighteenth-century historical writing, amounts to a major shift in perspective. Hume's articulation of the naturalistic position was a mid-century culmination of the challenge to Christianity that had begun early in the century by the English deists and even rationalist-oriented Anglicans.[14] Hume's *Natural History* presented the case for religious naturalism. It became a major work of the Enlightenment. The ultimate critique of religion, as Leo Strauss notes in his *Spinoza's Critique of Religion*, is an explanation of it as an outgrowth of human nature.[15] Religion then as a manifestation of human culture becomes a natural phenomenon studied in a naturalistic and reductive way. Frank Manuel's *The Eighteenth Century Confronts the Gods* devotes an entire chapter to "Mr. Hume's *Natural History*." "Of all the attacks upon the dominant religions of Europe this [the *Natural History*] was the

---

[14]Roland Stromberg, *Religious Liberalism in Eighteenth-Century England* (London: Oxford University Press, 1954), 1-10. Also see Gay, *The Rise of Modern Paganism*, 145. Gay provides a good, brief synopsis of the development of a naturalistic perspective toward the world from the latter part of the seventeenth-century through the eighteenth. "In 1691 the Dutch pastor Balthasar Bekker had attacked the widespread belief in the devil with his *De betooverte Wereld*—The Enchanted World, and five years later John Toland had published his first deist tract under the title *Christianity not Mysterious*. This tone echoes through the eighteenth century: Voltaire wrote a *philosophical* dictionary; Hume a *natural* history of religion; Raynal, a *philosophical* history of European expansion in the Indies; Kant, an essay on religion *within the limits of reason alone*; Holbach, a whole *system of nature*."

[15]Leo Strauss, *Spinoza's Critique of Religion*, trans. E.M. Sinclair (New York: Schocken Books, 1965), 86. Gaskin, *Hume's Philosophy of Religion*, 187, argues that Hume should be credited as the first modern thinker to treat religion completely from a psychological and anthropological perspective. James Collins, *The Emergence of the Philosophy of Religion* (New Haven, CT: Yale University Press, 1967) 6, writes that for Hume, "the study of religion is philosophically relevant by reason of its own direct contributions to our apprehension of man's makeup and aspirations."

most telling."[16] The *Natural History*, enormously influential throughout Europe, was quickly translated into French and German and became a classic in reductive religious naturalism.[17] For the French atheists in the latter half of the eighteenth century it was canonical.[18]

Gibbon cites the *Natural History* at key junctures in the *Decline and Fall* where he attempts to show how some facet of religious history conforms to a generalizable aspect of human nature. An example gives some sense of how closely tied Gibbon is to Hume in this regard. Chapter twenty-eight, though one of the shortest, is pivotal. It deals with two important historical circumstances; the final destruction of paganism, and the introduction among the Christians of the worship of saints and relics. Paganism's collapse was significant, and this event (catastrophic in Gibbon's view) marks off a major stage in the decline and fall of the empire. "The ruin of Paganism, in the age of Theodosius, is perhaps the only example of the total extirpation of any ancient and popular superstition; and may therefore deserve to be considered as a singular event in the history of the human mind." (*DF-28*, III, 198) Gibbon gives the eclipse of pagan religion very high billing. It is a truly remarkable event and is suggestive of the power of Christian fanaticism. The triumph of Christianity over paganism, however, reverberates in Gibbon's telling of it with a certain irony as manifest in the emergence of saint and relic worship. Upon delving into the miserable and pathetic details of the growth of miracles surrounding relics and saints, Gibbon pens the following summative observation which continues the echo of corruption and decline. "The imagination, which had been raised by a painful effort to the contemplation and worship of the Universal Cause, eagerly embraced such inferior objects of adoration as were more proportioned to its gross conceptions and imperfect faculties. The sublime and simple theology of the primitive Christians was gradually corrupted; and the monarchy of heaven, already clouded by metaphysical subtleties, was degraded by the introduction of a popular mythology, which tended to restore the reign of polytheism." (*DF-28*, III, 225) The irony expressed here in political imagery lies in the reference to the descent after the "painful effort" of Christian theologians to raise the imagination to a perfect though abstract concept of God into grosser more tangible conceptions and ultimately back down to something resembling polytheism. Indeed, the political imagery points to a parallelism we find frequently

---

[16]Frank E. Manuel, *The Eighteenth Century Confronts the Gods* (Cambridge, MA: Harvard University Press, 1959), 180.

[17]See Brown, *Cult of the Saints*, 13. Brown is very critical of Hume's *Natural History of Religion* for bequeathing a completely disparaging view of the religious ideas and sentiments of common, i.e., non-philosophical people, as irrational and superstitious and hence unworthy of consideration.

[18]Manuel, *The Eighteenth Century Confronts the Gods*, 168-170.

in the *Decline and Fall*; political *and* spiritual decay. Politics and spirituality have an unstable though close relationship.

The observation turns critically on the Humean notion articulated in the *Natural History* that religious ideas are invariably and inevitably shaped by human needs. The direction of influence in the formation of religious belief travels one way; *from* the emotional requirements and imaginative limitations of believers *to* the particular configuration of their religious ideas and attitudes. At the conclusion of these remarks Gibbon cites Hume saying, "Mr. Hume observes, like a philosopher, the natural flux and reflux of polytheism and theism." (*DF-28*, III, 225, n.92) Gibbon thus pays high tribute to Hume as a philosopher, but more importantly, he applies to his own history of Christianity the explanation of the originative process of religious beliefs laid out by Hume in the *Natural History*. Hume says "that the principles of religion have a kind of flux and reflux in the human mind, and that men have a natural tendency to rise from idolatry to theism, and to sink again from theism into idolatry." (*NHR*, 56-57) This is the "flux-reflux" notion of Hume's cited by Gibbon.[19] Hume says that: "[m]en's exaggerated praises and compliments still swell their idea upon them; and elevating their deities to the utmost bounds of perfection, at last beget the attributes of unity and infinity, simplicity and spirituality." (*NHR*, 57) Gibbon's above remark noting the Christians' "painful effort" of the imagination to conceive a perfect "Universal Cause" stands out as a specific historical instance of a general pattern of religious practice observed by Hume whereby objects of worship are gradually elevated to high and abstract levels of perfection. However, God's elevation to the pinnacle of perfection turns him into an incomprehensible deity who is far beyond the imaginative capacity of most individuals. Theoretically refined and perfect as He may be, this God can demonstrate little practical significance for human beings. In a letter to William Mure Hume says: "from this Circumstance of the Indivisibility and Incomprehensibility of the Deity [one] may feel no Affection towards him. And indeed I am afraid, that all Enthusiasts mightily deceive themselves. Hope & Fear perhaps agitate their Breast when they think of the Deity; or they degrade him into a Resemblance with themselves, and by that means render him more comprehensible." (*Letters*-H, I, 51)

Pressure within human experience unfailingly exerts itself to bring God into a more tangible, sensible, comprehensible form. Hume describes it this way. "Such refined ideas, being somewhat disproportioned to vulgar comprehension,

---

[19]Pocock, "Superstition and Enthusiasm in Gibbon's History of Religion," 89, says: "[w]hat occurs in chapter 28 is purely Humean: the greatest recorded example of that flux and reflux of polytheism and monotheism, superstition and enthusiasm, which Gibbon's master—for such Hume was in a number of ways—had declared inherent in the *Natural History of Religion*."

remain not long in their original purity; but require to be supported by the notion of inferior mediators or subordinate agents, which interpose betwixt mankind and their supreme deity. These demi-gods or middle beings, partaking more of human nature, and being more familiar to us, become the chief objects of devotion, and gradually recal that idolatry, which had been formerly banished by the ardent prayers and panegyrics of timorous and indigent mortals." (*NHR*, 57-58)

This anthropomorphic transformation of divine entities, as theorized here by Hume, is precisely what has taken place within the historical unfolding of the Christian religion, so Gibbon argues, in line with Hume's account. The phenomenon of saint and relic worship is an instance of this gradual recalling of idolatry, an interposing of intermediary gods that are more accessible to the mind. In order to stress just how far Christianity had departed from its pure and perfect notion of God, Gibbon shrewdly plays to the imagination of the reader by conjuring up the ghosts of some early Christians heroes to contemplate the "progress" of Christianity after about four hundred years. "If, in the beginning of the fifth century, Tertullian or Lactantius had been suddenly raised from the dead, to assist at the festival of some popular saint or martyr, they would have gazed with astonishment and indignation on the profane spectacle, which had succeeded to the pure and spiritual worship of a Christian congregation . . . . The most respectable bishops had persuaded themselves that the ignorant rustics would more cheerfully renounce the superstitions of Paganism, if they found some resemblance, some compensation, in the bosom of Christianity. The religion of Constantine achieved in less than a century the final conquest of the Roman empire; but the victors themselves were insensibly subdued by the arts of their vanquished rivals." (*DF-28*, III, 225-27)

Gibbon's acute, historical sense of time helps to dramatize his ongoing theme of the decline of Christianity. What may over many years be an imperceptible or gradual change becomes with this telescoping act of imagination quite startling. Christianity has departed significantly from its originative ideals. These are the final words of chapter twenty-eight which appropriately enough culminate with the ultimate expression of irony. The chapter describes the "final destruction of paganism," but Christianity finds itself with the tables turned. Human nature has rudely impressed itself on the Christianizing process and the supreme, unified God has been multiplied and metamorphosed into less abstract, less powerful, more tangible beings for the convenience of the worshipers. Emerging from the Hume-Gibbon version of religious naturalism is its unpalatable consequence for the Christian: man creates god in his own image.[20]

---

[20]This point raises the specter of Cicero, a favorite of both Hume and Gibbon. "Nor indeed do I understand why Epicurus preferred to say that gods are like men rather than that men are like gods.

II. Superstition and Enthusiasm

And this fear of things invisible, is the natural seed of that, which every one in himself calleth religion; and in them that worship, or fear that power otherwise than they do, superstition.

Thomas Hobbes

For the enthusiast, there is only one church, a church 'invisible.'

Ronald Knox

Christianity's ascendancy as a political and spiritual force and the vast social and political upheavals that followed in the wake of its ascent is a well worked theme in Hume and Gibbon. While the violence and destruction in Christian history erupted in part as a struggle for doctrinal supremacy—the power to define "true" Christianity—there were also, as both Hume and Gibbon interpreted the history of Christianity, specific types of emotive religiosity involved in the long history of conflict—two to be precise—"superstition" and "enthusiasm." Superstition and enthusiasm, designated specifically as religious emotions, play starring roles (sometimes tragic, sometimes burlesque) on the Hume-Gibbon stage of religious naturalism. Christians in Hume's *History of England* and Gibbon's *Decline and Fall* were frequently infused either with superstition or enthusiasm. Superstition and enthusiasm operate as technical terms, though wielded in a general and somewhat rough way. They mark out for the philosophic historian a broad typology of religious pathology.[21] Superstition in its post-classical world form was closely linked with popery and loosely described as a religious mentality rooted in ignorance and fear, expressed in abject subservience to oppressive, corrupt religious hierarchies. Enthusiasm, conversely, was seen by many eighteenth-century defenders as well as critics of Christianity like Hume and Gibbon to be a social toxin, a stimulus of religious anarchy and political levelling. The enthusiast was a reckless fanatic, made dangerous by his unfaltering confidence in his own

---

'what is the difference?' you will ask me, 'for if A is like B, B is like A.' I am aware of it; but what I mean is, that the gods did not derive the pattern of their form from men; since the gods have always existed, and were never born—that is, if they are to be eternal; whereas men were born; therefore the human form existed before mankind, and it was the form of the immortal gods. We ought not to say that the gods have human form, but that our form is divine." Cicero, *De Natura Deorum*, trans. H. Rackham, (Cambridge, MA: Harvard University Press, 1933), 87-89.

[21]Superstition and enthusiasm are widespread categories in the discussion of religion in the eighteenth century. See Susie I. Tucker, *Enthusiasm: A Study in Semantic Change* (Cambridge: Cambridge University Press, 1972), 18-19, and Ronald Knox, *Enthusiasm: A Chapter in the History of Religion* (Westminster, MD: Christian Classics, 1983).

special favor with God. The enthusiast for Hume and Gibbon was the nemesis of tradition and authority.[22]

In Hume and Gibbon we see a heavy focus on what they view as the socially disruptive workings of religion. They saw a close connection between the strong emotions of religious believers and social disruption and upheaval. Religion in its "proper" form is less interesting, less spectacular, and unremarkable. Their observations of religious emotionalism and its connections with fanaticism that came out of their study of Christianity were in part the likely cause for Gibbon's and Hume's aversion to the emotive side of Christianity. This was a typical view of eighteenth-century British thinkers toward religious emotionalism. E. Tillyard writes that Gibbon's entire intellectual community had an intense dislike of enthusiasm, a community that included orthodox Churchmen as well. Frank Manuel notes that the English deists came to view enthusiasm as a kind of madness.[23] And so the Christian history written by Hume and Gibbon turns out to be, remarkably, a chronicle of Christian emotive excess, a study of superstition and enthusiasm in myriad manifestations. *Their* Christianity often exhibits itself in one or the other of these excesses.[24] One could say that Hume and Gibbon are hard pressed to discover a Christianity that would be normal or non-aberrational religion in the sense that the lives of the practitioner's are free from some sort of excess or deficiency. Again, Hume admonishes that in attempting to understand religion "we must treat of Religion, as it has been commonly found in this World." Taking this to heart here though yields something of a paradox. Normal religion—normal in the sense of being what is usually the practice, what is "commonly found in this World"—is, historically viewed, as corrupt or perverted. Recall Gibbon's "melancholy duty," a study directed toward the practice of religion by a "weak and degenerate race of beings." "True Religion," Hume says, "has no such pernicious Consequences," i.e., wars, persecutions, bigotry, etc. The problem is that the

---

[22]Stromberg, *Religious Liberalism in Eighteenth-Century England*, 13-14. Caution here, however, should be noted in characterizing enthusiasts as enemies of religious tradition or authority. See Conal Condren, "Radicals, Conservatives and Moderates in Early Modern Political Thought: A Case of Sandwich Islands Syndrome?", *History of Political Thought* 10, no. 3 (autumn 1989): 536. "Battles in political religious discourse begin to look like fights not between radicals and conservatives, but between claimants to the mantle of authentic conservation; the rhetorical goal is to be recognized as custodian of legitimate tradition." This raises the question as to whether eighteenth-century critics of religious enthusiasts such as Hume and Gibbon were sufficiently historically appreciative of the spiritual yearnings of the "enthusiasts" (ancient or modern) or simply condemning what they saw as an excess emotion.

[23]E. M. W. Tillyard, *The English Epic and Its Background* (New York: Oxford University Press, 1966), 522; Frank Manuel, *The Eighteenth Century Confronts the Gods*, Chapter 3.

[24]Pocock, "Superstition and Enthusiasm in Gibbon's History of Religion," 83-84, says: "[s]ince enthusiasm is the idolatry of the Word, and superstition the idolatry of the Word made Flesh, there is not much room left for an authentic Christianity between them."

historian struggles to find many instances of it. The contemplation of religion presents an unpalatable paradox, so it would seem. Though religion exists as a testimony to the highest of spiritual aspirations, its normal practice is immersed in fanaticism and superstition: it is an institutional expression of human degeneracy and corruption.

The religious naturalism of Hume's *Natural History* makes its way into the *Decline and Fall* and exerts itself interpretatively in Gibbon's panoramic account of the religious history unfolding over one thousand years. Like Hume, Gibbon's rendition of religion is "as it has commonly been found in the world," with the most depressing disparity between the professed ideals and the historical reality. Religion as it is commonly found in the world manifests itself in these two corrupted forms of enthusiasm and superstition. And so with the contemplation of corruption comes the melancholy work of the moralist. The moral point of view brings disapprobation and condemnation. The *History of England* dwells with revulsion upon the Marian persecutions and the fanatical excesses of the Puritan revolution. The *Decline and Fall* is immersed in religious violence; wars, persecutions, pogroms, and the like. At the individual level in both of these works we are confronted by the religious fanatic, the pious opportunist, the hypocrite, and the death-embracing monk. The naturalism of these works is thus slanted heavily toward the scrutiny of religious belief as a kind of mental pathology. Such a pathology focuses on the emotive features of religion; its origins in fear,[25] its fanatical manifestations in euphoric hope.

Superstition and enthusiasm oppose *normal* or, what Hume calls in his essay, "Of Superstition and Enthusiasm," "true religion." This essay opens: "[t]*hat the corruption of the best things produces the worst*, is grown into a maxim, and is commonly proved, among other instances, by the pernicious effects of *superstition* and *enthusiasm*, the corruptions of true religion."(*Essays*, 73, original italics) "True religion" in this context, as suggested above, has a special meaning for Hume (a partly ironic one it would seem) since first, he held no revealed religion to be true and, second, his rejection of natural theology precludes the possibility that he would be referring to any specific demonstrably "true" set of theological propositions. True religion means for Hume what it very likely does for Gibbon, namely "normal" religion, normal in the sense that its practitioners are not led by it to depart from established, conventional social norms of self-restraint. True religion does not seem to have much positive content for Hume. Honesty, for

---

[25]D. Jordan, *Gibbon and His Roman Empire*, 108, says that the "first gods of polytheism were created through fear. This was an idea borrowed from David Hume. It gave Gibbon a psychological understanding of the importance of religion, and he built up his picture of polytheism from this assumption."

example, is a conventional norm that fanatics frequently discard. The zealous spurning of conventional norms is a frequent feature of Gibbon's history of Christianity and the basis of much of his criticism. Consider his expostulation against Justinian's persecutory policies as he approvingly quotes Procopius. "[From Procopius] Justinian might have learned, '*that* religious controversy is the offspring of arrogance and folly; *that* true piety is most laudably expressed by silence and submission; *that* man, ignorant of his own nature, should not presume to scrutinize the nature of his God; and *that* it is sufficient for us to know that power and benevolence are the perfect attributes of the Deity.'" (*DF-47*, V, 142, original italics) If we compare this to Hume's remarks through Cleanthes in the *Dialogues*, that "[t]he proper Office of Religion is to regulate the Heart of men, humanize their Conduct, and infuse the Spirit of Temperance, Order and Obedience" (*Dialogues*, 251), the socially conservatory function that both Hume and Gibbon see as appropriate for religion is apparent.

The superstition-enthusiasm categorization employed by Hume and Gibbon is certainly not original. That superstition is a perversion of religion, born of and nurtured by terror and apprehension, is an ancient observation. Cicero was one of the major classical sources for this critical eighteenth-century notion. Superstition for Cicero "implies a groundless fear of the gods," and is distinguished from proper religion "which consists in piously worshiping them."[26] The distinction is based on emotion and attitude. Frank Manual writing on the eighteenth-century confrontation between the philosophes and traditional Christians notes that: "[o]ne grand subterfuge was a study of superstition as distinguished from true religion, a field in which Bayle and the English deists labored with passion . . . ."[27] Religion in its degraded, superstitious, pagan forms could be scrutinized as a naturalistic phenomenon and safely criticized. For Protestant polemicists, Catholicism, insofar as it could be characterized as superstitious, was also open to attack. (Ibid., 22)

Superstition's perversity is closely linked to its origins in fear and its nurture by ignorance. Primitive peoples in the face of the uncertainties of existence and in the unavoidable path of natural calamities attribute the evils which befall them to malevolent or offended gods that must be appeased. (*NHR*, 33) Hume argues that superstition is the oldest of religions and is an invention of terror stricken, ignorant people, who abase themselves as a benighted strategy for deflecting divine displeasure or wrath. "Weakness, fear, melancholy, together with ignorance, are therefore, the true sources of superstition." (*Essays*, 74) The *Natural History,* as noted in the very first sentence, is an attempt to deal with religion "concerning its origin in human nature." (*NHR*, 25) Hume contends that early people were

---

[26]Cicero, *De Natura Deorum*, 113.

[27]Manuel, *The Eighteenth Century Confronts the Gods*, 21.

polytheists ("idolaters"), and that their intellectual primitiveness made it unlikely that they possessed the more abstract and sophisticated notions associated with monotheism.[28]   Moreover, a contemplation of their modes of worship and conceptions of the gods suggests that the primary shaping force in these things was the emotion of fear. Helpless, vulnerable to every imaginable catastrophe, the life of early man was immersed in fear. His terrified imagination invented beings which he attempted to appease through worship and sacrifice. "We may conclude . . . that, in all nations, which have embraced polytheism or idolatry, the first ideas of religion arose not from a contemplation of the works of nature, but from a concern with regard to the events of life, and from the incessant hopes and fears which actuate the human mind." (*NHR*, 31) Fear then is a primary motivational force for religion, particularly superstitious religion. "The mind of man is subject to certain unaccountable terrors and apprehensions, proceeding either from the unhappy situation of private or public affairs, from ill health, from a gloomy and melancholy disposition, or from the concurrence of all these circumstances." (*Essays*, 73) Hume observed the impact of superstition on his fellow Scots and how the fear-infused Calvinism that reigned in Scotland was an ineluctable element in the collective melancholia that gripped his people.   Henry Grey Graham describes the "melancholic despair" so prevalent in eighteenth-century Scotland, a response to the Calvinist preoccupation with the fear of damnation and with a real and imaginatively vivid picture of hell.[29]

Enthusiasm, like superstition, is a key part of the eighteenth-century vocabulary for the discussion of religious conduct in emotivist, naturalistic terms. For people in the eighteenth century, Susie I. Tucker writes, "enthusiasm" meant a religious fervor and passion that was always excessive.[30] Enthusiasm, again like superstition, is something perverse. It refers to unbridled, benighted, highly energized religious emotion. The deist Anthony Collins viewed enthusiasm as springing from ignorance and error and an aversion to inquiry. (Ibid., 39-40) The excessive nature of enthusiasm makes it an object of disapprobation. Intense emotions heighten the unpredictability of human action and undermine important qualities of character like constancy, self-control and reliability, all of which contribute to sociability. Hume's Puritan enthusiasts in their rebellion against Charles I and Gibbon's early Christian enthusiasts in their rejection of pagan gods are rash, bold, unpredictable, and destructive. Gibbon had great approbation for the Roman pagan religions with their built-in traditional constraints on the

---

[28]Gaskin, *Hume's Philosophy of Religion*, 184, says that Hume's statement that early men were all polytheists is open to some qualifications, but could be fixed up to be acceptable.

[29]Graham, *Social Life of Scotland*, 400-404.

[30]Tucker, *Enthusiasm: a Study in Semantic Change*, 4.

expression of religious emotion. Underlying the rites and practices of these ancient ceremonies was the assumption that an immoderate venting of religious expression undermined the social order.[31] Enthusiasm is similar to superstition in its immersion in ignorance. However, the emotions giving rise to it are opposite ones. The central emotive feature of enthusiasm is not fear, as it is with superstition, but confidence, supreme, overweening, and frequently blind, confidence. "Hope, pride, presumption, a warm imagination, together with ignorance, are, therefore, the true sources of enthusiasm." (*Essays*, 74) With enthusiasm, the causal framework involving the emotions is somewhat different than it is with superstition. The primary emotions of superstition are caused by *external* events (natural disasters, calamities, accidents, etc.). In the face of the unpredictable, uncontrollable caprices of nature arises feelings of fear, helplessness, abjection, and the like. But to enthusiasm Hume attributes the causes which give rise to the actuating emotions as internal to the mind. "But the *mind of man* is also subject to an *unaccountable* elevation and presumption, arising from prosperous success, from luxuriant health, from strong spirits, or from a bold and confident disposition." (*Essays*, 74, italics added) The cause of enthusiasm is some mental aberration, yet unknown ("unaccountable") phenomenon from which this excessive self-confidence emerges. Enthusiasm, indeed, comes off as a kind of mental illness or disease. As a form of religious exuberance enthusiasm is viewed here in fully naturalistic terms. Locke's account of enthusiasm in the *Essay Concerning Human Understanding*, which Hume and Gibbon had read, resorts to a physiological explanation of enthusiasm, appropriate perhaps, given Locke's medical background. "This I take to be properly Enthusiasm, which though founded neither on Reason, nor Divine Revelation, but rising from the Conceits of a warmed or over-weening Brain, works yet, where it once gets footing, more powerfully on the Perswasions and Actions of men, than either of those two, or both together."[32] Locke's "enthusiasm" is a kind of pathological brain-state. The superstitionist's angry, vengeful acting gods spring from his experience of their displeasure visited in the form of some tragedy or natural catastrophe. By contrast, the god of the enthusiast, as Locke suggests, is the fruit of mental aberration, an imaginary deity catering to violent or uncontrollable emotions caused by malfunctions of the brain. So, Locke explicitly, and Hume implicitly, attribute this phenomenon of enthusiasm to some physiological cause which accounts for the fanatical behavior of the enthusiast.

---

[31]See Alan Wardman, *Religion and Statescraft Among the Romans*, (Baltimore: Johns Hopkins University Press, 1982) 21.

[32]John Locke, *Essay Concerning Human Understanding*, ed. Peter H. Nidditch (Oxford: Clarendon Press, 1975), 699.

Enthusiasm is a more bewildering, less understandable phenomenon because of its unknown, unpredictable causes. In contemplating the different effects of superstition and enthusiasm this is an important consideration. Enthusiasm, by Hume's account, is more unpredictable, volatile, dangerous, and violent than superstition. But precisely because of that volatility the destructive political and social effects have a much shorter duration than those of superstition. Superstition is more predictable, more enduring than enthusiasm.

The supreme confidence and restless energy of enthusiasm reside in egotistical, overreaching personalities who spurn conventional norms. The enthusiast, believing himself to be God's chosen agent, feels justified, indeed bound to contravene law and conventional morality. "In a little time, the inspired person comes to regard himself as a distinguished favourite of the Divinity; and when this frenzy once takes place, which is the summit of enthusiasm, every whimsy is consecrated; Human reason, and even morality are rejected as fallacious guides." (*Essays*, 74) The enthusiast emerges from Hume's portrayal as an unrestrained purveyor of religiously inspired anarchy, and as a highly energized fanatic, spurning conventional morality and willing to assault the established institutions with an unshakable confidence in his divine mandate.

In contrast with enthusiasm, which gives each believer a feeling of divine recognition, superstition spawns an elite class with claims to intercessory powers. The rise of this class—"the priestly class," as Hume calls it—is attributable to the workings of the emotions which evoke the superstitious outlook. "As superstition is founded on fear, sorrow, and a depression of spirits, it represents the man to himself in such despicable colours, that he appears unworthy, in his own eyes, of approaching the divine presence, and naturally has recourse to any other person, whose sanctity of life, or, perhaps, impudence and cunning, have made him be supposed more favoured by the Divinity . . . . Hence the origin of Priests . . . ." (*Essays*, 75)

Superstition supports ecclesiastical hierarchies that invite corruption. In the face of the unpredictable calamities of life, the weak, the helpless, the credulous, turn to the more powerful, the more clever, the more capable in their midst who become the intercessors. Intercessors enjoy divine favor. Where high value attaches to divine favor, the divinely-favored are greatly valued. Because superstition is a religion based in fear, the greater the superstition the more intense the fear. The more acute the helplessness and ignorance the greater the intercessor's power. "But the stronger mixture there is of superstition, the higher is the authority of the priesthood." (*Essays*, 75) It is apparent if we look, as Hume does, at the superstitious priestly class as a power elite with the foundations of their power resting upon their perceived special intercessory abilities, then this priestly class has a vested interest in nourishing those emotions which make their followers dependent upon them. No one in this class could be blamed for fiercely resisting any and all efforts to dispel ignorance, raise hope, and alleviate that sense of personal helplessness. The feeling of helplessness on the part of those who are controlled by the elites is what makes the services of this class valuable and necessary.

Hume can hardly conceive of the dynamics of superstitious religion in any other way than he does. Because of the intercessors' vested interest in having people hold religious beliefs which justify *their* (the intercessors') prerogatives, they by necessity are called upon to use the most egregious instruments of tyranny, oppression, and violence. "Superstition . . . steals in gradually and insensibly; renders men tame and submissive; is acceptable to the magistrate, and seems inoffensive to the people: Till at last the priest, having firmly established his authority, becomes the tyrant and disturber of human society, by his endless contentions, persecutions, and religious wars." (*Essays*, 78)

Enthusiasm begets fanatics and anarchists; superstition, miserable craven-types and tyrants. The contrast (with its political implications) is stark and apparent. Enthusiasm in its most extreme forms manifests itself in attacks on the established order. Superstition frequently serves tyrants as an instrument to rationalize privilege, legitimize cruelty, criminalize doubt, and exalt credulity. Enthusiasm, as Hume describes it, attempts the levelling of economic and social class distinctions: superstition in contrast remains the insidious agent of reaction and aims at the perpetuation of *extremes* of social differentiation through repression and persecution.

"Of Superstition and Enthusiasm" speculates on the causes of these two perversions of religion as well as their effects, their "influence," most significantly, "on government and society." Hume develops three comparative generalizations of superstition and enthusiasm, all of which have profound implications for the impact of religion on society.

(1) "[S]uperstition is favourable to priestly power, and enthusiasm not less or rather more contrary to it, than sound reason or philosophy." (*Essays*, 75)
(2) "[R]eligions, which partake of enthusiasm are, on their first rise, more furious and violent than those which partake of superstition; but in a little time become more gentle and moderate." (*Essays*, 76)
(3) "[S]uperstition is an enemy to civil liberty, and enthusiasm, a friend to it." (*Essays*, 78)

In generalization (1) Hume indicates what was suggested above, that superstition and enthusiasm are opposite in the sense that superstition is associated with ultra-authoritarianism while enthusiasm is aligned with egalitarianism and social levelling. Hume stakes out the boundaries of normal religious behavior somewhere between the poles of repression and anarchy. While the superstitious hold their priests to be divinely inspired, each enthusiast arrogates to himself special consideration with God. Enthusiasm, Hume suggests, is so strongly opposed to superstition that it leads individuals seized by it not to consider themselves bound by any authority other than their own. The *History of England* shows how enthusiasm drives a society toward anarchy with the breakdown of norms that encourage self-restraining conduct.

Such are the effects of extreme enthusiasm. Because the "inspiration" is completely subjective and wholly self-justifying, its supremacy brings about a state of affairs where each individual can recognize no authority other than his own.[33] While being opposed to ecclesiastical tyranny, Hume appears to make a case for what might be called "traditional authority." Certainly traditional authority can have large religious components: this was the case with the pagan religions and with the emotionally low key Anglicans of the Laudian persuasion. Traditional authority constitutes the grounding for norms by which conduct can be regulated and by which consistent, coherent policy can be determined and pursued. While the superstitious blindly and cravenly submit to authority, enthusiasts, Hume seems to suggest, overreact and destroy useful authority structures.

In generalization (2), Hume attempts to show that the zeal, fervor, and the emotional intensity characteristic of the enthusiast are unsustainable. "When the first fire of enthusiasm is spent, men naturally, in all fanatical sects, sink into the greatest remisses and coolness in sacred matters; there being no body of men among them endowed with the sufficient authority, whose interest is concerned to support the religious spirit." (*Essays*, 77-78) This is another expression of Hume's near overriding concern with the issue of authority! Enthusiasm batters those useful and valuable relations of authority. There is also a harkening back to an earlier point made that the causes that bring about the emotions of enthusiasm are different in that they arise inexplicably from within. Enthusiasm, as we have seen, is more difficult to understand, attributable to less easily detected and recognized contingencies. Also, as suggested in the immediately above quotation, enthusiasm, by its very inexplicable and mercurial nature, cannot be expected in most cases to maintain its furious intensity.

---

[33]This is a problem raised by Catholic polemicists in their conflicts with the Reformers. See, Popkin, *History of Scepticism*, Chapter One, "The Intellectual Crisis of the Reformation," for an extensive historical treatment of the problem of justifying religious authority for truth-claims.

Enthusiasm wanes more easily than superstition. It does not to the extent that superstitious religions do support classes who profit exclusively from the heightening of religious emotion. Also, enthusiasm tended to be the religion of the rising, status-hungry, industrious middle class. The virtues attending the ascending Puritans—self-improvement, industry, self-denial—were particularly suited for moving them toward economic prosperity.[34] But material success brought a declining interest in spiritual concerns.[35] Enthusiasts in their early appearances on the scene seem to pose more danger to the body politic, yet with time their fanaticism usually dissipates somewhat and they become more moderate. Superstition thus over long periods compares unfavorably with enthusiasm. Superstitionists remain less amenable than enthusiasts to moderating, ameliorating modifications. Enthusiasm's rigors are more inherently unstable because enthusiastic emotion is less predictable, more volatile, and hence is more difficult to promote and cultivate than the superstitious variety, and is more likely to decompose into moderate and milder forms.

Hume's third generalization ("Superstition is an enemy to civil liberty, and enthusiasm a friend to it") is the most striking and important. And, he adds, "enthusiasm, being the infirmity of bold and ambitious tempers, is naturally accompanied with a spirit of liberty; as superstition, on the contrary, renders men tame and abject, and fits them for slavery." (*Essays*, 78) Where enthusiasm predominates, free government is more likely to emerge in the long run than where superstition reigns. But why is this the case? Why would enthusiasts with their convictions of near infallibility in the truth of their religious beliefs be a "friend" of civil liberty which demands the toleration of other "false" religious beliefs? Hume's explanation is not completely illuminating. "We learn from English history, that, during the civil wars, the *independents* and *deists*, though the most opposite in their religious principles; yet were united in their political ones, and

---

[34]Max Weber, *The Protestant Ethic and the Spirit of Capitalism*, trans. Talcott Parsons (New York: Charles Scribner's Sons, 1958), drew the connections between the origins of capitalism and the Protestant view of the world. See also Gellner, *Reason and Culture*, 51, 138-9. Gellner argues that Weber's great insight regarding the Protestant ethic is that the *inner* conviction that drove the Protestants toward those virtues that undergirded capitalism—sobriety, willingness to save, modestly, hard work, etc.—was born from un—reason. Capitalism is one of history's great works of unintended consequence. Enthusiastic religiosity begat prosperity.

[35]Some theorists see a link between what was called "backsliding," or a cooling in religious zeal, and devotion, and material success. Backsliding was a problem, particularly for the Protestant Puritan divines who frequently complained about this tendency. Hume saw it as inevitable in fanatical religions. For a discussion of the "backsliding" or "retrogression" phenomenon as it affected the covenant theology of the New England Puritans, see Perry Miller, *The New England Mind: The Seventeenth Century* (Cambridge, MA: Harvard University Press, 1939), 473, where Miller writes: "[t]hat success breeds sloth, that prosperity relaxes spirited efforts, were lessons of experience even to Puritans."

were alike passionate for a commonwealth. And since the origin of *whig* and *tory*, the leaders of the *whigs* have either been *deists* or profest *latitudinarians* in their principles; that is friends to toleration, and indifferent to any particular sect of *christians*." (*Essays*, 78-79, original italics) What we have here seems more like a description than an explanation. The "passion for a commonwealth" comes from a realization on the part of the various sects that they simply lack the power to impose their "religious principles" on those with different principles. Civil liberty and mutual religious toleration are a second-best strategy for those who understand that they do not have the power to prevail completely.[36] Significant in Hume's treatment of superstition and enthusiasm is the thoroughgoing naturalism. Three main elements enter into his analysis and inform the discussion; emotions, the behavior connected with the emotions, and the social and political impact of the behavior. The relevancy of the content or substance of theological ideas and thinking is limited to their effect on the emotional disposition of the religious believer. Such an approach to the study of religion is inevitably reductivist. It seeks to explain religious behavior through general causal statements that link certain kinds of emotions to particular types of behavior. Hume's effort thus amounts to a cross-cultural, comparative approach to the study of religion, and he attempts to construct a social-psychological vocabulary that discusses religion as a complex social manifestation of human emotions. Superstition and enthusiasm as terms of discussion take on a greater primacy than terms like Christianity, Islam, or paganism. Religions themselves become types for comparison. We can thus speak of Christian superstition, Islamic enthusiasm or pagan superstition.

As broad, general categories of religious pathology, superstition and enthusiasm were cast by Hume and Gibbon into particular historical contexts in which they take on added dimensions of significance. The Protestant Reformation with all of the violence inspired by conflicting religious convictions was the setting Hume used to create the rich historical coloration for his notions of superstition and enthusiasm. The following text from the *History of Great Britain* gives a specific sense of how he sees superstition and enthusiasm at work in the modern history of Christianity.

---

[36]Gellner, *Plough, Sword and Book*, 114-15 points out this problem with Hume. Hume "says that unitarians are enemies of liberty, and then he says that their zeal is a friend of it. A cogent argument makes unitarian scripturalism anti-liberal in general, but a friend of liberty *on one occasion*. Hume notices this, but his attempt to deal with it is feeble. The real answer would seem to be that it is important for the zealous enthusiasts to be defeated but not crushed. The defeat converts them to toleration . . . . The fact that their defeat is not total helps them secure toleration. A spiritual as well as political balance of power helps maintain a situation in which central coercion is not exercised to the full."

Before the reformation, all men of sense and virtue wished impatiently for
some event, which might repress the exorbitant power of the clergy all
over Europe, and put an end to the unbounded usurpations and
pretensions of the Roman pontiff: But when the doctrine of Luther was
promulgated, they were somewhat alarmed at the sharpness of the remedy;
and it was easily foreseen, from the offensive zeal of the reformers, and
defensive of the church, that all christendom must be thrown into
combustion. In the preceding state of ignorance and tranquillity, into
which mankind were lulled, *the attachment to superstition*, tho' without
reserve, was not extreme; and, like the *antient pagan idolatry*, the popular
religion consisted more of exterior practices and observances, than of any
principles which either took possession of the heart, or influenced the
conduct. It might have been hoped, that learning and knowledge, as of
old in Greece, stealing in gradually, would have opened the eyes of men,
and corrected such of the ecclesiastical abuses as were the grossest and
most burthensome. It had been observed, that, upon the revival of letters,
very generous and enlarged sentiments of religion prevailed thro'out all
Italy; and that, during the reign of Leo, the court of Rome itself, in
imitation of their illustrious prince, had not been wanting in a just sense
of freedom. But when the *enraged and fanatical reformers* took arms
against the papal hierarchy, and threatened to rend from the church at
once all her riches and authority; no wonder she was animated with equal
zeal and ardor, in defence of such antient and invaluable possessions. At
the same time, that she employed the stake and gibbet against her avowed
enemies, *she extended her jealousy even towards learning and
philosophy*, whom, in her supine security, she had formerly overlooked,
as harmless and inoffensive. Hence, the severe check which knowledge
received in Italy: Hence, its total extinction in Spain: And hence, the slow
progress, which it made, in France, Germany, and England. From the
admiration of antient literature, from the inquiry after new discoveries, the
minds of the studious were everywhere turned to polemical science; and
in all schools and academies, the furious controversies took the place of
the calm disquisitions of learning. (*HGB*, 96-97, italics added)[37]

This passage attempts to explain the origins of the most tragic, most protracted
conflict in the history of Christianity. Hume features it as a violent and momentous
collision of a particular kind of superstition, i.e., medieval Catholicism, with the

---

[37]This passage was deleted from the latter editions of the *History of England*. Hume was
attempting, perhaps, to soften the critical tone of his remarks about the Reformers.

fanatical enthusiasm of the Protestant reformers. The conflict begins as a classic case of the abuse of power. Here, captured in impressive historical dimensions, is a thoroughly corrupted papacy. Christianity had long departed from its primitive purity and simplicity. Like Gibbon, Hume insists on the inevitable human corruption of the spiritual aspirations of Christianity. The problem, Hume argues, was obvious to everyone with any elemental sense of the dynamics of social interaction. Medieval Catholicism, as a form of superstition, is compared to ancient, pre-Christian superstition, or, "pagan idolatry." Superstition in its original, earliest form is the polytheism of primitive peoples. Medieval superstition in this context resembles pagan idolatry in that it has become an "exterior" religion, a religion of social-ceremonial function and is not taken in deep seriousness as a "source of principles" that might guide or control human conduct. The flux-reflux phenomena are at work: Catholicism has devolved from its earlier, fanatical, monotheistic origins to something resembling pagan idolatry. Catholic superstition, Hume argues, *could* have been gently and gradually rolled back. Attachment to it was "not extreme" and classical learning was being rediscovered. The fanaticism of the Reformers with a violent, all out frontal assault on the ancient church, however, provoked an ugly but predictable reaction. "No wonder," says Hume, Catholicism "was animated with equal zeal and ardor, in defence of such antient and invaluable possessions."

So, two different forms of superstition are at work in this passage: the first, a milder, more tolerating superstition—a ceremonial, external religion. Pre-reformation Catholicism, at the popular level, in many ways resembled pagan idolatry. The second form of superstition, however, turns out to be more virulent. It is the superstition of post-Reformation Catholicism—defensive, reactionary, driven toward the use of philosophy as a polemical tool with which to battle the Protestants. Philosophy as we have seen earlier (Chapter Five) badly serves religion by making its pronouncements into logically coercive claims for universal truth. Hence, the "furious" and fruitless "controversies of theology" that "took the place of calm disquisitions of learning."

The superstition and enthusiasm described by Hume were the powerful forces at work during Christianity's most ideologically-combative, most violent period of history. They stand as antipodes: the former representing reaction and attachment to privilege, the latter a rejection of it. "The first reformers, who made such furious and successful attacks on the Romish Superstition and shook it to its lowest foundations, may safely be pronounced to have been universally inflamed with the highest Enthusiasm. These two species of religion, the superstitious and fanatical, stand in diametrical opposition to each other; and a large portion of the latter must necessarily fall to his share, who is so courageous as to control authority, and so assuming as to obtrude his own innovations upon the world. Hence that rage of dispute, which every where seized the new religionists; that disdain of ecclesiastical subjection; that contempt of ceremonies, and of all the exterior pomp and splendor of worship. And hence too, that inflexible intrepidity, with which they braved dangers, torments, and even death itself; while they preached the doctrines of peace, and carried the tumults of war, thro' every part of Christendom." (*HGB*, 71-72)

Here then is Christianity manifest in its two corrupted forms, Christian enthusiasm and Christian superstition. The Protestants and their enthusiastic excesses, though, seem to intrigue Hume the most. His characterization of the Reformers links three important elements. First is their courage, inspired by enthusiasm and based upon a strength of personal conviction, that makes them fearless in their confrontation with established authority. That a single person would be, as Hume says, "so assuming as to obtrude his own innovations upon the world," suggests just how powerful and uncontrollable this "new" religion is. The conduct of Protestant enthusiasts for Hume would seem to have no connections to any deep social roots of tradition.[38] At work, as Hume sees it, are vanity, egoism and individualism driven to the most anarchical extremes. Second, is the revulsion with all the ceremonial accouterments of worship ("that contempt of ceremonies, and of all the exterior pomp and splendor of worship"). The Reformers eschewed "the flesh" as a contaminated piece of the physical world. Worship had to be directed away from things associated with that sinful world toward the abstract and philosophical. No priest or intercessor is needed.[39] "Ecclesiastical subjection" can have no place and must be utterly repudiated because ecclesiastical or clerical rankings are based on the notion that the knowledge of God requires an expertise of human mediation. To a Protestant with an intense belief in his own direct contact with God, this is an insulting and horrifying sacrilege which attributes divine properties to humans. Priests were vain, conniving impostors! The third

---

[38]Whether Hume is fair in his characterization of the Reformers as reckless innovators, however, raises a question alluded to above. See Condren, "Radicals, Conservatives and Moderates in Early Modern Political Thought," 536. The Reformers, Condren argues, claimed to be clearing away a "tangled undergrowth of illegitimate tradition," work which the reformation had but begun in breaking with Rome. Although this work needed to go to the extremity (suggesting radical in the harmless sense) of rooting out episcopacy, the claims were, nevertheless, focused on the need to conserve what was valuable." Did Hume, because of his disdain for the religious emotion of the Reformers, fail to comprehend historically the nature of their theological grievances?

[39]Pocock, "Superstition and Enthusiasm in Gibbon's History of Religion," 83, characterizes enthusiasm as "the worship of the ideas or scriptures in which the godhead is apparent to men, and occurs when the mind is alone with these ideas or scriptures and no sensory, priestly, or civil authority is permitted to act as mediator . . . ."

linking element is the fanaticism, that "inflexible intrepidity," as Hume calls it, with which these "new" reformed Christians confront all the horrors of persecution.

So the events of the Protestant Reformation, historically reconstructed by Hume as a social explosion, resulted from two diametrically opposed religious dispositions. The irony is that much of the content of the opposing faiths was remarkably similar: it was the intense emotional attachment to the differences that generated the conflict. Christianity at this point in its history looms as a confrontation of two corrupted forms of religion. Behind the conflict were the religious emotions that gave the two contenders for power their own character and support. Fear and abasement remained as the reservoir of superstitious support for the Catholic hierarchy: the emotional intensity of feeling direct contact with God fueled the Protestant inspiration for the rejection of popery.

The naturalistic model Hume used in his analysis of the Protestant Reformation—Protestant, levelling enthusiasts versus a corrupted, established superstitious Catholic hierarchy is in some key respects similar to the one Gibbon employed in dealing with the rise of early Christianity and its challenge to the Roman empire. Gibbon charged that the early persecution of Christians, from the reigns of Nero through Diocletian, was incurred as a result of the Christians' own religious enthusiasm and concomitant separatism. Chapter sixteen opens with an implicit skepticism about Christian claims regarding the motives the Roman officials had in persecuting them. "The sectaries of a persecuted religion, depressed by fear, animated with resentment, and perhaps heated by enthusiasm, are seldom in a proper temper of mind calmly to investigate, or candidly to appreciate, the motives of their enemies, which often escape the impartial and discerning view even of those who are placed at a secure distance from the flames of persecution." (*DF-16*, II, 77)

Gibbon attempts to demonstrate his concern (expressed with his adverbs, "calmly" and "candidly") to proceed with impartiality and moderation. We cannot, he suggests, trust the testimony of the early Christians: here is another instance of Gibbon's *ad hominem* attack on Christianity. Why they were persecuted at all is something of an historical puzzle given the usually tolerant posture of Roman polytheism. The motives for persecution are to be attributed, Gibbon insinuates, to something other than simple disdain or hatred by the persecutors. The solution to this puzzle lies in the traditionalist nature of the superstition of the persecutors. Hume, recall above, characterizes the "antient pagan idolatry" as religion consisting more of "exterior practices and observances," not one which takes "possession of the heart." Gibbon characterizes it as a religion "supported by custom rather than by argument." (*DF-28*, III, 216) Such a religion is the furthest removed from enthusiasm which infuses the believer with a deeply felt, personal conviction. The persecution by the Roman state launched against the early Christians was thus a defensive reaction directed toward a new type of religionist whose intensity of belief expressed itself in deliberate and open provocation against the venerable traditions. Just as Hume observes, above, that the violent reaction of medieval Catholicism against the assault by the Protestant Reformers on their ancient religion was understandable ("no wonder she was animated with equal zeal and ardor, in defence of such antient and invaluable possessions"), so, Gibbon argues, was the reaction of the Roman government. "It has already been observed that the religious concord of the world was principally supported by the implicit assent and reverence which the nations of antiquity expressed for their respective traditions and ceremonies. *It might therefore be expected* that they would unite with indignation against any sect of people which should separate itself from the communion of mankind, and, claiming the exclusive possession of divine knowledge, should disdain every from of worship, except its own, as impious and idolatrous." (*DF-16*, II, 77, italics added)[40] The early Christians incurred the wrath of the Roman state for two reasons; separatism and exclusive claims for the truth of their religion. These are the defining characteristics of extreme enthusiasm; both are openly divisive and provoke resentment. They mark both Hume's early Protestant Reformers and Gibbon's early Christians. They are also attributes of Gibbon's Jews.

The Jews, like the Christians, experienced persecution, and Gibbon looks at the history of the persecution of this sect of enthusiastic religionists in order to make better sense of what happened to the early Christians. (Ibid., x)[41] "[T]he consideration of the treatment which they [i.e., the Jews] experienced from the Roman magistrates will serve to explain how far these speculations are justified by facts, and will lead us to discover the true causes of the persecution of Christianity." (*DF-16*, II, 77-78)[42] More naturalism is in evidence here with the

---

[40]Frend, *Martyrdom and Persecution in the Early Church*, 5, confirms Gibbon's observation. He notes that the impetus for early incidents of persecution of Christians came initially from their unpopularity with the pagans. Of the persecution of Christians at Lyons in 177 he says: "during the early summer of 177, feeling in Lyons gradually seethed up against the Christians. First, they were subjected to a series of social and semi-religious sanctions as though they were polluted persons."

[41]Frend says: "Gibbon's sixteenth chapter of the *Decline and Fall* remains one of the finest summaries of the history of the relations between the primitive Church and the Empire ever written. In the sentence 'The Jews were a people which followed the Christians, a sect which deserted the religion of their fathers', Gibbon puts his finger on the central weakness of the Christian position in the first three centuries."

[42]Frend, *Martyrdom and Persecution in the Early Church*, 34, points to three features of Jewish martyrdom that were emulated by Christians. First, martyrdom involved the notion of being a personal witness to the truth against heathen forces, a witness that involved personal suffering. Second, there was a hope of personal resurrection and vengeance against the persecutors. Third, the struggle

absence of any notion of divine providence at work in Gibbon's attempt to explain
the career of Christianity. The appeal is to facts; the underlying assumption is that
natural-causal forces are at work.

Jewish religion gets a rough handling from Gibbon. He shows little regard for
the Christian-supported notion of their status as a chosen people, another aspect of
his naturalistic approach. "[W]e are tempted to applaud the severe retaliation
which was exercised by the arms of the legions against a *race of fanatics*, whose
dire and credulous superstition seemed to render them the implacable enemies not
only of the Roman government, but of human kind." (*DF-16*, II, 78, italics added)
This harshness in the characterization of the Jews as a "race of fanatics" and as
"enemies" of "human kind" is due to Gibbon's view of their unbridled fanaticism
and misanthropy, a peculiar manifestation of enthusiasm. What offends Gibbon
is not Jewish theology or doctrine but precisely what he sees as its fanaticism. The
Jews are the first monotheists, and the development of monotheistic religions, as
Hume notes, is marked by intolerance. "The intolerance of almost all religions,
which have maintained the unity of god, is as remarkable as the contrary principle
in polytheists. The implacable, narrow, spirit of the *Jews* is well known.
Mahometanism set out with still more bloody principles; and even to this day, deals
out damnation, tho' not fire and faggot, to all other sects. And if, amongst
Christians, the *English* and *Dutch* have embraced the principles of toleration, this
singularity has proceeded from the steddy resolution of the civil magistrate, in
opposition to the continued efforts of priests and bigots." (*NHR*, 60-61, original
italics) The movement toward toleration in monotheistic religions, Hume argues,
comes from external forces, i.e., monotheism is not self-moderating.[43]

Jews, Christians, followers of Islam, all of them are monotheists and all of
them, contrary to polytheists, are intolerant. The fanaticism of the Jews made their
religion the object of Roman persecution, but it was the outright resistance to the
state by Jewish enthusiasts that provoked the Roman government into harsh
reprisals against them and led to the destruction of the Temple by Hadrian. This
punishment, Gibbon argues, eventually put a brake on their fanatical excesses.
"Notwithstanding these repeated provocations, the resentment of the Roman
princes expired after the victory; nor were their apprehensions continued beyond
the period of war and danger. By the general indulgence of polytheism, and by the
mild temper of Antoninus Pius, the Jews were restored to their ancient privileges,

against the persecutors was seen in cosmic terms as one against demonic forces of evil.

[43] See A. H. Armstrong, "The Way and Ways: Religious Tolerance and Intolerance in the Fourth Century A.D." *Vigiliae Christianae* 38, no 1 (1984), 1. "In general I do not think that any Christian body has ever abandoned the power to persecute and repress while it actually had it. The acceptance of religious toleration and freedom as good in themselves has normally been the belated, though sometimes sincere and whole-hearted recognition of a *fait accompli*."

and once more obtained the permission of circumcising their children, with the easy restraint that they should never confer on any foreign proselyte that distinguishing mark of the Hebrew race." (*DF-16*, II, 79)

The contrast is apparent here between the mild tolerating polytheists—in this case the victorious polytheistic Roman emperors—and the vanquished enthusiastic sect of the monotheistic Jews. Gibbon then adds: "[a]wakened from their dream of prophecy and conquest, they assumed the behaviour of peaceable and industrious subjects. Their irreconcilable hatred of mankind, instead of flaming out in acts of blood and violence, evaporated in less dangerous gratifications." (*DF-16*, II, 79) This is another Humean-flavored observation. Enthusiasm is mercurial and unsustainable. Enthusiastic religions are, "on their first rise more furious than those which partake of superstition; but in a little time become more gentle and moderate." Gibbon is describing the waning of enthusiastic Judaism, an inevitable process from which the believer gradually emerges more gentle and moderate. Over time the radicalism of Judaism with its implacable hostility toward rival religionists dissipated and the Jews assumed a more civilized posture.

The early Christians were, like the Jews, enthusiasts, but with this extremely important difference: the "Jews were a *nation*; the Christians were a *sect*." (*DF-16*, II, 80, original italics) The Jews were a separate nation and culture, and as such could be granted toleration as long as they were peaceable. The Christians, however, were Roman subjects first and their open and vehement rejection of their ancestral religion brought them into open conflict with the state. "By embracing the faith of the Gospel, the Christians incurred the supposed guilt of an unnatural and unpardonable offense. They dissolved the sacred ties of custom and education, violated the religious institutions of their country, and presumptiously despised whatever their fathers had believed as true, or had reverenced as sacred."[44] (*DF-16*, II, 80)

The pagan world, as Gibbon attempted to show, found Christianity to be repugnant and difficult to comprehend. "Their gloomy and austere aspect, their abhorrence of the common business and pleasures of life, and their frequent predictions of impending calamities, inspired the Pagans with the apprehension of some danger which would arise from the new sect, the more alarming as it was the more obscure." (*DF-16*, II, 84) The Christians, initially, were believed to be atheists because the "pure and sublime idea which they entertained of the Supreme Being escaped the gross conception of the Pagan multitude, who were at a loss to

---

[44]Again, see Frend, *Martyrdom and Persecution in the Early Church*, 9, who confirms Gibbon's observations. "[A]s always in the second and early third centuries, there is popular hatred, the prime mover of anti-Christian outbreaks. The intense fury of the people and their fear that somehow or other the Christians might triumph over the gods, stands out on every page of the confessors' story."

discover a spiritual and solitary God, that was neither represented under any corporeal figure or visible symbol, nor was adored with the accustomed pomp of libations and festivals, of altars and sacrifices." (*DF-16*, II, 81) This God of the Christians was a more philosophically refined deity than most of the pagans could comprehend, one that was stripped of any sensuous aspect of existence. The new Christianity that confronted the pagan world was strangely otherworldly, its central ideas foreign and abstract. Jesus's "mild constancy in the midst of cruel and voluntary sufferings, his universal benevolence, and the sublime simplicity of his actions and character were insufficient, in the opinion of those carnal men, to compensate for the want of fame, of empire, and of success." (*DF-16*, II, 83) There is a subtle irony in this vivid contrast between the invisible world morality of Christianity and the common morality of regular, "carnal men" preoccupied entirely with conventional, material modes of success. The irony lies in the incommensurability of the concepts of the two worlds that Gibbon conjoins in the sentence. The insinuation, faintly registered perhaps, is that Christianity in its most pure, exemplary form is too rare ever to take a hold in the material world. It is fated for a rapid and inevitable corruption. But the stress here is indeed on the complete incomprehensibility of Christianity to the disbelieving pagans. "Though [the Christian's] situation might excite the pity, his arguments could never reach the understanding, either of the philosophic or of the believing part of the Pagan world." (*DF-16*, II, 81)

Christianity could stir the emotions and engender raging enthusiasm and craven superstition, but it embraced a perspective that was completely at odds with and foreign to that of the pagan religionist. Christianity, as Gibbon admits, could not be comprehended by pagan philosophers, nor did it seem to speak to the pagan devotees of superstition. Yet Christianity was to triumph over paganism.

III. Religious Naturalism and Religious Conversion

*Religious change is effected not by arguments but by a predisposition to
receive them.*

E. H. Lecky

What is one to make of the triumph of Christianity over pagan Rome? For Gibbon
it is a large and haunting event, and it indelibly marks the course of his entire
history. Because the *Decline and Fall* is very much about the conversion of the
Roman world to Christianity, the experience of religious conversion becomes a
phenomenon that has to be somehow accounted for by Gibbon, the philosophic
historian. For religious naturalists like Hume and Gibbon, religious conversion is
a most remarkable phenomenon. Divine intervention as an explanation is out of
court for them, and, since religion is primarily an affair of the passions, the work
of rationality in conversion can be of little efficacy. Hume, as has been discussed,
stressed the enormous attraction of the invisible world with its altogether new
"scenes, and beings and objects" over the more confining, somewhat more
predictable visible world. The strength of religion lies in its capacity to draw upon
all the resources of the human imagination in the creation of invisible world models
of explanation for the events that shape human existence. For Hume it was
Puritanism that impressed him with its power to convert believers. For Gibbon it
was the conversion of pagan Rome to Christianity.

Christianity, as Gibbon presented it in chapter fifteen, possessed a novel,
compelling invisible world model. Paganism was ancient, worn, if you will. Its
novelty had ebbed and its imaginative appeal was diminished. "When Christianity
appeared in the world, even these faint and imperfect impressions had lost much
of their original power." (*DF-15*, II, 59) Skepticism regarding the ancient and
venerable deities, Gibbon continues, had seeped into the Roman consciousness and
had eroded somewhat the power of the pagan gods over the imagination. However,
skepticism for all but a few philosophers is an intolerable state. Gibbon, like
Hume, believed that human beings by inclination are credulous. Gibbon goes on
to argue that a discredited superstition merely clears the way for another one. New
gods arise to replace the fallen ones. "But the practice of superstition is so
congenial to the multitude that, if they are forcibly awakened, they still regret the
loss of their pleasing vision. Their love of the marvellous and supernatural, their
curiosity with regard to future events, and their strong propensity to extend their
hopes and fears *beyond the limits of the visible world*, were the principal causes
which favoured the establishment of Polytheism." (*DF-15*, II, 59, italics added)
The establishment of the pagan gods was through the love of wonder; their

displacement by the Christian God was accomplished because the new God had a stronger appeal to the imagination.

The phenomenon of religious conversion, conditioned as it is by the activity of the imagination, is nevertheless an event in which one set of beliefs supersedes another, or, if you will, overturns another set of beliefs. Since this superseding or overturning process does not in Hume and Gibbon's view appear to be rational, just what is one to make of religious belief? All belief relative to experience, Hume argues, is based on custom, not reason. "All inferences from experience, therefore, are effects of custom, not of reasoning." (*EHU*, 43) Beliefs that arise out of practical interaction with the world are based on custom or habit which is itself a product of the experience of uniformities of nature. "It is that principle alone, [custom] which renders our experience useful to us, and makes us expect, for the future, a similar train of events with those which have appeared in the past." (*EHU*, 44)

When it comes to providing bases for religious belief, the work that custom does becomes especially problematic because the supernatural objects of religious belief are not directly experienced. And yet religious beliefs, as Hume was well aware, are among the most strongly and passionately held of any kind of beliefs. How does this come about? Consider the following: "[s]o close and intimate is the correspondence of human souls, that no sooner any person approaches me, than he diffuses on me all his opinions, and draws along my judgment in a greater or lesser degree. And tho', on many occasions, my sympathy with him goes not so far as entirely to change my sentiments, and way of thinking; yet it seldom is so weak as not to disturb the easy course of my thought, and give an authority to that opinion, which is recommended to me by his assent and approbation." (*Treatise*, 592)

Sympathy, our capacity to feel in real, albeit fainter form, the emotions of others is such that mere exposure to someone giving strong "assent and approbation" to an opinion works upon the mind a disposition to believe that opinion. Assent and approbation are, as well, felt and expressed in degrees of strength and forcefulness. Indeed, vehement expressions of approbation and assent will have strong effects on the disposition to believe. Ironically, nowhere do we find stronger, more impassioned believers than religious believers. Yet, the multiplicity of religions suggests that the truth of these beliefs is far from being established with the sort of fixity that other kinds of belief have. Paradoxically, it would seem that the greater the passion invested in an idea, the less certain its truth. Sympathy with its capacity for emotive communicability is what accounts for the process of religious conversion. Strong, emphatic, expressions of belief are extremely important for a new religion in order for it to gain authority.

Hume describes the Puritan religious conversion experience in the *History of England*. There, Hume captures the contagion of the religious fever of the Puritans. The power of the Puritan religion to convert followers and gain believers, as Hume describes it, lay in its emotive capacities. "It had frequently been the practice of puritanical clergymen to form together certain assemblies, which they called *prophesyings*; where alternatively, as moved by the spirit, they displayed their pious zeal in prayers and exhortations, and raised their own enthusiasm, as well as that of their audience, to the highest pitch, from that social contagion, which has so mighty an influence on holy fervors, and from the mutual emulation, which arose in those trials of religious eloquence." (*HGB*, 76, original italics) Hume's entire description here turns on emotive processes whereby individuals assume the intensity of the religious feeling ("pious zeal") of their fellows by participating in ceremonies engineered to arouse the most intense and communicable emotions. The religious beliefs of the Puritans were intense and their conveyance was made not by argumentation but by an emotionally emulative process which created the "social contagion" to which Hume refers.

Gibbon also viewed religious conversion as a form of social contagion. Beliefs, such as the immortality of the soul, beliefs which are speculative and non-demonstrable, beliefs which are at least for individuals in some cultures matters of indifference, become for others something to die for. Gibbon's haunting question is, how did Christianity come to triumph over paganism?

The rigid, austere conduct of the early Christians (one of Gibbon's five secondary causes for the triumph of Christianity) was shaped largely by a kind of superstitious terror and by expectations of the destruction of the world and a final judgment. Both the fearful, superstitious message and the severe character of the devout, energized Christians who were delivering that message made the pagan religions weaken under the assault. "The careless Polytheist, assailed by new and unexpected terrors, against which neither his priests nor his philosophers could afford him any certain protection, was very frequently terrified and subdued by the menace of eternal tortures. His fears might assist the progress of his faith and reason; and, if he could once persuade himself to suspect that the Christian religion might possibly be true, it became an easy task to convince him that it was the safest and most prudent party that he could possibly embrace." (*DF-15*, II, 29)

Religious conversion for Gibbon, as for Hume, is essentially an emotive process involving sympathy. Beliefs are shared in a very basic and primal sense through emotion, particularly through strong emotions like fear and hope. What Gibbon calls the "progress of the Christian religion" in chapter fifteen was achieved by Christianity's capacity to affect converts with its religious passion. "The superstitious observances of public or private rites were carelessly practised, from education and habit, by the followers of the established religion. But, as often as they occurred, they afforded the Christians an opportunity of declaring and confirming their *zealous opposition.* By these frequent protestations, their attachment to the faith was continually fortified, and, in proportion to the *increase of zeal,* they combated with the more ardour and success in the holy war which they had undertaken against the empire of the dæmons." (*DF-15*, II, 20, italics added) Powerful emotion, a "zealous opposition," was what drew the early Christians into a tight community and energized their confrontation with non-Christians with the ultimate victory going to Christianity. Moreover, as Gibbon seems to suggest, the pagans, with their "carelessly practiced" rites were themselves deficient in religious ardor and hence susceptible to the entreaties of the impassioned Christians. With the dread-inspiring conviction that the world would soon end and be succeeded by a new one in which deep conviction and belief would be rewarded, the Christians catered skilfully to the emotion of wonder and fear in their the pagan rivals. The dynamic of conversion depicted here does indeed rely heavily on the motivations of hope and fear. The salient feature of the Christian proselytizer was not the force of his arguments but the strength of powerful emotions. "The Christian, who founded his belief much less on the fallacious arguments of reason than on the authority of tradition and the interpretation of scripture, expected it with terror and confidence, as a certain and approaching event . . . ." (*DF-15*, II, 28) Christianity predicted "new," "unexpected" terrors for the unbeliever. And terror was a powerful instrument for conversion. Hope was also at work. "The ancient and popular doctrine of the Millennium was intimately connected with the second coming of Christ . . . . So pleasing was this hope to the mind of believers that the *New Jerusalem,* the seat of this blissful kingdom, was quickly adorned with all the gayest colours of the imagination . . . . Though it might not be universally received, it appears to have been the reigning sentiment of the orthodox believers; and *it seems so well adapted to the desires and apprehensions of mankind* that it must have contributed, in a very considerable degree, to the progress of the Christian faith." (*DF-15*, II, 25-26, italics added) The doctrine, Gibbon notes, prevailed because it touched powerfully upon the hopes and fears of people. The Christian agents of conversion evinced strong convictions in the reality of the prospects for eternal rewards and punishments, convictions, Gibbon seems to suggest, that were effectively communicated, and ultimately efficacious in the conversion process.

The ancient, pagan world, prior to the emergence of Christianity, was a superstitious one, and this pagan superstition was, as Gibbon notes with a certain Humean locution, a religion of "custom" not of "opinion." Pagan superstition or idolatry did not present systematic, philosophically defensible sets of beliefs or dogmas. Pagan religions, as Hume had described them, "could never be ascertained by fixt dogmas and principles." The religionists of these non-philosophical, non-dogmatic, traditional forms of superstitious worship initially greeted the appearance of Christianity with puzzlement. Gibbon describes an incommensurability of belief between pagans and Christians. "The whole body of Christians unanimously refused to hold any communion with the gods of Rome, of the empire, and of mankind. It was in vain that the oppressed believer asserted the inalienable rights of conscience and private judgment." (*DF-16*, II, 80) The inevitable confrontation assumed dramatic proportions as the pagans came to understand that the success of the Christian enthusiasts meant the destruction of their traditions. "The zeal and rapid progress of the Christians awakened the Polytheists from their supine indifference in the cause of those deities whom custom and education had taught them to revere." (*DF-16*, II, 126) The resentful reaction of the pagans to the success of Christianity was akin to that described by Hume (above, of the dynamics of the Reformation) of the Catholics when provoked by the Protestants. "The habits of justifying the popular mythology against the invectives of an implacable enemy produced in their minds some sentiments of faith and reverence for a system which they had been accustomed to consider with the most careless levity." (*DF-16*, II, 126) The pagan posture of "careless levity" toward the traditional religions was much like that of the medieval Catholics' attachment to their superstition, which, as Hume describes it, "was not extreme," consisting principally of "exterior practices and observances." In its confrontation with Christianity the careless levity of the pagans gave way to a more serious endeavor to combat the new religionists with the tools of philosophy. "Philosophy, her most dangerous enemy, was now converted into her most useful ally. The groves of the academy, the gardens of Epicurus, and even the portico of the Stoics, were almost deserted, as so many different schools of scepticism or impiety; and many among the Romans were desirous that the writings of Cicero should be condemned and suppressed by the authority of the senate." (*DF-16*, II, 127)

Here is the tergiversation of philosophy. The skeptical, non-dogmatic philosophers embraced lives of moderation, eschewed emotive excess, and were little troubled by the subject of their future in the afterlife. This kind of philosophy, as Gibbon notes, was "most dangerous" to religion. The new alliance reversed this adversarial relationship. "The prevailing sect of the new Platonicians judged it prudent to connect themselves with the priests, whom perhaps they despised, against the Christians, whom they had reason to fear." (*DF-16*, II, 127) Gibbon, in a speculative mode, cynically attributes purely self-seeking motives to the Platonist philosophers. "These fashionable philosophers prosecuted the design of extracting allegorical wisdom from the fictions of the Greek poets; instituted mysterious rites of devotion for the use of their chosen disciples; recommended the worship of the ancient gods as the emblems or ministers of the Supreme Deity; and composed against the faith of the Gospel many elaborate treatises, which have since been committed to the flames by the prudence of orthodox emperors." (*DF-16*, II, 127)

Hume, recall, in his description of the Catholic-Protestant confrontation observed that the Catholic Church took up philosophy as an intellectual weapon to supplement its political battles against the Reformers. "At the same time she employed the stake and gibbet against her avowed enemies, she extended her jealousy even towards learning and philosophy, whom in her supine security, she had formerly overlooked, as harmless and inoffensive." What Hume describes here—an embrace of learning and philosophy by Catholicism, reversing its former indifference—is mirrored by Gibbon in his description of paganism's reactionary embrace of Platonic philosophy as a polemical weapon. In both cases philosophy disintegrated as an independent critical endeavor. The outcome of the Christian-pagan confrontation was that the Christians and pagans "mutually concurred in restoring and establishing the reign of superstition." (*DF-16*, II, 126-27)

Pagan superstition lacked a systematic ideational structure and hence was not philosophically defensible. Gibbon characterized the "temper" of polytheism as "loose and careless," while of its substance, Hume says, that it "seemed to vanish like a cloud, whenever one approached to it, and examined it piecemeal." (*NHR*, 75) Since the attachment to the ancient superstitions was based on tradition rather than on an arguable rationale, the vulnerability of this attachment became obvious with the appearance of rival religionists, armed not only with polemical weapons but with a superior confidence in their faith born of a fanatical intensity of emotion. Moreover, paganism was less suited than Christianity to endure persecution since the efficacy of idolatrous pagan worship was tied closely to its visible symbols and its rituals. These symbols and rituals, as Gibbon notes, while useful in translating the abstractions of religious belief into a more concrete object of worship, are also vulnerable. "The popular modes of religion that propose any visible and material objects of worship have the advantage of adapting and familiarizing themselves to the senses of mankind; but this advantage is counterbalanced by the various and inevitable accidents to which the faith of the idolater is exposed. It is scarcely possible that, in every disposition of mind, he should preserve his implicit reverence for the idols or the relics which the naked eye and the profane hand are unable to distinguish from the most common productions of art or nature; and, if, in the hour of danger, their secret and miraculous virtue does not operate for their own preservation, he scorns the vain apologies of his priest, and justly derides the object, and the folly, of his superstitious attachment." (*DF-28*, III, 213)

The power and sacredness possessed by these "visible and material objects of worship," as Gibbon well recognized, rest upon the strength of convention, a common agreement that these objects do indeed possess these sacred, supernatural qualities. Certainly, they may in a variety of circumstances and perspectives be vulgar and profane ("the most common productions of art"). But it is the convention, in this instance the tradition of belief that invests these objects with power. "The hour of danger" is that time when that convention is challenged in a forceful way. The attack on the pagan god, Serapis, is Gibbon's dramatic example. "The colossal statue of Serapis was involved in the ruin of his temple and religion . . . . It was confidently affirmed that, if any impious hand should dare to violate the majesty of the god, the heavens and the earth would instantly return to their original chaos." (*DF-28*, III, 212-13) Note that Gibbon alludes to the "confidence" held in the power of this god and his capacity to destroy the world in retaliation for impiety. Yet, "[a]n intrepid soldier, animated by zeal and armed with a weighty battle-axe ascended the ladder; and even the Christian multitude expected, with some anxiety, the event of combat. He aimed a vigorous stroke against the cheek of Serapis; the cheek fell to the ground; the thunder was still silent, and both the heaven and earth continued to preserve their accustomed order and tranquillity." (*DF-28*, III, 213)

This assault was a hard test even for the Christians. But the vulnerability of idols as this account shows, is painfully obvious. Support for the belief in the power of the god collapses when the impotence of the symbol is demonstrated. Serapis's "mangled carcase was burnt in the Amphitheatre, amidst the shouts of the populace; and many persons attributed their conversion to this discovery of the impotence of their tutelar deity." (*DF-28*, III, 213) This episode captures the primacy of superstitious fear. Serapis's respect was commanded by his perceived power to destroy the earth in retaliation for impiety. But the challenge revealed his actual impotence. His followers transferred their allegiance to the Christian god of the courageous soldier. In a footnote Gibbon comments that the history of the Reformation follows a similar iconoclastic course where enthusiasts, in this case the Protestant Reformers, attack impotent idols. "The history of the Reformation affords frequent examples of the sudden change from superstition to contempt." (*DF-28*, III, 213, n.58)

The importance of Gibbon's frequently-used categories of superstition and enthusiasm with all their naturalistic assumptions becomes obvious in his account of the conflict between Christianity and paganism. Christianity's triumph over paganism is what a philosophic historian would predict given the understanding of how the mentality and behavior of superstitionists and enthusiasts typically work. Religious behavior is a part of human behavior, which has a discernable regularity or pattern. Hume, in the first *Enquiry*, says that the "same motives always produce the same actions: The same events follow from the same causes." (*EHU*, 83) Human motivation and human action, complex as they are, have a causal relationship which, in Humean parlance, is observed regularity. Without that assumption, Hume argues, no practical knowledge of human affairs could even be possible. "But were there no uniformity in human actions, and were every experiment which we could form of this kind irregular and anomalous, it were impossible to collect any general observations concerning mankind; and no experience, however accurately digested by reflection, would ever serve to any purpose." (*EHU*, 85)

Religious behavior, like human behavior in general, has observable patterns and regularities that move across the spectrum of history and culture. These regularities form a basis for making generalizations about motivation and behavior. Determining why someone at a given point in history takes up a particular religious view, involves some attempt at discerning his or her motivation for the affirmation of their beliefs and the action which follows from them. The phenomenon of religion makes this complicated because those things with which religionists are typically occupied—the gods and their expectations for human beings, the proper ways to worship them, etc.—cannot be experienced or dealt with in the same way that the various material contingencies are. Why an extremely hungry person drops everything else in the search for food, or why an angry person may retaliate against someone who has injured him at least *seems* apparent and obvious given an elementary understanding of how human beings are physically constituted. The phenomenon of a hungry person trying to obtain food is not questionable in the same way as that of someone worshiping god through, say, the ritual of holy communion. Why someone worships one god rather than another, or acts as if he were a favorite of god rather than despised by him is a puzzling matter. Tradition at one level accounts for it. Beliefs, including religious beliefs, are just part of the culture and are taken up, by most with little reflection. But Gibbon, as well as Hume, is more interested in how religious beliefs change, how culture itself changes. How, indeed, do the ancient, socially conserving, traditional pagan religions of ancient Rome give way to a religion whose adherents, at least initially, seem to be completely preoccupied with an invisible reality? Explanation of religious belief and behavior certainly cannot be exact or precise. Again, we have Hume's affirmation that "the empire of all religious faith over the understanding is wavering and uncertain . . . ." There is always thus a large element of unpredictability in religion, but what Gibbon attempts to do, following Hume, is to deal at a general level with the emotional disposition and outlook of religionists and determine how the disposition comes to play in a larger configuration of human activities, interests, and motives. In chapter twenty-eight of the *Decline and Fall*, on the final destruction of paganism by Christianity in the late fourth century, Gibbon provides an explanation for this phenomenon which takes into account a variety of basic motives (e.g., fear, love, desire for power, etc.) that are typical and universal in human social interaction. Of the conversion of the Roman senate under Theodosius in 394, Gibbon makes an observation. "The hasty conversion of the senate must be attributed either to *supernatural* or to *sordid* motives." (*DF-28*, III, 204, italics added) The couplet of "supernatural" and "sordid" motive is, of course, completely facetious. Supernatural motives may indeed be at work, but the sordid variety will be sufficient to account for the event. Gibbon then adds: "they were gradually fixed in the new religion, as the cause of the ancient religion became more hopeless; they yielded to the authority of the emperor, to the fashion of the times, and to the entreaties of their wives and children, who were instigated and governed by the clergy of Rome and the monks of the East." (*DF-28*, III, 204-205) Here is a list of the usual kind of motives at work in human interaction; fear, affection, desire for social approbation. Supernatural causes may have been in effect, but we have all these natural motives that seem to explain the conversion.

IV. The Death of Paganism and the Five 'Secondary' Causes

Passions make for the keenest of observations but for miserably defective conclusions.

Jean Paul

The religious history of the early empire is the story of moribund pagan superstition in rivalry with enthusiastic Christianity. The dynamics of the encounter of fear-dominated, *superstitious* paganism and its limited, highly anthropomorphic version of the gods with *enthusiastic*, otherworldly primitive Christianity is a big piece of Gibbon's story of the final destruction of paganism. Gibbon, as one writer argues, "forced the hands of the apologists of the type of Warburton and Paley. He pulverized their evidential arguments, and, covertly denying the supernatural origin of Christianity, opened the road to proving that progress, or whatever else we chose to call it, is explicable by human agencies and human agencies alone."[45] These dynamics are at work in the infamous five "secondary" causes Gibbon gives for the "rapid growth of the Christian church" in chapter fifteen. The five causes are:

1. "The inflexible, and, if we may use the expression, the intolerant zeal of the Christians, derived, it is true, from the Jewish religion, but purified from the narrow and unsocial spirit which, instead of inviting, had deterred the Gentiles from embracing the law of Moses." (the intolerant zeal cause)
2. "The doctrine of a future life . . . ." (the future life cause)
3. "The miraculous powers ascribed to the primitive church." (the miracles cause)
4. "The pure and austere morals of the Christians." (the exemplary morals cause)
5. "The union and discipline of the Christian republic, which gradually formed an independent and increasing state in the heart of the Roman empire." (the political discipline cause) (*DF-15*, II, 3)

These five causes, as will become apparent, are interdependent and ultimately rooted in enthusiasm. Christianity inherited the fanaticism of Jewish monotheism. Gibbon makes a great deal of this and expends approximately seventeen pages documenting the historical process by which the enthusiasm of Judaism is transmitted to Christianity. "An exclusive zeal for the truth of religion and the unity of God was as carefully inculcated in the new as in the ancient system; and

---

[45]Edward Clodd, *Gibbon and Christianity* (London: Watts and Co., 1916), 62.

whatever was now revealed to mankind, concerning the nature of God concerning the nature and designs of the Supreme Being, was fitted to increase their reverence for that mysterious doctrine. The divine authority of Moses and the prophets was admitted, and even established, as the firmest basis of Christianity." (*DF-15*, II, 7)

Gibbon here argues for both the emotive and the doctrinal continuity of Judaism and Christianity.[46] Christianity absorbs the monotheism and enthusiasm (the "exclusive zeal") of Judaism and its otherworldly preoccupations and exclusivist tendencies. The emergence of Christianity from Judaism as a new and distinct religion is, as Gibbon portrays it, a kind of sectarian free-for-all involving enthusiasts of various persuasions; Jews, Gnostics, orthodox, and the like, quarreling and persecuting each other, yet united in their hatred of the traditional idolatrous religions. "But, whatever differences of opinion might subsist between the Orthodox, the Ebionites, and the Gnostics, concerning the divinity or the obligation of the Mosaic law, they were all equally animated by the same exclusive zeal and by the same abhorrence for idolatry which had distinguished the Jews from the other nations of the world." (*DF-15*, II, 16) From this seventeen-page narrative with its complex account of Christian orthodoxy being accomplished the reader does not observe this historical spectacle as a divine plan, but rather as a theater of the absurd in which fanaticism and ambition recklessly and wildly play themselves out.

The "abhorrence for idolatry" for the Christian, practically, involved him in relentless confrontation with the idolaters. And, because idolatrous religion pervaded social life, conflict was everywhere. "The Christian, who with pious horror avoided the abomination of the circus or the theatre, found himself encompassed with infernal snares in every convivial entertainment, as often as his friends, invoking the hospitable deities, poured out libations to each other's happiness . . . . Every art and every trade that was in the least concerned in the framing or adorning of idols was polluted by the stain of idolatry; a severe sentence, since it devoted to eternal misery the far greater part of the community, which is employed in the exercise of liberal or mechanic professions." (*DF-15*, II, 18)

The connections between the intolerant zeal cause and the future life cause, the miracles cause, and the exemplary morals cause become apparent. Christians, inheriting from the Jews their monotheistic enthusiasm (intolerant zeal) and the concomitant fear of spiritual contamination through association with idolaters, needed a personal discipline to sustain themselves in their efforts to achieve their separation from the society they were repudiating. Such a discipline would have to be particularly rigorous given their minority status and the social dimensions of

---

[46]Frend, *Martyrdom and Persecution in the Early Church*, 20-22, 34-35, 56.

their repudiation—hence the exemplary morals cause. "Any particular society that has departed from the great body of the nation or the religion to which it belonged immediately becomes the object of universal as well as invidious observation. In proportion to the smallness of its numbers, the character of the society may be affected by the virtue and vices of the persons who compose it; and every member is engaged to watch with the most vigilant attention over his own behaviour and over that of his brethren, since, as he must expect to incur a part of the common disgrace, he may hope to enjoy a share of the common reputation." (*DF-15*, II, 35) Gibbon's religious naturalism is particularly evident here. He begins this observation with the broadest generalizing intent—"Any particular society"—and proceeds to an explanation which turns on the assumptions he makes about how the motivation of human beings gets translated into social dynamics. There is nothing unique here about Christianity.

In their quest to attain moral exemplary status, the early Christians were also motivated by the promise of "repentance for their past sins." (*DF-15*, II, 34) Repentance becomes an extremely important business especially when the repenter believes himself to be headed toward an immortal future. "As they emerged from sin and superstition to the glorious hope of immortality, they resolved to devote themselves to a life, not only of virtue, but of penitence." (*DF-15*, II, 35) We can see a connection between the exemplary morals cause and the future life cause. The importance of the future life overrides the present one. Belief in the possibility of a glorious immortality provides the support for the formidable discipline and iron determination needed to pursue the self-denying, austere, morally pure life characteristic of Gibbon's enthusiastic early Christian. "The ancient Christians were animated by a contempt for their present existence, and by a just confidence of immortality, of which the doubtful and imperfect faith of modern ages cannot give us any adequate notion." (*DF-15*, II, 24) Here we have the combination of a "contempt for their present existence" with a "just confidence" in immortality. This just confidence is the work of enthusiasm.

One of the important characteristics of enthusiasm, as has been noted above, is its anti-hierarchal tendencies. As Hume notes, "the inspired person comes to regard himself as a distinguished favourite of the Divinity." (*Essays*, 74) Gibbon's discussion of the miracles cause as one of the five secondary causes of the "rapid growth of the Christian church" begins with the observation that divine inspiration was for all believers direct and unmediated. Each believer, in the words of Hume, could regard himself as a distinguished favourite of the Divinity. Gibbon notes this of the early believers. "The divine inspiration, whether it was conveyed in the form of a waking or of a sleeping vision, is described as a favour very liberally bestowed on all ranks of the faithful, on women as on elders, on boys as well as upon bishops." (*DF-15*, II, 30) With regard to miracles, this means that each and every believer is a potential source of demonstration for and affirmation of the miraculous power of the church. "When their devout minds were sufficiently prepared by a course of prayer, of fasting, and of vigils, to receive the extraordinary impulse, they were transported out of their senses, and delivered in extasy what was inspired, being mere organs of the Holy Spirit, just as a pipe or flute is of him who blows into it." (*DF-50*, II, 30) Gibbon clearly works here with a Lockean-Humean interpretation of enthusiasm as a kind of dementia. The enthusiastic confidence of faith and the intense belief nurtured by appropriate rituals created the disposition to view the world all around as a miraculous place subject to a divine intervention that could be called down. "The primitive Christians perpetually trod on mystic ground, and their minds were exercised by the habits of believing the most extraordinary events." (*DF-15*, II, 33) The enormous power and strength of Christian belief enabled the believers to reconstruct the world and all its happenings as a manifestation of God's will. "Credulity performed the office of faith; fanaticism was permitted to assume the language of inspiration, and the effects of accident or contrivance were ascribed to supernatural causes." (*DF-15*, II, 33) Credulity and fanaticism are what Gibbon sees here as the dominate features of the Christian mentality. Fanaticism *assumes* the language of inspiration. Miracles are a product of delusion.

With the fifth cause, the political discipline cause, Gibbon argues that the development of the church as a powerful political institution came about as a rechanneling of initial otherworldly-directed enthusiastic energy. One of Hume's observations of enthusiasm, it may be recalled, is that it is on a long-term basis unsustainable. Enthusiastic religions are "on their first rise, more furious and violent than those which partake of superstition; but in a little time become more gentle and moderate." This observation is at the heart of Gibbon's account of the political discipline cause. "But the human character, however it may be exalted or depressed by a temporary enthusiasm, will return, by degrees to its proper and natural level, and will resume those passions that seem most adopted to its present condition." (*DF-15*, II, 41) The enthusiasm of the early Christians, with its initial and wholly otherworldly focus, gives way imperceptibly, "by degrees," to what Gibbon says is a "proper and natural level." The implication of these terms is that the emotive state of the early Christians is *improper* and *unnatural*, but that the passage of time takes care of it. The forces and pressures of the visible world exert themselves over the hopes and aspirations for the invisible one. While the initial enthusiastic passions for the next world become naturally moderated over time, the ever present and irrepressible agency of human ambition rechannels itself toward the mastery of the present one. "The primitive Christians were dead to the business and pleasures of the world; but their *love of action*, which could never be entirely extinguished, soon revived, and found a new occupation in the government of the church." (*DF-15*, II, 41-42, italics added) The object of enthusiasm has shifted from the preparation of the soul for its fate in the next world to creation of the church as a political institution.   "The safety of that society, its honour, its aggrandisement, were productive, even in the most pious minds, of a spirit of patriotism, such as the first of the Romans had felt for the republic, and sometimes, of a similar indifference in the use of whatever means might probably conduce to so desirable an end." (*DF-15*, II, 42) Gibbon effects a remarkable equation of motivation here which takes him even further along in a naturalistic interpretation of the development of Christianity. The early Christians and the early republican Romans are comparable as agents driven by pride and ambition and in their susceptibility to corruption. Lurking in this statement is the general pessimism of Gibbon: institutions are, from the perspective of the philosophical historian, inevitably corrupt. The early Christians differed from the Republican Romans in that the Christians possessed transcendental spiritual aspirations, but, alas, these also do not hold up. The institutionalization of the church makes spirituality the handmaiden of politics. "The ecclesiastical governors of the Christians were taught to unite the wisdom of the serpent with the innocence of the dove; but, as the former was refined, so the latter was insensibly corrupted, by the habits of government." (*DF-15*, II, 42) The striking imagery and the subtle pronouncement of the inevitability of the corruption of spirituality by politics conjures up a feeling of melancholy. Human beings, it must never be forgotten, are flawed.

Each of the secondary causes, as we have seen, is linked in an essential way to the enthusiastic character of early Christianity. Christianity prospered and eventually triumphed over a social order whose mode of religion was based on traditional superstition and idolatrous worship, and it was the combination of these five causes, Gibbon argues, that actually explains the success.   Christianity inherited a monotheistic view of the world from the Jews and a concomitant fanaticism that came from conceiving of God as a jealous being who punishes disbelief in other gods. Such a view makes idolatry into criminality. The belief in immortality and the preoccupation with one's future in the next life was derived from an "unnatural" contempt for the present world born of enthusiastic faith. The corrupt material world could compare only invidiously with the perfect future world. With the enthusiastic message of the gospel every Christian could claim direct divine inspiration. This unconstrained and unmediated enthusiasm, along with a view of the present world as a quickly fading existence, made it a theater for the miraculous: the imagination could freely run. The enthusiastic conviction behind that separatism provided the motivation for the creation and enforcement of a pure, austere and highly exemplary form of social morality.   The natural moderating process, observed by Hume, which enthusiasm as an extreme passion undergoes, was, as Gibbon observed, redirected into the institutionalization of the church.

CHAPTER TEN

ATTACKING CHRISTIANITY: BY WAY OF ISLAM

I must admit that I have not noticed among the Christians that lively faith in their religion which one finds in Mussulmen. With them there are great distances from profession to belief, from belief to conviction, and from conviction to practice. Their religion is less a subject of sanctification than a subject for dispute, which is open to everyone. Courtiers, soldiers, even women rise up against ecclesiastic, demanding that they prove to them what they have resolved not to believe.

Montesquieu

Gibbon contemplated the anti-Catholic Gordon Riots of 1780 with considerable disdain and some personal uneasiness. To his stepmother he wrote: "[a]s the old story of Religion has [caused] most *formidable* tumults in this town, and as they will of course seem much more formidable at the distance of an hundred [miles], you may not be sorry to hear that I am perfectly safe and well: my known attachment to the Protestant Religion has most probably saved me." (*Letters*-G, II, 242, original italics) The rioters, perhaps along with Hume's literary assistance, had conjured up in Gibbon's imagination the ghost of Oliver Cromwell. "[F]orty thousand Puritans such as they might be in the time of Cromwell have started out of their graves." (*Letters*-G, II, 243) Gibbon had a new, very practical reason to celebrate his recantation of Catholicism of many years past.

The tumult launched by Gordon's resurrected Puritan rioters,[1] pillaging and burning to the chant of "no popery," was a modern manifestation of a phenomenon that Gibbon had copiously explored and descanted upon in the *Decline and Fall*, namely religious enthusiasm. This dismal scene was, indeed in Gibbon's view, a recrudescence of the "old story of Religion," a manifestation of religion's ever present affinity for fanatical self-expression. While much of his historical attention was focused on the development of Christianity in its enthusiastic, as well as superstitious variants, Gibbon was intrigued with the enthusiasts of Islam and with the life of its founder. "The genius of the Arabian prophet, the manners of his nation, and the spirit of his religion involve the causes of the decline and fall of the Eastern empire; and our eyes are curiously intent on one of the most memorable revolutions which have impressed a new and lasting character on the nations of the

---

[1]For a short, fascinating account of the Gordon riots, see, Dobson Austin, "The Gordon Riots," in *Twentieth Century Essays and Address*, ed. William A. J. Archbold (1927; reprint, New York: Books for Libraries Press, 1970) 82-104.

globe." (*DF-50*, V, 332) The rise of a new, powerful religion—Islam—just like the rise of Christianity, was to have profound consequences for the history of the Roman empire. Moreover, Christianity and Islam would come to a confrontation of epic proportions. "The existence of Islam," writes medievalist R. W. Southern, "was the most far-reaching problem in medieval Christendom."[2] To write historically of the rise of this great world religion, with its enormous historical impact and its contest with Christianity, also set Gibbon up to indulge his animus toward the superstition of medieval Catholicism. He, indeed, seemed happy to make the history of Islam cast dark shadows over the Faith of Christianity. Gibbon presented Islam as more rational than Christianity, free of the latter's priestly hierarchy, and less susceptible to sectarian division and conflict. (*DF-50*, V, 361, 370).[3] With this prejudice, as Bernard Lewis points out, Gibbon was operating with many of the myths and distortions of Islam that were the legacy of centuries of Christian hostility to its chief rival. Gibbon was constricted in part by his ignorance of Semitic languages and a heavy reliance on defective sources in his ability to exercise his usual critical powers on the history of Islam. "Gibbon recognized the late and legendary character of much of the Arabic material made available to him in Latin translations and attempted some critical analysis of its content. However, his own imperfect knowledge and the defective state of European scholarship at the time hampered his work and sometimes blunted the skepticism which he usually brought to the sources and subjects of his historical inquiries." (Ibid., 71) In his account of the rise of Islam and his portrait of Muhammad we find Gibbon perhaps less capable than anywhere else in his work in carrying out his self-affirmed role as the skeptical, impartial philosophic historian. "The chapter on Muhammad and on the beginnings of Islam is still much affected by myths, and in this, more visibly than in the chapters on Rome and on Byzantium, Gibbon gives expression to his own prejudices and purposes and those of the circles in which he moved." (Ibid., 71)

Gibbon, as we have noted, understood the significance of religion as a complex phenomenon, and throughout the *Decline and Fall* attempts to show how

---

[2]R. W. Southern, *Western Views of Islam in the Middle Ages* (Cambridge, MA: Harvard University Press, 1962), 3.

[3]Bernard Lewis, "Gibbon on Muhammad," in *Edward Gibbon and the Decline and Fall of the Roman*, 70. "[A] point which Gibbon is at some pains to impress upon his readers is the stability and permanence of the Islamic faith in the form in which it was founded by the Prophet—that is to say, it is free from subsequent and local accretions such as have overlaid the message of Christ and retains its pristine content and character. In this, of course, he was greatly mistaken, as he could have ascertained by some attention to Islam as practiced in various parts of the Islamic world in his own day. Linked with this is his insistence that Islam is a faith with few dogmas and without priesthood or church and, therefore, by implication much freer and better than Christianity, which is heavily burdened by all these. This is slightly better than a half truth."

the religious beliefs and practices of the various European, African, and Asiatic peoples with whom he deals have a profound effect on their cultural histories.[4] However, the two religions of most significance in the *Decline and Fall* are Christianity and Islam. Both were major forces in the decline and fall of the Roman empire. Also, both came into massive mutual conflict. Christianity and Islam were fierce and direct competitors at least two levels; militarily-politically and religiously-philosophically. The earliest threat by Islam to Christianity was in fact military. "The first generations of Christians to face Muslim invasions see Muslims as a formidable political and military force, but know and care little about their religious beliefs. It is only in the following generations, as the Christian majority assimilate to Arabic culture and convert in large numbers to Islam, that Islam becomes a religious threat . . . ."[5] Christendom and Islam militarily contested a vast common territory over hundreds of years including the Middle East, North Africa, Spain, and finally southeastern and central Europe.[6] In the seventh and eighth centuries Muslims had captured much of the Christian world. Until the Turks were turned back by Poland's John Sobieski at the gates of Vienna in 1683 (only a half-century before Gibbon's birth), Islam had represented a persistent expansionist threat to Christian Europe.[7]

Islam represented a rival civilization not just a rival faith. Culturally—especially in philosophy, mathematics, and medicine—Islam had much for the Christians to envy: Muslim scholars had access to and took advantage of Greek, Persian, and Hindu learning hundreds of years before their Latin Christian counterparts in the West.[8] Islam was a phenomenal cultural success. Its pace of growth and far-reaching influence was spectacular. Muslims relentlessly persisted in their faith and stalwartly resisted Christendom's attempts at both conquest and conversion.[9] The philosophic rivalry was as intense and bitter as the military: both

---

[4]See Jemielity, "Gibbon among the Aeolists, 168-69, "The application to Christianity of the evaluative norms and principles of the *General Observations* and of chapter 2 is a familiar story. Less familiar, perhaps, is the consistency and degree to which Gibbon thinks comparably about religions other than Christianity and Judaism in the *Decline and Fall*. Any religion introduced into the history, first of all, appears always for the same reason: because its fortunes somehow influenced the fortunes of the Roman Empire. The religions that enter the history also permit Gibbon to provide a comparative study of the civil and ecclesiastical orders, which so often intersect in the course of his narrative."

[5]John Tolan, introduction to *Medieval Christian of Perceptions of Islam: A Book of Essays* (New York: Garland, 1996), xii.

[6]Shaul Bakhash, review of Islam and the West, by Bernard Lewis, *New York Review of Books* 40, no. 16 (October 7, 1993): 43.

[7]R. R. Palmer and Joel Colton, *A History of the Modern World* (New York: Alfred A. Knopf, 1965), 189-90.

[8]Tolan, introduction to *Medieval Christian of Perceptions of Islam*, xi.

[9]Southern, *Western Views of Islam*, 5.

Christians and Muslims claimed to possess exclusive universal truth. This conjunction of exclusivity and universality distinguished them from other great world religions whose practitioners did not view themselves as possessors of universal truths. "The Jews, Buddhists and Hindus did not aim at converting all of mankind to their faith."[10] Gibbon's interest in Islam, as Lewis has observed, began at a very early age.[11] In his *Memoirs* he somewhat boastfully recounted his curiosity and extensive reading in oriental studies as a teen. "Mahomet and his Saracens[12] soon fixed my attention: and some instinct of criticism directed me to the genuine sources. Simon Ockley, an original in every sense, first opened my eyes, and I was led from one book to another till I had ranged round the circle of Oriental history. Before I was sixteen I had exhausted all that could be learned in English of the Arabs and Persians, the Tartars and the Turks, and the same ardour urged me to guess at the French of d'Herbelot, and to construe the barbarous Latin of Pocock's *Abulpharagius*." (*Memoirs*, 72) These "genuine" sources Gibbon consulted for his history of the Prophet and Islam were, as Lewis notes, the work of Western observers and critics of Islam; many of them were heavily polemical and biased.[13] Ockley, whom Gibbon so happily credits with opening his historical eyes, Bury writes, relied heavily on the Al Wakidi, who was more mythologist than historian. (*DF*, I, xi)

The late eighteenth century was a time when important changes were taking place in Europe in the Christian view of Islam and its founder. Reaching back into the Middle Ages there had long been an interest in the West in Islam. There were two basic motives for this interest. The first was a desire to learn what the Arabs had to teach about Greek philosophy and science. The second was polemical. Islam, as noted above, was the great rival. Christians wanted to learn about Islam in order to confute it and to convert its faithful to Christianity.[14] With the Renaissance came a new motive that fueled interest in Islam, that of a disinterested intellectual curiosity, a desire to understand the workings and mentality of a

---

[10]Bakhash, review of Islam and the West, 43.

[11]Lewis, "Gibbon on Muhammad," 61.

[12]Gibbon's use of "Saracens" is consistent with an earlier European Christian practice that showed a preference for names that were ethnic rather than religious. As Bernard Lewis points out, "Saracen" is obscure in its origin but is certainly ethnic since it is pre-Christian and pre-Islamic. Lewis, "Gibbon on Muhammad," 61. Also, Tolan, introduction to *Medieval Christian Perceptions of Islam*, xi, notes that few Christian writers used the terms "Islam" or "Muslim." They preferred ethnic or linguistic designations such as "Saracen," "Hararene," "Arab," "Turk," etc.

[13]Lewis, "Gibbon on Muhammad," 62-66.

[14]Bernard Lewis, "The State of Middle Eastern Studies," *American Scholar* 48 (summer 1979):365.

foreign, even hostile culture. (Ibid., 366)[15] The Reformation, as well, stimulated an interest in the West in the study of Arabic both for the polemical resources it might lend in Christianity's own sectarian struggles and in the value that Arabic as a Semitic language provided in the study of the Old Testament. (Ibid., 367) These motives, old and new, polemical, scholarly, and sectarian were the mixture behind the Western curiosity in Islam. Added to these in the eighteenth century was a growing critical posture toward Christianity on the part of Western thinkers. Islam became a subject of a kind of reverse polemics which provided Western anti-Christian thinkers a path on which to attack Christianity indirectly. "[The] image of Muhammad as a wise, tolerant, un-mystical, and undogmatic ruler became widespread in the period of the Enlightenment, and it finds expression in writers as diverse as Goethe, Condorcet, and Voltaire—who, in some of his writings, condemns Muhammad as the terrible example of fanaticism, but in others praises him for his wisdom, rationality, moderation, and tolerance."[16] Also, by the time Gibbon was writing, Islam no longer represented a military threat to the West. In his "General Observations on the Fall of the Roman Empire in the West," Gibbon, quite pridefully, affirmed the safety of the civilization of his contemporary Europe from the future predations of barbarians. "The reign of independent Barbarism is now contracted to a narrow span; and the remnant of Calmucks or Uzbecks, whose forces may be almost numbered, cannot seriously excite the apprehensions of the great republic of Europe." (*DF-38*, IV, 177)[17] Islam was no longer a political or military threat to Gibbon's "great republic of Europe" and was now especially suitable as a subject for inquiry by the detached and impartial European philosophic historian. Gibbon here does emit a half-hearted warning. "Yet this apparent security should not tempt us to forget that new enemies, and unknown dangers, may *possibly* arise from some obscure people, scarcely visible in the map of the world. The Arabs or Saracens, who spread their conquests from India to Spain, had languished in poverty and contempt, till Mahomet breathed into those savage bodies the soul of enthusiasm." (*DF-38*, IV, 177, original italics) It was, ironically, enthusiastic religion that wrought the transformation of desert barbarians

---

[15]Lewis writes: "[t]he Renaissance initiated an entirely new phase in the development of Islamic and Middle Eastern studies in the Western world. Perhaps the most important new factor was a kind of intellectual curiosity that is still unique in human history. For until that time, no comparable desire had been felt and no effort made to study and understand alien, still less hostile, civilizations."

[16]Lewis, "Gibbon on Muhammad," 65.

[17]See Ernest Gellner, *Conditions of Liberty: Civil Society and Its Rivals* (New York: Penguin Books, 1994), 63-4. Gellner makes note of Gibbon's shortcoming of insight here. Gibbon's contemporary, Adam Ferguson, was wiser than Gibbon: Gibbon thinks that civilization is advanced enough or strong enough to repel barbarianism from without. Ferguson realizes that the roots of barbarism are in civilization. This perhaps is a failure of Gibbon to apply consistently enough his view of mankind as a "degenerate race of beings."

into rivals to Christianity. Southern notes that: "[d]espite this cautionary word we can sense that Mahomet and his savage enthusiasts have been safely relegated to the realm of legend with Tamburlaine and the great conquerors of antiquity. Intellectually and physically Europe felt safe."[18]

It was in this context that Gibbon labored on his life of Muhammad and the rise of Islam. The year of 1788 saw the publication of the last three volumes of the *Decline and Fall*. The completed work not only brought him praise, it was also the occasion for a new series of attacks on him. Gibbon's ignominy persisted. He was a libeler of Christianity. Previous criticism had been directed in great part at the fifteenth and sixteenth chapters. These later attacks maligned Gibbon's handling of certain topics in the second half of the book, which included the rise of Islam, the life and character of Muhammad, and the history of the Crusades.[19] The Rev. William Disney, a former Regius Professor of Hebrew from Cambridge University, preached a sermon at the University in 1789 attacking Gibbon for his countenance of Muhammad and Islam. He accused the historian of a gross partiality toward "Mohammedism" and complained that the portrayal of Islam was more akin to that of a "slave of the Grand Seignior," rather than of a subject of the "English King, a Defender of the Faith." (Ibid., 149)

Disney had cause for complaint. Gibbon's account of the birth and development of Islam, his biography of Muhammad, and his comparison of Islam with Christianity in no way dissimulated an admiration for Islam. Disney, like many of Gibbon's critics and detractors at that time, thought that his analysis was motivated by a desire to denigrate Christianity, to defame it, in this case, by holding up its main competitor for praise. "By the time Gibbon began to write, there was a vacancy for an Oriental myth. Islam was in many ways suitable. While China was ceasing to impress, Islam no longer terrified, and it had the further advantage of being the intimate enemy of the church. The mythopoeic process began with an attempt by historians to correct the negative stereotypes of the Middle Ages and to recognize the contributions of Islamic civilization to mankind."[20] Gibbon, as a philosophic historian desirous to be free of religious prejudice and cultural parochialism, was susceptible to reverse-stereotype myths that were gaining currency: Islam, in contrast to Christianity was a priest-free, undogmatic religion. (Ibid., 98) Gibbon's Islam and Gibbon's Muhammad would be additional components in his attack on Christianity. (Ibid., 70)[21]

---

[18]Southern, *Western Views of Islam*, 13.

[19]McCloy, *Gibbon's Antagonism to Christianity*, 144-145.

[20]Lewis, "Gibbon on Muhammad," 70.

[21]Lewis writes: "[t]he honor and reputation of Islam and its founder were protected in Europe neither by social pressure nor by legal sanction, and they thus served as an admirable vehicle for anti-

Islam presents a certain challenge for the historian of religion. Compared with most other world religions, including Christianity, its foundations and origins have, relatively speaking, a good historical documentation. Ernest Renan observed that the creation of Islam was the last and best known of mankind's major religions. So while the origins of other religions were immersed almost entirely in fable and myth, Islam possessed a documented history that opened it more widely to detailed historical scrutiny. (Ibid., 66) Muhammad was himself a historically documented figure with no claim to being a divine being. Wilfred Cantwell Smith writes that Islam is unique of the world religions in its being deliberately founded.[22] This rich historical character of Islam was of great importance for Gibbon. It meant that he could look at Islam more completely and directly as the creation of a human being, a religion which carries the unique stamp of the character and personality of its founder.[23] In fact, the life of the prophet that emerges in the *Decline and Fall* is entirely consistent with Gibbon's naturalistic approach to the history of Christianity. But Gibbon's account of Muhammad and Islam also reflects a partiality and admiration for a religion that he sees as less constrained by dogma and priests. Gibbon's account begins with a compact ethnological study of the pre-Islamic Arabs. He then moves to a biography of Muhammad and his religious experience and follows the transformation of Islam into a world religion that changed the Roman empire. And finally, he develops an account of the sectarian progression of Islam after Muhammad's death and its military and political triumphs. In two chapters of the *Decline and Fall* (chapters fifty and fifty-one) comprising approximately two hundred pages, we have a history of Islam, a special history, as it turns out, of an enthusiastic religion.

Gibbon's account of Muhammad and the emergence of Islam begins with his laying out an ethnological foundation for the study of the religion and the life of its founder. The history of Islam is to be grounded in both the physical and cultural conditions of Arabian life. The character of the Arab is sketched out in a somewhat idealized form—the picture of a rough and independent desert nomad carving out an existence with the most adroit use of scarce and primitive resources.

---

religious and anti-Christian polemic. Gibbon occasionally accomplished this purpose by attacking Islam while meaning Christianity, more frequently by praising Islam as an oblique criticism of Christian usage, belief, and practice. Much of his praise would not be acceptable in a Muslim country."

[22]W. Smith, *The Meaning and End of Religion*, 106.

[23]Carl Brocklemann, *History of the Islamic Peoples*, trans. Joel Carmichael and Moshe Perlmann (London: Routledge and Kegan Paul, 1948), 36, says that: "Muhammad's religion must not, of course be judged only by the Qur'an . . . . His intellectual world was his own only to the smallest degree; it stemmed mostly from Judaism and Christianity, and was skilfully adapted by him to the religious needs of his people. In doing this he raised them to a higher level of intuitive belief and moral sensitivity."

The camel, for example, played a central role in Arab life. "Alive or dead, almost every part of the camel is serviceable to man; her milk is plentiful and nutritious; the young and tender flesh has the taste of veal; a valuable salt is extracted from the urine; the dung supplies the deficiency of fuel; and the long hair, which falls each year and is renewed, is coarsely manufactured into the garments, the furniture and the tents, of the Bedoweens." (*DF-50*, V, 337)

This picture of Arab resourcefulness and economy is put up against the backdrop of the hostile physical world they inhabited. "But in the dreary waste of Arabia, a boundless level of sand is intersected by sharp and naked mountains, and the face of the desert, without shade or shelter, is scorched by the direct and intense rays of a tropical sun. Instead of refreshing breezes, the winds, particularly from the south-west, diffuse a noxious and even deadly vapour; the hillocks of sand which they alternately raise and scatter are compared to the billows of the ocean; and whole caravans, whole armies, have been lost and buried in the whirlwind." (*DF-50*, V, 333-34)

Both the rhythm and the imagery of the narrative is vivid and stark—"dreary waste," "sharp and naked mountains," "noxious and even deadly vapour"—conveying a sense of loneliness, fear, and vulnerability—entire armies "lost and buried in the whirlwind." Against the backdrop of this vast, unfriendly region Gibbon depicts a tough, courageous, self-sufficient people who had mastered the arts of survival. In this austere, formidable world Gibbon's Arab remains above all a free and independent character. "The slaves of domestic tyranny may vainly exult in their national independence; but the Arab is personally free; and he enjoys, in some degree, the benefits of society, without forfeiting the prerogatives of nature." (*DF-50*, V, 342) No dissimulation of admiration is attempted here. The people of these desert tribes lived lives untrammeled by the formal apparatus of political authority, but they were sufficiently foresighted and sociable so as to create the kinds of associations that served their needs. Gibbon draws an invidious comparison—holding up the "slaves" who live in independent nations against the "free Arabs"—in order to lay as much stress as possible on freedom as a prominent feature of the Arab's desert society. "Their spirit is free, their steps are unconfined, the desert is open, and the tribes and families are held together by a mutual and voluntary compact." (*DF-50*, V, 343) This emphasis on the free and independent spirit of the Arab also evokes comparisons with the early Roman republicans who were also tough, independent, and uncontaminated by excesses of luxury. The suggested comparison helps explain why Gibbon does indeed appear to have admired these early Bedouins. Yet, Gibbon is nevertheless careful to distinguish Roman from Arab freedom. "But their simple freedom was of a very different cast from the nice and artificial machinery of the Greek and

Roman republics, in which each member possessed an undivided share of the civil and political rights of the community." (*DF-50*, V, 343) The distinction is an important one. Roman freedom is an artifice, a convention ("nice and artificial"). Arab freedom, it would seem, is a more primitive, natural freedom rooted in the primal experience of desert life and a tribal society. "In the more simple state of the Arabs the nation is free, because each of her sons disdains a base submission to the will of a master. His breast is fortified with the austere virtues of courage, patience, and sobriety; the love of independence prompts him to exercise the habits of self-command; and the fear of dishonour guards him from the meaner apprehension of pain, of danger, and of death." (*DF-50*, V, 343) Gibbon seems intent on upholding this distinction and making the reader understand that he is in fact describing a primitive people, politically less sophisticated than the early Romans, whose freedom originated more in the natural conditions of climate and ethnology, than in the development of political institutions.

Gibbon's emphasis on freedom as a prominent feature of the Arab personality has, I believe, another reason. The freedom, which Gibbon takes great pains to show is an important moral characteristic of these desert people, is the basis for a striking comparison that he establishes between Islam and Christianity, a comparison much to the detriment of Christianity. While Islam, in its emergence as a fanatical monotheistic religion became characteristically intolerant, similar to Christianity, it, unlike Christianity, remained free of priestly hierarchy. "But the Mahometan[24] religion is destitute of priesthood or sacrifice; and the independent spirit of fanaticism looks down with contempt on the ministers and the slaves of superstition." (*DF-50*, V, 370) Here we see the connection between the basic freedom-loving character of the Arab and the Islamic disdain for priesthood. Priests, for Gibbon, as we have seen, are the agents of superstition, the enemies of freedom. The shaping of the religion of Islam with its own unique character, Gibbon would have us believe, was tethered to the primal Arab life of the desert and the independent, freedom-loving personality that came from that experience.

The religious world into which the founder of Islam was born was dominated by traditional pagan idolatry. Idolatry, as Hume observed, is characteristic of all primitive peoples. Gibbon applies this generalization to the pre-Islamic Arabs. "The religion of the Arabs, as well as of the Indians, consisted in the worship of the sun, the moon, and the fixed stars; a primitive and specious mode of

---

[24]With the use of this terminology Gibbon carries on the Christian tradition of falsely attributing to Muslims a worship of Muhammad analogous to the Christian worship of Christ. See Lewis, "Gibbon on Muhammad," 61. "Then, by false analogy, they [Christians] called them Muhammadans and their religion Muhammadanism, on the totally false assumption that Muslims worshiped Muhammad as Christians worshiped Christ."

superstition." (*DF-50*, V, 349)[25] Behind all superstition, pagan or otherwise, is fear, and in the life of the typical Arab there is much to dread. "The life of a wandering Arab," Gibbon remarks, "is a life of danger and distress . . . ." (*DF-50*, V, 337) The forms of worship, the deities that emerge as objects of worship, the practices and accouterments of early Arab religion were the natural outgrowth of a people who lived in a harsh, unpredictable world. Gibbon is openly contemptuous of the particularities of pre-Islamic Arab idolatry. "I am ignorant, and I am careless, of the blind mythology of the barbarians; of the local deities, of the stars, the air, and the earth, of their sex or titles, their attributes or subordination. Each tribe, each family, each independent warrior, created and changed the rites and the object of his fantastic worship; but the nation, in every age, has bowed to the religion as well as to the language, of Mecca." (*DF-50*, V, 349-350) The pre-Islamic superstition has a carelessness and looseness that parallels pre-Christian pagan superstition. Here Gibbon is able to strengthen the Humean contrast between the mythopoeic, tolerating character of polytheistic religions and the intolerant, persecuting nature of monotheistic faiths. Islam, like Christianity, commanded assent to its doctrines.

Islam and Christianity bear important resemblances in their origins and progress. Monotheistic Christianity with an enthusiastic fanaticism invaded the Roman world of traditional religions and ultimately destroyed them. Likewise, the history of Islam depicts the course of monotheistic zealotry—in its beginnings the possession of a small fanatical band of believers—and its ultimate triumph over the traditional idolatrous religions and its emergence as a major force in shaping world history. The theme is the same: enthusiasm confronts and defeats traditional superstition and polytheism. This is not to say that monotheistic ideas were unknown in the Arab world at the time of Muhammad's birth in the late sixth century. In fact, in Gibbon's description of the religious climate into which Muhammad was born we see a highly diverse range of religious systems and ideas. "Seven hundred years before the death of Mahomet, the Jews were settled in Arabia . . . . The Christian missionaries were still more active and successful: the Catholics asserted their universal reign; the sects whom they oppressed successively retired beyond the limits of the Roman empire; the Marcionites and the Manichæans dispersed their *phantastic* opinions and apocryphal gospels; the churches of Yemen, and the princes of Hira and Gassan, were instructed in a purer creed by the Jacobite and Nestorian bishops." (*DF-50*, V, 354, original italics) So, in addition to all of the traditional superstitions, the sixth-century Arab had

---

[25]See Bernard Lewis, *The Arabs In History* (New York: Oxford University Press, 1993), 20. In pre-Islam, "the religion of southern Arabia was polytheistic and bears a general, though not detailed, resemblance to those of the other ancient Semitic peoples."

Christianity with all its heretical and heterodoxical variants as well as Judaism from which to choose. "The liberty of choice was presented to the tribes: each Arab was free to elect or to compose his own private religion; and the rude superstition of his house was mingled with the sublime theology of saints and philosophers." (*DF-50*, V, 354) But in spite of the presence of monotheistic ideas and systems (that mingling of "sublime theology"), the typical Arab was mired in idolatry. "The most rational of the Arabs acknowledged his [i.e., God's] power, though they neglected his worship; and it was habit rather than conviction that still attached them to the relics of idolatry." (*DF-50*, V, 354)

Muhammad's amazing life and extraordinary career were irresistible topics for Gibbon who seems throughout the *Decline and Fall* to have been fascinated by charismatic religious and political leaders. Julian and Athanasius are two of Muhammad's predecessors in the *Decline and Fall* as major religious-political personalities. Both of these men are rich, forceful personalities who combined otherworldly religious idealism with this-worldly political ability. With Muhammad, Gibbon, the historian of religion, had at his disposal and for his examination the actual flesh and blood creator of a militant world religion, a man whose inspiration in less than one hundred years carried religious warriors across three continents. Gibbon's life of Muhammad explores the enigmatic personality of the prophet as it inspired and shaped the enthusiastic faith that he created and imposed on a larger and initially resistant superstitious world. Also, Gibbon's biography of Muhammad presents itself as a kind of counterpoint to his Christian biographers for whom the details of life of this "false prophet" were evidence of the Islam's falsehood and nefariousness. As Norman Daniel writes: "[t]he life of Muhammad was seen as an essential disproof of the Islamic claim to revelation. It was often treated as the most important disproof of all."[26] Muhammad for Christians *had* to be a villain: his flaws *had* to represent a sufficiently large scale of evil commensurate with the threat that Islam mounted against the goodness of Christianity.

Near the beginning of his biography of Muhammad Gibbon tells us that the Prophet, "[f]rom his earliest youth . . . was addicted to religious contemplation; each year, during the month of Ramadan, he withdrew from the world and from the arms of Cadijah; in the cave of Hera, three miles from Mecca, he consulted the spirit of *fraud* or *enthusiasm*, whose abode is not in the heavens, but in the mind of the prophet." (*DF-50*, V, 360, italics added) It is quite clear here that the ideas of Muhammad were his own unique creation, the product of his hermetic speculation. But with the disjunctive, "fraud or enthusiasm," Gibbon employs two

---

[26]Daniel Norman, *Islam and the West: The Making of an Image* (Edinburgh: Edinburgh University Press, 1960), 79.

general concepts of the philosophic historian which are frequently at work in the *Decline and Fall* in the discussion of religion. Enthusiasm, as we have seen, is a kind of dementia, an excess of religious emotion, the foundation of religious fanaticism. Fraud is an element frequently conjoined with enthusiasm (Recall Hume's Puritans full of "ardour and fraud"): fraud is what the philosophic historian searches for in politics and religion as he uncovers in human nature the typical motives of ambition. Once again, Gibbon is looking at religion as the historian, not the theologian, finds it; a work of a "weak and degenerate race of beings." Fraud and enthusiasm are instrumental for Gibbon in writing religious history—Christian or otherwise. This is certainly the case in interpreting Muhammad's role as the creator of a great religion, and his career as an apostle-warrior. Muhammad's founding role and his evangelizing success involve the astute, cunning work of the consummate *fraud*, and the delusional product of religious madness—*enthusiasm* at its outermost limits. Also, near the end of his biography of Muhammad, in his summational remarks on the Prophet's character, Gibbon points to these important elements of fraud and enthusiasm. "At the conclusion of the life of Mahomet, it may perhaps be expected that I should balance his faults and virtues, that I should decide whether the title of *enthusiast* or *impostor* more properly belongs to that extraordinary man." (*DF-50*, V, 400, italics added) Muhammad is in fact for Gibbon another world historical figure, like Constantine, who is emblematic of religion itself. Gibbon viewed the history of religion, along with Hume, as a strange product of an often interweaving of madness and ambition. Ambition works its far ranging effects in religion as it does in other realms of life, and, when corrupted by enthusiasm or superstition, is the powerful engine of fraud. The scrupulous biographer of one of the world's greatest religious leaders, one who rivals the great frauds of his own Christian heritage, must expect to confront fraud and ambition as they manifest themselves in his life and career. Also, the traditional Christian interpretation of the life of Muhammad of which Gibbon was aware and which he had to balance against his own attempt to be impartial, was that the Prophet was, pure and complete, a fraud. For Christian detractors: "[t]he three marks of Muhammad's life were thought to be the violence and force with which he imposed his religion; the salacity and laxness with which he bribed followers whom he did not compel; and finally his evident humanity, which it was constantly believed to be necessary to prove . . . . It was on these three points that the total fraud seemed to based; fraud was the sum of Muhammad's life."[27] Gibbon had to contend with the Christian-apologist view of Muhammad as a pure fake, a view, as a critic of Christianity, he would certainly resist. Thus, Gibbon begins his narrative of Muhammad's religious career agnostically by leaving it open as to

---

[27]Daniel, *Islam and the West*, 107.

whether "fraud" or "enthusiasm" was the force behind the Prophet's work, and he ends the account by posing the question as to which of the two categories, he could, as an historian, accurately apply. Gibbon declines to make the choice. "From enthusiasm to imposture the step is perilous and slippery; the dæmon of Socrates affords a memorable instance, how a wise man may deceive himself, how a good man may deceive others, how the conscience may slumber in a mixed and middle state between self-illusion and voluntary fraud." (*DF-50*, V, 400-01) Enthusiasm at its height, as Hume has noted, is unsustainable. It gives way to more regular, less violent emotions. Gibbon here, with the imagery of a kind of natural winding-down process, characterizes the progress of enthusiasm as a course of dissipation: enthusiasm—pure and intense—gives way, gradually, inevitably, to imposture, a more complex and perplexing dimension of human experience. Pure, otherworldly religious fervor becomes mixed with this-worldly ambition. Gibbon thus recreates the life of Muhammad so that it is neither an affair of pure fraud (the Christian version) with the dominance of ruthless and unprincipled ambition nor pure enthusiasm with its intense and self-illusionary state, but very probably a combination or mixture of both.

Gibbon's inclination to look at Muhammad, as he does with other major religious figures in the *Decline and Fall*, as a muli-faceted character in which competing, even contradictory forces are at work, is underwritten with a distinct philosophical vision of how the moral universe is constituted. This philosophical vision is part of the equipment of the philosophic historian who looks at human nature as a mixture of good and evil. Human beings, as revealed by historical observation, generally tend to be mixtures of good and evil. Saintliness and deviltry are the products of theologically oriented historians who seek to make human beings cosmological reflections of moral extremes. Hume, in his own attempt to write religious history, articulates the philosophical notion of human beings as a moral mix. "Good and ill are universally intermingled and confounded; happiness and misery, wisdom and folly, virtue and vice. Nothing is pure and entirely of a piece. All advantages are attended with disadvantages. A universal compensation prevails in all conditions of being and existence." (*NHR*, 92) Human beings confront a world that is an interwoven fabric of good and evil, advantage and disadvantage, virtue and vice. Such a world makes life itself complicated and decisions far from clear cut and easy. "And it is scarce possible for us, by our most chimerical wishes, to form the idea of a station or situation altogether desirable . . . . The more exquisite any good is, of which a small specimen is afforded us, the sharper is the evil, allied to it; and few exceptions are found to this uniform law of nature." (*NHR*, 92-93) The apparent goods that human beings pursue, the aspirations they conceive, may likely be tainted or compromised. "The most sprightly wit borders on madness; the highest effusions of joy produce the deepest melancholy; the most ravishing pleasures attended with the most cruel lassitude and disgust; the most flattering hopes make way for the severest disappointments."(*NHR*, 93) And so, for Gibbon, Muhammad is a rich historical personality whose character is a complex mixture of good and evil. He is not the evil genius of Christian apologists; neither is he the inspired Prophet of Islamic panegyrists.

One of the primary theological points of contention between Christianity and Islam is over the unity of God. "The creed of Mahomet is free from suspicion or ambiguity; and the Koran is a glorious testimony to the unity of God." (*DF-50*, V, 361) But this sublime doctrine of the unity of God, for all its theological sophistication and philosophical acuity, as Gibbon goes on to suggest, provides little help for the understanding of what God actually is, what his attributes might be. "A philosophic Atheist might subscribe the popular creed of the Mahometans: a creed too sublime perhaps for our present faculties. What object remains for the fancy, or even the understanding, when we have abstracted from the unknown substance all ideas of time and space, of motion and matter, of sensation and reflection?" (*DF-50*, V, 362) These remarks are reminiscent of Hume's description of the abstract doctrine of the Puritans, so devoid of sensibility and imagery that it could only defy rational comprehension and inspire awe and terror.[28] "Even the English church, though it had retained a share of popish ceremonies, may justly be thought too naked and unadorned, and still to approach too near the abstract and spiritual religion of the puritans." (*HE*, V, 186)

The unity-of-God doctrine therefore certainly does not, as Gibbon interprets it, contribute to the understanding of God, but it does have enormous importance for the conduct of his apostles. "The God of nature has written his existence on all his works and his law in the heart of man. To restore the knowledge of the one, and practice of the other, has been the *real* or *pretended* aim of the prophets of every age . . . ." (*DF-50*, V, 362, italics added) The doctrine of the unity of God does little, as Gibbon suggests, "to restore the knowledge of the one." What remains then is the restoration of the "practice" of the God's law through the authority of his apostles. Thus, what the unity of God means for Muhammad, God's final apostle, is that his authority (Muhammad's) is to be recognized as the voice of God's law. Muhammad brings both authority and a simplicity of belief. Muhammad's interpretation of the absolute unity of God positions him against Christianity whose trinitarianism makes the issue of God's unity quite problematic. "The mysteries of the Trinity and Incarnation *appear* to contradict the principle of

---

[28]"Thus, Catholic polemicists accused Calvin of Islamizing tendencies, and Calvinists in Geneva tried to bring the same charges against Servetus." Lewis, "Gibbon on Muhammad," 72, n.3.

the divine unity." (*DF-50*, V, 361, original italics) Here again is Gibbon pointing to the tendency of Christianity to degenerate into doctrinal anarchy. The invidious contrast with Christianity is apparent, and Gibbon is quick to point it out. "The Christians of the seventh century had insensibly relapsed into a semblance of paganism; their public and private vows were addressed to the relics and images that disgraced the temples of the East; the throne of the Almighty was darkened by a cloud of martyrs, and saints, and angels, the objects of popular veneration; and the Collyridian heretics, who flourished in the fruitful soil of Arabia, invested the Virgin Mary with the name and honours of a goddess." (*DF-50*, V, 361) Islam's insistence on the unity of God is a great advance over Christianity. In his earlier chapters readers will recall the scorn Gibbon unleashes on the theological disputes over the trinity. The doctrine of the trinity was a vast and cumbersome machinery of professional interpretation. The advantage with Islam, as Gibbon seems to be arguing here, lies with the simplicity of its theology. The less complex God is, the less there needs to be said about him.[29] Strict monotheism is less likely to produce theological and semantical battles over the nature of its deity. The comparison is an unhappy one for Christianity. The doctrine of trinity turned sanguinary for the Christians. "In their obvious sense they introduce three equal deities, and transform the man Jesus into the substance of the son of God; an orthodox commentary will satisfy only a believing mind; intemperate curiosity and zeal had torn the veil of the sanctuary; and each of the Oriental sects was eager to confess that all, except themselves, deserved the reproach of idolatry and polytheism." (*DF-50*, V, 361)

Christianity from Muhammad's perspective was idolatrous. Jesus, a prophet, was falsely worshiped as a god. "Yet Jesus was a mere mortal; and, at the day of judgment, his testimony will serve to condemn both the Jews, who reject him as a prophet, and the Christians, who adore him as the Son of God." (*DF-50*, V, 364) From Muhammad's periods of hermetic "religious contemplation" he emerges as the final and ultimate apostle of God. "The piety of Moses and of Christ rejoiced in the assurance of a future prophet, more illustrious than themselves; the evangelic promise of the *Paraclete*, or Holy Ghost, was prefigured in the name, and accomplished in the person, of Mahomet, the greatest and last of the apostles of God." (*DF-50*, V, 364, original italics)

---

[29]See John A. Hall, *Powers and Liberties: The Causes and Consequences of the Rise of the West* (Berkeley, CA: University of California Press, 1985), 84. "Islam is scripturalist, egalitarian, and very strictly monotheist. It is also very simple . . . . There are no mysteries needed to be interpreted by a formal ecclesiastical organization."

"In all religions," observes Gibbon, "the life of the founder supplies the silence of his written revelation . . . ." (*DF-50*, V, 366) Muhammad's life, as we have seen up to this point, was the work of enthusiasm and ambition. Just how these two elements were combined, and the extent to which Muhammad's ambition was corrupted by artifice and fraud are matters of ambiguity, open questions for the reader. But these two elements were definitely behind Muhammad's achievement. "Mahomet, with the sword in one hand and the Koran in the other, erected his throne on the ruins of Christianity and of Rome." (*DF-50*, V, 332)[30] The sword and the Koran remain as visible material symbols for Gibbon of the ambition and enthusiasm at work in the life of Muhammad and in the propagation of the Islam. In the early stages of his success, while his following was still small, Muhammad—making virtue out of necessity—urged a freedom of religious conscience and condemned religious violence. "Conscious of his reason and of his weakness, he asserted the liberty of conscience, and disclaimed the use of religious violence . . . ." (*DF-50*, V, 377) But this appeal was the work of expediency and prudence. Muhammad was merely bidding his time. Once Muhammad gained a strong and zealous following, his revelations changed, reflecting a boldness and confidence that comes with the acquisition of power. "The imperfection of human rights was supplied and armed by the plenitude of divine power; the prophet of Medina assumed, in his new revelations, a fiercer and more sanguinary tone, which proves that his former moderation was the effect of weakness: the means of persuasion had been tried, the season of forbearance was elapsed, and he was now commanded to propagate his religion by the sword, to destroy the monuments of idolatry, and, without regarding the sanctity of days or months, to pursue the unbelieving nations of the earth." (*DF-50*, V, 382-383)

The fanatical or enthusiastic elements of Islam were dissimulated until the time was right for the Muslims to impose the truth of the Koran with threat of the sword. Gibbon's narrative then moves to a description of how religious enthusiasm combined quite nicely with the typical ambitions of human martial enterprises. "From all sides the roving Arabs were allured to the standard of *religion and plunder* . . . . The intrepid souls of the Arabs were fired with enthusiasm; the picture of the invisible world was strongly painted on their imagination; and the death which they had always despised became an object of hope and desire. The

---

[30]Lewis, "Gibbon on Muhammad," 72, notes a significant manifestation of ignorance on Gibbon's part with this statement. "'Mahamot,' of course, is here used metonymically for the empire of the Caliphs. Even so, the statement is remarkably inaccurate. Both Christianity and Rome survived the advent of Islam; the Qur'an did not become a book until some time after Muhammad's death; only a left-handed swordsman could brandish both, since no Muslim would hold the sacred book in the hand reserved for unclean purposes—and most important of all, there was a third choice, the payment of tribute and acceptance of Muslim rule."

Koran inculcates, in the most absolute sense, the tenets of faith and predestination, which would extinguish both industry and virtue, if the actions of man were governed by his speculative belief." (*DF-50*, V, 384, italics added)

Gibbon makes it quite clear that the elements of ambition and religion are impossible to sort out. He links "religion *and* plunder" to one standard. The language employed to describe the conduct of these conquering, new religionists is the language of passion and imagination, the same kind used by Hume in his characterization of the typical enthusiast. The emotions are of the strongest kind, reversing even the natural fear of death into a fearless, fanatical willingness to embrace it. The conquering Arabs possessed an enthusiastically inspired intrepidity which came from their belief that they were the special favorites of God. "In a little time," says Hume, "the inspired person comes to regard himself as a distinguished favourite of the Divinity." The central motive attributed to the Arabs by Gibbon was hope conjoined to a stimulated imagination, which, as Hume notes, is the driving force of the enthusiast. "Hope, pride, presumption, a warm imagination, together with ignorance, are, therefore, are the true sources of enthusiasm." Gibbon also suggests that the actual doctrines or teachings of the Koran if put consistently into practice would have the effect of eradicating conventional morality ("extinguish both industry and virtue"). The destruction of conventional morality by religious enthusiasm is one the main features noted by Hume. "Human reason, and even morality are rejected as fallacious guides."

Here then, unleashed upon the Roman empire in the seventh century, was a full blown enthusiastic religion with all the distinctive features associated with fanatical, monotheistic believers. But Gibbon, with his extensive description of the physical and cultural conditions of Arab existence and his biography of the Prophet, recreates historically the birth of Islam in such a way that its uniqueness as a cultural creation emerges. Islam bore the stamp of the personality of its founder and exhibited the effects of a militant ferocity that one would expect an independent, freedom-loving desert people to bring to it. Both Islam and Christianity were in their origins enthusiastic religions and are to be understood as productions of enthusiasm and ambition. Yet they exhibit many points of profound difference giving confirmation to Hume's dictum that the "empire of all religious faith over the understanding is wavering and uncertain, subject to all varieties of humour, and dependent on the present incidents, which strike the imagination." From Gibbon's perspective, the most profound of the differences from Christianity is the dominance of enthusiasm over superstition.[31] Islam remained enthusiastic:

---

[31]Gellner, *Conditions of Liberty*, 50, makes an comparative observation about Christianity and Islam that is resonant with Gibbon's presentation. Islam is at its center enthusiastic and thus puritan and scripturalist. At its edges is variant and ritualistic superstition. Christianity is the reverse; superstitious

Christianity become heavily superstitious. Christian superstition had developed and joined to itself a vast theological apparatus that expressed itself institutionally in an equally complex hierarchy. Moreover, Christian superstition was more virulent than pagan superstition precisely because of Christianity's affinity for theology. Pagan superstition, as Gibbon had argued, was oriented primarily toward the social and the civic, while Christian superstition had developed a perpetually contentious, theoretical preoccupation with the next world.[32] Islam's was enduringly enthusiastic, and enthusiasm, with its affinity for egalitarianism and eschewal of hierarchy was at the heart of its difference with Christianity. "To Western ideals essentially celibate, sacerdotal, and hierarchical, Islam opposed the outlook of a laity frankly indulgent and sensual, in principle egalitarian, enjoying a remarkable freedom of speculation, with no priests and no monasteries built into the basic structure of society as they were in the West."[33] Sensuality, as Southern notes, is a profoundly different matter in Islam and Christianity. Consider how Gibbon characterized the sensuality of Islamic paradise. "It is natural enough that an Arabian prophet should dwell with rapture on the groves, the fountains, and the rivers of paradise; but, instead of inspiring the blessed inhabitants with a liberal taste for harmony and science, conversions and friendship, he idly celebrates the pearls and diamonds, the robes of silk, palaces of marble, dishes of gold, rich wines, artificial dainties, numerous attendants, and the whole train of sensual and costly luxury, which becomes insipid to the owner, even in the short period of this mortal life." (*DF-50*, V, 374)

This description of paradise characterizes in a quite revealing way the cultural attainments and aspirations of the Prophet and gives added force to Gibbon's religious naturalism. Such a conception of heaven is what one would expect from an semi-literate desert nomad, one in which science and conversation and friendship are of less significance than objects of material affluence. It is also the kind of heaven envisioned by a people living in the conditions of the physically austere and hostile world described by Gibbon. But there is an even more important sensual feature of the Islamic paradise. "Seventy-two *Houris*, or black-eyed girls of resplendent beauty, blooming youth, virgin purity, and exquisite sensibility, will be created for the use of the meanest believer; a moment of

---

at its center and enthusiastic at the margins. It was this Christian mix, Gellner argues, that produced secularization.

[32]Gellner, *Anthropology and Politics*, 109-110, refers both to Hume and Gibbon in a discussion of how models of explanation have developed from the magical to the religious to the scientific. Hume and Gibbon recognized, claims Gellner, that pagan religion was primarily sociological and functional. Christianity as an axiological religion moves away from function and toward theorizing, and bad theorizing at that.

[33]Southern, *Western Views of Islam*, 7.

pleasure will be prolonged to a thousand years, and his faculties will be increased an hundred-fold to render him worthy of his felicity." (*DF-50*, V, 374)[34] Never perhaps have the rewards of a religious paradise catered so perfectly to the libidinous inclinations of the religion's founder. Muhammad's sexual appetite, Gibbon writes, was enormous, and he employed special revelation to indulge it even beyond the constraints he had set for his own followers. "[B]ut in his private conduct Mahomet indulged the appetites of a man and abused the claims of a prophet. A special revelation dispensed him from the laws which he had imposed on his nation; the female sex, without reserve, was abandoned to his desires; and this singular prerogative excited the envy, rather than the scandal, the veneration, rather than the envy, of the devout Musulmans." (*DF-50*, V, 403)

Gibbon describes a very carnal Muslim paradise, which he links directly to the Arab libido. "The heat of the climate inflames the blood of the Arabs; and their libidinous complexion has been noticed by the writers of antiquity." (*DF-50*, V, 402-403) This carnality, Gibbon seems happy to note, had been an object of vehement disparagement by Christian polemicists who decried the sexual immorality. "This image of a carnal paradise has provoked the indignation, perhaps the envy, of the monks: they declaim against the impure religion of Mahomet; and his modest apologists are driven to the poor excuse of figures and allegories." (*DF-50*, V, 374) Gibbon, the hater of monasticism, could not resist this cynical little piece of irreverence as he insinuates envy as well as indignation of the prurient Christian celibates. This flagrant sensuality is even, as he notes, something of an embarrassment to Muhammad's later Islamic followers. But Gibbon himself holds up this paradise of seventy-two *Houris* as fully consistent with the Koranic doctrine of resurrection. "But the sounder and more consistent party adhere, without shame, to the literal interpretation of the Koran; useless would be the resurrection of the body, unless it were restored to the possession and exercise of this worthiest faculties; and the union of sensual and intellectual enjoyment is requisite to complete the happiness of the double animal, the perfect man." (*DF-50*, V, 374) Christianity like Islam teaches the resurrection of the body, and although Gibbon does not mention Christianity, his implicit disdain for its asceticism is apparent. Muhammad's paradise, Gibbon seemed to argue with some satisfaction, properly embraced sexuality as a worthy feature of humanity in contrast with the Christian monks who have mortified the flesh. Gibbon had taken a traditional, long-standing Christian practice, the vilification of Muhammad via

---

[34]Daniel, *Islam and the West*, 148. "It must be said that it was usual for Christians to allow themselves a rather purple rendering of the gardens and precious metals of Paradise, though usually not of the virgins so beloved of later romanticism. There is a genuine latinisation here, that in one aspect recalls the lapidaries, and, in another, some of the background of romance, the legend of the Reine Sybille, a hint of the native pagan idyll."

his supposed immoral sexuality, and given it a reverse thrust so that it results in an aspersion against Christianity.[35]

Near the end of chapter fifty-one, the longest in the *Decline and Fall*, where the seventh-century conquests of Islam are detailed, Gibbon explores the means by which Islam is propagated. Again, Gibbon draws Christianity into invidious comparison with Islam. "The wars of the Moslems were sanctified by the prophet; but, among the various precepts and examples of his life, the caliphs selected the lessons of toleration that might tend to disarm the resistance of the unbelievers." (*DF-51*, V, 516) Religious toleration, Gibbon argues, became under the calculations of Muhammad's epigones, primarily a political issue. There is more discrete invidious comparison here as Gibbon follows the movement of Islam into its full institutional stage. Its policies of religious toleration, though contrived to make the imposition of Islam irresistible, admitted greater toleration of other religions that its chief rival, Christianity. "Thus, Muhammad's violence was essential, in the Christian position, to his religion, although Christians and Muslims alike practiced holy war, and only Islam effectively tolerated other religions within itself, admittedly granting only second-class citizenship."[36] Jews and Christians, Gibbon points out, could convert or they could pay tribute and be "entitled to the freedom of conscience and religious worship." (*DF-51*, V, 516) But it is in Gibbon's rhapsodic presentation of Christianity and Islam as choices of belief where he draws his sharpest criticism of Christianity. "But the millions of African and Asiatic converts, who swelled the native band of the faithful Arabs, must have been allured, rather than constrained, to declare their belief in one God and the apostle of God. By the repetition of a sentence and the loss of a foreskin, the subject or the slave, the captive or the criminal, arose in a moment the free and equal companion of the victorious Moslems. Every sin was expiated, every engagement was dissolved: the vow of celibacy was superseded by the indulgence of nature; the active spirits who slept in the cloister were awakened by the trumpet of the Saracens; and, in the convulsion of the world, every member of a new society ascended to the natural level of his capacity and courage." (*DF-51*, V, 517)

Gibbon here distills for the reader his own version of the elements of these two faiths. Here he can again animadvert against the monks. The comparison effected

---

[35] See, Daniel, *Islam and the West*, particularly Chapter III, "The Life of Muhammad: Polemic Biography" for the details of the interpretation that Christian polemicists put on the life of Muhammad including his "immoral" sexuality. "The picture of the licentious hypocrite took shape inevitably. What clerical writers, always aware of the problems of moral and pastoral theology, most feared was the doctrinal justification of sexual acts which are already attractive to men who believed them to be wrong. This explains the virulence of educated Christian feeling about Muhammad, which always excluded charity and usually excluded the complete truth." (102)

[36] Daniel, *Islam and the West*, 274.

is one of vitality, strength, and enjoyment against enfeeblement and constraint. The imagery, full of Gibbon's devious irony, is that of death and resurrection. The Saracen trumpet blows and awakens from cloistered death the Christian somnambulist whose active spirits have been shrouded in guilt and whose natural desires have languished. Celibacy and all of the abnegating effects that monkish practice conjures up give way to a "natural" indulgence.

We then find Gibbon drawing a somewhat more abstract comparison of Islam with its other competitor religions. "More pure than the system of Zoroaster, more liberal than the law of Moses, the religion of Mahomet might seem less inconsistent with reason than the creed of mystery and superstition which, in the seventh century, disgraced the simplicity of the gospel." (*DF-51*, V, 517) The comparison here is, despite the euphemistic use of the subjunctive, quite straight forward. Seventh-century Christianity unlike Islam has descended into superstition. Gibbon has made these Saracen aggressors into spiritual liberators.

Gibbon also, in his review of Islamic miracles, poses problematic aspects of them that end up reverberating critically against Christianity. Muhammad was trapped by his followers who wanted him "to call down from heaven the angel or the volume of his revelation, to create a garden in the desert, or to kindle a conflagration in the unbelieving city." (*DF-50*, V, 367) Muhammad had to dissemble, and, he "appeals to the internal proofs of his doctrine, and shields himself behind the providence of God, who refuses those signs and wonders that would depreciate the merit of faith and aggravate the guilt of infidelity." (*DF-50*, V, 367) This shrewd, special pleading is betrayed by a tone of exasperation in the Koran, unwittingly to the advantage of Islam. "But the modest or angry tone of his apologies betrays his weakness and vexation; and these passages of scandal establish, beyond suspicion, the integrity of the Koran." (*DF-50*, V, 367) Here we have a curious causal connection asserted; "scandal" establishing "integrity." The scandal is obvious to the historian looking back at this conspicuous piece of fraud on the part of Muhammad, yet, ironically, the vexed tone of the Koranic apologia turns out to be a kind of evidence that gives the Koran credibility. This is stressed in an appended note. "Maracci, with a more learned apparatus, has shewn that the passages which deny his miracles are clear and positive, and those which seem to assert them are ambiguous and insufficient." (*DF-50*, V, 367, n.102) Gibbon here has applied the philosophic historian's method of making judgments about events based upon a knowledge of human passion and motivation. The uncertainty and ambiguity surrounding miracles (the passions of the votaries and the motivations of Muhammad) are, given the circumstances, what one would expect. Thus the Koran is a more credible document than if it were to affirm, as do the Old and New

Testaments, the performance of miracles. Gibbon's judgment on the "integrity of the Koran" implies just such an invidious comparison.

Yet, in spite of this integrity, a tradition of miracles did grow up around Muhammad. "The votaries of Mahomet are more assured than himself of his miraculous gifts, and their confidence and credulity increase as they are farther removed from the time and place of his spiritual exploits." (*DF-50*, V, 367) Islamic miracles seem to resemble Jewish and Christian ones (the naturalism is again at work) in that the strongest believers in the miracles are the ones that are farthest removed, temporally, from their occurrence. These believers: "affirm that trees went forth to meet him; that he was saluted by stones; that water gushed from his fingers; that he fed the hungry, cured the sick, and raised the dead; that a beam groaned to him; that a camel complained to him; that a shoulder of mutton informed him of its being poisoned; and that both animate and inanimate nature were equally subject to the apostle of God." (*DF-50*, V, 367)

Thus, we contemplate with increasing cynicism the full range of miracle working, including the traditional curing of the sick, raising of the dead, and the arbitrary command over the natural forces. Muhammad, in his miraculous powers, resembled Christ. The reminder of that resemblance perhaps further diminishes the credibility of Christian miracles. Belief in miracles seems more and more to be a predictable attribute of credulous religionists.

Gibbon does tie this tradition of miracles exclusively to the vulgar. "The vulgar are amused with these marvelous tales; but the gravest of the Mussulmen doctors imitate the modesty of their master, and indulge a latitude of faith or interpretation. They might speciously allege that, in preaching the religion, it was needless to violate the harmony of nature; that a creed unclouded with mystery may be excused from miracles; and that the sword of Mahamet was not less impotent than the rod of Moses." (*DF-50*, V, 368) With few words, Gibbon says a great deal, in a comparative vein, about Christianity and Islam. Moreover, his choice of words was deliberately draped in ambiguity so as to make the comparison rich and suggestive. Islam, unlike Christianity with the miraculous entry of Christ into the world and his subsequent death and resurrection, is not bound in a foundational way to miracles. Islam was powerful enough without the invention of miracles ("it was needless to violate the harmony of nature"). Muhammad's sword was no less impotent that the rod of Moses, but in what sense, temporal or spiritual? The sword of Muhammad symbolizes for Gibbon his military and temporal power, and certainly the martial virtues equaled that of Christianity. Yet, "a creed unclouded with mystery may be excused from miracles." Islam remains a purer, simpler creed. The mysterious and miraculous aspects of Christianity were precisely for Gibbon those elements responsible for its degeneracy and decline.

At work in Christianity as well was the large element of ambition which became increasingly corrupted as Christianity took on an institutional form and became immersed in the acquisition, preservation, and extension of power. Christianity's original enthusiasm, comparable in its energy to that of Islam's, had given way to enervating superstition. Gibbon used the early history of Islam to sustain his argument that Christianity, after seven hundred years, had, like the Roman empire, undergone a process of decline. The Islamic soldier-evangelists are in some curious respects similar to the barbarians who had invaded Rome in the fourth and fifth centuries. "The hatred of the Christians, the love of spoil, and the contempt of danger were the ruling passions of the audacious Saracen; and the prospect of instant death could never shake his religious confidence, or ruffle the calmness of his resolution, or even suspend the frank and martial pleasantry of his humour." (*DF-50*, V, 448) Bold, disdainful of authority, motivated by gain—material as well as spiritual—the Islamic armies invaded the Christianized Roman empire and confronted a people that had lost their martial edge. Gibbon describes the invasion of Christian Syria: "[c]onfident in their strength, the [Christian] people of Bosra threw open gates, drew their forces into the plain, and swore to die in the defence of their religion. But a *religion of peace* was incapable of withstanding the fanatic cry of 'Fight, fight! Paradise, paradise!' that re-echoed in the ranks of the Saracens; and the uproar of the town, the ringing of the bells, and the exclamations of the priests and monks increased the dismay and disorder of the Christians." (*DF-51*, V, 445, italics added)

This reference to "a religion of peace" makes for double irony. Peace appears as a never-realized ideal of the early Christians, and the history of Christianity that Gibbon has presented in the *Decline and Fall* is one of bitter, hate-inspired warfare, internecine as well as against external foes. But also, the "religion of peace" is really a euphemism for a religion of weakness and impotence. It is a pacific religion not by design, but because its followers have no capacity to make war. The "priests and the monks," the spiritual leaders of the Christians, provide no leadership and exert no authority. They resemble the enervated, corrupted Roman Senators, unable to protect Rome from the onslaught of the Goths. As presented here, they are weak and enfeebled, incapable in this time of grave crisis to do anything but succumb to confusion and emit "exclamations" which merely contribute to their impending destruction.

Christianity then, just like the Roman empire, emerges from Gibbon's pages as a social institution vulnerable to every form of human corruption. The decline and fall of the Roman empire is not just about political decline but moral and spiritual decadence as well. Over pagan Rome Christianity achieved political triumph, but in its future was the corruption of its own moral and spiritual authority through the invention of a priestly hierarchy ambitious for the goods of this world and superstitiously fearful of the evils in the next.

Conclusion

How fares the Truth now?--Ill?
Do pens but slily further her advance?
May one not speed her but in phrase askance?
Do scribes aver the Comic to Reverend still?
Thomas Hardy, Lausanne In Gibbon's Old Garden: 11-12 p.m.

A study of the Hume-Gibbon attack on Christianity is ultimately an account of a unique eighteenth-century phenomenon—philosophic history. Its consummation is found in the work of Hume and Gibbon. Hume's philosophical critique—skeptically boring away at the metaphysical foundations of Christianity and morally accusing its practitioners of excess—finds its complement in Gibbon's historical critique. Gibbon put his extraordinary erudition to work in an exposé that deliberately drew attention to all of Christianity's shortcomings adumbrated in rich historical detail. It was Hume principally who developed and refined the outlook characteristic of philosophic history defined by its thoroughgoing naturalism, its skepticism of theology and metaphysics, and its pessimism of human nature. Gibbon absorbed all the elements of this philosophic perspective and, with elegance and irony, applied them iconoclastically to the particularities of fifteen hundred years of history. His intent was to explain the decline of one civilization—the pagan classical—and the rise of another—Christianity, a task complicated by his affinity for the former and his ambivalence toward the latter. Gibbon linked the rise of Christianity to the political decline of Rome, and thus much of the *Decline and Fall* is devoted to exploring the political significance of religion and the religious dimensions of politics.

Philosophic history was a self-conscious, deliberate work of iconoclasm but was above all else critical. It defined itself largely in opposition to, and operated against, the philosophical ambitions and historical perspectives of medieval Christianity. Its methods of inquiry were affirmed to be undergirded by the norm of impartiality. This was in contrast to the Christian apologists who were *required*, by virtue of their membership in the unassailable Citadel of Truth, to find in every historical event an exclusive affirmation of Christianity, "descended from Heaven, arrayed in her native purity." Philosophic history's practitioners were self-declared foes of the church, disdainful of its long-enforced monopoly on religious truth and moral wisdom. And so the attack on Christianity was an essential, inevitable feature of philosophic history. Philosophic history was a mode of philosophizing, an attempt to understand the past. Past events, properly interpreted, had moral value and could be used to teach human beings how to act; or, more importantly, how not to act. Here Christianity came to the fore. Philosophic history held up—from its study of centuries of Christian history—the folly of religious enthusiasm and the enervation of superstition as important lessons to be gleaned from the study of religion. Because Christianity was its primary instructive model of the excesses of religion, philosophic history was also a profound exercise in disillusionment.

The Christian interpretation of the past represented for Hume a major obstacle to understanding the human condition: *its* mode of interpretation was theological—grounded in concepts with no experiential points of reference—and hence *its* philosophizing was condemned to perpetuate itself in fruitless attempts to extract systematic knowledge and moral certainty from a world that was the domain of the poets—a world of imagination and fancy. Hume's response was to develop a philosophical critique that struck at Christianity's claims to be defensible through the instrument of reason. Faith and reason were incompatible. Attempts to *demonstrate* the truth about the principal concerns of Christianity—the goodness and justice of God, immortality, the nature of the soul, etc.—could never succeed; only dispute and sectarian rancor would follow. Theology turned out to be a vain—and as philosophic history seemed to be intent on showing—and often pernicious exercise.

Gibbon, as we have seen, shared Hume's skepticism about the work of the Christian theologians. Christianity, too, for Gibbon was an obstacle to his ambitions to be impartial and truthful, the two objectives of philosophic history. The Christian past constructed by the apologists—particularly the origins of Christianity—was a distortion, a made-up version of events that was incompatible with the historian's quest to make sense of the all the sources. The pagan writers (history's losers) had contributed their versions of the early days of Christianity: Gibbon wanted to take these into account. Christian apologists made history the servant of theology. And not only was theology, as Hume had argued, a misguided attempt to extend reason beyond its limits, it was, as Gibbon attempted to show, subject to all the usual forces of corruption that had ever persisted in human society. Theology as an ambitious quest to comprehend the otherworld became an instrument of ambition for this one. Christianity became a vehicle for converting metaphysical constructs into political forms, principally through coercion. Christianity's political high point was the nadir of the freedom of thought in the history of the West. Christianity's entry into the world, its subsequent development, and its presentation by its apologists were a source of irony that Gibbon was to exploit throughout the *Decline and Fall*.

Gibbon's irony is a most important consideration: it is an essential element in the linkage of Hume and Gibbon in this study. While Hume had forged the philosophical argumentation against many important elements of Christianity—miracles, immortality, martyrdom, theological reasoning—it was

Gibbon's ironic historical narrative—operating with the naturalistic Humean presuppositions—that set the stage for what turns out to be a moral inversion of Christianity. The ironic insinuation, so pervasive in the *Decline and Fall*, turned Christianity's strengths into its weaknesses. Miracles, profound evidence of Christian truth, were doubted away—fabrications of the superstitious and credulous. Belief in immortality fueled the fanatical, otherworldly excesses of the early Christians and corroded the social fabric of the classical world. Christians suffered persecution, but they were also ferocious persecutors—a moral equation Gibbon set up to diminish further official, i.e., apologetic history. Gibbon's accounts of theology and doctrine were masterful studies in opportunism and fanaticism—open to cynical and derisive portrayal. Even Christianity's chief rival, Islam, emerged from Gibbon's purview in comparative favor. Where the apologists had sought to elevate Christianity, Gibbon, in his project of moral inversion, held up for historical inspection its weaknesses and vulnerabilities.

The Hume-Gibbon attack on Christianity developed on two major fronts. The first was epistemological. The objects of Christian knowledge—God, his nature, and his designs for mankind—were unknowable. Hume's analysis of causality and his attack on miracles had assaulted the substantial theological and metaphysical edifice that provided the intellectual and apologetic underpinnings of the Christian Faith. Gibbon's version of the history of Christianity had attempted to demonstrate the heavy influence of extra-philosophical elements at work in defining Christian doctrine. Gibbon had created a historical critique which argued for the essential irrationality of Christianity, one which corroborated Hume's philosophical version. The disputes over the Trinity, the Incarnation, and other elements of theological knowledge were shown ultimately to be political battles, contests of will and skill decided by the various contingencies of the personalities and characters of the contestants and the fortuity of events. In his accounts of the doctrinal and institutional battles, Gibbon took considerable effort to expose the high degree to which fanaticism played a determining role. All of Gibbon's Christians—the good ones as well as the bad—were tainted in some degree by superstition or enthusiasm. Gibbon, aided by his accumulation of historical learning, had made theological truth and certainty a casualty of historical contingency.

Miracles were the product of superstition and fraud, a part of that "inevitable mixture of error and corruption" which the historian discovered in the study of religion. Hume formulated a philosophical critique that raised the issue of the credibility of accounts of the miraculous to the forefront. Gibbon treated the events of Christ's own miraculous death and resurrection with an artfully ironic suspicion. Thus, Hume and Gibbon were to confront Christianity, founded in the miraculous and buoyed up by a massive bulwark of theology, with a collective skepticism that was wholesale and extremely damaging, both philosophically and historically. The spiritual causality at work behind the all events of history was cast into doubt. Hume made this point generally and philosophically; Gibbon did it with historical particularity. The skepticism of Hume and Gibbon, directed as it was against the spiritual causality of Christianity, fell back upon the causality of the natural world, expressed "noumenally" by Gibbon as "secondary" causality. No one was fooled. Philosophic history was thoroughgoing in its attack on historical and dogmatic Christianity: it injected into the consideration of its claims philosophic skepticism and historical doubt.

The second problem followed from the first, but in some respects was more important—that of the practical or moral problem of Christianity. The thrust of the Hume-Gibbon attack, as the preceding pages have shown, is with its social and political significance. The history of Christianity was a vast arena of politics and religion. Christianity was not simply a speculative mode of belief. It was a source of profound inspiration. Its believers had changed the course of history. Christianity defined the culture of all of Europe. As we have seen, both Hume and Gibbon were very much preoccupied not simply with the beliefs of Christianity but with the behavior of Christians. The history of Christianity was a cultural lesson with enormous implications for morals and politics. Gibbon devoted many pages of his history to the ridicule of the theologians, a piece of the entertainment he saw as a necessary element of good history. However, it was the conduct of the Christians that Gibbon held up as an important lesson on religion and its potential for corruption.

The history of Christianity was thus an extremely important subject for philosophic history. Indeed the history of Christianity presented itself in the eighteenth century as the ultimate theater of polemic. The establishment view, the Christian self-protected view of its own history, was in direct conflict with the reading of Hume and Gibbon who sought to expose its limitations. In their rendition, acutely expressed in Gibbon's moral inversion, the Christian miracles were fraudulent; the martyrs were fanatics; the saints were flawed; the Christian rulers were bigots and persecutors. Among Gibbon's more interesting Christians were the fanatical early ones who rejected the traditional religions of their ancestors and assisted in the destruction of the Roman empire. Hume's Christians were the Puritan enthusiasts of the seventeenth-century who confronted superstitious Catholicism. Indeed, Hume and Gibbon attacked Christianity by making the conduct of Christians scandalous. Early Christianity featured the destruction of the political order by fanaticism. Medieval Christianity was a story of religious decadence, a study of superstition and the exploitation of it by priests.

Monasticism was the ultimate tergiversation of classical values. The Reformation was a dismal scene of civil war and destruction.

Much of the history of Christianity for Hume and Gibbon is a study of religious passion embodied in superstition and enthusism. The critique directed skeptically against the supernatural claims affirmed by traditional Christianity was also extended into a naturalistic explanation of the origin of religious practice. The history of Christianity as a divine plan became in Hume's and Gibbon's study of it a contingent object of anthropology. No longer could its representatives sustain the claim to being privileged cognitive specialists or unspotted moral virtuosos. Religion, as it comes to be expressed socially and politically, Hume and Gibbon argued, is grounded largely on two primary emotions, fear and hope—both arising out of the contingency of human existence. From the natural phenomenon of the human fear of uncertainty comes the invention of a supernatural order and a sacerdotal class that explains the workings of that order. Fear is the originating cause of superstition, and superstition works to the benefit of tyrants. Religious hope is the emotive underpinning of religious fanaticism or what Hume and Gibbon call enthusism. Enthusism, more than any other religious phenomenon captured the attention and fascination of Hume and Gibbon. In large part this was due to the effects of enthusiastic religion on the social and political order. Enthusiastic Jews brought down the wrath of the Roman state. Enthusiastic Christians contributed to the decline of Imperial Rome. Enthusiastic Puritans had toppled the Stuarts. The enthusiasm of an illiterate desert prophet ignited a contagion and created hosts of warrior-apostles who swept over three continents and for centuries threatened Christendom.

Behind the fascination of Hume and Gibbon for religious enthusiasm was a generalized apprehension of the susceptibility of human beings to religious passion. Human beings were primarily creatures of passion and the passion of religious enthusiasm had a large element of the unpredictable and inexplicable, manifesting itself, as it often did, in a disposition to depart from the norms that usually governed human beings. Christian history, as we have noted, was in large part for Hume and Gibbon a study of the work of Christian enthusiasts. It is in their grappling with Christian enthusiasts that their antagonism to Christianity is most profound because the behavior of enthusiasts reflects a more general problem with religion, one with its roots in human nature. Human beings are flawed—an element of pessimism pervades the work of Hume and Gibbon. They are creatures with limited benevolence and operate with a practical myopia, a short-sightedness that is due largely to the fact that they are driven by the impulses of emotion. From social and political life human beings can reap many benefits and advantages. To do so, however, requires through norms and rules, the imposition of self-restraint over what is generally a natural human inclination to overreach. Human society and culture, even at its very best, works through constraint. That is the best that can be asked for. Enthusiasm is so pernicious from the standpoint of Hume and Gibbon precisely because it attacks norms of self-restraint, the glue that makes social and cultural life possible. This was the basis of Gibbon's criticism of the conduct of the early Christians and of Hume's "generous tear for the fate of Charles I and the Earl of Strafford." This is also the foundation for what has been described as the secular conservatism of Hume and Gibbon. To them, religion shaped by philosophy—Christianity as the prime example—is dangerous because of the tendencies of philosophical religion to penetrate politics, i.e., to sweep away established rules and norms of self-restraint in the quest for social perfection or utopia.

Christianity, in its various quests for perfection, had shown itself to the philosopher Hume and historian Gibbon to be an enemy of freedom. And thus Hume and Gibbon emerge as philosophers of freedom and in this we see a fundamental complementary character in their opposition, as philosophic historians, to Christianity. Freedom is essentially a historical concept. In Hume's philosophy all moral judgments are based on experience, i.e., history: it is history that helps supply the moral wisdom that allows human beings, "weak and degenerate" though they may be, to carry out their projects.

BIBLIOGRAPHY OF SOURCES CITED

Acton, John Emerich Edward Dalberg-Acton, Baron. "Protestant Theory of Persecution." In *Essays on Freedom and Power*, edited by Gertrude Himmelfarb. Gloucester, MA: Peter Smith, 1972.

Addinall, Peter. *Philosophy and Biblical Interpretation: A Study in Nineteenth-Century Conflict*. Cambridge: Cambridge University Press, 1991.

Africa, Thomas W. "Gibbon and the Golden Age." *The Centennial Review* 3, no. 3 (summer 1963): 273-81.

Allan, David. *Virtue, Learning and the Scottish Enlightenment: Ideas of Scholarship in Early Modern History*. Edinburgh: Edinburgh University Press, 1993.

Armstrong, A. H. "The Way and the Ways: Religious Tolerance and Intolerance in the Fourth Century A.D." *Vigiliae Christianae* 38, no. 1 (1984): 1-17.

Aron, Ramond. *The Opium of the Intellectuals*. Translated by Terence Kilmartin. New York: Doubleday, 1957.

Austin, Dobson. "The Gordon Riots." In *Twentieth Century Essays and Address*, edited by William A. J. Archbold. 1927. Reprint, New York: Books for Libraries Press, 1970.

Bagehot, Walter. *Collected Works of Walter Bagehot*. Edited by Norman St. John-Stevas. 8 vols. Cambridge, MA: Harvard University Press, 1965.

Bakhash, Shaul. *Review of Islam and the West*, by Bernard Lewis, *New York Review of Books* 40 (October 7, 1993): 43.

Beckwith, Francis J. *David Hume's Argument Against Miracles: A Critical Analysis*. Lanham, MD: University Press of America, 1989.

Berlin, Isaiah. "Hume and the Sources of German Anti-Rationalism." In *Against the Current: Essays in the History of Ideas,* edited by Henry Hardy. New York: Penguin, 1980.

Black, J. B. *The Art of History*. New York: F.S. Crofts and Co., 1926.

Boesche, Roger. "The Politics of Pretence: Tacitus and the Political Theory of Despotism." *History of Political Thought* 8, no. 2 (summer 1987): 189-210.

Bond, Harold. *The Literary Art of Edward Gibbon*. Oxford: Clarendon Press, 1960.

Bongie, Laurence. *David Hume: Prophet of the Counter-Revolution*. Oxford: Clarendon Press, 1965.

Bourke, Vernon J. *History of Ethics*. Garden City, NY: Doubleday, 1968.

Braudy, Leo. *Narrative Form in History and Fiction*. Princeton, NJ: Princeton University Press, 1970.

Brockelmann, Carl. *History of the Islamic Peoples*. Translated by Joel Carmichael and Moshe Perlmann. London: Routledge and Kegan Paul, 1948.

Brown, Peter. *Augustine of Hippo: A Biography*. New York: Dorset Press, 1986.

_____. *The Cult of the Saints: Its Rise and Function in Latin Christianity.* Chicago: University of Chicago Press, 1981.

_____. "Gibbon on Culture and Society." In *Edward Gibbon and 'The Decline and Fall of the Roman Empire,'* edited by G. W. Bowersock, John Clive, and Stephen R. Graubard. Cambridge, MA: Harvard University Press, 1977.

Brownley, Martine Watson. "Gibbon's Memoirs: The Legacy of the Historian." *Studies on Voltaire and the Eighteenth Century* 201 (1982): 209-20.

Bryson, Gladys. *Man and Society: The Scottish Inquiry of the Eighteenth Century.* 1945. Reprint, New York: August M. Kelley, 1968.

Buckle, Henry. *On Scotland and the Scotch Intellect.* Edited by H. J. Hanham. Chicago: University of Chicago Press, 1970.

Burckhardt, Jacob. *The Age of Constantine the Great.* Translated by Moses Hadas. Berkeley, CA: University of California Press, 1949.

Burke, Edmund. *Reflections on the Revolution in France.* Indianapolis, IN: Bobbs-Merrill, 1955.

Burns, R. M. *The Great Debate on Miracles: From Joseph Glanville to David Hume.* Lewisburg, PA: Bucknell University Press, 1981.

Burrow, J. W. *Gibbon.* New York: Oxford University Press, 1985.

Byrne, Peter. *Natural Religion and the Nature of Religion: The Legacy of Deism.* London: Routledge, 1989.

Cameron, Averil. *Christianity and the Rhetoric of Empire: The Development of Christian Discourse.* Berkeley, CA: University of California Press, 1991.

Carmichael, Joel. *Stalin's Masterpiece: The Show Trials and Purges of the Thirties —The Consolidation of the Bolshevik Dictatorship.* London: Weidenfeld and Nicolson, 1976.

Carnochan, W. B. *Gibbon's Solitude.* Stanford, CA: Stanford University Press, 1987.

Cassirer, Ernst. *The Philosophy of the Enlightenment.* Translated by C. A. Koellin and James P. Pettegrove. Boston: Beacon Press, 1951.

Chadwick, Owen. "Gibbon and the Church Historians." In *Edward Gibbon and 'The Decline and Fall of The Roman Empire,'* edited by G. W. Bowersock, John Clive, and Stephen R. Graubard. Cambridge, MA: Harvard University Press, 1977.

Charron, William C. "Convention, Games of Strategy, and Hume's Philosophy of Law and Government." *American Philosophical Quarterly* 17, no. 4 (October 1980): 327-34.

Chitnis, Anand C. *The Scottish Enlightenment: A Social History.* London: Croom Helm, 1976.

Cicero. *De Natura Deorum*. Translated by H. Rackham. Cambridge, MA: Harvard University Press, 1933.

Clark, J. C. D. *English Society 1688-1832: Ideology, Social Structure and Political Practice During the Ancien Regime*. Cambridge: Cambridge University Press, 1985.

Clodd, Edward. *Gibbon and Christianity*. London: Watts and Co., 1916.

Clover, Wayne. Note on the Text to *Natural History of Religion*, by David Hume. Oxford: Clarendon Press, 1976.

Coady, C. A. J. *Testimony: A Philosophical Study*. Oxford: Clarendon Press, 1992.

Cochrane, Charles Norris. *Christianity and Classical Culture: A Study of Thought and Action from Augustus to Augustine*. London: Oxford University Press, 1944.

Cohn, Norman. *The Pursuit of the Millenium*. Fair Lawn, NJ: Essential Books, 1957.

Collins, James. *The Emergence of the Philosophy of Religion*. New Haven, CT: Yale University Press, 1967.

Commission of the Central Committee of the C.P.S.U. *History of the Communist Party of the Soviet Union (Short Course)*. New York: International Publishers, 1939.

Condren, Conal. "Radicals, Conservatives and Moderates in Early Modern Political Thought: A Case of Sandwich Islands Syndrome?" *History of Political Thought* 10, no. 3 (autumn 1989): 525-42.

Coulton, G. C. *Inquisition and Liberty*. Boston: Beacon Press, 1959.

Craddock, Patricia. *Edward Gibbon: A Reference Guide*. Boston: G.K. Hall, 1987.

____. *Edward Gibbon: Luminous Historian, 1772-1794*. Baltimore: The Johns Hopkins University Press, 1989.

____. *Young Edward Gibbon: Gentleman of Letters*. Baltimore: The Johns Hopkins University Press, 1982.

Cragg, Gerald C. *Reason and Authority in the Eighteenth Century*. Cambridge: Cambridge University Press, 1964.

Cross, John G. *Social Traps*. Ann Arbor, MI: University of Michigan Press, 1980.

Danford, John. *David Hume and the Problem of Reason: Recovering the Human Sciences*. New Haven, CT: Yale University Press, 1990.

Daniel, Norman. *Islam and the West: The Making of an Image*. Edinburgh: Edinburgh University Press, 1960.

Darnton, Robert. "In Search of the Enlightenment: Recent Attempts to Create a Social History of Ideas." *Journal of Modern History* 33, no. 1 (March 1971): 113-32.

Davie, George E. *The Scottish Enlightenment and Other Essays*. Edinburgh: Polygon, 1991.

Dawson, Christopher. "Edward Gibbon: Annual Lecture on a Master Mind, Henriette Hertz Turst." *Proceedings of the British Academy*, 159-80, 1934.

DeBeer, Gavin. *Gibbon and His World*. London: Thames and Hudson, 1968.

Dickinson, H. T. "The Politics of Edward Gibbon." *Literature and History* 8, no. 4 (1978): 175-96.

Dijksterhuis, E. J. *The Mechanization of the World Picture: Pythagoras to Newton*. Translated by C. Dijkshoorn. Princeton, NJ: Princeton University Press, 1986.

Drake, H. A. "Lambs Into Lions: Explaining Early Christian Intolerance." *Past & Present* 153 (November 1996):3-34.

Drucker, Peter. *The End of Economic Man: A Study of the New Totalitarianism*. New York: John Day Co., 1939.

Dyson, A. E. *The Crazy Fabric: Essays in Irony*. London: Macmillan, 1965.

Evnine, Simon. "Hume, Conjectural History, and the Uniformity of Human Nature." *Journal of the History of Philosophy* 31, no. 4 (October 1993): 589-606.

Farr, James. "Hume, Hermeneutics, and History: A 'Sympathetic' Account." *History and Theory: Studies in the Philosophy of History* 17, no. 3 (1978): 285-310.

Fearnley-Sander, Mary. "Philosophical History and the Scottish Reformation: William Robertson and the Knoxian Tradition." *The Historical Journal* 33, no. 2 (1990): 323-38.

Ferreira, M. Jamie. "Hume's *Natural History*: Religion and 'Explanation.'" *Journal of the History of Philosophy* 33, no. 4 (1995): 593-611.

Flew, Anthony. *Hume's Philosophy of Belief: A Study of His 'First Inquiry'*. New York: Humanities Press, 1961.

Forbes, Duncan. *Hume's Philosophical Politics*. Cambridge: Cambridge University Press, 1975.

____. Introduction to *History of Great Britain: The Reigns of James and Charles I*, by David Hume. Middlesex, England: Penguin, 1970.

Foster, Stephen Paul. "Different Religions and the Difference They Make: Hume on the Political Effects of Religious Ideology." *Modern Schoolman* 46, no. 4 (May 1989): 253-74.

Frend, W. H. C. "Edward Gibbon (1737-1794) and Early Christianity." *Journal of Ecclesiastical History* 45, no. 4 (Oct. 1994): 661-72.

____. *Martyrdom and Persecution in the Early Church: A Study of a Conflict from the Maccabees to Donatus*. Garden City, NY: Doubleday, 1967.

Furet, Francois. "Civilization and Barbarism in Gibbon's History." In *Edward Gibbon and 'The Decline and Fall of The Roman Empire,'* edited by G. W. Bowersock, John Clive, and Stephen R. Graubard. Cambridge, MA: Harvard University Press, 1977.

Garrison, James D. "Gibbon and the Treacherous Language of Panegyrics." *Eighteenth Century Studies* 11, no. 1 (fall 1977): 40-62.

Gaskin, J. C. A. *Hume's Philosophy of Religion.* 2nd ed. Highlands, NJ: Humanities Press International, 1988.

Gay, Peter. *The Enlightenment: An Interpretation.* Vol. 1, *The Rise of Modern Paganism.* New York: W. W. Norton, 1966.

_____. *The Enlightenment: An Interpretation.* Vol. 2, *The Science of Freedom.* New York: W. W. Norton, 1969.

_____. *Style in History.* New York: W.W. Norton, 1974.

Gellner, Earnest. *Anthropology and Politics: Revolutions in the Sacred Grove.* Oxford: Blackwell, 1995.

_____. *Conditions of Liberty: Civil Society and Its Rivals.* New York: Penguin Books, 1994.

_____. *Plough, Sword and Book: The Structure of Human History.* Chicago: University of Chicago Press, 1988.

_____. *Reason and Culture: The Historic Role of Rationality and Rationalism.* Cambridge, MA: Blackwell, 1992.

Giarrizzo, Giuseppe. "Toward the *Decline and Fall*: Gibbon's Other Historical Interests." In *Edward Gibbon and 'The Decline and Fall of the Roman Empire,'* edited by G.W. Bowersock, John Clive and Stephen R. Graubard. Cambridge, MA: Harvard University Press, 1977.

Gibbon, Edward. *The English Essays of Edward Gibbon.* Edited by Patricia Craddock. Oxford: Clarendon Press, 1972.

_____. *The History of the Decline and Fall of the Roman Empire,* in seven volumes. Edited by J. B. Bury. 7 vols. London: Methuen and Co., 1909-1914.

_____. *The Letters of Edward Gibbon.* 3 vols. Edited by J. E. Norton, London: Cassell and Co., 1956.

_____. *Memoirs of My Life.* Edited by Betty Radice. London: Penguin, 1984.

_____. *The Miscellaneous Works of Edward Gibbon.* 5 vols. London: John Murray, 1814.

Gillispie, Charles Coulston. "Science and the Enlightenment." In *The Edge of Objectivity: An Essay in the History of Scientific Ideas.* Princeton, NJ: Princeton University Press, 1960.

Goodman, Dena. "The Hume-Rousseau Affair: From Private *Querelle* to Public *Procès.*" *Eighteenth-Century Studies* 25, no. 2 (winter 1991-92): 171-201.

Goodman, Martin. *The Ruling Class of Judaea: The Origins of the Jewish Revolt Against Rome A.D. 66-70.* Cambridge: Cambridge University Press, 1987.

Gordon, Daniel. *Citizens Without Sovereignty: Equality and Sociability in French Thought, 1670-1789.* Princeton, NJ: Princeton University Press, 1994.

Gossman, Lionel. *The Empire Unpossess'd: An Essay On Gibbon's 'Decline and Fall'.* Cambridge: Cambridge University Press, 1981.

Grafton, Anthony. "The Footnote from De Thou to Ranke." *History and Theory: Studies in the Philosophy of History.* Theme Issue 33, *Proof and Persuasion in History* (1994): 53-76.

Graham, Henry Grey. *The Social Life of Scotland in the Eighteenth Century.* 1901. Reprint, New York: Benjamin Blom, Inc., 1971.

Grant, Michael. *Constantine the Great: The Man and His Times.* New York: Charles Scribner's Sons, 1993.

____. *The Fall of the Roman Empire.* New York: Macmillian, 1990.

Guterman, Simeon L. *Religious Toleration and Persecution in Ancient Rome.* 1951. Reprint, Westport, CT: Greenwood Press, 1971.

Halévy, Elie. *The Birth of Methodism in England.* Translated and edited by Bernard Semmel. Chicago: University of Chicago Press, 1971.

Hall, John A. *Powers and Liberties: The Causes and Consequences of the Rise of the West.* Berkeley, CA: University of California Press, 1985.

Hardy, E. G. *Christianity and the Roman Government: A Study in Imperial Administration.* London: Longmans, Green and Co., 1894.

Hayek, F. A. *The Constitution of Liberty.* Chicago: University of Chicago Press, 1960.

____. *Law, Legislation and Liberty.* Vol. 2, *The Mirage of Social Justice.* Chicago: University of Chicago Press, 1976.

____. "The Legal and Political Philosophy of David Hume." In *Studies in Philosophy, Politics and Economics.* Chicago: University of Chicago Press, 1967.

Haynes, E. S. P. *Religious Persecution: A Study in Political Psychology.* London: Duckworth and Co., 1904.

Hazard, Paul. *European Thought in the Eighteenth Century: From Montequieu to Lessing.* Translated by J. Lewis May. New Haven, CT: Yale University Press, 1954.

Hume, David. *The Dialogues Concerning Natural Religion.* Edited by John Valdimir Price. Oxford: Clarendon Press, 1976.

____. *Enquiries Concerning Human Understanding and Concerning the Principles of Morals.* Edited by L. A. Selby-Bigge. 3rd ed. Oxford: Clarendon Press, 1975.

____. *Essays Moral, Political and Literary.* Edited by Eugene F. Miller. Indianapolis: Liberty Classics.

____. *The History of England From the Invasion of Julius Caesar to the Revolution in 1688.* 6 vols. Boston: Little, Brown, and Co., 1854.

____. *The History of Great Britain: The Reigns of James I and Charles I.* Edited by Duncan Forbes. England: Penguin, 1970.

____. *The Letters of David.* Edited by J. Y. T. Greig. 2 vols. Oxford: Clarendon Press, 1932.

____. *The Natural History of Religion.* Edited by Wayne Colver (Oxford: Clarendon Press, 1976).

____. *New Letters of David Hume.* Edited by R. Kilbanski and E. C. Mossner. Oxford: Clarendon Press, 1954.

____. *A Treatise of Human Nature.* Edited by L. A. Selby-Bigge. 2nd ed. Oxford: Clarendon Press, 1978.

Hutton, Edward. "The Conversion of Edward Gibbon." *The Nineteenth Century* 91, no. 661 (March 1932): 362-75.

Jefferson, Thomas. *The Life and Selected Writings of Thomas Jefferson.* Edited by Adrienne Koch and William Peden. New York: Random House, 1944.

Jemielity, Thomas. "Gibbon Among the Aeolists: Islamic Credulity and Pagan Fanaticism in *The Decline and Fall.*" *Studies in Eighteenth-Century Culture* 19 (1989): 165-83.

Jordan, David. *Gibbon and His Roman Empire.* Urbana, IL: University of Illinois Press, 1971.

____. "Gibbon's 'Age of Constantine' and the Fall of Rome." *History and Theory: Studies in the Philosophy of History* 8, no. 1 (1969): 71-96.

Jordan, Wilbur. *The Development of Religious Toleration In England.* 4 vols. 1932-40. Reprint, Gloucester, MA: Peter Smith, 1965.

Kampf, Louis. "Gibbon and Hume." In *English Literature and British Philosophy: A Collection of Essays.* Edited by S. P. Rosenbaum. Chicago: University of Chicago Press, 1971.

Kemp Smith, Norman. "Hume's Arguments Against Miracles, and His Critique of the Argument From Design, in the 'Enquiry.'" *Dialogues Concerning Natural Religion,* by David Hume. Edited by Norman Kemp Smith. Indianapolis, IN: Bobbs-Merrill, 1947.

Keynes, Geoffrey. *The Library of Edward Gibbon: A Catalogue.* 2nd ed. N.p.: St. Paul's Bibliographies, 1980.

Knox, Ronald. *Enthusiasm: A Chapter in the History of Religion.* Westminster, MD: Christian Classics, 1983.

Lamprecht, Sterling P. "Naturalism and Religion." In *Naturalism and the Human Spirit*, edited by Yervant H. Krikorian. New York: Columbia University Press, 1944.

Lane Fox, Robin. *Pagans and Christians*. New York: Alfred A. Knopf, Inc., 1989.

Lecky, W. E. H. "Edward Gibbon." *Warner Library*. Vol. 11. New York: Warner, 1917.

Letwin, Shirley Robin. *The Pursuit of Certainty: David Hume, Jeremy Bentham, John Stuart Mill, Beatrice Webb*. Cambridge: Cambridge University Press, 1965.

Levine, Michael P. *Hume and the Problem of Miracles: A Solution*. Dordrecht: Kluwer Academic Publishers, 1989.

Lewis, Bernard. *The Arabs In History*. New York: Oxford University Press, 1993.

____. "Gibbon on Muhammad." In *Edward Gibbon and `The Decline and Fall of the Roman Empire,'* edited by G. W. Bowersock, John Clive, and Stephen R. Graubard. Cambridge, MA: Harvard University Press, 1977.

____. "The State of Middle Eastern Studies." *American Scholar* 48 (summer 1979): 365-80.

Livingston, Donald. *Hume's Philosophy of Common Life*. Chicago: University of Chicago Press, 1984.

____. "On Hume's Conservatism." *Hume Studies* 21, no. 2 (November 1995): 151-64.

Locke, John. *Essay Concerning Human Understanding*. Edited by Peter H. Nidditch. Oxford: Clarendon Press, 1975.

Low, D. M. *Edward Gibbon, 1737-1794*. London: Chatto and Windus, 1937.

Lucas, F. L. *The Art of Living: Four Eighteenth-Century Minds*. New York: Macmillan Co., 1960.

Manuel, Frank E. "Edward Gibbon: Historien-Philosophe." In *Edward Gibbon and 'The Decline and Fall of the Roman Empire,'* edited by G. W. Bowersock, John Clive, and Stephen R. Graubard. Cambridge, MA: Harvard University Press, 1977.

____. *The Eighteenth Century Confronts the Gods*. Cambridge, MA: Harvard University Press, 1959.

Martin, Marie A. "Hume on Human Excellence." *Hume Studies*, 18, no. 2 (November 1992): 383-99.

McClelland, J. S., ed. and trans. *The French Right: From De Maistre to Maurras*. New York: Harper and Row, 1970.

McCloy, Shelby T. *Gibbon's Antagonism to Christianity*. Chapel Hill, NC: University of North Carolina Press, 1933.

McNeil, Gordon H. "The Anti-Revolutionary Rousseau." *American Historical Review* 58, no. 4 (July 1953): 808-23.

____. "The Cult of Rousseau and the French Revolution," *Journal of the History of Ideas* 6, no. 2 (1945): 197-212.

Medvedev, Zhores. *The Rise and Fall of T. D. Lysenko.* New York: Columbia University Press, 1969.

Meinecke, Frederich. *Historism: The Rise of a New Historical Outlook.* Translated by J. E. Anderson. New York: Herder and Herder, 1972.

Miller, David. *Philosophy and Ideology in Hume's Political Thought.* Oxford: Clarendon Press, 1981.

Miller, Perry. *The New England Mind: The Seventeenth Century.* Cambridge, MA: Harvard University Press, 1939.

Miller, Stephen. "The Death of Hume." *Wilson Quarterly* 30 (summer 1995): 30-39.

Momigliano, Arnaldo. *The Classical Foundations of Modern Historiography.* Berkeley, CA: University of California Press, 1990.

____. *Essays in Ancient and Modern Historiography.* Middletown, CT: Wesleyan University Press, 1977.

____. "Introduction. Christianity and the Decline of the Roman Empire." In *The Conflict Between Paganism and Christianity In the Fourth Century: Essays* edited by Arnaldo Momigliano. Oxford: Clarendon Press, 1963.

____. "Pagan and Christian Historiography In the Fourth Century A.D." In *The Conflict Between Paganism and Christianity In the Fourth Century: Essays* edited by Arnaldo Momigliano. Oxford: Clarendon Press, 1963.

____. *Studies in Historiography.* London: Weidenfeld and Nicolson, 1966.

Morison, James Cotter. *Gibbon.* London: Macmillan, 1904.

Mossner, Ernest Campbell. *The Life of David Hume*, 2nd ed. Oxford: Clarendon Press, 1980.

____. "Philosophy and Biography: The Case of David Hume." *Philosophical Review* 5, no. 2 (April, 1950): 184-201.

____. "Was Hume a Tory Historian? Facts and Reconsiderations." *Journal of the History of Ideas* 2 (1941): 225-36.

Muecke, D. C. *The Compass of Irony.* London: Methuen, 1969.

Newman, Jay. *Fanatics & Hypocrites.* Buffalo, NY: Prometheus Books, 1986.

Nicol, D. M. "Byzantine Political Thought." In *The Cambridge History of Medieval Political Thought, c. 350--c. 1450*, edited by J. H. Burns. Cambridge: Cambridge University Press, 1988.

Nisbet, Robert. *Conservatism: Dream and Reality.* Minneapolis, MN: University of Minnesota Press, 1986.

____. *Twilight of Authority.* New York: Oxford University Press, 1975.

Nock, A. D. *Conversion: The Old and the New in Religion from Alexander the Great to Augustine of Hippo.* Oxford: Clarendon Press, 1933.

Norman, Daniel. *Islam and the West: The Making of an Image.* Edinburgh: Edinburgh University Press, 1960.

Norton, David Fate. *David Hume: Common-sense Moralist, Sceptical Metaphysician.* Princeton, NJ: Princeton University Press, 1982.

Norton, J. E. *A Bibliography of the Works of Edward Gibbon.* London: Oxford University Press, 1940.

Noxon, James. "Hume's Concerns with Religion." In *David Hume: Many-sided Genius,* edited by Kenneth R. Merrill and Robert W. Shahan. Norman, OK: University of Oklahoma Press, 1976.

____. *Hume's Philosophical Development.* Oxford: Clarendon Press, 1973.

Oakeshott, Michael. *Rationalism In Politics and Other Essays.* Indianapolis, IN: Liberty Press, 1991.

Palmer, R. R. *Catholics and Unbelievers In Eighteenth-Century France.* Princeton, NJ: Princeton University Press, 1939.

____. and Joel Colton. *A History of the Modern World.* New York: Alfred A. Knopf, 1965.

Parke, Catherine N. "Edward Gibbon by Edward Gibbon." *Modern Language Quarterly* 50, no. 1 (March 1989): 23-37.

Parkinson, R. N. *Edward Gibbon.* New York: Twayne, 1973.

Pattison, Robert. *The Triumph of Vulgarity: Rock Music in the Mirror of Romanticism.* New York: Oxford University Press, 1987.

Pelikan, Jaroslav. *The Excellent Empire: The Fall of Rome and the Triumph of the Church.* San Francisco: Harper and Row, 1987.

Pocock, J. G. A. "Between Machiavelli and Hume: Gibbon as Civic Humanist and Philosophical Historian." In *Edward Gibbon and `The Decline and Fall of the Roman Empire,'* edited by G. W. Bowersock, John Clive, and Stephen R. Graubard. Cambridge, MA: Harvard University Press, 1977.

____. "Gibbon and the Idol Fo: Chinese and Christian History in the Enlightenment." In *Sceptics, Millenarians and Jews,* edited by David S. Katz and Jonathon I. Israel. Leiden: E.J. Brill, 1990.

____. "Gibbon's *Decline and Fall* and the World View of the Late Enlightenment," In *Virtue, Commerce, and History: Essays on Political Thoughts and History, Chiefly in the Eighteenth Century.* Cambridge: Cambridge University Press, 1985.

____. *The Machiavellian Moment: Florentine Political Thought and the Atlantic Republican Tradition.* Princeton, NJ: Princeton University Press, 1975.

____. "Superstition and Enthusiasm in Gibbon's History of Religion." *Eighteenth-Century Life*, n.s. 8, no. 1 (October 1982): 83-94.

Popkin, Richard H. *The High Road to Pyrrhonism*. San Diego: Austin Hill Press, Inc., 1980.

____. *The History of Scepticism From Erasmus to Spinoza*. Berkeley, CA: University of California Press, 1979.

____. "Hume: Philosophical Versus Prophetic Historian." In *David Hume: Man-sided Genius*, edited by Kenneth R. Merrill and Robert W. Shahan. Norman, OK: University of Oklahoma Press, 1976.

____. "Skepticism and the Study of History." In *David Hume: Philosophical Historian*. Edited by David Fate Norton and Richard H. Popkin. Indianapolis, IN: Bobbs-Merrill, 1965.

Porter, Roy. *Edward Gibbon: Making History*. London: Weidenfeld and Nicolson, 1988.

____. "Gibbon, the Secular Scholar." *History Today* 36 (September 1986): 46-51.

Price, John Vladimir. "David Hume's 'Dialogues Concerning Religion,' Composition and Publication." *Dialogues Concerning Natural Religion,* by David Hume. Oxford: Clarendon Press, 1976.

____. *The Ironic Hume*. Austin, TX: University of Texas Press, 1965.

Quinton, Anthony. *The Politics of Imperfection: The Religious and Secular Traditions of Conservative Thought From Hooker to Oakshott*. London: Faber and Faber, 1978.

Radcliffe, Elizabeth S. "Hume on Motivating Sentiments, the General Point of View, and the Inculcation of 'Morality.'" *Hume Studies* 20, no. 1 (April 1994): 37-58.

Redwood, John. *Reason, Ridicule and Religion: The Age of Enlightenment in England, 1660-1750*. London: Thames and Hudson, 1976.

Robertson, J.M. *Gibbon*. London: Watts and Co., 1925.

Rotwein, Eugene. Introduction to *David Hume: Writings on Economics* Madison, WI: University of Wisconsin Press, 1955.

Rousseau, Jean-Jacques. *Du Contrat Social*. Edited by Ronald Grimsley. Oxford: Clarendon Press, 1972.

Rudolf, Kurt. *Historical Fundamentals, and the Study of Religion*. New York: Macmillan, 1985.

Russell, Bertrand. *A History of Western Philosophy: And Its Connection with Political and Social Circumstances from the Earliest Times to the Present Day*. New York: Simon and Schuster, 1945.

Russell, Paul. "Epigram, Pantheists, and Freethought in Hume's *Treatise*: A Study in Esoteric Communication." *Journal of the History of Ideas* 54, no. 4 (October 1993): 659-73.

Saunders, Dero A. Introduction to *The Portable Gibbon: The Decline and Fall of the Roman Empire*. Edited by Dero A. Saunders. New York: Penguin, 1977.

Schapiro, Leonard. *The Communist Party of the Soviet Union*. 2nd ed. New York: Random House, 1971.

Schopenhauer, Arthur. "The Christian System." In *The Pessimist's Handbook: A Collection of Popular Essays*. Translated by T. Bailey Saunders, edited by Hazel E. Barnes. Lincoln, NE: University of Nebraska Press, 1964.

Sher, Richard B. "Professors of Virtue: The Social History of the Edinburgh Moral Philosophy Chair in the Eighteenth Century." In *Studies in the Philosophy of the Scottish Enlightenment*, edited by M. A. Stewart. Oxford: Clarendon Press, 1990.

Smith, Adam. *The Correspondence of Adam Smith*. Edited by Ernest Campbell Mossner and Ian Simpson Ross. Oxford: Clarendon Press, 1987.

Smith, David Dillon. "Gibbon in Church." *Journal of Ecclesiastical History* 35, no. 3 (July 1984): 452-63.

Smith, Wilfred Cantwell. *The Meaning and End of Religion: A New Approach to the Religious Traditions of Mankind*. New York: Macmillan, 1963.

Southern, R. W. *Western Views of Islam in the Middle Ages*. Cambridge, MA: Harvard University Press, 1962.

Stephen, Leslie. *History of English Thought in the Eighteenth Century*. 2 vols. London: Smith, Edder and Co., 1902.

Stewart, John B. *Opinion and Reform in Hume's Political Philosophy*. Princeton, NJ: Princeton University Press, 1992.

Strachey, Lytton. *Eminent Victorians*. New York: G. P. Putnam's Sons, 1918.

____. *Portraits in Miniature and Other Essays*. New York: Harcourt, Brace, and Co., 1931.

Strauss, Leo. *Persecution and the Art of Writing*. Glencoe, IL: Free Press, 1952.

____. *Spinoza's Critique of Religion*. Translated by E. M. Sinclair. New York: Schocken Books, 1965.

Stromberg, Roland. *Religious Liberalism in Eighteenth-Century England*. London: Oxford University Press, 1954.

Swain, Joseph Ward. *Edward Gibbon the Historian*. New York: St. Martins Press, 1966.

Tacitus. *The Annals*. Translated by John Jackson. Loeb edition. 3 vols., Cambridge, MA: Harvard University Press, 1931.

Tillyard, E. M. W. *The English Epic and Its Background.* New York: Oxford University Press, 1966.

Tolan, John. Introduction to *Medieval Christian of Perceptions of Islam: A Book of Essays.* New York: Garland, 1996.

Toynbee, Arnold. *A Study of History.* Vol. 9. London: Oxford University Press, 1954.

Trevor-Roper, Hugh. "Gibbon and the Publication of the *Decline and Fall of the Roman Empire,* 1776-1976." *The Journal of Law and Economics* 19, no. 3 (October 1976): 489-504.

_____. "The Historical Philosophy of the Enlightenment." *Studies in Voltaire and the Eighteenth Century* 27 (1963): 1667-87.

_____. Introduction to *The Decline and Fall of the Roman Empire.* 3 Vols. New York: Alfred A. Knopf, 1993.

Trotsky, Leon. *The History of the Russian Revolution.* Translated by Max Eastman. Vol. 3. New York: Monad, 1932.

Tucker, Susie I. *Enthusiasm: A Study in Semantic Change.* Cambridge: Cambridge University Press, 1972.

Turnbull, Paul. "The 'Supposed Infidelity' of Edward Gibbon." *The Historical Journal* 5, no. 1 (March 1982): 23-41.

Vartarian, Aram. "The French Enlightenment and Its Nineteenth-Century Critics." *Studies in Burke and His Time* 18, no. 1 (winter 1977): 3-26.

Walbank, F. W. *The Aweful Revolution: The Decline of the Roman Empire in the West.* Toronto: University of Toronto Press, 1969.

Ward, A. W. and A. R. Wallin, eds. "Edward Gibbon." *Cambridge History of English Literature.* Vol. 10. New York: G.P. Putnam's Sons, 1913.

Wardman, Alan. *Religion and Statescraft Among the Romans.* Baltimore: The Johns Hopkins University Press, 1982.

Waugh, Scott L. and Peter D. Diethl, eds. *Christendom and Its Discontents: Exclusion, Persecution, and Rebellion, 1000-1500.* Cambridge: Cambridge University Press, 1996.

Weber, M. Andreas. *David Hume und Edward Gibbon: Religionssoziologie in der Aufklarung.* Frankfurt am Main: Hain, 1990.

Weber, Max. *The Protestant Ethic and the Spirit of Capitalism.* Translated by Talcott Parsons. New York: Charles Scribner's Sons, 1958.

_____. *The Sociology of Religion.* Translated by Ephriam Fischoff. Boston: Beacon Press, 1993.

Wells, G. A. *Belief and Make-Belief: Critical Reflections on the Sources of Credulity.* La Salle, IL: Open Court, 1991.

Wexler, Victor G. *David Hume and the History of England*. Philadelphia: American Philosophical Society, 1979.

_____. "David Hume's Discovery of a New Scene of Historical Thought." *Eighteenth-Century Studies* 10, no. 2 (winter 1976/77): 185-202.

Whelan, Frederick G. *Order and Artifice in Hume's Political Philosophy*. Princeton, NJ: Princeton University Press, 1985.

White, Hayden. *Metahistory*. Baltimore: The Johns Hopkins Press, 1973.

_____. *Tropics of Discourse: Essays in Cultural Criticism*. Baltimore: The Johns Hopkins University Press, 1978.

Wills, Gary. *Explaining America: The Federalist*. New York: Penguin, 1981.

_____. *Inventing America: Jefferson's Declaration of Independence*. New York: Vintage Books, 1978.

Wind, Edgar. *Hume and the Heroic Portrait: Studies in Eighteenth-Century Imagery*. Edited by Jaynie Anderson. Oxford: Clarendon Press, 1986.

Wolin, Sheldon S. "Hume and Conservatism." In *Hume: A Re-evaluation*, edited by Donald W. Livingston and James T. King. New York: Fordham University Press, 1976.

Womersley, David. "Gibbon's Unfinished History: The French Revolution and English Political Vocabularies." *The Historical Journal* 35, no. 1 (1992): 63-89.

_____. *The Transformation of the Decline and Fall of the Roman Empire*. Cambridge: Cambridge University Press, 1988.

Woolf, Virginia. "The Historian and 'The Gibbon.'" In *Collected Essays*, Vol. 1. New York: Harcourt Brace and World, 1967.

Wooton, David. "Hume's 'Of Miracles': Probability and Irreligion." In *Studies in the Philosophy of the Scottish Enlightenment*, edited by M. A. Stewart. Oxford: Clarendon Press, 1990.

_____. "Narrative, Irony and Faith in Gibbon's *Decline and Fall*." *History and Theory: Studies in the Philosophy of History*. Theme Issue No. 33, *Proof and Persuasion in History* (1994): 102.

Yandell, Keith E. "Hume on Religious Belief." In *Hume, A Re-evaluation*, edited by Donald W. Livingston and James T. King. New York: Fordham University Press, 1976.

INDEX

ARCHIVES INTERNATIONALES D'HISTOIRE DES IDÉES

*

INTERNATIONAL ARCHIVES OF THE HISTORY OF IDEAS

63. G. Defaux: *Pantagruel et les Sophistes*. Contribution à l'histoire de l'humanisme chrétien au 16ᵉ siècle. 1973   ISBN 90-247-1566-0
64. G. Planty-Bonjour: *Hegel et la pensée philosophique en Russie (1830-1917)*. 1974
                                                                                      ISBN 90-247-1576-8
65. R.J. Brook: *[George] Berkeley's Philosophy of Science*. 1973   ISBN 90-247-1555-5
66. T.E. Jessop: *A Bibliography of George Berkeley*. With: *Inventory of Berkeley's Manuscript Remains* by A.A. Luce. 2nd revised and enlarged ed. 1973
                                                                                      ISBN 90-247-1577-6
67. E.I. Perry: *From Theology to History*. French Religious Controversy and the Revocation of the Edict of Nantes. 1973   ISBN 90-247-1578-4
68. P. Dibbon, H. Bots et E. Bots-Estourgie: *Inventaire de la correspondance (1631–1671) de Johannes Fredericus Gronovius* [1611–1671]. 1974
                                                                                      ISBN 90-247-1600-4
69. A.B. Collins: *The Secular is Sacred*. Platonism and Thomism in Marsilio Ficino's *Platonic Theology*. 1974   ISBN 90-247-1588-1
70. R. Simon (éd.): *Henry de Boulainviller*. Œuvres Philosophiques, Tome II. 1975
                                                                                      ISBN 90-247-1633-0
    For Œvres Philosophiques, Tome I see under Volume 58.
71. J.A.G. Tans et H. Schmitz du Moulin: *Pasquier Quesnel devant la Congrégation de l'Index*. Correspondance avec Francesco Barberini et mémoires sur la mise à l'Index de son édition des Œuvres de Saint Léon, publiés avec introduction et annotations. 1974   ISBN 90-247-1661-6
72. J.W. Carven: *Napoleon and the Lazarists (1804–1809)*. 1974   ISBN 90-247-1667-5
73. G. Symcox: *The Crisis of French Sea Power (1688–1697)*. From the *Guerre d'Escadre* to the *Guerre de Course*. 1974   ISBN 90-247-1645-4
74. R. MacGillivray: *Restoration Historians and the English Civil War*. 1974
                                                                                      ISBN 90-247-1678-0
75. A. Soman (ed.): *The Massacre of St. Bartholomew*. Reappraisals and Documents. 1974   ISBN 90-247-1652-7
76. R.E. Wanner: *Claude Fleury (1640-1723) as an Educational Historiographer and Thinker*. With an Introduction by W.W. Brickman. 1975   ISBN 90-247-1684-5
77. R.T. Carroll: *The Common-Sense Philosophy of Religion of Bishop Edward Stillingfleet (1635-1699)*. 1975   ISBN 90-247-1647-0
78. J. Macary: *Masque et lumières au 18ᵉ [siècle]*. André-François Deslandes, Citoyen et philosophe (1689-1757). 1975   ISBN 90-247-1698-5
79. S.M. Mason: *Montesquieu's Idea of Justice*. 1975   ISBN 90-247-1670-5
80. D.J.H. van Elden: *Esprits fins et esprits géométriques dans les portraits de Saint-Simon*. Contributions à l'étude du vocabulaire et du style. 1975   ISBN 90-247-1726-4
81. I. Primer (ed.): *Mandeville Studies*. New Explorations in the Art and Thought of Dr Bernard Mandeville (1670-1733). 1975   ISBN 90-247-1686-1
82. C.G. Noreña: *Studies in Spanish Renaissance Thought*. 1975   ISBN 90-247-1727-2
83. G. Wilson: *A Medievalist in the 18th Century*. Le Grand d'Aussy and the Fabliaux ou Contes. 1975   ISBN 90-247-1782-5
84. J.-R. Armogathe: *Theologia Cartesiana*. L'explication physique de l'Eucharistie chez Descartes et Dom Robert Desgabets. 1977   ISBN 90-247-1869-4

ARCHIVES INTERNATIONALES D'HISTOIRE DES IDÉES
*
INTERNATIONAL ARCHIVES OF THE HISTORY OF IDEAS

85. Bérault Stuart, Seigneur d'Aubigny: *Traité sur l'art de la guerre*. Introduction et édition par Élie de Comminges. 1976   ISBN 90-247-1871-6
86. S.L. Kaplan: *Bread, Politics and Political Economy in the Reign of Louis XV*. 2 vols., 1976   Set ISBN 90-247-1873-2
87. M. Lienhard (ed.): *The Origins and Characteristics of Anabaptism / Les débuts et les caractéristiques de l'Anabaptisme*. With an Extensive Bibliography / Avec une bibliographie détaillée. 1977   ISBN 90-247-1896-1
88. R. Descartes: *Règles utiles et claires pour la direction de l'esprit en la recherche de la vérité*. Traduction selon le lexique cartésien, et annotation conceptuelle par J.-L. Marion. Avec des notes mathématiques de P. Costabel. 1977   ISBN 90-247-1907-0
89. K. Hardesty: *The 'Supplément' to the 'Encyclopédie'*. [Diderot et d'Alembert]. 1977   ISBN 90-247-1965-8
90. H.B. White: *Antiquity Forgot*. Essays on Shakespeare, [Francis] Bacon, and Rembrandt. 1978   ISBN 90-247-1971-2
91. P.B.M. Blaas: *Continuity and Anachronism*. Parliamentary and Constitutional Development in Whig Historiography and in the Anti-Whig Reaction between 1890 and 1930. 1978   ISBN 90-247-2063-X
92. S.L. Kaplan (ed.): *La Bagarre*. Ferdinando Galiani's (1728-1787) 'Lost' Parody. With an Introduction by the Editor. 1979   ISBN 90-247-2125-3
93. E. McNiven Hine: *A Critical Study of [Étienne Bonnot de] Condillac's* [1714-1780] *'Traité des Systèmes'*. 1979   ISBN 90-247-2120-2
94. M.R.G. Spiller: *Concerning Natural Experimental Philosphy*. Meric Casaubon [1599-1671] and the Royal Society. 1980   ISBN 90-247-2414-7
95. F. Duchesneau: *La physiologie des Lumières*. Empirisme, modèles et théories. 1982   ISBN 90-247-2500-3
96. M. Heyd: *Between Orthodoxy and the Enlightenment*. Jean-Robert Chouet [1642-1731] and the Introduction of Cartesian Science in the Academy of Geneva. 1982   ISBN 90-247-2508-9
97. James O'Higgins: *Yves de Vallone* [1666/7-1705]: *The Making of an Esprit Fort*. 1982   ISBN 90-247-2520-8
98. M.L. Kuntz: *Guillaume Postel* [1510-1581]. Prophet of the Restitution of All Things. His Life and Thought. 1981   ISBN 90-247-2523-2
99. A. Rosenberg: *Nicolas Gueudeville and His Work (1652-172?)*. 1982   ISBN 90-247-2533-X
100. S.L. Jaki: *Uneasy Genius: The Life and Work of Pierre Duhem* [1861-1916]. 1984   ISBN 90-247-2897-5; Pb (1987) 90-247-3532-7
101. Anne Conway [1631-1679]: *The Principles of the Most Ancient Modern Philosophy*. Edited and with an Introduction by P. Loptson. 1982   ISBN 90-247-2671-9
102. E.C. Patterson: *[Mrs.] Mary [Fairfax Greig] Sommerville* [1780-1872] *and the Cultivation of Science (1815-1840)*. 1983   ISBN 90-247-2823-1
103. C.J. Berry: *Hume, Hegel and Human Nature*. 1982   ISBN 90-247-2682-4
104. C.J. Betts: *Early Deism in France*. From the so-called 'déistes' of Lyon (1564) to Voltaire's 'Lettres philosophiques' (1734). 1984   ISBN 90-247-2923-8

ARCHIVES INTERNATIONALES D'HISTOIRE DES IDÉES
*
INTERNATIONAL ARCHIVES OF THE HISTORY OF IDEAS

105. R. Gascoigne: *Religion, Rationality and Community*. Sacred and Secular in the Thought of Hegel and His Critics. 1985   ISBN 90-247-2992-0
106. S. Tweyman: *Scepticism and Belief in Hume's 'Dialogues Concerning Natural Religion'*. 1986   ISBN 90-247-3090-2
107. G. Cerny: *Theology, Politics and Letters at the Crossroads of European Civilization.* Jacques Basnage [1653-1723] and the Baylean Huguenot Refugees in the Dutch Republic. 1987   ISBN 90-247-3150-X
108. Spinoza's *Algebraic Calculation of the Rainbow* & *Calculation of Changes*. Edited and Translated from Dutch, with an Introduction, Explanatory Notes and an Appendix by M.J. Petry. 1985   ISBN 90-247-3149-6
109. R.G. McRae: *Philosophy and the Absolute*. The Modes of Hegel's Speculation. 1985   ISBN 90-247-3151-8
110. J.D. North and J.J. Roche (eds.): *The Light of Nature*. Essays in the History and Philosophy of Science presented to A.C. Crombie. 1985   ISBN 90-247-3165-8
111. C. Walton and P.J. Johnson (eds.): *[Thomas] Hobbes's 'Science of Natural Justice'*. 1987   ISBN 90-247-3226-3
112. B.W. Head: *Ideology and Social Science*. Destutt de Tracy and French Liberalism. 1985   ISBN 90-247-3228-X
113. A.Th. Peperzak: *Philosophy and Politics*. A Commentary on the Preface to Hegel's *Philosophy of Right*. 1987   ISBN Hb 90-247-3337-5; Pb ISBN 90-247-3338-3
114. S. Pines and Y. Yovel (eds.): *Maimonides [1135-1204] and Philosophy*. Papers Presented at the 6th Jerusalem Philosophical Encounter (May 1985). 1986   ISBN 90-247-3439-8
115. T.J. Saxby: *The Quest for the New Jerusalem, Jean de Labadie [1610-1674] and the Labadists (1610-1744)*. 1987   ISBN 90-247-3485-1
116. C.E. Harline: *Pamphlets, Printing, and Political Culture in the Early Dutch Republic*. 1987   ISBN 90-247-3511-4
117. R.A. Watson and J.E. Force (eds.): *The Sceptical Mode in Modern Philosophy*. Essays in Honor of Richard H. Popkin. 1988   ISBN 90-247-3584-X
118. R.T. Bienvenu and M. Feingold (eds.): *In the Presence of the Past*. Essays in Honor of Frank Manuel. 1991   ISBN 0-7923-1008-X
119. J. van den Berg and E.G.E. van der Wall (eds.): *Jewish-Christian Relations in the 17th Century*. Studies and Documents. 1988   ISBN 90-247-3617-X
120. N. Waszek: *The Scottish Enlightenment and Hegel's Account of 'Civil Society'*. 1988   ISBN 90-247-3596-3
121. J. Walker (ed.): *Thought and Faith in the Philosophy of Hegel*. 1991   ISBN 0-7923-1234-1
122. Henry More [1614-1687]: *The Immortality of the Soul*. Edited with Introduction and Notes by A. Jacob. 1987   ISBN 90-247-3512-2
123. P.B. Scheurer and G. Debrock (eds.): *Newton's Scientific and Philosophical Legacy*. 1988   ISBN 90-247-3723-0
124. D.R. Kelley and R.H. Popkin (eds.): *The Shapes of Knowledge from the Renaissance to the Enlightenment*. 1991   ISBN 0-7923-1259-7

ARCHIVES INTERNATIONALES D'HISTOIRE DES IDÉES
*
INTERNATIONAL ARCHIVES OF THE HISTORY OF IDEAS

125. R.M. Golden (ed.): *The Huguenot Connection*. The Edict of Nantes, Its Revocation, and Early French Migration to South Carolina. 1988   ISBN 90-247-3645-5

126. S. Lindroth: *Les chemins du savoir en Suède*. De la fondation de l'Université d'Upsal à Jacob Berzelius. Études et Portraits. Traduit du suédois, présenté et annoté par J.-F. Battail. Avec une introduction sur Sten Lindroth par G. Eriksson. 1988
    ISBN 90-247-3579-3

127. S. Hutton (ed.): *Henry More (1614-1687)*. *Tercentenary Studies*. With a Biography and Bibliography by R. Crocker. 1989   ISBN 0-7923-0095-5

128. Y. Yovel (ed.): *Kant's Practical Philosophy Reconsidered*. Papers Presented at the 7th Jerusalem Philosophical Encounter (December 1986). 1989   ISBN 0-7923-0405-5

129. J.E. Force and R.H. Popkin: *Essays on the Context, Nature, and Influence of Isaac Newton's Theology*. 1990   ISBN 0-7923-0583-3

130. N. Capaldi and D.W. Livingston (eds.): *Liberty in Hume's 'History of England'*. 1990
    ISBN 0-7923-0650-3

131. W. Brand: *Hume's Theory of Moral Judgment*. A Study in the Unity of *A Treatise of Human Nature*. 1992   ISBN 0-7923-1415-8

132. C.E. Harline (ed.): *The Rhyme and Reason of Politics in Early Modern Europe*. Collected Essays of Herbert H. Rowen. 1992   ISBN 0-7923-1527-8

133. N. Malebranche: *Treatise on Ethics* (1684). Translated and edited by C. Walton. 1993
    ISBN 0-7923-1763-7

134. B.C. Southgate: *'Covetous of Truth'*. The Life and Work of Thomas White (1593–1676). 1993   ISBN 0-7923-1926-5

135. G. Santinello, C.W.T. Blackwell and Ph. Weller (eds.): *Models of the History of Philosophy*. Vol. 1: From its Origins in the Renaissance to the 'Historia Philosphica'. 1993   ISBN 0-7923-2200-2

136. M.J. Petry (ed.): *Hegel and Newtonianism*. 1993   ISBN 0-7923-2202-9

137. Otto von Guericke: *The New (so-called Magdeburg) Experiments* [Experimenta Nova, Amsterdam 1672]. Translated and edited by M.G.Foley Ames. 1994
    ISBN 0-7923-2399-8

138. R.H. Popkin and G.M. Weiner (eds.): *Jewish Christians and Cristian Jews*. From the Renaissance to the Enlightenment. 1994   ISBN 0-7923-2452-8

139. J.E. Force and R.H. Popkin (eds.): *The Books of Nature and Scripture*. Recent Essays on Natural Philosophy, Theology, and Biblical Criticism in the Netherlands of Spinoza's Time and the British Isles of Newton's Time. 1994   ISBN 0-7923-2467-6

140. P. Rattansi and A. Clericuzio (eds.): *Alchemy and Chemistry in the 16th and 17th Centuries*. 1994   ISBN 0-7923-2573-7

141. S. Jayne: *Plato in Renaissance England*. 1995   ISBN 0-7923-3060-9

142. A.P. Coudert: *Leibniz and the Kabbalah*. 1995   ISBN 0-7923-3114-1

143. M.H. Hoffheimer: *Eduard Gans and the Hegelian Philosophy of Law*. 1995
    ISBN 0-7923-3114-1

144. J.R.M. Neto: *The Christianization of Pyrrhonism*. Scepticism and Faith in Pascal, Kierkegaard, and Shestov. 1995   ISBN 0-7923-3381-0

145. R.H. Popkin (ed.): *Scepticism in the History of Philosophy*. A Pan-American Dialogue. 1996   ISBN 0-7923-3769-7

ARCHIVES INTERNATIONALES D'HISTOIRE DES IDÉES
*
INTERNATIONAL ARCHIVES OF THE HISTORY OF IDEAS

KLUWER ACADEMIC PUBLISHERS – DORDRECHT / BOSTON / LONDON